TATTOO

TATTOO
A MEMOIR OF BECOMING

W. PATRICK LANG

iUniverse®

TATTOO
A MEMOIR OF BECOMING

This memoir in its present form was cleared by the U.S. Government for publication after a security review.

iUniverse books may be ordered through booksellers or by contacting:

iUniverse
1663 Liberty Drive
Bloomington, IN 47403
www.iuniverse.com
844-349-9409

ISBN: 978-1-6632-0766-1 (sc)
ISBN: 978-1-6632-0768-5 (hc)
ISBN: 978-1-6632-0767-8 (e)

Library of Congress Control Number: 2020924103

Print information available on the last page.

iUniverse rev. date: 12/30/2020

Tattoo is a bugle call that signals that all light in squad rooms be extinguished and that all loud talking and other disturbances be discontinued within 15 minutes, at which time Taps should follow.

https://www.youtube.com/watch?v=SZyj2amkOU0 Courtesy of David Sensing, United State Air Force Heritage Band

https://www.youtube.com/watch?v=XzyRVic9h1Y United States Navy Band

"The Life So Short, the Craft So Long to Learn"
Hippocrates

For
John Henry Lang
A Sailor Man

Contents

Introduction

By Alan Farrell

"I do all that becomes a man; he who does more is none." Or so says Macbeth. Here's the life story of a man, (small *m*) who's done all that becomes us and in an epic (small *e*) adventure that spans recent history and retrieves in capsule the identity of American manhood from the fifties with its tapestry of sprawl and confusion and yes, goddam it, glory, and now its bafflement for a new age (small *n,* small *a*) that seems to have no comprehension of that nation from which this man and so many others emerged and no patience for the values they embodied and for which they fought and suffered.

I say epic (small *e*) since this life follows the pattern we have identified as epic through all the great and eternal sagas of manhood and coming of age over time: *separation, initiation, return.* The hero (small *h* though heroes by definition search to demonstrate Heroism with that capital *H* and speak to us from memory on that very account that they do just that, as this man has) rises from a community whose values he absorbs at the hands of a father and other mentors, takes his leave from them often ceremonially but sometimes by dint of real pain—an atonement with the father that can leave scars over the years and that produces a rare vulnerability in our hero—on the threshold of departure, has adventures in the broader world beyond the village precinct and over the horizon of youth's development, undergoes learning, has adventures--to include the discovery of a magical woman, sometimes a life's companion, sometimes not—in the darkness out there, then wiser and marked by his ordeal comes back home to tell the tale, and in his turn, prepare another generation of young men for experience in their turn and for their contribution to the tribe.

Walter Lang, born into a soldier's family, lives a soldier's life, the contours of which are less and less familiar to an America where soldiers, serving and out of service, represent an infinitesimally small fraction of the population, an anomaly in a culture gone ganging after immediate pleasures and well-being and for which the deliberate pursuit of challenge, the willing deferment of gratification, the purposeful submission to discomfort and risk have become incomprehensible. For this reason alone—that it tells a tale uncommon these days—the life of Walter Lang would be instructive. Yet Lang's epic was not that uncommon in an America bygone and from whose towns and villages and cities young men of his generation faced the same expectations from their family and from their nation and embarked on the same ages-old odyssey of departure, war, and reintegration, often—like the voyager in that original *Odyssey*—painful reintegration. To hear Lang's story is to retrieve the authenticity of that earlier time and a simplicity which, if stark, had purity to it we might well envy now.

What makes this adventure particularly compelling is that this young man who made the traditional stations of the Cross along with his brothers from the epoch (hunting with the uncle, forging through formal education, securing life's love) somehow also contrived to be not merely witness to, but major player, in the grandest events along the timeline of his century, most significantly the war that traumatized America, the one we did not win, the one that contested our most cherished notions of ourselves and that provoked in an Army considered the foremost in the world internal turmoil, anguish, schism.

Lang, who had early on revealed a diffidence and fierce integrity, honed by his durance at the Virginia Military Institute, bastion of antebellum notions of Honor and Nobility already alien to the greedy, silly, duplicitous society into which it released its young gentlemen of the Old Way, stood on one side of this schism, disapproving the template mentality of the worst of Uncle Sam's officer corps, committed to the prosecution of a war into which he'd been thrust with dignity, intelligence, humanity but with ferocious courage and unrelenting determination in the path he saw toward victory. We remember that Siegfried, Rodrigo Diaz de Vivar, Roland, even Beowulf stood each one at odds with his countrymen, done in ultimately by their enmity. If Lang does not get done in by his fellows, he certainly provokes enmity sufficient to place him squarely in that paradigm as loner among comrades not always willing or able to discriminate finely.

It's perhaps the best tribute to America that an Army, a society ultimately and at every turning of the path, did discriminate and did discern in Walter Lang (and, if we can take him as a *beau ideal*, other men with the integrity and courage to stand alone upon principle …if Walter Lang is not the figment of someone's imagination, if a man of flesh and blood actually lived the events recounted so dutifully here, if we could have any clue to the possible identity of such a man) the qualities it needed in a leader and shunted him from post upward to post with ever-enhanced responsibility for his brothers in arms and for the destiny of the republic. This story, of a man's, of a hero's, of *our* journey out of... *what?* and into... *what?*

Brigadier General (Ret.) Alan Farrell
Virginia Military Institute

Prologue

"The Iraqis don't want to see you," the civilian intelligence man said. "They say they don't want to hear your name."

"That's what Claire George said as well," Lang replied, "but that's not what the Iraqi embassy, and the Saudi ambassador says in Washington. That's not what the Iraqis tell our Defense Attaché here."

"George is the Director of Operations," the local intelligence boss answered with a condescending smile.

"Your operations, not ours," Lang answered. "I am here at the direction of the National Security Council and the Secretary of Defense to take charge of this mess."

The US ambassador listened. He and Lang had known each other for a long time in many Arab countries. He looked inscrutably diplomatic. He said nothing. The meeting occupied the undistinguished room that served him as an office. The embassy was in a side street, hidden from public view and closed at both ends of the block by movable barriers and government security forces.

"There is no 'mess,'" the civilian spook hissed. "We have had limited goals here in helping the Iraqis in their 'problem' with Iran."

"Yes, I know," Lang said. "You give them 'chicken feed' to keep your case officers in contact with their people. I understand that. You might get lucky and recruit one. Unfortunately for this program, Ollie North and his pals used information the Iraqis gave you to try to 'make nice' with Iran. The Iranians 'tried out' this gift as they were urged to do by North, and as a result the Iraqis lost a thousand men in repelling the Iranian experiment. Now, the Iraqis believe you betrayed them."

"We did not!"

"No, you did not. The White House betrayed them, but you are blamed. As a result, Iraq wants nothing further to do with you," Lang continued. They have made that clear. At the same time, there is a great and perhaps unreasoning fear in Washington and Riyadh that Iran will break through somewhere south of Baghdad soon and arrive on Kuwait's border."

"You don't believe that?"

"No. I think the crisis in the war has passed. The Iraqis are greatly improved, but… orders are orders. I am going to the general headquarters in half an hour. Do you want to come along?"

"I forbid you to go!"

"I've seen his instructions, and mine, Jim. You can't forbid him to do anything," the ambassador interjected. There was something about the look on his face that revealed how much he enjoyed saying that. Unsurprisingly, the Agency man chose to join Lang's convoy of cars en route to the military headquarters.

"Why have you come to visit us Mister Lang?" His Iraqi host enquired when they had arrived. "Have you come to change history? The Saudis insist that you could do that, and the Jordanians passed us your critique of our dispositions north of Basra on the Shatt al-Arab. You were correct, and we made the change you suggested to King Hussein. Why are you here? Your government is already represented in our capital?" The Iraqi army major general hosting the meeting carefully ignored the American civilian intelligence chief.

The room was bright with light from big windows. There were flowers in cut glass bowls on the long table as well as the little dishes of fruit, candy and nuts that were indispensable at Arab meetings. Their absence would have indicated something less than genuine welcome.

"Did you and your major watch the news last night in the hotel?" the Iraqi general asked. He appeared to want to know something.

"I think you know we did," Lang responded in a friendly, offhand way.

"What did you think of the combat footage from the North, from east of the big lake?"

"A hard-fought action; you lost cameramen in this, did you not? It was impressive the way the infantry swept the top of the mountain in that waist high brush."

"Yes, ma'raka mumtaza!" The Iraqi then remembered that some of his guests might not understand Arabic. "It was an excellent battle, excellent!"

"My government fears for your survival as a country," Lang replied to an earlier question about purpose for his visit. "I have been sent to make sure that this concern is unjustified."

"Well, that is a refreshing change. What are you prepared to do to help us? Our embassy in Washington suggests something specific."

While they chatted, the six senior officers on the Iraqi side of the table had not been able to avert their eyes from the large document tube that Lang's deputy held in his hands.

"We will need space."

The table was cleared.

From the tube emerged a variety of materials designed to direct the Iraqi air force to targets that would cripple any Iranian drive towards Saudi Arabia and Kuwait.

"We can use these?" the general asked. "There will be more?"

'Yes, certainly, but I must mention conditions," Lang answered. "We will not help you in your struggle with the Kurdish separatists. We will not help you select weapons for the strikes, and you must tell me if you want this help. You must say the words."

The Iraqi side sat silent for a moment. Suspicion seemed to war with hope in their souls.

"I see," the general finally said while looking at the civilian intelligence man. "I see. We have similar difficulties on our side. Yes, yes, and yes. We accept any conditions, any."

He stood and offered his hand across the table. "The Jordanians say that your luqab, your 'nickname,' is Antar."

"That is so. I was 'named' by my first Arabic teacher, named for the warrior poet."

"But you are not black," the general said and laughed.

"Perhaps my soul is dark enough."

The grey-haired man looked down at the table. "We know that feeling here. Six years of this war has darkened all our souls. Welcome, Antar, welcome."

CHAPTER ONE

The Far Shore

May 1969

Buildings have a life of their own. Some have a look that conveys the collective effect of decades or even generations of careful, perhaps loving attention. Well-polished brasses, clean, highly waxed floors, new and tasteful carpets, these things all create an atmosphere of prosperous well-being and self-assurance. Other buildings "speak" of decline and neglect, of money denied for repairs.

This old hotel looked as if it might have been built in the early twentieth century. There were occasional reflections of the art-deco era in elevator doors and obscure sculptural references in the lobby's corners.

The young man wondered if this relic had been put up in the 1920s. In a childhood filled with different lives, lived in strange places, he had developed a lot of interests that might have seemed odd to his peers. One of them was architecture and its history. He noticed that the dirty and water stained marble was leaning away from the wall in places and was loose in an angle of the lobby cornice near the ceiling. He examined the reception staff while he waited with his father. They were as seedy as the building.

He was a soldier. His father was also a soldier. They were professional soldiers. The father was now long retired and completely devoted to such preoccupations as dog walking and television news.

An elevator door opened, and the young man's uncle appeared. The little man had aged a lot, but his back was still straight. His head was still held high, but he had lost a lot of weight and seemed pale. The uncle was yet another military man. In his case, the US Navy had been the main devotion in his life, devotion so pure and true that he was thought by many to be one of the navy's greatest heroes. His name was John.

The brothers shook hands and greeted each other with few words. There was no embrace. It was not their way.

"Uncle," the young man said extending his hand. "It has been too long, far too long."

John looked at him, looked at him from head to foot. "You've grown tall. You were such a skinny little kid. I was always afraid that we might ask you to do things that were too hard for you... No uniform? I hoped that you would wear your uniform." He looked saddened.

The nephew regretted his choice of clothing...

They rode a dirty elevator to the roof. The car smelled of old vomit, and the red carpet was stained brown in places. The door opened at the top offering relief and escape into a larger space.

The roof top saloon was surrounded by slabs of plate glass. A rectangular bar was covered on its sides with red vinyl and corroded brass covered studs. Shabby wooden tables were scattered around the room in no obvious pattern. There were a dozen old men and women in the room drinking. It was ten in the morning.

The uncle spoke to the bartender. "Good morning, George, my family has come to visit. This is my brother, Walt, and his son, Walter Patrick." It was clear from his manner with the barman that they knew each other well. The light brown man was dressed in a white jacket and black pants. When they had arrived, he was standing at the end of the bar with his hands behind him contemplating the streets below.

George nodded gravely, "Good to meet you, gentlemen. Any friends of Mister Lang are welcome at my counter."

And why not, the young man thought. *Why not? He spends enough time here, doesn't he?*

From a perch between the brothers, he found that he felt a child again, closed in and there to be examined for some reason. *Why am I here? Why have I been summoned here?* He wondered.

Outside, beyond the streaked glass walls, the sky was lead grey and depressing... The building they sat in was a residence hotel, a place for "warehousing" the elderly and poor while waiting for God to collect them. The Long Beach shoreline could be seen stretching away into the distance. There was a fishing pier in the close foreground. Beyond that was an amusement park. Yet farther away was a cluster of two-story stucco buildings that he had driven by on the way to the hotel. He remembered that it was a navy hospital. Surf broke on the beach by the legs of the iron pier. A Ferris wheel turned slowly in the distance. A large carousel was closer. He remembered this carousel. His grandmother had brought him to the amusement park once or twice, and his father had brought him a few more times. He particularly remembered the beautifully carved horses and all the other fantastic beasts. He could still "hear" the lilting steam calliope music ringing in his head. *How old was I then? I was nine or ten when we came back from Frankfurt. We left for Maine when I was thirteen. It was somewhere in between.*

At this moment, while seated in the bar, he was three days back from the war. A week earlier, he had handed over command of his unit to someone he found unsatisfactory, someone who feared everything and who talked openly of moving the teams into secure compounds. He had told the man that it would be impossible to operate from such places, but he could see that this had no meaning for one so fearful. By the time he climbed aboard a helicopter to go to the coast and home, he knew, and his men knew, that the grand game they had played together on the Cambodian border was over.

Sitting in the shoddy bar, he was still far away, absent in that other life across the ocean. The memory of that life and the yet lingering result of illnesses that had come with the very air in the mountains of Viet Nam were still with him. He had commanded a unit of military intelligence troops on the border. The mission had been to recruit locals to infiltrate Viet Cong and North Vietnamese Army lines of supply so as to provide targets for air attack, artillery fire and ground operations.

The Republic of Vietnam government held scattered towns in jungle covered country throughout his area. His men had operated from the towns, towns surrounded by VC and by North Vietnamese Army soldiers. The enemy's forces were always present outside these towns, always waiting outside the towns and often in the towns as well. The enemy persistently "leaned" against the barbed wire and fortified lines of the towns and villages. There were daily attacks by fire with mortars and artillery rockets. From time to time, a ground "probe" overran sections of the perimeter of the towns. These limited attacks took place several times a month. Counterattacks drove the intruders out again in actions that always lost men. He had led several such counterattacks. A number of times that year, the enemy had tried to seize towns in which he had soldiers. None succeeded. There were no roads that were safe to travel. All were "ambushed" by men who waited and waited and waited. There were roadside bombs everywhere outside the perimeters. Every ground trip outside "the wire" was a patrol or an operation looking for a fight. It had been a long year, a year-long, seven days a week fight that had been broken at midpoint by a week-long leave in Hawaii with his wife.

Most soldiers never see the enemy. Even those said to be in combat never see the enemy. The Cambodian borderlands had been different. The enemy's lines of supply ran through his area from across the border. The "opposition" wanted to keep RVN and US forces "bottled up" in the towns. To that end they engaged every effort to go out into the countryside. This meant that face to face fights at close range were commonplace. There had been a lot of killing and wounding, and he had done more than his share both personally and through his men.

While preparing to leave that place of sorrow and adventure, he was offered two very different assignments. One was to the army general staff in Washington and the other was to Europe. He chose Europe, even though he knew the other was more likely to lead to sponsorship for promotion by some powerful general. As a result, he had orders to a nice, quiet job in Germany where he intended to rest, go skiing and shelter in the warmth of his marriage while readying himself for a certain return to the war. He and his wife were going to travel to Europe by steamship in a few weeks. A first-class cabin on the SS United States was a tangible reward for his recent promotion and new rank.

He wrote his father from Vietnam to inform him of the date of his return to the United States. This was an unusual thing for him to do. He and his father were not close. They had not been close for a long time. As a boy, he felt that his father cared deeply for him, but that had ended. It ended when he was something like 13, and near the time when the family moved to his mother's home place in Maine. His father retired ill from the army after 34 years and did not seem interested in finding employment in California. The mother's hometown was a bustling industrial center of the textile industry. Perhaps his father thought he could find work there as an accountant. He was a CPA and had been a finance department officer, but soon after they arrived the factory was sold, and that prospect disappeared. They lived far out in the Maine woods for several years, until the father found work in another state. In the woods, the father taught his son the lumberman's skills. He had worked as a lumberjack in his youth, but in spite of doing hard physical work together every day, a barrier arose between them. There was less and less talk while working until there was none. That distance remained over the years. Nothing he did pleased his father. Nothing was ever good enough. This included his marriage to the beautiful, accomplished woman who waited for him in Boston, waited while he wasted time in California.

Surprisingly, the father wrote back asking him to stay a few days in California for a visit. His wife said that he should do that. She said that they could wait a few more days. It grieved her that his father did not appreciate him, and she hoped for reconciliation. He flew to Santa Barbara, but after a few hours at his parents' home he knew that nothing had changed. His efforts to tell them of his year were met by silence and efforts to change the subject. Finally, he was told the truth. "Your uncle John asks to see you. He wants to talk to you." This was a surprise. He had been planning to leave the next day, but this changed everything, even though he had not seen the man for a long time. The truth was that John Lang was one of his favorite people.

The father had been stationed in Los Angeles for five years after his return from occupation duty in Germany. John lived nearby at that time as did another brother, Gordon. This other uncle was also a retired navy man. In those childhood years in southern California, the young Walter came to know John well. The three Lang brothers often congregated for backyard feasts and beer around a big built-in barbecue constructed by a previous owner of the house. Stories of China, the Philippines and Borneo were told and retold over steaks to the wonderment of the boy.

John eventually began to pay attention to this child. One day he reminded him of the occasion at Fort Devens, Massachusetts in 1942, when little Walter had vomited beer on John's dark blue navy jacket.

In fact, the boy remembered the jacket and the rows of gold braid that marked a chief petty officer's rank.

"Ah, you made him drink it," Gordon said.

"Only a sip," John laughed with his head thrown back, "Then he grabbed the glass and drained it. You don't remember that, do you?" he asked the boy.

He began to teach the child to tie knots, seaman's knots. They made a wooden board and mounted the knots on the board. After a few months, John told the boy that he knew so many knots that he could "sit" for the exam for "bosun's mate."

John had lost both kneecaps in the taking of Saipan. They were rebuilt for him during a year in hospital. When they had finished their work, the doctors told him that he had a choice. He would walk a lot, or he would not walk at all. He had a Master Mariner's license as a merchant marine captain and could have found a job as master of a merchant vessel. He laughed at the thought. "Merchant Marine sailors! Hooligan sailors!" he laughed.

He used his disabled veteran's advantage to find work for the Los Angeles County flood control system as a hydrographer. This was a fancy description for someone who walked around in the San Gabriel Mountains near Los Angeles, measuring the depth of water in the ponds behind flood control dams.

One day he asked the boy if he would like to go with him on one of these hikes in the wilderness. The father was present and gave his assent. He gave it so readily that a carful observer might have thought this had been arranged in advance.

Someone in the bar asked the young man a question. He looked at his father and uncle... Their faces told him little. The Lang habit of impassivity shrouded their thoughts. He glanced at the barman. "What did you say?" he asked the smiling, waiting presence.

"What'll it be, sir? And can I see some ID?"

The soldier retrieved his military identification and handed it across the wooden counter. "I'll have whatever my uncle drinks at this time of day," he said.

"You are a major in the army?" the bartender asked. He looked uncertain about his own question.

"Yup, let's see, three months ago. Four months next week."

The man was still holding the ID card and looking at it. "You are twenty-eight?"

Photo Credit: W. Patrick Lang

"Don't you think it looks like me?" The major asked. The deep hostility that was always there biding its time began to float towards the surface.

"Give it back, George," his uncle said quietly from his left. "Give it back... We will have Scotch and water."

"Not me," the major's father said from his bar stool to the right. "You know I don't drink any longer."

"No, not anymore," John said. "Not anymore..."

"You live here?" The major asked. "You live in this hotel, with... George?" He realized that he was watching George work with more than casual interest.

George looked uncomfortably aware of that attention. "This is quite a bar, George," the major said straight faced. "You have a pretty view up and down the beach and all-over Long Beach. Is that the navy hospital over there beyond the Ferris wheel? I'll bet you were a navy man. You were, weren't you, George?"

George nodded.

A steward, the major thought but did not say. He tasted his drink. "Excellent, thank you, George."

He turned to his uncle. "I was sorry to hear of Lorraine's death. I hardly knew her, but it is a great loss for you I am sure."

I remember the trip to Big Bear Lake. I remember the log cabin with the wooden dock. Lorraine was from hardscrabble Texas You picked her up somewhere, somewhere like this. She brought a rabbit from a butcher shop for that Lang family weekend. My parents did not eat rabbit. You handed me the rabbit and a knife in the kitchen and told me to deal with it. Father got up and came to watch me cut the rabbit into frying pieces. You and he and my mother continued to watch while I finished the job. You told your wife to let me cook. I dusted the parts with corn flour and fried it up as you taught me to do in the mountains when we were lucky enough to kill one with the slingshot you carried in the knapsack. First the slingshot to stun the little creature and then the wrung neck and a discussion of the merits of wild rabbit. My rabbit cookery was said by Lorraine to be "tasty."

Photo Credit: W. Patrick Lang

The scarred, pale little man sat silent beside him and studied him, seeking something, something.

It was probably something that the major did not want to reveal. *Ah, it's not fifteen years,* he thought. *He came by the Santa Barbara house for a few hours when I was there for the summer in 1960.*

"Do army majors have 'scrambled eggs' on their caps?" the uncle asked.

The new major, a combat man through and through, felt a deep impatience, an annoyance with what seemed to be worries about trivialities of dress.

"Yes, I suppose I will have to buy one eventually."

"You don't care?"

"No. I don't care. Would you care?" He then saw, looking from one to the other, that they would care. He began to grasp an important notion, an idea that he should have understood. *They struggled so long for what has been given me in just a few years. I must be more careful in what I say.* "I remember our hydrographic expeditions to the mountains" he told John.

The uncle waited glass in hand to hear what else he would say and while waiting ordered another round from George who stood waiting and listening.

Customers walked by and greeted the uncle in the hearty way that people always assumed when they met him.

"Would you like to hear about what I have been doing?" the young man asked. He knew before he inquired that the response would be different from that in Santa Barbara.

"Of course, I want to know," John replied. "Sorry you have to listen to this again, Walt," he told his brother. An embarrassing silence hung over them all.

"George," the major said. "Does he still drink a lot?"

"Yassuh," the man said instinctively using his own true voice. "They's a navy doctuh ovah theah in the hospitul. He tol' him not to stop, an' that the shock to his system would be too much for him if he did, considerin' his... injuries."

"Start," John said, "Start at the beginning when you trained for this, somewhere. I want to hear it all."

The telling took several hours. The story was full of spying, blood, death and comradeship. It was filled with love for the men he had left behind in the hands of a fool.

Halfway through the tale, they took a break for lunch in a neighborhood bar and grill favored by John. It was another beer stained dump, filled with the smell of old grease. They ate fried abalone, something the brothers dearly loved. The major picked up the tab, determined to show that he was no longer the boy they remembered... His father was pleased, not for the demonstration of maturity, but because he was tight fisted by nature and had always been.

While they ate, the major remembered the trips to the mountains, particularly the first. *We walked up the long trail to the first dam. The sun was warm, but the air was cold with the bite of the snow-covered peaks above. You cut a sapling and made it into a walking stick with a fork at the end. You limped a lot when we started up, but that eased as the ruined legs warmed. Near the first dam, you told me to be careful because animals came to drink or to hunt those that did. Something moved nearby, and you chased it into the undergrowth. "Come here," you called. I found you in a thicket where you had pinned a diamondback rattlesnake to the ground with the stick. The fork held it down, pinning it behind the head. The snake was about six feet long. It thrashed unhappily. You watched me and then picked up the animal, holding it behind the head. You held it three feet high with most of the creature thrashing and rattling fiercely. The jaws opened and closed, opened and closed, the fangs extending as the mouth opened. "Do you want to hold it?" you asked. I knew what the answer had to be and knew this was a test... I reached for it... "Hold it tight with both hands. Don't let go!" After a few minutes' discussion of the finer points of diamondbacks as opposed to sidewinders and other vipers, you took it back, and broke the neck. The snake continued to writhe on the stony ground among the piñón needles. You handed me a knife and watched while I cut off the rattle. The rattle went into a Mason jar from your pack. This rattle had nine segments. We took a foot of the diamondback to grill for lunch. Nine rattles, nine years old you told me, "almost as old as you." We fished behind the third dam. The pond was stocked with small mouthed bass. A piece of line, a lead weight, a plastic float, a hook and pink salmon eggs were all that was needed. I cleaned the fish on the gravel shore, and we cooked them on sticks cut nearby. When we returned to the car, we had a Mason jar nearly filled with rattles.*

The major laughed aloud; his head thrown back.

The two old men looked up in surprise. They had been content in their lunch and quiet as they ate.

"I was just thinking of my mother and the rattles."

"What is this about?" John asked.

The father shrugged in resignation at the need to tell his brother something not known, something hidden. "She found ten or twelve jars of rattles in the garage. She went crazy, demanded I come home from the office. She knew I did not do that except for emergencies. She knew that... Your friend here had told her all about it. She demanded that I 'have it out with you' over this."

John waited.

The major watched them; waiting for something he had not seen between them, something loving. It did not appear. With an audible sigh. he told John that his brother had explained to his nearly hysterical wife that this was a matter between the boy and his brother, and that he would not interfere.

"You might have told me," John said to the father. "I wondered why I could not take him to the mountains any longer. You could have told me."

The major saw that his uncle looked like he might cry. This man of unending courage and perseverance in the face of suffering was red in the face, and the water in his eyes welled up so because he had been shut out of that important moment in his brother's family life.

They returned to the big, ugly building that pretended to be a hotel.

The father asked for John's room key so that he might rest.

In the bar, the "snake hunters" had another drink. The major bought George one as well.

"A rare privilege," John said. "He generally does not drink with anyone but navy people. I would have preferred that you had gone into the navy. I could have helped with that... Now tell me what is bothering you..."

"What do you mean?"

The bartender walked to the end of the bar and once again stood with his hands clasped behind him looking at the wind and rain swept beach. The Ferris wheel had closed for the day.

"Don't fool around. Tell me. Tell me while he is gone. He is not a good listener for things like this. He never was."

"I lost a friend..."

"We lose many. Tell me."

"I told you of the big fight in my detachment headquarters town three months ago."

John nodded. "Yes. The province senior advisor went out into the battle and was killed the first night. What of it?"

"I tried to convince him of what was coming. I tried to tell him how many there would be. I failed. He had a wife and five children at Clark Air Base in the Philippines. He went home to be with them often."

"Ah... Listen to me. Men die in our business. Sometimes they kill themselves for reasons known only to them. An officer on one of my ships decided to kill himself. He went down to his stateroom and lined up his head with the porthole before he shot himself. We were grateful and thought him a gentleman. Your friend willfully killed himself after you warned him. You cautioned him, but he did not listen to you. You are not responsible... Do you hear me? Do you? You are not responsible. He killed himself."

The major heard. It felt as though a great weight was taken from the burden of death that he carried. He thought for a moment. "Why am I here?" he asked at last. "Why did you send for me?"

John glanced down at the liquor stained wood of the bar. "I wanted to know. I wanted to see what you had become. Now I know. You are one of us, a member of my company. You are a warrior."

'What does that mean for me?"

"You know what it means. You must be what you are. Tell your wife that I would come live near the two of you, but that does not seem to be 'in the cards.'"

"I could get out. I could support my family. I could do that. We could make money..."

John laughed. "No, that is not for you and me. We are what make the army and navy work in combat. Dressed up phonies with high rank hate us, but they know we make it work, and they can't bring themselves to get rid of us. Remember that the civilians who come in to serve in wartime are just doing their civic duty, but they are like sheep ready for the knife. We make victory happen. I am finished. Now it is your turn. You will make it happen. Do your duty. Never forget this. Now let us collect my brother. I am happy to have seen you."

The word, *father,* welled up in the major's soul. It struggled to be said. He desperately wanted to call the little man what he really was.

John watched and reached for his hand. "That is his. You know that. I understand. Thank you."

Five months later, Marguerite Lang opened the door of her apartment in Frankfurt to find her husband in the living room. He seldom returned before the end of the duty day. Today he sat with a glass in one hand and a letter in the other. He said that the letter was from her father-in-law. She saw grief in his face. She had been shopping for Christmas presents downtown. She took a moment to put her packages on the dining room table before sitting with him. He watched her move around the room. It was a pleasure to watch her. She sat beside him and reached for the letter.

"John died in his sleep two weeks ago," her husband said. "His ashes were scattered on the California Current west of Catalina Island. A group of his old shipmates did that hoping that some part of him might reach the far shore."

"I thought he had been in fairly good health recently," she whispered.

He raised his glass.

"I see," she said. "He stopped drinking."

CHAPTER TWO

The Dancing Carabao

*"Oh, the monkeys have no tails in Zamboanga, Oh, the monkeys
have no tails in Zamboanga, Oh, the monkeys have no tails,
They were bitten off by whales,
Oh, the monkeys have no tails in Zamboanga."*

27th Infantry Regiment (Wolfhounds) Marching Song

The date was October 12, 1924. The place was the city of Zamboanga, on Mindanao Island in the Department of the Philippines. Zamboanga was then a city of one hundred thousand souls. Colonial Spanish architecture predominated. There was a "Plaza Mayor" in which the Inquisition had burned relapsed *Conversos* from Islam. There was a cathedral on one side of this square. It was built in a style popular in Spain in the 18ᵗʰ Century. Dominican friars, now mostly of Filipino descent, were still seen in the streets in their black and white habits.

In the city's three-hundred-year-old Presidio, Spanish troops had been replaced by Americans as a result of victory in the war against Spain some twenty-five years before. Now the garrison was an 800-man Philippine Scouts battalion of regular US troops, once again of mainly Filipino descent.

Outside the town, the countryside was policed by the mounted gendarmerie of the Philippine Constabulary. This rural police force was led by US Army sergeants promoted to officers' commissioned ranks.

Some US commissioned officers served as well in the senior positions. The constables were all Filipinos and representative of the local population in whatever district they served. They fought a lot against *ladrones*, non-Filipino tribesmen of such interesting groups as "Ifugaos," "Igorots," "Negritos," and the occasional Moro "sultan" wrapped in the emotional comfort of the idea of "jihad." These were the most worrisome of the Constabulary's usual foes. Itinerant mosque preachers spread notions from India and Arabia of the duty of Muslims to fight for the *"Umma"* in Mindanao and the islands that stretched away southwest to Borneo.

There was a tavern in the city, just next to the big, blue-domed mosque paid for by the Turkish sultan in the 19ᵗʰ Century. It was called "The Dancing Carabao." A garishly painted sign hung over the old, metal studded Spanish door. It depicted the ubiquitous Southeast Asia domesticated water buffalo standing placidly in a muddy wallow. The stone walls of the inn were covered in tan stucco. They were thick and easily carried the weight of the mahogany door that hung on wide strap hinges. The bar was owned by a retired US Navy chief petty officer and his Chinese wife. She was from Shanghai. He was Chicago born. He had served in the "Yangtze River Patrol" in USS Palos, a gunboat built in Manila, and then in the cruiser flagship of the Navy's Asiatic Squadron. This ship usually was on station at Shanghai so that it could command the river patrol gunboats and other fleet units in the China Sea. He had been a ship's cook and at the end was chef of the admiral's mess on board the cruiser.

His wife had been a waitress in Shanghai. The "Carabao" was a favorite "retreat" for constabulary officers, sergeants from the army garrison and those Filipino soldiers who had developed a taste for American food and company. US Army officers and their wives were not seen there. They preferred their clubs and mutual entertainments. This was understandable. The upper floors housed the owners and a thriving bordello. The Chief's wife had imported girls from China. They were popular with the soldiers and constabulary. She was a splendid hostess and known for her "mothering" of injured soldiers. Many a man with injured hands or arms had enjoyed the experience of having her feed him his dinner with chopsticks.

The mosque looked like the *"Suleimaniyah"* in Istanbul. A great many Muslims worshipped there weekly. The town was nearly equally divided in faith between the followers of Islam and Catholics. The Americans, of course, were mainly Protestants, if anything.

Four Constabulary officers assembled there the evening of the 11th. It was their custom to spend the night there monthly, taking refuge from isolation and loneliness within the tavern's walls, feasting on the cook's American dishes, and sampling the girls on the third floor.

They were friends. Two of them, Walt Lang and Jim Davis, were from the upper Midwest. They were from Minnesota and North Dakota respectively. They had served together in the 7th Cavalry Regiment in Mexico in the Punitive Expedition of 1917.

Another, Douglas Burns, had been a Canadian soldier but came south into the United States to escape prosecution for a disciplinary offense involving another man's wife. He transferred to tanks in 1918 to serve with the "1st US Tank Brigade" in France. He would have stayed with tanks after the war, but the US Army got rid of them all, hoping to save money when faced with the reality of peace time budgets. The fourth, Geraldo Martinez, was from California. He had been a captain in the National Guard there. He had served with honor in Europe in World War I. He had asked to be brought on active duty in 1922 and sent to the Constabulary when he could not find work suitable to a gentleman in California... His family had been *hidalgos* in the *pueblo* of Los Angeles when the first *gringos* arrived, but that meant little to the horde of Texans and Oklahomans now flowing like the proverbial river into his homeland. To them, he was just another "beaner." He knew the other three from a few months that he had served at Fort McKinley. This post was Philippine Department Headquarters near the city of Manila.

They ate, drank and played pinochle into the morning hours. After dawn, they woke in their rooms on the third floor to screaming, shouting and shots in the streets. Dressed, they left their Chinese women friends hiding under the beds. It soon became clear that a mutiny of Moro soldiers of the Philippine Scouts raged in the streets of Zamboanga. The garrison battalion was mixed. Most of the troops were Filipino Christians, but there was also an infantry company of Moro Scouts.

Some units of the Scouts regiments were made up altogether of Muslims from Mindanao and the Sulu Archipelago, but most included Moro companies within majority Christian battalions. The Moro soldiers were fierce fighters, but their feeling of allegiance to the uniform they wore was fragile and some imagined cause constantly carried the potential for friction. In this case, a newly assigned and recently commissioned American officer had made what seemed to him a trivial comment about local custom. The "issue" brewed for a bit, and then the offended parties found the lieutenant walking down a street and stabbed him to death. Realizing that retribution was inevitable when the Army discovered this murder, the soldiers and the rest of their company broke into the arms room, took their rifles and ran amok in the streets looking for more Americans.

When the American patrons of the "Carabao" reached the ground floor, they found that three Military Policemen from the provost guard had taken shelter in the bar with their sergeant. They had broken the glass of the windows so that they could shoot up and down the street, especially at the open space in front of the mosque. They quite reasonably believed that trouble would likely come from that direction.

The innkeeper and his wife stood, or perhaps crouched, behind the bar. The Chinese lady shouted in rage that the "bastid MPs" had broken her windows. Who would pay for this, she demanded?

Second Lieutenant Lang walked to the swinging doors and started out into the street. One of the MPs grabbed his arm and pulled him back into the barroom.

A bullet smacked into the doorframe near his head. The report of the rifle arrived. The marksman was far off, perhaps in a tall structure like the cathedral's bell tower.

The wiry little lieutenant staggered back into the room. "What the hell is going on?" he asked.

"Moros," the MP Sergeant replied. "They have gone *juramentado* and are killing people all over town. We came in here to get away from snipers in the buildings. The garrison commander is organizing a counter-attack to clear the streets, but it will take a while…."

The four officers looked at each other, and then at the lady owner.

"Any chow, Mai?" Davis asked. "Mighty hungry…"

"And hung over," Burns added.

"You good custommahs, don't break nussing, don' beat up girls. I send Henry to kitchen. Bacon, egg, good?" Henry Brown, her husband, left for the kitchen to see what there was in the iceboxes.

"Yer a good woman, Mai," Davis said in a low voice. "If it wasn't fer Henry…"

"Hmmphh!" she sniffed, while looking at him with a slight smile.

"Now you go back and see to it that Henry doesn't spit in our eggs," Lang told her. "And bring some for the MPs!"

She waved as she went through the kitchen doors.

About the time they finished breakfast, the shooting seemed to die down a little in the street.

A couple of the Chinese girls came down the stairs and could not be "shooed" back upstairs.

The four men decided to take shelter under a table where they could continue their gaming and conversation. They had changed into uniform; khaki shirts with red and gold shoulder straps, riding britches, cavalry boots with short, blunt, Army spurs. Their broad brimmed campaign hats lay on the table.

The two girls were joined by two more. They all sat with their backs pressed to "their men" and chattered in Chinese amongst themselves.

"Henry! Bring us a bucket of suds! San Miguel, not that British swill from Singapore… Eight glasses, *por favor,* and keep it coming, right Mai?" Davis had his way, and the beer flowed freely in an endless supply of pails "Thanks, Mai, you're a sweetie," he said. He was always her favorite among the four.

She kept looking at him as he sat under the table with a pretty girl.

Mai's husband was rooted behind the bar. He looked thoroughly afraid. "What if they…?"

'Don't worry, Chief," Martinez laughed. "We'll protect your home. Won't we boys?" he asked the MPs.

They were happy with their breakfasts and looked enviously at the beer and girls.

Martinez' girl had come downstairs wearing a blue silk *cheongsam* with embroidered gold and silver flowers across the body and skirt. She looked a little older, or perhaps the right description would have been that she looked more mature, than the other three. Those were clearly adolescents.

"What's her name?' Lang asked Martinez. He was both appreciative and envious.

"Lin. Why?" Geraldo Martinez was shuffling several packs of cards together and did not look up.

The girl who was being discussed looked at Lang, then at Martinez and then returned to her chat with the other girls.

"Walt, where were you last month?" Davis asked. "We missed you. Mai and Henry missed you. Those Igorots can't be all that wonderful that you would forget your old friends?"

"No, they are a hard lot. My district has almost nothing in it but tribesmen except in a few towns in the valleys. My constables are all Filipinos. They can't stand people smaller and darker than they are. And, now I have about a dozen "Old Maid" schoolteachers from New England in the towns. They are all Protestants. The Mullahs and Catholic priests hate them…"

"Aren't you Catholic?" Martinez asked.

"That's the rumor," Lang replied. "I'm not much for that kind of thing… I was in Manila with my two Navy brothers. We don't see each other much. Gordon is on a submarine at Cavite, and the other one, John, is at Shanghai waiting for a new gunboat to come out of the yard there. We got a little tight, and Gordon drove his car off a pier in *Intramuros* in the middle of the night. It was an open car so we swam to the pier, but the car is somewhere on the bottom of the bay. Last I heard the two of them were still trying to 'square' this with the Manila police. I left as soon as I could to come home.

Davis looked at the tan colored wall beside his elbow. Motion had attracted his attention. He picked a tiny chameleon lizard called a *gecko* off the wall and dropped it in a dice cup they had under the table for the purpose of shooting "craps." He put his hand over the open end of the cup, shook it a few times and then rolled the lizard out on the cloth on which they were dealing cards. "Snake eyes!" he laughed. The lizard lay on its back. Davis prodded it with a fingertip. "The engineers are building an iron bridge over the Sindagan River," he said. "I am trying to keep the locals quiet enough to let them finish it in peace."

The lizard staggered to its feet and wandered off toward the wall.

"What'll that do?" Burns asked.

"It'll open up the market towns in the interior of the island," was the response.

"And let us get troops into the mountains to keep the tribes quiet," Burns commented.

Under the table, the gambling continued as the sound of mayhem outside the inn waxed and waned throughout the morning.

"What do you think will happen here," Martinez asked.

"Oh, the garrison will bring enough force in to clear out the mutineers," said Lang.

"No, I mean in P.I. generally? Are they going to fight us again for independence?"

Burns recited:

"Oh, he may be a little brown brother to big Bill Taft, but he ain't no brother of mine."

Everyone laughed except Martinez. Even the Chinese women laughed.

Martinez asked if they thought the American administration of the islands was doing anything for the various peoples.

"I think they will be much the same when we are gone as they were when we arrived," said Burns.

"What do you mean we? You're Canadian," laughed Martinez.

"Not any longer. Ottawa took that when I joined the US Army. No, I am going to live in coastal California when I have enough time to retire."

"When will that be?" Lang enquired.

"1935, but I might stay on for thirty years. The retired pay is a lot better. That would be 1945."

"Little brown brother, you don't really mean that," Martinez protested.

They all just looked at him.

"Well, maybe not," Davis said. He was looking at the Chinese whore in the beautiful blue silk dress.

At 11 o'clock, one of the MPs yelled. "Here they come! There's dozen of 'em." Rifle fire rang through the room. Bullets came through the door and windows, striking the walls and wooden bar.

The owners cowered on the floor behind it.

A bayonet stab through a window wounded one MP in the back.

Lang picked his service automatic up from the floor and shot the mutineer in the face. Three more of them broke down the door and charged into the room with rifles and bayonets. They were screaming *"Allahu Akbar! Allahu Akbar!"* The MPs fought them around the door, but a hail of .45 pistol bullets from the men under the table killed all three.

Lang and Davis got up, stretched and walked to the door where they and the MPs threw the bodies out into the street. They rejoined the others and called for another pail of San Miguel.

"Good pistol, the .45 Colt," Burns said. "Good pistol."

There were still pools of liquid blood on the floor.

'Yes, a good pistol," said Davis. "Did you hear that Sergeant Major Keene retired from department headquarters?"

"Who's that?" Lang asked.

"You're joking," said Davis.

"No, who is he?"

"He was a corporal in the Wolfhounds in 1912. They were fighting some sultan on Jolo in the Sulu Islands. They reached the sultan's 'capital.' It was on a mountaintop. It had a six-foot wooden stockade around it. It was a little place, maybe a thousand people; maybe, they couldn't get close enough to break down the wall with rams. There was no artillery, just rifles and pistols. The Moros made a couple of charges out the gate with those little nets tied around their nuts and twisted until they go mad with the pain. They were yelling and screaming as usual and swinging those wavy swords. They were driven back every time, but it looked like a stand-off."

"So, what happened?" Lang pressed.

"Some genius came up with the idea of throwing a man over the wall to open the gate from the inside…"

"Jesus wept…"

"Probably he did. The officers asked for volunteers. You know how that goes, 'well, men, for the regiment…'"

"Keene volunteered?"

"Yup, Keene weighed a hundred pounds soaking wet back then. So, they gave him four .45s. They were new guns. Two in his fists and two tied to his belt. His pockets were full of magazines. Then, the six biggest men in the regiment picked him up, ran forward under covering fire and hurled him over the fence…"

"And he was killed…"

"No. There was a tremendous noise of firing inside, along with a lot of *"Allahu Akbar"* as well, and then silence. After a moment, the gate slowly swung open. Keene staggered out and collapsed. Inside the gate were a dozen

Moro *juramentados* on the ground. The regiment charged through the gate and the whole thing was over in a few minutes."

"Medal of Honor?" asked Lang.

"Oh yes, and a nice job in headquarters, he's been there ever since, as a kind of museum exhibit." Martinez laughed at his own joke.

"Lin" looked at him over her shoulder and smiled.

"Here come the troops!" yelled the MP sergeant.

The Constabulary officers went to the door in time to see a skirmish line of Filipino Scouts sweep by with fixed bayonets. Their sergeants and officers strolled along behind the line. Some had not even drawn their pistols.

Another line could be seen converging on the mosque. It was suddenly all over, finished.

"Next month boys?" Lang asked as they paid their bills at one end of the now bullet-scarred bar.

"Lin" stood next to Martinez looking up at him. There was something wistful in her pretty face. She looked gorgeous in the slim Chinese dress. The high collar and the slit along the outside of a thigh were marvelous to behold.

Captain Martinez tried not to look at her, but it was impossible, just impossible.

"She tell you her name Lin?" Mai asked. She had been watching the scene between the captain and this girl. "Her name Mary, not Lin anymore. She Christian from Shanghai. Her father big man in *Kuomintang*. He killed by communists. That why she whore. She speak English real good."

Martinez waited.

"Yes, my name is Mary," the young woman began. "My father was a Nationalist officer. He made the revolution against the emperor. I went to school with nuns until my family was gone… Please take me with you, please, please."

"You never told me, all night…"

Mary looked at the floor.

Martinez looked at Mai enquiringly.

She held out a hand, palm up. "You pay her bill to me, then take her. She too fancy for my house. I want her gone." She looked sideways at her husband in a way that carried meaning.

Henry seemed fascinated by a spot near the bathroom door.

"My credit good?" Martinez asked.

"All time," Mai answered. "You take her."

"I command a police district in the mountains," Geraldo told Mary. "I have fifty mounted constables and two hundred square miles of territory to police. I have a small set of quarters and two servants. You would not be a servant."

Mary put her arm through his. She looked almost shy.

In front of the "Carabao," they all saw that the sign had bullet holes in it and had been knocked off one hinge.

Mai waved her arms in anger and went back in the bar.

His friends lifted Mary up and put her on the horse behind Captain Martinez. She clung to his back as they rode away, returning to his post.

> *"Damn, damn, damn the Filipinos.*
> *Cross eyed kakiak ladrones.*
> *Underneath the starry flag, Civilize'em with a Krag,*
> *And return us to our own beloved homes."*
> *By Unknown*

CHAPTER THREE

Chrysanthemum

In April 1928, China was in chaos. The 1912 revolution against the ancient imperial government had triumphed. It succeeded beyond the dreams of the insurgents. Dr. Sun Yat Sen was their leader in that revolt, but he had not been able to create a unified national government to replace the emperor's rule. What had emerged was an increasingly savage struggle between the nationalist forces in the *Kuomintang* Party and the communist faction of that party led by Mao Tse Tung. A further complication was the existence of autonomous warlords. These freebooter generals controlled large private armies. The warlords' "game" was to play the Nationalists and Communists against each other while seeking power and wealth. Among them was one Zhang Zuolin, known ironically as the "Christian Warlord."

Nanking, far up the Yangtze River from Shanghai, was the capital of the Republic of China. The Nationalists among the *Kuomintang* had held the city for most of the previous year, but in this spring, Communist forces approached the city and made clear their intention to occupy it.

Adding to the confusion, "General" Zhang occupied a quarter of the town while he negotiated with both the Nationalists and the Communists.

The city had many foreign residents. There were large diplomatic and business communities in Nanking. Foreign news organizations were present. Several of these distributed "newsreels" in which Chinese soldiers belonging to the contesting parties declared their desire to kill foreigners and sack the city.

In response, the "Treaty" countries that maintained forces in China assembled a naval force on the river at Nanking to protect their nationals and interests. There were twenty ships with several thousand troops embarked. There were ships from: Britain, France, Japan, the Netherlands and the United States. Most of these countries maintained shallow draft vessels on the Yangtze on a permanent basis. These gunboats were usually less than two hundred feet in length. For this operation the "powers" brought larger vessels to Nanking. There were two light cruisers, eight destroyers and the usual swarm of gunboats.

The assembled force watched for a day as the violence in the city grew to unacceptable levels. Patrols from the ships reported that there were dead civilians throughout the business district, and that General Zhang's men had reached the riverbank in a number of places.

At dawn on 26 April, Zhang's artillery began to fire "ranging" shots at the ships. A shell struck the French destroyer, *Indomitable,* above the waterline and well aft.

The ships then began lowering their boats while the main batteries of the larger ships engaged visible Chinese artillery pieces on the riverbank. These were located in parks and other open spaces. Several Chinese guns were hit. They flew into the air like broken toys.

Sitting in his boat, tiller in hand, Quartermaster's Mate John Lang waited for the order to embark his complement of troops for the landing. His principal duty in the gunboat, USS Palos, was to steer the ship and to help with her navigation. To qualify him as a "pilot" on the Yangtze, the Navy had sent him to a maritime college in Hong Kong. He had served on the river for seven years and knew the Yangtze better than any of the Navy officers on board.

One of Lang's additional duties in Palos was to act as coxswain of one of the ship's boats. His boat, a twenty-foot, clinker-built, "Boston Whaler" with an inboard motor, was alongside at the ship's "waist." The motor "ticked" over reassuringly. Blue smoke dribbled from it in the morning air. The distinctive exhaust smell was familiar and almost "sweet."

Nanking and the dirty river did not stink more of sewage and refuse than usual.

USS Palos was 165 feet long. Built at Mare's Island, California, she was shipped in pieces across the Pacific and reassembled in Shanghai. Her shallow draft, powerful engines and two three-inch guns, fore and aft, gave her admirable characteristics in the service she was designed for. She was a major unit of the Yangtze River Patrol of the US Navy's Asiatic Fleet. Her ship's company was 47 officers and men in strength. She was normally commanded by a lieutenant. Palos never left the river. Her officers' families followed the ship from home port to home port as the "stationing "of the ship changed. The wives rented Chinese houses along the river. The life was adventurous but comfortable. Life was pleasant and highly social in the upper-class Chinese and foreign communities in which the officers' families lived. Petty officers like Lang and the sailors of the crew lived for and on their ship and found their recreation and solace in the public houses of the ports. A few had Chinese women and families ashore.

The ship was home ported at Nanking in 1927. Palos' people had many of those they cared for most ashore in the burning city.

Gunfire could be heard across the town.

For the landing, USS Palos had 150 souls aboard. In addition to the ship's company, there were 100 Japanese marines of the "Imperial Special Naval Landing Force."

The combined flotilla had embarked a variety of troops at Shanghai. National identity was not a major factor in deciding which troops each ship would transport in the expedition. There were a lot of soldiers to carry, and the ships varied a great deal in capacity. A lot of "mixing and matching" to make them all fit had been necessary. There was also the problem of the draft of the larger vessels. Some of them could not "stand in" close to the river bank for the landing.

Palos' Japanese marine contingent looked formidable as they stood in ranks, waiting to disembark. The enlisted marines were almost all Koreans. Their Japanese officers, in contrast, were all from the home islands of Japan.

Lang looked up at them from the tiller of his boat. He had two US sailors as crew. The Japanese, in return, looked down at him from the American warship. The marines were noticeably taller than their officers. Dressed in dark green and loaded down with equipment, they looked fearsome.

Lang would land a ten-man squad on the riverbank. These marines were a small fraction of the force to be landed. Some of their comrades would go ashore in other boats from Palos, and some from other ships. In the landing force, there would also be US Marines, British infantry from Hong Kong, French *Infanterie de Marine* and some nationalist Chinese from Chiang Kai Shek's army.

A signal flag "broke" at the yardarm on HMS Mantis, the flotilla flagship.

The loudspeaker system on Palos came to life. "Land the landing force. Troops will disembark. Boats will assemble at the line of departure. Good luck." The ship's three-inch guns then opened fire against the stretch of riverbank that her boats would assault. The noise was deafening but reassuring.

The marines climbed down the netting into the boats. Their rifles were slung across their backs, but they managed to avoid being tangled in anything.

Lang was grateful for that. He was uncertain about these strange Asian soldiers and wanted to deliver them to the shore without any unnecessary complications.

The marines were led by a stocky Korean sergeant who came aft to sit next to the coxswain.

They nodded at each other, each hoping for some sign of mutual confidence.

John Lang ran away from home in the Dakotas in 1916. An oppressive father was the motivating force behind the "escape." Sixteen years old, he made his way to Milwaukee where he enlisted in the Canadian Army. He served in Flanders in the Canadian Black Watch, and he reckoned that he could tell a competent infantry sergeant when he saw one. This one looked like a fat little man with three "stripes."

Oh, well, Lang thought, *Soon I will know, very soon.*

The river bank was 300 yards away. There were fires burning in the two- and three-story brick buildings "inland" from the waterfront... The capital of the Republic of China smoldered under a cold, grey blanket of cloud that obscured the sun. The oily water looked silvery grey in the light from an overcast sky.

The six boats from Palos went to join twenty more from other ships. They lined up on an imaginary line in the water. They made a long, shaky line facing the shore. A British boat with a sub-lieutenant on board established the right of the line.

The ships' guns continued to fire at the shore.

Smoke would be nice, old soldier Lang thought.

The British officer blew his whistle, and the line of boats accelerated toward the "beach."

Other groups of boats could be seen to port and starboard. They were all headed for the riverbank.

Lang sat on his little "U" shaped seat and held the hickory tiller. He liked small boats. He had always liked them, even when there were only North Dakota rivers in his life. He hoped desperately that the motor wouldn't quit in the middle of all this....

The Chinese were having a good time shooting at the boats. Bullets hummed in the air and splashed in the water. One struck the boat somewhere forward. One of the marines was hit and cried out in unintelligible words.

Lang and his human cargo were a hundred feet from shore when the boat was struck by a shell from what he later thought was a small artillery piece.

As he recalled the event in later years, "One minute I was steering for the bank and thinking about "idling" the engine while "they" got off my boat, and the next minute I was standing in brown water up to my chest with no sign of the boat except for some sinking wreckage."

The Japanese marines were wading toward the shore and from instinct Lang waded with them.

When the water was knee deep, he realized that he was holding the broken off tiller in his right hand.

The "beach" was gravel and two feet wide. There was a low wall. It was four feet high and made of brick.

Lang remembered that someone's lawn was beyond the "seawall." He threw the tiller away and looked around.

The Korean sergeant floated near the water's edge. His rifle was still slung across his body.

Lang was armed with a service .45 automatic pistol and nothing else. He crawled out into the river to retrieve the rifle and ammunition. Sitting with his back to the wall, he contemplated the situation.

Two US sailors and nine Japanese marines were on the "beach." All were looking at him, waiting.

Briefings on Palos had been thorough. Lang knew where the "beachhead line" would be inland. This was yet another imaginary line. This one had depicted on the briefing map the localities where the landing force would stop before advancing to finish its work.

Fortunately, Lang knew Nanking well from many happy liberty trips ashore.

Oh, well, he thought, *why not?* He crawled along the "beach" giving instructions in a mixture of: hand and arm signals, pidgin Chinese, and a little English. This last was dimly understood by several of the Koreans. With that done, he got them up and over the wall.

He did that by going over the wall first.

A businessman's stucco villa complete with red tile roof was fifty yards away behind a tennis court and driveway.

A dark figure with a rifle fired at them from an upstairs window and was shot by a marine.

They charged across the grass, going around or over the Adirondack chairs and other lawn furniture. They broke down the back door of the house.

Chinese soldiers were running out the front door into the street.

The Koreans caught several of them just outside the house. Screaming and clubbing sounds died away after a minute.

The house was beautifully furnished with European furniture, flocked wallpaper and a marble fireplace in the living room. A statue of Kuan Yin stood beside the fireplace.

I might come back for that, Lang thought.

Abandoned in the street was a British made Vickers machine gun on wheels. Next to it was a pushcart loaded with ammunition for the gun. The Chinese must have just entered the house when the marines arrived.

Lang knew this machine gun from World War I. He got it turned around to cover the street that ran away from the front door.

The Japanese also knew this weapon and the squad soon had a potent weapon with which to sweep the street.

Their objective was a half mile "inland."

Lang organized the group into a machine gun team made up of several Japanese and one American sailor. Another group was composed solely of men with rifles, pistols and bayonets. His method was simple, as are all good military plans. The machine gun would fire into the next area they would occupy and then shift its fire to an area above or beyond while the rifle group moved forward. Lang would lead the rifle group.

Three hours later, they were on their tiny portion of the "Beachhead Line."

This was a diagonal across an intersection of two streets. Lang had the men push several motor vehicles into a line across the intersection to make a barrier and shelter. They then built a "nest" for the machine gun by piling up bricks and stones just in front of the vehicles. From there, the Vickers could fire up and down the connecting streets as well as at the buildings to the front. He then posted a man on the top floor of the building behind them to watch for movement and to shoot at snipers. Having done all this, he considered his work largely done and sat down with his back to a wheel where he could oversee what the machine gun crew did. He was hungry. He looked in his musette bag and found the sandwiches and fruit that the galley on Palos had issued to the boat crews.

Seeing him eat, the marines produced their field rations of cooked rice, bits of dried fish and various Japanese vegetables.

There was some trading back and forth of rations.

Lang liked the Japanese food better than his own. After eating, he went to find the units on either flank of his blocking position. These were all Japanese marines. He and his two sailors were alone in a vast Asian city with "comrades" who did not comprehend much of what needed to be communicated.

Chinese troops attacked the roadblock several times in the first hours, but each group soon departed, retreating down the streets from which they had come after losing men to the rifles and machine gun.

About four PM, a lieutenant of the Imperial Japanese Special Naval Landing Force appeared on the scene. He walked into the roadblock coming from the eastern flank "boundary" unit that Lang had found. The officer wore a dark green uniform with his rank on his collars. He wore white "drill gloves" and carried his sword reversed in his left hand. On his head was the strange little soft peaked cap favored by the Japanese. He was about five foot, five inches tall and quite slender. He looked at the group behind the vehicles and around the machine gun, then up at the roof where the rifle of the marksman could be seen protruding over a low wall. He asked the Japanese marines something and when they pointed at Lang, he approached.

John stood to attention.

"Your name?" the Japanese officer asked in English. A volley of Chinese rifle fire buzzed like a swarm of bees over the vehicular obstacles. The lieutenant did not flinch, and John was careful not to flinch. He knew that in this situation it was necessary to show, as he put it years later, "that I, too, was brave."

"You brought these men up here from the river?"

"Yes, sir, I did."

"How do you know how to do this? You are a sailor."

"I was a corporal of infantry in the Great War, sir. Your sergeant was killed…"

The lieutenant nodded. His face was a mask. "You will hold this corner?" he asked. "It is the hinge of our position."

"Yes, sir, I will."

"We will advance tomorrow morning to clear our zone. We will advance with the other countries. Do you wish to lead these men?"

John felt lightheaded. He knew it would be sensible to say no and return to Palos, still at anchor in the river. "I would be honored," he replied to the offer.

The Japanese officer bowed slightly. "I will see to it that you are given instructions in English."

He turned to continue down his line.

"Sir?" Lang called after him.

"Yes?"

"May I ask how you speak English this way?"

The lieutenant smiled. "I was born in California. My parents brought me home when I was ten." He walked away.

The Japanese marine battalion fought for a week as part of the combined force. They cleared the central part of the city of all Chinese troops. There was much close fighting amidst the low, European style buildings, telephone poles and markets.

When the city had been secured, Lang was relieved of his small command. To his surprise, he had been given more and more reinforcement from among the marines and sailors of the Japanese ships of the flotilla. At the end he had thirty men and was beginning to learn Korean from listening to them talk to each other.

Behind his final fighting position, Lang found a bar and bordello called "The White Crane." He used the bar as headquarters and waited there for what might come next. He let the men come into the bar for a beer and a short trip upstairs after counseling each with regard to behavior. There were no complaints.

The saloonkeeper, a White Russian, was glad to be protected from the bedlam that had ruled in the streets before allied troops fought their way to his establishment.

After relief, Lang was escorted to the command post of the battalion by the Japanese lieutenant from California.

After an exchange of salutes, the Imperial Navy commander bowed and said, "You are Samurai."

The US Navy awarded John Lang the Navy Cross based on Japanese reports of his behavior.

He thought little more of this. He was scheduled to sit for examination for promotion to Chief Petty Officer in his rating. This filled his thoughts and study filled his days.

After six months, he sat for the examination aboard the flagship of the Asiatic Fleet. This was the heavy cruiser USS Augusta. She was at anchor at Shanghai, swinging around her "hook" off the International Quarter quays.

The Asiatic Fleet Commander in Chief, Rear Admiral Mark Bristol, summoned him to his flag cabin the day after the examination. "Sit down, Lang," he began. "You are promoted, congratulations, Chief."

This was a great relief. Only a few promotions were available in the small navy, and competition was fierce.

"I have a telegram from US Embassy Tokyo," Bristol said. "We waited to tell you of it until you had taken the test. I am asked to send you up there. The Japanese want to give you a medal." The admiral looked up from the file folder. "Do you have a tailor in Shanghai?"

Lang replied that he did not.

The admiral wrote a name and address on a card.

"Tell him to make you a beautiful chief's uniform of the best cloth and to send me the bill. The Navy will pay. You are booked on Pan American's China Clipper on Friday. Luigi will have your clothes ready by then. Don't forget to take your medals."

In Tokyo, Lang was lodged in the embassy guesthouse and was soon escorted by the ambassador and naval attaché to the palace where he was invested with the Grand Cordon of the Order of the Chrysanthemum. The order was received from the hand of the god-emperor himself. An equerry of the Imperial Court draped the sash across his upper body, and an aide de camp to the emperor pinned on the star. John bowed to his imperial majesty. The American ambassador and naval attaché were at his side and bowed also. His majesty smiled. John Lang from Casselton, North Dakota was from that moment a Japanese knight. He wore the ribbon during World War II until the Japanese wounded him out of the war in 1944.

The order brought with it a monthly stipend that was greater than his US Navy pay. The Imperial Japanese Government paid him the stipend through the Swiss until their government was destroyed. In 1953, after a treaty of peace was signed between Japan and the United States, the payments resumed and continued until his death in 1969.

CHAPTER FOUR

A Boot Full of Blood

Photo Credit: W. Patrick Lang

(Off Nanking, China – 12 December 1937)

USS Panay's alarm bells rang in the early dawn.

The loudspeaker system spoke. "Action stations! Action stations! This is not a drill! This is not a drill!"

Chief Petty Officer John Lang woke in his bunk and "caught" the end of this announcement from the bridge. He listened and heard the sound of aircraft engines. He put on yesterday's "wash khaki" and went out on deck.

With five other Chief Petty Officers he lived in a small wooden structure on the weather deck behind the sick bay and overlooking the stern. Each of the senior enlisted men had a curtained cubicle in which to sleep. There were several comfortable chairs around a central table. A Chinese steward had the job of bringing their meals while they played cards or discussed the day's events. A short-wave radio was on a corner shelf. It was usually tuned to the Imperial Service of the BBC.

He heard engine noise to starboard and went to that side of the ship. At the rail he looked up and found himself looking at the nose of a Japanese aircraft approaching the ship in a shallow dive. He could see the pilot's face through the windscreen. There was another, similar aircraft behind the first.

As he watched, a bomb detached from the plane. The bomb fell 50 yards off the starboard quarter of the ship and threw up a fountain of dirty river water. The bomber turned hard to port. He could see the red, rising sun insignia of Japan on the bottom of the wings as it banked left.

At least one machine gun was firing from somewhere near Panay's bridge. Holes opened in the belly of the aircraft. It "wobbled" away, losing altitude.

Lang thought the second aircraft's bomb might strike the ship where he stood, so he went to the port side and wrapped his arms and legs around a stanchion. He hoped for a "dud," but a dull "boom" shook the ship and she began to list to starboard.

As Quartermaster, his place of duty was in the wheelhouse. Going forward, he passed several Lewis machine guns mounted on the rails of the uppermost deck. Sailors were firing at the planes. Many of them were still in their underwear.

There were a number of passengers on Panay that day. The Chinese and Japanese were at war. The longstanding desire of the Japanese to acquire Chinese resources and labor had brought war earlier in the year. The Japanese Army was literally at the gates of Nanking, the Chinese capital. The city was thought to be too dangerous for foreigners. Panay was ordered there to evacuate diplomats, business managers and a Life magazine crew. The attack was unexpected. The United States was at least officially neutral in the Sino-Japanese War, and the US Embassy believed it had arranged safe passage with the commander of Japanese forces.

USS Panay was Shanghai built and 191 feet long. There were 59 officers and men in her crew. She was thought to be the "Princess of the Yangtze," fast at 18 knots, spacious, beautifully fitted out, and the recipient of every prize and award the Navy could bestow on her. Her gleaming bronze metalwork and hand rubbed teak decks were immaculate. Dressed for a celebration with colored lights strung from every "yard," she was an adornment for any river port entertainment. Command of PR-5 was a prize widely sought among US officers. All who served aboard loved her.

Nearing the wooden wheelhouse, Lang saw that the structure had been blown away by the bombing. The brass and wooden wheel was untouched, and the stand to which the log was chained remained, but the three members of the bridge watch were dead. The commanding officer, Lieutenant Commander James Hughes, lay on the wheelhouse deck. He was badly wounded in the legs.

The airplane noises sounded different. Looking up, Lang saw that the earlier planes had left and had been replaced by other bombers now in the process of "rolling over" and diving out of the sky.

Sailors were gathering on the weather deck. Some were looking up at the bombers. "Get on the damned guns," Lang yelled.

They then began to form up in lines behind the machine guns waiting for a turn and opportunity to shoot at the Japanese.

Lang lashed the wheel over toward the side of the river that the Chinese still "owned" and then picked up Commander Hughes. He put him over a shoulder. The journey to the sickbay was hard because the deck was slippery, and the ship was listing more. Lang was small and Hughes was large. He smiled at the thought that he had never touched the captain before, not even to shake his hand. He was on his way back to the bridge when several more bombs burst aboard wounding him severely in the legs, face and back.

He freed the wheel, put Panay on a hard course for the left bank and called the engine room. "All ahead," he ordered.

"Who is this?" was the answer.

"It's Lang. I am going to beach her. The 'old man' is gone. I think his legs are... finished."

There was a momentary pause. "This is Lieutenant Johnson," a voice said from the engine room. "Are you sure?"

"Aye, sir, we're done, she'll be on the bottom soon," Lang answered.

"Right, all ahead," Johnson replied. "Put her on the beach."

"Thank you, sir," said Lang.

The machine guns continued to fire. Sailors brought ammunition up from the magazine and stacked the open metal cans beside the guns. The Lewis guns were firing so much that they were very hot. Crewmen poured buckets of river water over them. The water hissed and boiled on all parts that were exposed to the air. This would ruin the guns, but that did not matter.

Standing at the wheel, the Quartermaster stared at the wooden stand to which the open logbook was chained.

Another Japanese air attack screamed down from above.

He logged the attack with details of: direction, damage, and hits on aircraft. When he finished, he noticed that he was dripping blood on the page. He tried to rub it off with his hand.

The Chinese-held bank seemed impossibly far away.

Another attack struck the ship.

He logged that one as well and resolved to log them all.

The bottom of the hull dragged on the gravel of the riverbed.

The Japanese were still making passes at Panay but seemed to be losing interest. There were fewer planes.

The ship's undamaged boats came up to the weather deck rail. Panay was now resting on the bottom but moving with the current and rolling from side to side as though she wished to live.

He unchained the log, put it under an arm and walked aft.

A sailor helped him over the rail and into a boat.

"Jesus, Chief, can you walk?" the man asked.

He felt a little faint, but other than that, was just angry.

The boat moved to the riverbank.

When it "grounded," Lang climbed out into the cold, thigh deep water. He shook off attempts to help him. Clutching the log, he struggled up the bank, and turned to sit where he could contemplate his beloved home. She was now leaning far to one side with smoke and steam pouring from many wounds.

Someone asked him to open his mouth and then tied a bandage around his lower face. "You've been shot through the face," the man said.

Lang looked up and saw that it was the ship's medical officer. "What, what did you say?"

"A bullet passed through your cheeks, right behind your mouth, and another through your upper lip. You have lost several teeth. I am giving you some morphine…"

He had not felt the face wounds, but he knew that this was common in the heat of action. He probed his mouth with his tongue. The tongue hurt. It was damaged toward the back, near its "root." There was a hole in each cheek, a mess where his lip should be, and the broken teeth were jagged.

One of the news photographer passengers approached and took his picture. This man helped him to his feet so that he could leave the riverbank.

He walked unsteadily until he reached a farm road a few yards away.

Commander Hughes' stretcher was there. The captain was unconscious.

Lang felt that his feet were wet. Looking down, he saw something surprising. He had recently bought a fine pair of black calf Wellington boots from his old friend Luigi, the Italian *clothier,* in Shanghai. Red blood was welling up and running over the top of one of these ten-inch boots. "I think I will sit down," he said to the doctor.

The survivors of Panay's company walked for a day until they reached a Chinese village. They carried their wounded. Lang walked with them. They were rightly afraid that the Japanese would kill them if they could to conceal as much of their deed as possible by eliminating witnesses

Eventually, Chinese Army medical help arrived at the village to transport them to a rendezvous with a US Navy destroyer downstream.

Three months later Lang was still in the small US Navy hospital at Shanghai. His wounds were healing. The broken teeth were gone, and he was growing a mustache to hide some of the holes in his face.

The Navy had awarded him another Navy Cross.

The US and Japan came close to war over the destruction of Panay. The Japanese government of 1937 did not want that. Profound apologies were offered and accepted for this terrible "mistake." Japanese school girls sent letters of sorrow and sympathy for the suffering of the crew. The emperor's government agreed to pay for the ship and to pay reparations to all those attacked.

John decided to buy a Packard convertible loaded with all options when he arrived in California. He was soon involved in the process of ordering the car with delivery at the pier.

The Japanese Army Air force which had ordered the attack on Panay refused to take notice of the problem they had caused. The Japanese Navy air arm decided to send their pilots to the hospital to apologize. The Imperial Navy command wrote to ask for an appointment.

On the day agreed, Lang asked the ward nurse to put his dress coat on a chair in such a way that the medal ribbons would face those in the room. He then asked her to put the chair next to the "head end" of the bed. The dark blue of the jacket and the bright colors of the ribbons made a pleasing contrast to the white walls.

The pilots brought flowers. There were chrysanthemums in the bouquets. The Navy nurse brought vases, and soon the room stank of flowers.

The four young officers stood at the foot of the bed in their blue uniforms. It was clear that they could see nothing but the glory of the "Order of the Chrysanthemum" among Lang's ribbons. He had been given it by the "son of heaven" himself. "What can we do to make amends?" the senior lieutenant asked.

Lang sat up in bed and grasping his hands together mimed the act of *seppuku* by "stabbing" himself in one side of the belly and then drawing his hands across to the other side.

The four pilots grew very still. One trembled slightly.

After a moment Lang laughed aloud. "No. No," he said. "You come back when I am better, and you can take me out on the town…"

They bowed.

And, that is what they did.

CHAPTER FIVE

Casablanca

USS Massachusetts

Chief Petty Officer John Lang reported aboard USS Massachusetts (BB-59) when she was still an empty steel hull in the shipyard at Quincy, Massachusetts. There were no decks when he boarded. Construction had started in 1940 and by March 1941 progress had been made toward a launch planned for the summer.

Lang came to Boston from recruiting duty in the mid-West and upper South. He had been stationed in Cincinnati since his return from China in 1938. In his new job he traveled in grand style in the touring car the Japanese reparations money bought him. The Japanese government paid him a lot of money as his part of their reparations for bombing and sinking the gunboat USS Panay. He showed the newsreel of the sinking of Panay in hundreds of towns in Ohio, Tennessee, Kentucky and Virginia. There were many recruits to be had for the navy. These were depression days. Life was difficult for many, and he projected just the right image of the "old sea dog" and the chance for a life of high adventure.

The work was easy. He met a beautiful blonde girl in Nashville, Tennessee. He met her in a bar. This was not surprising. He spent a lot of time in bars. She was attracted to the scarred little man in navy blue. Women often were. They never seemed to care that his mustache had been grown to cover the scars made by a Japanese bullet that knocked out several of his teeth. Women felt that this little man would care for them and protect them. They were correct. He and his brothers helped to support his widowed mother all her days. He and the blond were married two weeks later before a Justice of the Peace in Bristol, Virginia. They honeymooned in the Shenandoah Valley as Lang "worked" all the little towns on the road north. She was still with him when he reported in Boston. He knew that would probably not last much longer, probably not longer than his first long time at sea. She was already looking around, and stalwart loneliness did not seem her style. Her Christian names were May Belle. The names fit her admirably.

Lang had orders that named him Quartermaster of the battleship under construction. He would be responsible for the steering crew and much of the navigation of this 35,000-ton behemoth. The vessel was of the South Dakota class and armed with 16-inch naval rifles. He had a separate set of orders that awarded him the rank of Warrant Officer. This would take effect when the ship was launched. Those meant he would henceforth live in Officers' Country, have a stateroom of his own, stewards to look after him and would be a member of the officers' wardroom mess. He liked that. This privilege had been a long time coming in the small peacetime navy of the '20s and '30s. John himself appeared an exceedingly gentle and self-effacing man. He rarely raised his voice. His manners were impeccable, something rare in a man so long "before the mast" and then a chief petty officer. Nevertheless, those who knew John well understood that beneath the tranquil surface was another soul. That other man was someone who started with little in life and who made his way through courage and generosity toward a distant and largely unknown goal of recognition and responsibility.

John found a small apartment near the shipyard and began the long days of supervision of the building and fitting out of the ship. As a member of the commissioning crew, he would, by navy tradition, own a plank in her and forever feel identified with her.

By chance, two of his brothers were stationed nearby. His younger brother Gordon was also a navy chief petty officer. He was at the naval experimental torpedo station at Newport, Rhode Island. Gordon was a submariner, and a torpedoman. He had spent years in the S boats of the Asiatic Fleet. His older brother, Walter, was an army Finance Corps man in the garrison of Fort Devens, Massachusetts a few miles away.

The three made an occasion to gather at Walter's quarters at Fort Devens. This residence was a small brick house within the army post on a quiet, tree lined street. Since they had last seen him, the eldest had acquired a wife and a son. This seemed strange. He had never seemed a family man, never the marrying type. Altogether, Walter had spent 14 years in the Philippines, North China and Borneo. In 1937 he decided to ask to be returned to the US Army to become a warrant officer in the Finance Corps. He was a proud man, and sensitive to status. They knew he had enjoyed his rank as a police captain. Why he had left that was a mystery to them.

Sitting at his table at Fort Devens, the two younger brothers found themselves trapped in drama. Gordon was a solitary, seemingly destined to be a permanent bachelor. Not surprisingly, he drove alone to the gathering.

John brought his beautiful young wife.

At opposing ends of the dinner table sat their brother Walt and his handsome French-Canadian wife, Rollande. She was 17 years his junior. At her left sat her sister, Jeanne, visiting from Maine. The baby, Walter junior, occupied a highchair between the sisters.

At Marie's right was John's wife, May Belle.

The sisters had been reared in the rigidly moral atmosphere of Jansenist Catholicism then prevalent in northern New England. John's wife fascinated them in much the same way that a wild animal seen in a zoo fascinates the viewers. They did their best to avoid staring, but her blatant and seemingly unconscious sensuality made it difficult not to stare as she flirted uninterruptedly with John's brothers. She looked a lot like Jean Harlow.

"How does it feel to be a warrant and almost a gentleman?" Gordon asked Walter. "John is looking forward to the sensation."

"Pretty damned good, pretty damned good," their older brother laughed. He had drunk several glasses of beer and his face was a familiar shade of red. "The only problem with it is that when I was appointed, the senior sergeants who normally 'own' this row of quarters began agitating for us to move to an officer's section of the post. My wife was unaccustomed to this kind of foolishness in the civilian world and does not want to move."

"I will not move," Rollande said clearly. "Let them come move me."

There was a moment of silence while all absorbed the mental image of MPs at the door.

"Why not move to an officer's house?" Gordon asked. He had always been the sensible, practical one. "It would be larger...."

"There are none," Walt replied. "The whole 1ˢᵗ Infantry Division has assembled here and there is not an empty house. This post was never built for so many people. The Army reckons war is coming soon. We know what is happening for John. The navy must believe the same thing. What's in your future, Gordon? You are not going to 'homestead' at Newport are you?"

"I wouldn't mind if they left me there. I have bought a couple of beach properties that rent well. I believe I will keep those." His talent for saving money and investing it was an enigma for his brothers. "But, the Bureau of Personnel tells me that I will go to 'new construction' on an aircraft carrier as soon as they pick one. I, too, will be a warrant officer within a few months. So, I guess we are all rising in the world."

"Since we are revealing things," Walt said. "I should tell you that 'the powers' have decided to make me a captain in September. It is a wartime appointment, but I will take it. We will be gone, gone somewhere soon after that. We three will have little time together. It will be a long war. Let us make good use of the months that we have.

"You should go overseas when war begins," his wife commented. "I may not know much about the Army yet, but I know that the chance for improvement will be larger for those overseas."

The two navy men waited for his reply.

Walter looked at his plate and said nothing.

"His old friends forced him to take the captain's rank," Marie exclaimed. "Now they want to make him the Finance Officer of the 1st Division. The division is here now, and they will be with the first to go to the war.... Tell him! I have nagged him and picked on him for weeks over this."

Her sister looked embarrassed.

After a few seconds May Belle said, "Go on, Walt, she's tellin' you the truth, you know that. You can see it in her face. You're not goin' to listen to her?"

Walter raised his head. His face was a dark, brick red. For a moment, it seemed certain that he would lash out at his sister-in-law. Then he focused on John's face and subsided. "I will not go overseas. I am finished with all that...."

The navy men left the next day. Outside the gate of the fort they stopped their cars to talk.

"We know this thing," John began. "We have seen it many times..."

Gordon nodded and looked away.

"Well, tell little me," May Belle demanded. "I never saw nothin' like that before. You said he was a brave man," she told her husband.

"Every man has only so much courage," Gordon said to her. "He has come to the end of his."

His brother nodded and they drove away.

There are occasions in which it is better to be ignorant than informed. In this case this was very true. John's wife mercifully never learned that she was forever after referred to in Walter's household as Daisy May from Dogpatch, Tennessee. Perhaps that reflected his inability to deal with her questions.

A year and a half later, USS Massachusetts (big Mamie to her crew) sortied from Boston to join the fleet gathered off French North Africa for Operation Torch, the invasion of Morocco and Algeria. The big ship crossed the Atlantic without escort. She was so fast that no destroyer could stay up with her, and for that reason it was thought that speed and her armor were better anti-submarine defenses than any other.

John's stateroom was aft the bridge and near that of the captain. It was large enough to contain his bunk, a desk and built in cabinets for clothes and his other possessions. His responsibility for the ship's steering meant that he must be immediately available to both captain and the watch standers. He was the most highly decorated man in the ship's company and the best-qualified watch officer on board. For these reasons, the captain gave him the honor of guiding the ship as she left her homeport for the war zone. Dressed with every signal flag available and with the ship's company manning the rail in whites, the big ship passed slowly from view.

May Belle waited on the pier until she could no longer see the grey hull in the distance.

"Mamie" joined Task Force 34 off Casablanca on the 6th of November 1942. From a position out on a bridge "wing," John counted the ships in TF 34. The carrier "Ranger" was to port in the assembly area, and beyond her was USS Augusta, the heavy cruiser in which the task force commander flew his flag. John remembered Augusta well. She had long been flagship of the Asiatic Fleet. In the screen for the big ships there were dozens of destroyers and many, many troop ships sheltering behind them.

The battleship came to join the covering force for the landing for one specific reason. There was a French Navy battleship, the *Jean Bart* in dry dock at Casablanca. French forces in North Africa were still loyal to the government of occupied France. This government functioned under German supervision and with German toleration that constantly threatened complete German military occupation of the country. The threats were particularly specific with regard to German insistence that the "puppet" government should defend its colonial territories against the "Allies." The French armed forces in Morocco knew of this threat to their people at home and seemed prepared to defend Morocco against invasion by their former and perhaps future friends. It appeared likely that the French army units dug in on the beaches around Casablanca would resist the landings, but the major doubt in allied command headquarters was uncertainty over what French Navy actions would be when the moment of truth arrived.

There were several shore batteries under navy control at Casablanca. The largest was at a place called *Al-Hank*. This battery of shore artillery flanked the planned landing beaches. This fort and several others had guns that could sink every ship in the American task force if given the chance. The battleship *Jean Bart* was in the naval shipyard but possessed one 15-inch turret that could be fired. Lighter French naval units positioned in the harbor of Casablanca included a light cruiser and at least six destroyers.

At dawn on the 8th of November, American destroyers opened fire against the smaller shore defenses. This fire was returned from *Al Hank*. Shore battery fire straddled the American battleship. Massachusetts then began firing its 16-inch main battery into *Al Hank*.

Observing this, *Jean Bart* fired a salvo from its one turret at USS Augusta and at USS Massachusetts. The American battleship returned fire and after a few rounds damaged the French ship's aiming mechanism so severely that *Jean Bart* played no further role in the fighting.

While this happened, John Lang stood on a bridge wing. high in the ship's superstructure. There, he had a good view of the action. The bombardment did not require him to do anything, and the helmsman who was his responsibility was only a few feet away. Massachusetts was moving parallel to the shore to provide a stable platform for the guns.

Ten feet below, the captain and the executive officer of the ship, a commander by rank, paced up and down and across the ship. Like everyone else in the ship's company, they wore steel helmets because of the danger posed by shell fragments. The executive officer, a stern man who was given to frequent anger directed at subordinates for minor infractions of routine and uniform, was an object of thinly concealed disdain for John who noticed that French fire arriving in the covering force area made the commander flinch at the sound of water bursts.

The captain ignored the tumult and his executive officer's reaction and strolled back and forth across the ship, passing through the bridge itself on each traverse.

A crafty smile appeared on John's scarred face. He went below and returned in a few minutes with a six-inch steel bolt. He held it behind his back and waited for an alignment to occur in which the placement of the executive officer below him matched an incoming French salvo. When this occurred, he leaned over the rail and with unerring aim launched the bolt in a trajectory that struck the XO in the center of the top of his helmet. The man prostrated himself on the deck screaming, "My God, my God I am killed," while rolling from side to side in his "death agony."

The captain looked up, shook his head, and with several others helped his second in command to his feet. Watching the XO stagger around as officers and men sought to conceal their amusement; John began to think that his prank had not been a good idea.

The loudspeakers broke their silence, "Enemy squadron sortieing from port!"

Seven or eight French ships were coming out of the harbor of Casablanca at high speed. Several held a course that would take them into the convoy of troop-carrying freighters. A light cruiser and three destroyers turned toward Massachusetts.

As John watched, the four warships moved from column formation to in-line abreast and accelerated. The bow waves of the four rose and rose until the forward parts of the ships could hardly be seen. These standard bearers of French ideals of honor looked like greyhounds coursing across a meadow in pursuit of a rabbit. The tricolor could be seen at the mastheads and the cruiser began to sound its horn. This war whoop spread from vessel to vessel until the four ran at the American battleship howling like Comanches.

"Lay us across the destroyers' bow," said the voice in John's headphones.

The super dreadnought heeled as she turned to lay perpendicular to the direction of the attack.

The 16-inch turrets swung until the rifled cannon stared at the small attackers with their nine unwinking "eyes."

As he watched them come, John could see that the French ships were making an "all-ahead" torpedo attack on the battleship. There would be two torpedo tubes "forward" on each vessel and two more on the four stern decks. Eight torpedoes would be fired in the run in, and then when the attack turned away, eight more. The French ships began to make smoke to cover their withdrawal. This meant that the torpedo launch was imminent.

The nine 16-inch rifles "spoke" with one voice. The secondary batteries of Massachusetts joined the choir.

USS Augusta added the weight of her metal to the fire.

In the next instant, the French attack was over. The four ships lay burning on the water. Two were sinking.

My God, John thought. *That's the bravest thing I have ever seen. My God, who would believe that they would do that...*

Ships all over the American covering force put their boats in the water as quickly as they could.

French seamen soon came up the ladders, helped over the side by sailors and marines. Casualties were hoisted aboard in sling loaded stretchers.

A *capitaine de vaisseau* was brought to the bridge. He gravely saluted Massachusetts' commanding officer. The salute was returned, and a handshake followed. The American accepted the promise offered of good behavior and obedience to the captors' orders. On the weather decks below, cigarettes and "medicinal" brandy were passed around.

French Navy officers ate in the wardroom mess that night.

John remembered what he had learned of their language when an infantry soldier in World War I. His messmates smiled as he joked with the Frenchmen to cheer them and then took on the task of translating for some of the Americans.

The next day it was learned that the government of French North Africa had abandoned allegiance to Vichy, and that the "prisoners" aboard were allies once again. French ships came from the port to remove their people.

The landings were successful, and the advancing front line was far inland as Massachusetts turned away from Morocco to return to Boston.

On the way home John Lang found himself speaking to the captain in the "old man's" stateroom. Seated together over a cup of navy coffee, all seemed well until the captain announced that John would have to leave the ship.

"Commander Wilkins has learned of your foolishness with the bolt. He wanted to prefer charges against you on a variety of bases, but I persuaded him to desist. Your "joke" was not a smart thing to do. He could have charged you with something that would have required a general court-martial. As it is, I will be leaving the ship myself soon and Wilkins will be remaining..."

"Ah," John said to no one in particular. "Where do I go?"

"BUPERS wants you report to Washington, and they will work something out. This is unfortunate. A few more months and you would surely have been appointed a lieutenant."

John "detached" from Massachusetts in Boston. He walked down the gangway for the last time and stood looking at her grey magnificence.

At last, with sorrow in his heart, he went to his apartment. There he learned that She had gone and that he owed two months' rent.

CHAPTER SIX

The "Zebulon Pike"

The USNS Zebulon Pike was an auxiliary transport of the US Navy.

The Lang family rode this rusty old tub of a Liberty ship from Bremerhaven to New York. The passage was 17 days in the steady head winds and rough sea state of the North Atlantic. The ship wallowed and bucked her way through the swells and wind waves like an elephant trying to swim.

The trip to Europe with his mother several years earlier had been on another Liberty ship. That one was named "Zebulon Vance." As a result, young Walter Patrick Lang thought for a while that all Liberty ships were named "Zebulon..." On that voyage he and his very seasick mother had been berthed with several other officers' families. These women had not seen their husbands for a long time in some cases years. There was tension in the air that could be heard in their talk about their menfolk.

This trip was different. Major Walter Lang, senior, was a "field officer," and for that reason the three living members of the family had a private room, something that might be called a "stateroom" by the generously minded.

Somewhere down in the hold was a three-foot metal coffin that contained the fourth member of the family. That was an infant boy who had been conceived, born and died in Germany the previous year. He had perished of a heart defect beyond cure or hope.

Little Patrick Lang enjoyed the trip immensely. He liked the ship. He liked the grey, wind-driven sea. He liked the food served in the ship's mess facility where his parents ate with the merchant marine officers who ran the vessel as well as with other officer passengers. He particularly liked the breakfasts served there. The messmen soon learned that the boy would eat all they put on his tray. He was careful to thank them for his food. He had been taught to be courteous, especially to those who might somehow think he was arrogant or haughty. Scrambled eggs, bacon, sausage gravy on toast, stewed apples and biscuits; these were treasures to be consumed with relish. His mother did not like to cook and certainly not such food as this, and this was a rare opportunity.

The son passed many of the hours between meals and bedtime reading books and magazines from the ship's tiny library. Sitting on the "weather deck" of the old ship, he clutched cheap editions to him against the spray and gusts. There, he first read Hemingway, and a new world opened. This happiness came to an end when his mother expressed concern about the books and their worth.

Halfway across the Atlantic, a passing Army captain stopped to watch him play chess against another boy. The man asked to play the next game against young Walter Lang and seemed satisfied with this pastime until he lost. After that he was absent from the part of the deck where the child played with his friends.

The boy knew that several bad things had happened to his family in Germany. First and apparently most importantly, an infant brother had died. His death tore a wound in his parents' hearts; a wound that never healed. Second, there had been some dispute about his father's work as a finance officer. The boundaries of this difficulty were not clear to him, but he understood it to concern his father's unwillingness to "bend" regulations to the taste of a senior officer. Thirdly, his father had angered a general over an audit of the man's unit finances, and this man wished him gone. As a result, they were going home.

That made young Lang sad. He liked Germany and the larger Europe beyond the borders of the American Zone of Occupation. For an American child, the occupation of Germany had created an immense and fertile ground for learning, experience and play. It was true that the ruined towns and parts of towns were frightening, but the Germans were quickly recovering their ability to make and sell the things that children love. Wooden toys, Christmas ornaments, carved and marvelously wrought art that depicted their rich heritage of legend and myth; these were all things to delight a child's soul. The boy particularly remembered the carved altar in the Army chapel in which his family worshiped. The building was a simple Quonset Hut set in one of the many German municipal woodland parks. The altar was mounted on a pivot at the center. On one side in deep relief was a representation of "The Last Supper." On the other was a scene from the Old Testament to make the altar useful for Jewish services.

It snowed their first Christmas Eve in Germany. A choir of soldiers sang for midnight mass. The moon had emerged by the time mass ended. Brilliant moonlight made ice crystals in the snow glitter like tiny jewels. The crunch beneath their boots was wondrous.

In an unusual event, a child had been baptized at mass that night.

His mother wept as they walked home. His father "shushed" her to whimpers, telling her that she could cry when they were home but not in front of the Germans.

They lived in a large house "requisitioned" from the German owner. The house was in a street undamaged by Allied bombers. It had been left untouched because the planners for the post-war occupation had marked the neighborhood as one that would be needed for housing officials of the occupation

In a characteristically generous decision, his father decided to allow the owner to live in the housekeeper's apartment on the top floor. The man could often be heard there playing the baby grand piano that he moved upstairs. He played well and was particularly fond of Gershwin's work... Lang did not know who George Gershwin was, but his father explained. For major occasions like Christmas the owner was invited downstairs to eat in his own kitchen with the household staff that the occupation government required Lang's father to maintain. Employment was scarce in Germany.

There was a housekeeper, a professional "domestic," who ran the affairs of the household with rigor. She was a middle-aged woman who wore her grey hair in a "bun" and always seemed to be scowling.

There was a gardener.

There was a cook. She cooked wonderfully and was the housekeeper's cousin.

There was a housemaid. She was a pretty thing, blond and nineteen years old.

There was a driver for his father's staff car. The man's name was Walter Flick. In the war he had been a captain in the Luftwaffe and had flown FW-190s against the Soviets and Western Allies. He was in his forties and had been the owner of a major car sales dealership in Bremen before the war. He was the housemaid's older brother. Flick and the boy's father got on well, and young Patrick often rode on the front seat between them. Flick never talked about the war. The boy's mother hated Germans as well as the Japanese. She hated the household staff and usually hid from them in charity work or in parts of the big house that they knew she did not want to see them in. There was a constant, annoying series of hostile events between Lang's mother and the servants.

One involved a dog. At the father's request Flick brought a full-grown German Shepherd. The father wanted it for a watchdog. The mother did not want a dog, especially a German dog. Its name was Ulrich.

Flick said that it had been a guard dog on a German air base. He said the farmer who now owned it could not afford to feed it. This was probably a lie. It was probably the fighter pilot's dog. The big dog was under-nourished. The boy and the dog looked at each other while the parents tried to find words with which to say that the dog frightened them. The boy sat down cross legged on the parquet floor near the beast. The animal approached and lay down with his head in the boy's lap. It was decided that he could stay, at least for a while. The boy and the pilot took Ulrich to a slaughterhouse the next day where the dog drank most of a pail of blood and then licked Patrick's hand. The boy loved animals, and they always seemed to know that,

On another occasion loud arguments could be heard from the kitchen. The Langs rose from supper in the dining room to learn the cause. Flick and his sisters were shouting at each other across the kitchen table. He was red in the face and she was weeping. It was learned that the girl had been seen by her brother going to the military cinema with an American soldier. Her brother was enraged. The boy's mother flew into a rage of her own, telling Flick that he should be honored that an American liked his sister, considering… The Luftwaffe veteran absorbed that insult and then said "You must understand *Herr Major;* it is not because he is American. How would you feel if the situation were reversed?" His father told Flick to deal with this himself, but to make sure his behavior was impeccable. The former officer bowed slightly.

With all this as background, it was not surprising that Patrick's mother flew into a tirade against the former enemies of the United States once she reached her home on that snowy Christmas morning.

His father tried to quiet her, afraid the staff would hear, but there was no ending her anger.

She was particularly loud about the Japanese. "He should know what the damned filthy Japs did to John McDonnell! He should know!"

"What should I know?" the boy asked. His dog, Ulrich, sat beside him. They were almost the same height when the dog sat.

There was a pleasant blaze in the fireplace. It must have been set by one of the staff. The flickering yellow light reflected on the dark paneling of the room.

Photo Credit: Courtesy of permission of Lowell Sun

His father switched on the big Grundig radio that sat on a table near the fireplace. Bing Crosby was singing "White Christmas" on Armed Forces Radio. "The chaplain who baptized you," his father began, "Father John McDonnell was his name. He was a close friend of ours. This was at Fort Devens. He was captured by the Japanese Army on Bataan and died in captivity. There have been terrible rumors as to how he died after the Death March... He was a close friend and spent Christmas with us once at Devens when you were a baby. We should not speak of this on Christmas morning, perhaps some other time."

"What has this got to do with Flick or the people we know here?" the boy asked.

"Nothing! Not a damned thing! Go to bed. Take the dog with you. Now!"

As he lay in bed, his warrior dog warming his feet, he could still hear his mother wailing in the parlor.

Later that day they went to see Bob Hope's Christmas show in a big theater used by the US Army for movies. Coming out of the building later, the boy saw Flick's sister in the crowd. She was with her soldier friend. She saw him and held a finger to her lips. He smiled at her in what he hoped was reassurance.

Standing on the quay in New York, he watched his father supervise the loading of the little casket into a hearse.

The Zebulon Pike had carried him to a new stage in life. His childhood was ending.

CHAPTER SEVEN

Gunning

Deer tracks are like a book. They tell you all that you need to know. The White-Tailed deer live all over eastern North America. They live in the cold of the deep North and the swamps of the Florida Panhandle. The farther north you find them, the bigger they generally are. Perhaps that is caused by the "winter kill" of parasites and microbes. Maybe it is just the result of there being fewer human hunters in the northern forests.

Pat Lang learned to track deer from his uncles, his mother's brothers. These men lived in the Maine woods. They had spent a few years in the army, but except for that time, they lived in southern Maine all their lives. They worked in shipyards on the coast and in factories scattered across York County. When they were not so occupied, they concerned themselves with their growing families and pursuit of the huntsman's skills.

These men stalked deer. November was the month of the legal deer hunting season. That month was reserved for hunting or gunning as they would have said. They taught their nephew to stalk deer. From them he learned to read the footprints of deer. From them he learned to know if deer were male or female, calm or agitated, running or walking, old or young. He learned to find their sleeping nests and to search them for droppings that could speak of what they had eaten recently and how much. He learned to inspect the droppings if there was doubt about what they had been eating. Different feed led to different pellets. A deer that had been feeding on some particular item could be expected to be found at the place of production. It was easier to go to Farmer Moulton's apple orchard and wait for the animals to come than it was to follow the beasts through second growth forests and stone bottomed muskeg knee-deep in cold water.

Patrick learned quickly.

On a cold November day, he shot his first deer, a big doe. He was 14. The sun was slanting down in the late fall way it does in northern latitudes. There was a smell of leaf mold in the air. Clouds flew across the bright, pale blue sky. He and an uncle named Roger followed several deer though a wilderness of fallen treetops and stumps.

He liked this uncle. The man was a wild, nearly ungovernable ne'er-do-well who had been field first sergeant of an infantry company in the Korean War. He had a lot of combat medals but no ability at all to survive in the peacetime army. He was discharged involuntarily within six months of his return to the US. He fought with everyone after coming home and had almost been court-martialed several times.... It was his way.

Suddenly they were in the presence of a 10-point buck and his three does. "Pick a doe," the uncle said. "They are better eating…"

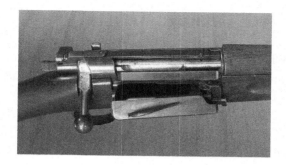

The boy shot the deer through the rib cage just behind the leg and the animal dropped like a stone. By the time he reached the doe, she was dead. When he gutted it later, it was clear that the .30-40 Krag bullet had gone straight through the heart. Standing over the carcass, he heard heavy breathing nearby.

The buck was 30 yards away watching them and his mate.

"You're a brave son of a bitch," his uncle told the stag. He picked up a loose stick and threw it.

The animal turned and walked into the underbrush.

"Why did he do that?" the boy asked. "Why did he stay? We could have killed him."

Roger shook his head. "They do that sometimes. He was waiting for her to get up."

They sat on stumps and waited for the heat of the kill to leave them. His uncle gave him one of the sweet cigars that he always carried. "Don't tell your mother," he muttered. "A dead first deer requires a celebratory smoke. Don't tell your father either." After a moment he looked at the boy and asked if he had any idea what made his father "tick."

"None at all, do you?"

Roger shook his head. "Rollande was always strange. She is stranger now. She can't seem to hang on to things long." He looked at the boy for confirmation. "She can't get over being the daughter of your grandfather's first wife, the one who died in the influenza, not our mother. Why aren't you going to the public high school?" he asked.

"I don't know. She wanted it and he did not say no. St Ignatius is a crummy school. I wanted to go to the public school"

Roger nodded. "OK. Let's do this."

They hung the doe by the neck so that the guts would fall out naturally. They had brought some rope. Patrick draped his red checked hunting coat over a broken branch and rolled his sleeves to above his elbow. With Roger watching, he cut into the doe's abdomen from breastbone to anus being careful to avoid piercing the bladder or intestines. His uncle had told him that if he cut into these, he would have a worse mess and they would have to drag the body to a stream to wash it. Once he finished the main incision, the intestines spilled out on the grass and leaves. He reached into the bloody hole to cut the major organs loose from inside the neck. Roger had brought a large plastic bag. They put the bullet- pierced heart and the liver in that and tied the bag shut with string. While Roger went to cut a pole for them to use in carrying the body to the road, the young man walked to a nearby creek to wash. The deer had been drinking from this stream when they surprised them. Deer blood quickly dries into a flaky, iridescent hardness that has an oddly pleasant feel and appearance. He washed his hands, forearms and knife in the stream. There were stubborn spots where the blood clung, but leaves helped in removing them. When he returned, he found that his uncle had tied the doe's fore and hind legs together with a pole between them. The bag of organs hung from the neck. The doe's eyes had turned gray and empty. There was a little dried blood on the fur, just a little.

The sky had turned gray and the temperature was dropping. "It's a mile to the road" his uncle said. "Looks like snow; we should get going. It'll be dark in an hour."

The light was steadily dimming.

Patrick slung the Krag across his back to have two free hands and bent for his end of the pole. They settled the weight on their shoulders and started back to the road.

Driving to a deer tagging station, Roger asked if he had a shotgun.

"No, I bought this rifle from grandpa for forty dollars. I saved my allowance for that and am still paying him for it."

Roger said nothing. He was intent on driving down the middle of the dirt and gravel road. He wanted to reach a gas station nearby where they could register the deer kill. It would close soon, and he did not want an unregistered deer on their hands overnight. He already had enough trouble with the police and game wardens.

"I have a .22 single shot that grandpa sold me for ten bucks," the boy said. "I shoot squirrels and rabbits with that."

Roger remembered about the shotgun. "Your cousin Joe has a closet full of old shotguns that he doesn't use any more. We'll see if we can talk him out of one. He has a nice Lefever 12-gauge side by side. We'll see...." He glanced at his nephew while still clutching the wheel on the rutted road. "Maybe you could offer to supply him with ducks and pa'tridge?"

"Of course. He doesn't hunt anymore?"

"Nope, bad arthritis."

"I'll do it."

When they reached the boy's home, they hung the deer in a Silver Birch tree on the front lawn. This display of the trophy was local custom.

The father came out of the house to watch.

They hoisted it high enough to keep it from scavengers.

"He shot it?" the father asked.

"Shot it and field dressed it. Who taught him to be so handy in the field?"

"My brother," the father said and turned away.

The mother watched from a window.

CHAPTER EIGHT

The Inferno

The small house stood in a clearing in the forest.

Fire surrounded it in a circle that seemed to besiege the little building. It was built of wood with composition shingles and roofing. It was something that a carpenter and a few helpers could build in a week once the foundation was in. It was the kind of house Pat Lang's father seemed always to buy. He could have bought something grander, but that would have made him uneasy…

The fire started far away in the second or third growth woodland. Lightning was the most likely culprit for ignition. Smoky the Bear, notwithstanding, lightning was usually the most probable cause.

Logging began in the 17th Century in southern Maine and continued ever after with pauses of a few decades needed to grow more trees, trees of ever diminishing stature. The forest was mixed, but the principal plants in it were Norwegian pines that were planted originally for the purpose of growing masts for sailing ships.

There were dry, long dead treetops everywhere in the forest, treetops and stumps.

When the fire came to burn the house in 1957, you could hear it approach roaring and moaning as it jumped from one feast to the next. The tops of standing trees exploded like bombs as the flames raced towards the house. At first sight it was a glow on the night horizon but soon it was at the edges of the clearing and sniffing for a way across the grass. There was a big pile of stumps near the clearing's edge. They had been bulldozed into a thirty-foot-high hillock when Lang's father and he cleared several acres of trees just after the family bought the house in the woods. The fire licked at the pile of stumps for a while and then found one tasty enough to devour. Within an hour. the whole "mountain" of stumps was burning in a spectacular Viking's funeral display.

The heat became intense. It was obvious that the roof would catch fire if the temperature remained so high.

Patrick and his Uncle Roger decided to save the house.

Lang's mother and sister had "evacuated" when the fire reached the clearing.

The two men looked at the burning trees and brush, looked at the house and made a wordless decision that the fire would not be allowed to devour the house. *"No pasaran!"* would have been in the spirit of the moment,

Patrick and his father had dug a well in the front yard. The soil was beach sand beneath the sod. This was evidence of the presence of an ancient sea.

The water "table" was only six or seven feet down and there was always water in the well.

Roger and his nephew dragged garden hoses from the shed behind the house. There were several outside water faucets. So long as there was electricity in the house there would be water under pressure in the hoses.

Pat and Roger wet each other down with the hoses. The heat of the fires was growing more menacing by the minute. They wet down the house thoroughly. The water steamed on the siding.

They climbed to the roof and drenched the hot shingles while walking back and forth under a continuous "rain" of cinders, burning pine needles and small branches.

Deer and a black bear came out of the fire to stand near the house. They looked up at the two humans on the roof. Lang told his uncle that they were like disciples of Orpheus summoning the beasts to come and be saved. There was an excellent endowed library in the old "mill town" seven miles away across the burning forest. This was the "Louis B. Goodall Memorial Library" and Patrick liked to read.

Roger said nothing. He accepted the idea that his nephew was an intellectual as well as a woodsman.

The smoke was a bitter grey fog.

The two "heroes" wrapped wet cloths around their lower faces.

The electricity supply never broke down. The water never stopped flowing and the fire finally "ate" its way through the available fuel and began to die away.

Eventually, there were just a few isolated ground fires burning across a landscape transformed into Dante's vision of the blasted terrain of hell.

Pat Lang's father arrived while the firefighters were wetting the roof again. He had been out of town on business.

The mother drove the car. The man had never learned to operate a motor vehicle.

Standing beside the car he asked what they were doing.

"Saving the house," his son replied, hose in hand.

"Why?" his father asked. "You should have let it burn. I could have collected the insurance on this place and moved into town..." Having spoken these words to the soot covered men who had saved his residence from nature's incendiarism. he got back in the car and was driven away. He left his son and brother-in-law standing on the roof.

"Well, I'll be damned!" Roger shouted at the smoky wreck of the forest. "Why the hell did my sister marry this asshole?"

"He wasn't always this way. He doesn't know how to say that he thinks we were crazy to do this, to risk ourselves to save this crummy house... He is a very unhappy man, unhappy with his life, unhappy with his life with your sister, unhappy with a lot of things, but he does have a sense of right and wrong. That has gotten him in trouble a lot."

Lang laughed aloud... After a moment he asked his uncle if he had ever told him about his visit to Dachau.

Roger looked blank.

"Maybe it is the burning forest. Maybe it's the animals that came out of the inferno to hide from the demons in the woods. I don't know, but this makes me think of Germany and my first glimpse of hell itself. I used to travel with him in Europe when we lived there. I was maybe eight or nine years old. Europe was a giant playground for kids like me. Even with the ruined cities and poor people everywhere, it was a paradise for a little American kid. He went to many places on government business and often took me with him. I think it worried him how much I enjoyed the experience, worried him because I did not understand the price of our experience there as the winners of the war, the conquerors."

"On a trip to southern Germany he took me to the concentration camp at Dachau. This is near Munich. The Army ran the place then. It was huge, a big camp for communists, Jews, Gypsies, all kinds of people that Hitler did not like much. An American master sergeant showed us around. He was one of the soldiers who had liberated the camp in 1945. I didn't really get the picture fully until we got to the crematoria where the murdered prisoners were burned. Then I understood."

On the way to the gate I asked him why he brought me there. He said it was part of my education, as much a part of my education as riding in trains to go to places like Paris or staying in fancy hotels. I asked why that was. He said that I needed to know that if they were allowed to do bad things, people were much worse than any animal in the jungle. He said that most people are 'no damned good.' He asked that I not tell your sister. I think we saw the sad man who said that here today."

"Does he drink at all?"

"No and does not smoke either. Maybe he should."

"Does he hit you?" the uncle asked.

"Oh, yeah, he does that, but now I am as strong as he is and that will have to stop. As a matter of fact it stops today; he and I will have to talk this out some day. I may end up in the marines yet."

"Jesus, not that," his uncle growled. "I have some Canadian Club in the truck, let's have a drink and go get something to eat."

CHAPTER NINE

"To The Last Man"

103rd Infantry Regiment (MEARNG)

Walter Patrick Lang, Junior joined the Maine Army National Guard when he was almost 16. That was an illegal act. He joined because some of his high school buddies joined as a group and they urged him to sign up with them. The boys who wanted to join belonged to a hot-rod club called the "Blue Suede Eagles," and although he did not belong to the club, their appeal touched him. The local National Guard unit was short of men and offered to make a rifle squad out of nine of them if they could find that many who wanted to join together.

Lang thought this sounded like fun. He had lived on army posts and liked what he had seen of the military. He asked his father's opinion.

Walter, senior was retired from the Regular Army, having served 32 years. "You think you can do this?" he asked. He looked doubtful, but perhaps hopeful. Of what he might be hopeful was not instantly plain. When his son did not respond, he chuckled and said, "Well, why not? I enlisted under-age the first time. If they catch you at this, they will just give you an honorable discharge and welcome you back when you are old enough."

"This was when you went to Mexico with Pershing?"

"Yes. I was 16, like you are now. I was a hard kid. You don't seem that to me."

"Why not? Don't I work out here in the woods with you? Didn't I work last summer at the beach?"

"Yes, but you don't do sports, and you let your mother and those two god-damned old maid aunts of hers dress you up as a woman for a Halloween party."

"I was St. Theresa, the Little Flower. It was a joke and I won. I was having fun thumbing my nose at the nuns and brothers. I won. I was almost the best-looking woman in the room."

The father shook his head. "When I was a trooper in the cavalry at your age, I had to fight off queers all the time. What did your classmates think?"

His son laughed. "They know I am a menace to their sisters. I'm their hunting and fishing buddy. I shoot better and kill more than any of them. I've been a class officer every year. I am a cadet major in the Civil Air Patrol."

His father stared at him. "The sergeant major of the 6th Cavalry Regiment made me a clerk in headquarters when I was 17. He used a corporalcy from a line troop to do that. I had to fight every noncom in that troop out behind the horse lines. After they broke my teeth in front, a collar bone and two ribs,

I gave up. They carried me to the post hospital. I told the sergeant major that he could shove the stripes up his Irish ass. I preferred to live. He knew I would not give their names and so did the officers. Are you up to that?"

"Yes."

"All right I will lie for you. We will say that you were born in 1938. I know a good deal about altering documents. We have a copy of your birth certificate. Your mother would not be happy with that. We were married a year later. Don't tell her about this. Bring the papers to me."

The completed enlistment forms came out of a back pocket.

Captain Prescott Osborne, commanding Company B, 103rd Infantry Regiment of the Maine Army National Guard was a fireman in everyday life. He was both a company fireman for the woolen mill and a backup fireman for the town. His wife, Veronica liked to speak of his colonial heritage and of ancestors who were at the siege of Boston and the Battle of Bennington. He was a plump little man who seemed confused at times.

When Lang came to enlist, Osborne looked at the forms in his hands and thought how unlikely it was that the birth date was accurate. On the other hand, the boy's father had signed.

The company armory was then in an old frame navy barracks building at a long abandoned anti-submarine airfield south of Sanford. There were runways, the barracks, an operations building complete with tower and a huge hangar. The town had sold the rest of the buildings for profit after the navy left. They had been disassembled by the buyers.

Captain Osborne's executive officer was a first lieutenant named Bernard Pepin. He was a thin, ascetic looking man who carried a vast hunger for status behind an iron reserve and a well-known "poker" face. He was a lawyer of no great distinction but educated at Bowdoin and Boston College Law. He was the first of his family to graduate from a university college in the United States. He thought his commanding officer to be an example of the degeneration of the founding Yankee stock. He was probably right.

Captain Osborne looked at the fraudulent papers. "You don't look this old," he said. "Have you ever fired a rifle?"

"I've been hunting since I was 14," Lang replied, "deer mostly but partridge and rabbits too."

The XO felt mocked. He saw his commission in the Guard as a credential that would help him achieve his ambition to be a state judge. He was not pleased that his company commander was a fireman, but the potential ridicule that would result from having boy soldiers in the company was a danger to his image. As a lawyer he was aware of the simple truth that all they needed to do with regard to Lang was to demand a certified copy of his birth certificate. He opened his mouth.

First Sergeant William Moulton was an apple farmer from the hilly country north of Sanford. His ancestors had probably sold fruit to Captain Osborne's family when the militia left town to join Washington's army at Boston. He was a big man, big and as strong as farmers must be in their daily lives. He had been in this company since 1940. When the 103rd Infantry Regiment fought in the Pacific, first in the Northern Solomons, then on New Georgia and finally in the Luzon campaign, he had been there, rising slowly until he was "first soldier" of his hometown unit. For him the two officers were an annoyance, but one that would eventually depart, leaving him in charge as always. The CO and XO were the only officers in the company. There were nine or ten sergeants who had been his comrades in the war against the Japanese. They were all French-Canadian woolen and shoe workers, Yankee farmers like him, or lumbermen. "Your father is retired army?" he asked the nervous, suddenly apprehensive boy.

"Yes, first sergeant," the boy answered. Such a response was instinctive for him. He had been raised to be a soldier. Some of those who had raised him for that life had not realized what they were doing, but they had accomplished this function, nonetheless. His reaction to Moulton's six chevrons with a diamond in the center was automatic. It had not occurred to Lang that anyone in uniform would doubt him.

"He wants you to do this?" Moulton asked.

"He accepts it. He thinks it will be good experience."

"He came from the ranks?" It was an inspired guess on Pepin's part. "What was your father's rank?" the lawyer asked, concerned that the signature on the fraudulent forms might be those of someone "important."

"Lieutenant colonel, sir."

For Pepin, this was a rank he could only aspire to at this point in his life. He grew unreasonably cautious.

Lang began to anger. His knowledge and feeling in military affairs began to "float" toward the surface. "My father ran away from home in Minnesota in 1916 to follow the flag into Mexico. He served for 17 years as an enlisted man and then was commissioned from the ranks. He was a sergeant major in the cavalry, the regular cavalry." He no longer cared if they wanted him or not. He was too young to be afraid.

"Wait outside," Captain Osborne told him.

Beyond the door, he waited. He was alone.

His friends had passed through the interview quickly, but not him. The friends waited on a lower floor, wondering what the delay might be.

His testicles hurt. He had recently called a senior at school an insulting name in a schoolyard confrontation. He had assumed that the older boy would "take" the affront and had been surprised when kicked in the crotch. His father asked him why he walked strangely that evening. When informed, the old soldier asked if he had won the fight. He had not.

"You told me to fight in California," the son had said. "You told me to fight when that kid in 4th grade pushed me around. I won that fight."

"Yes, you did. You did. Of course, he broke your arm..."

"I hurt him so bad he was in the hospital."

"And then he was your friend. He was your friend although I did have to talk to his parents and the nuns... It was well done."

On the other side of the company office door, his fate was being decided.

"We don't need this kid," Lieutenant Pepin began. "He is too full of himself and for no reason. He is just another high school kid. He is a know-it-all, and he knows nothing really. He looks like the child he is. We don't need that."

He and Osborne and the first sergeant were all dressed in the woolen olive drab uniform of the time. They wore brown boots with their trousers tucked in the top. The first sergeant had three rows of medal ribbons on his jacket. The officers had none.

"His buddies like him," Osborne said to no one in particular. "They all said they liked him. First sergeant?"

"He's not much to look at," Moulton said. "He looks like you could break him with one hand, a bookworm type. I talked to that that big black-haired kid who goes to school with him."

"And?"

"He said that Lang is no good at sports, but he's the best shot of any of them and has killed at least half a dozen white tails. He always kills does."

"Why?" Pepin enquired. He was not a hunter.

Osborne thought about that. He thought about how much of a city man his XO was. "He's a 'pot hunter,' like us," the CO muttered. "He doesn't care about the head. Get him back in here, first sergeant. We're wasting time. I need to go watch training."

"If you decide to do this, captain, we should give him something hard to do…"

"Young man, do you know what a B.A.R. is?"

"It's a Browning Automatic Rifle, sir, a squad light machine gun."

"Have you ever seen one?"

"Only in pictures, sir."

"Do you want to carry one in this company?"

"Yes sir, I sure do. I do."

Osborne looked as though he had made a decision."

Pepin opened a drawer, searched a bit and then handed Lang a small, flat metal object. "Explain that," he said.

"It is the insignia of this regiment, sir," Lang replied. He looked puzzled by the question.

Pepin hoped that there would be something strange about the boy's words, something unwanted.

"This regiment is the old 20th Maine infantry," Lang said. "The St. Andrew's Cross refers to the Civil War," he continued. "It is from the Confederate battle flag. The *fleur de lis* is for service in France in World War One. The motto is from Joshua Chamberlain's memoirs. He wrote that on Little Round Top; he thought they would fight "to the last man.""

There was silence for a moment.

"Where did you learn that?" Osborne asked.

"I went to the library last week, sir."

"*Tu parles Francais? J'ai remarqué ta prononciation de 'lis.'*" Pepin had not really meant this as a question.

"*Oui, mon lieutenant.*"

"*Ta mère est Canadienne?*"

"*Née à Quebec mais citoyenne des Etats Unis.*

Pepin glanced at Captain Osborne and shrugged. The gesture said all that was needed.

Sergeant Moulton nodded.

"Stand up and raise your right hand," the captain muttered.

In the next months, the company moved from the old naval airfield to a brand-new brick and stone armory building on the edge of Sanford. There was a drill hall useful for a range of civic events. There were classrooms, an arms room, a supply room, locker rooms and offices. Behind the building was a chain-link fence surrounding the motor pool with its treasured olive-green trucks and jeeps. The Maine woods closely approached the motor pool. The giant pines seemed to lean across the fence to see all within. Across the road from the armory was an artificial "pond," half a mile wide. A 19th century dam built by the woolen mill downstream held back the waters of the lake. This body of water was a great convenience in winter. Truck-mounted snowplows cleared it. Hockey was played there, and many a girl pretended to need skating lessons on its surface. The winter before he joined the National Guard, Lang experienced water on the knee from an injury experienced on that ice. He was goalie in a scratch game of hockey. The puck came up off the ice in a slap shot and struck his left knee. The knee swelled until he could hardly walk. His hockey playing friends thought it was funny.

While skating on the pond one winter day that year, he saw Marguerite Lessard, a girl a year behind him in high school at St. Ignatius. She was the object of his admiration and desire. A beautiful, auburn-haired paragon of feminine grace with a dancer's body, she was younger than her classmates because of years "skipped" and was an academic star as well as having been a ballet student in Portland for many years. He had often attempted to attract her attention but with little success. His luck in wooing her was no better that day on the ice. She simply ignored him after a few polite words

Lang found his new avocation fascinating. The clothing and equipment issue seemed like Christmas in May. He had a locker for all this in the troop dressing room and found that his mother was quite willing to help him keep his OD uniforms and fatigues in suitable condition.

The men in the company were a mixture of veterans from the Pacific and Korean wars as well as blue-collar workers of one kind or another. Drill pay was clearly an incentive for service, and the older men relished the thought of a pension someday.

His high school pals learned quickly that they were not going to be a distinct group and decided to accept that.

Lang was issued a Browning Automatic Rifle as had been promised. The company was almost entirely equipped with World War 2 weapons, and the BAR was no exception. This venerable "beast" was developed at the end of World War One as a machine gun fire support for a squad of nine riflemen. It shot a big rifle cartridge and was accurate over long distances. It weighed 20 pounds empty, and the ten magazines that came with it weighed 20 more pounds. He went to the training sergeant's office and signed out the Field Manual on the BAR. The sergeant, a full time National Guardsman, asked if he was going to read it or just look at it.

Two months later a Regular Army inspector visited the company on a drill night. As this major walked down the company's ranks in the drill hall, Captain Osborne and the first sergeant followed closely behind. The major looked bored. In "pinks and greens," the medium sized, grey haired man looked formidable behind rows of combat ribbons. He stopped several times to talk to soldiers. He came to a complete halt in front of Lang and laughed. "Why do they always make the littlest guy the BAR man?"

Lang was offended, but then, he was easily offended.

"Tell me about this weapon" the major asked Lang. He had learned to question the actual state of training in a lot of National Guard units.

Lang was prepared for this. He rattled off the description of the BAR that was in the manual.

"Have you fired it?"

"Not yet, sir, but I have fired many large bore rifles."

The answer from this boy intrigued the major. It was an early spring night. The outside temperature was frigid. He faced a long, dark, drive back to Portland and his quarters on an almost abandoned Army post. *Might as well have some fun with the 'raggedy assed militia.'* "Can you field strip it and assemble it?"

"Yes, major. I can."

"Do so."

A shelter half appeared and was folded into a neat rectangle on the tiled floor. The company was given "rest" as a command so that they could stand comfortably in ranks and watch.

Lang took the gun off his shoulder and laid it on the half tent. He extended the bipod and started to take the BAR apart. As he proceeded, he recited the steps listed in the manual.

The officers and First Sergeant Moulton stood around him, looming over the cloth on the floor and watched the parts come out of the gun.

Lang laid them out on the cloth in a specific order and in places designated in the manual. When he was done, he stood at "attention" behind the shelter half.

"Bring me the manual" the major said. With the book in his hand, he turned to the page with an illustration of how the disassembled gun should be laid out for inspection. After looking at the picture for a moment, he reached down and moved one small piece a foot. "Put it together," he said.

It went back together faster than it had come apart.

"Congratulations," the major said to Lang. "A fine showing captain," he said to Osborne and walked away.

Lang was feeling good after the company fell out until Moulton beckoned.

In a corner of the drill hall, the big man said that the performance had been remarkable, but that Lang had made an enemy of many in the company. "They know that most of them could not have done that without preparation. They are jealous. You should watch your back."

When he went home, his father said much the same thing. His mother listened uncomprehending.

Three weeks later, he was called to a meeting in the company commander's office. Waiting outside, he heard Lieutenant Pepin say that it was a mistake to let him think himself too much. The door opened and Pepin emerged. The officer did not look at him as he walked down the hallway.

Osborne gestured him to a chair. "We have to provide an instructor for BAR assembly and disassembly at summer camp this year. You will be that instructor. Any questions?"

"A battalion class, sir"

"No, regiment."

"Sir, I am a private soldier. Are there no others to do this?"

"A 'private soldier,' you read too much," Osborne said. "We will promote you to Specialist 4th Class before the summer. Anything else?"

"Thank you, sir."

"You may go."

As he closed the door behind him, he saw that Moulton watched him closely. He was careful to keep his face expressionless.

The company had the tradition of a dance at the armory in celebration of the US Army's "birth" in June 1775. Lang asked Marguerite Lessard to the dance. She listened and declined. He did not know why but suspected it had something to do with him personally. He took another high school girl to the dance but thought of Marguerite all night.

In July, the regiment assembled at Camp Drum, New York near the Saint Lawrence River. The big military reservation stretched for many miles across dense forest, abandoned farms and hard bottomed northern swamps. The summer air was thick with mosquitoes, and the tiny biting gnats called "no see-ums." The company moved into a collection of wooden buildings built for World War II. The cooks then began to pretend that they knew how to operate in the kitchen attached to the company mess. While in summer camp, they were required to prepare food prescribed by the army's worldwide master menu. Some of the dishes and ingredients were things they had never heard of. The results were hearty but, at times, unrecognizable.

Lang's class was one of a dozen taught on different aspects of the BAR. Every enlisted man in the regiment sat through it in groups of twenty. There were over 2,000 men in the regiment. There was general satisfaction with his lecture and the demonstration that accompanied it, although some of the older men looked surprised at his youth. The BAR "committee of instruction" was to teach for five days.

While he was in the field the second day, a "runner" brought Lang the kitchen police roster for the company for the rest of the stay in summer camp. He was on the roster the next three days in a row, beginning that night.

The KP detail worked through the night to clean the mess hall and especially the kitchen before breakfast.

Lang reported to the mess sergeant, a fisherman from Casco Bay and was assigned to "pots and pans" as a working position. This involved scrubbing out all the aluminum vessels in which the company's food was cooked. The standard of cleanliness was perfection, and the work was inspected by a regimental officer from the National Guard and an army veterinary officer from the Camp Drum garrison each morning.

Halfway through the night, Lieutenant Pepin arrived on the scene with First Sergeant Moulton. As XO, Pepin oversaw all administrative matters including the mess.

Lang had finished his work and was standing by one of the gleaming stainless-steel tables in the kitchen drinking coffee. Everyone in the room came to the position of "attention" while Pepin and Moulton inspected the work. Pepin spent a lot of time at the sinks. He was wearing white drill gloves and ran his hands over all the pots and pans looking for grease. It was clear that he had reserved the pots and pans job for Lang. There was no grease.

The slowest man in the detail had been given the worst task. This was the cleaning of the "grease trap." This "trap" was an iron box set on the floor between the two big steel sinks. Drainpipes ran into it from the sinks. The "trap" strained out the grease before the water went into the sewer system. By the end of the day six inches of sludge and grease filled the bottom of the black iron box. The Regular Army standard for cleanliness in that box before breakfast cooking began was the same white glove test that Pepin had given the pots and pans.

"Since you did so well with the 'pots and pans.' you can finish this," Pepin said completely straight-faced. "You have a couple of hours left. Is that enough time?" You could see the unthinking malice behind the stony face. *"Ca suffit, eh, mon petit?"* The French words slipped out. They betrayed a private agenda.

The mess sergeant was named Tremblay. He protested. *"Mais, lieutenant, il a fait son travail, et il l'a fait bien."*

"You heard me," the XO said and walked out the door into the dark.

The first sergeant and Tremblay talked in a corner for a few minutes while Lang got busy on the grease trap.

Several of the other KPs gathered to help him as they finished their work. At 5 a.m., the KP detail was released and fed breakfast before the company arrived. It was creamed chipped beef on toast, a dish Lang loved, a dish he relished from childhood breakfasts eaten with his father in army messes.

A runner waited for him to finish eating and then escorted him to the company commander's office.

"I'm filthy," Lang told the soldier. "I can't go in to see him like this."

"I was told to bring you without delay." The man went in to tell Osborne he was there.

Through the momentarily open door, he saw Osborne seated at his desk. Pepin was standing in front of it, and Moulton was seated to one side. The wooden walls were thin.

"It doesn't matter whether or not you like it," Osborne told someone, "Colonel Bartlett particularly complimented us on his classes. Do you understand? Now, sit down. Send him in."

Ten minutes later, Lang emerged as a corporal rather than a "Specialist." A "Specialist," although possessed of the same pay as a corporal, was not a non-commissioned officer. As a corporal, Lang would be exempt from fatigue details such as KP, unless he was the supervisor of the detail.

He went to the barracks to wash and dress for his teaching day. That night he moved out of the squad "bay" into a separate room with another non-com.

He went to the post Clothing Sales Store to buy corporal's stripes as soon as he could. A little old lady who worked in the store sewed them on for him. "Aren't you young for this?" she asked.

"I guess not," he said. "Thank you, ma'am."

That evening when he went to the company mess, he remembered his father's story of broken teeth following an early promotion and went to sit with his school friends at the ordinary tables.

Moulton crooked a finger at him from the "first three graders" table and then pointed at an open seat at another NCOs' table.

When he appeared there, two sergeants moved to make room for him to sit, and he knew he was "in."

The following school year seemed to last forever in the nearly "polar" Maine winter.

Lang continued to acquire academic distinctions and prizes, but his real interests resided in the National Guard, the Civil Air Patrol and Marguerite Lessard. She was as "remote" and unattainable as ever. He tried to talk to her when there were opportunities, but she was not interested.

Fortunately for him, the religious "brothers" who directed the boys' side of St. Ignatius High School decided that year to participate in the American Legion's national oratorical contest. The theme of the year for this "ladder" of competitions was "The Constitution, Ours to Defend." Lang's father was concerned about the erosion of constitutional law in the United States and talked about constitutional history a great deal. They discussed this subject frequently in the "back and forth" of what daily conversations they still had.

Lang wrote a speech centered on the preamble of the US Constitution and its meaning as he understood it.

The first round of competition was held in the school gymnasium. There was no real contest, and the whole business was unfair. Lang had lived across the world in many surroundings and with relatives deeply interested in government. His recent teaching experience gave him fluency as a speaker. He won hands down, but more importantly, he saw Marguerite seated in the audience with her mother.

The next day, she talked to him for half an hour on the sidewalk in front of the school. She wanted to know how he went about building his speech and how he dealt with the anxiety that preceded question and answer periods. The interest was not personal, but it was a beginning. Her interest was enough to make him want to do well in the competition. He moved from success to success across the state until he found himself at the state championship event at Augusta. There he was bested by an astute, sophisticated young man who carried the day by strolling to the edge of the stage and sitting with his legs crossed while answering questions. It was a masterstroke.

Lang thought that the Lessard girl's attention would vanish with that defeat, but that did not happen. They continued to talk and meet occasionally for tennis or some other wholesome outdoor activity until one day she surprised him by accepting an invitation to the "prom." The dance night was a magic affair complete with white dinner jackets, beautiful girls in ball gowns, and the inevitable orchid corsages. Lang thought everything went well. He did not grasp the mistakes he had made. In fact, Marguerite had not appreciated the way he had made a salad out of her orchid at an *après le bal* dinner with other couples. Nor had she thought well of his disparagement of Elvis Presley. The singer was then at the height of his first period of popularity. Within a week or so. she began to tell him that they should not see each other too much. and that she intended to have a real career and would not be interested in permanent relationships until she was thirty.

Lang brooded on that and resolved to change her mind someday.

In his senior high school year, he was elected president of what was admittedly a small class at St. Ignatius.

At the same time, he began to focus on the tightly knit group of senior noncoms who actually ran B Company of the 103rd Regiment. The company was entitled to six commissioned officers and never had more than two, the CO and XO, in all the time he served with the unit. All the platoon leaders were senior sergeants, as were most platoon sergeants. The supply sergeant, the mess sergeant and of course, the first sergeant made up the rest of the leadership.

He discussed this with his father. The father laughed and said that these noncoms were somehow blocking assignment of more officers in order to retain control. "I've seen this before. They have an ally somewhere up the chain of command."

Patrick began to understand that the tie that bound these men together was their service in this company in the South Pacific. They were all in their late 30s or early 40s. To Lang they seemed ancient but in reality, the war was only 12 years in the past.

From time to time the governor of the state called out the National Guard for emergencies of various kinds. Floods, landslides, storm damage or forest fires were the most common. Forest fires were a constant menace in Maine. Much of the forest was second or third growth, and the woodlands were covered with dried "slash" that seemed to be waiting for a chance to burn.

On one occasion when the battalion was engaged in fighting a big fire northwest of Portland, he happened to overhear a group of the senior NCO's discussing a place called Munda. Filled with the confidence of youth, he asked what or where Munda might be. After a moment's silence, the second platoon leader, a sergeant first class, told him that they were talking about Munda Airfield on New Georgia Island in the Northern Solomons.

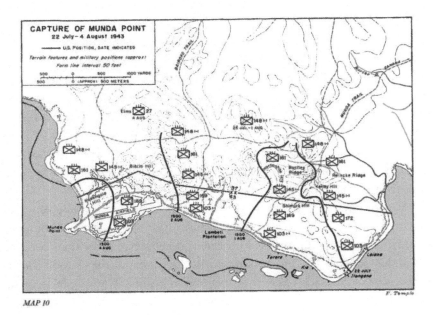

MAP 10

"This is the anniversary of the day we captured Munda in 1943," First Sergeant Moulton, told him. "It was our first real big fight. We were on the left of the line again, like at Gettysburg." He smiled at the thought. "The rest of the regiment and all of Fourteenth Corps stretched out to our right, but this company went into the Jap line at the airfield astride the coast road with our left flank just about on the beach. We were green as hell. and the Japs put up a hard fight. Why wouldn't they? They were determined to die there rather than lose the airfield. We had a company of marine light tanks with us in support of the regiment... We captured the field. Our company commander was killed among the airfield buildings. He was a lawyer from Alfred." He smiled. "You look a little like him... We had other, bigger, fights in the Philippines, but all of us remember Munda the best." He looked around. "OK. Let's go back to work!"

Looking at them that day in the smoky wood, Lang saw that their future would hold only the decimations of old age until all of these "brothers" were gone. He saw how truly irrelevant the two company officers were in the life of this unit. He never forgot that.

In September, he was moved to the 60 mm mortar section of the company's weapon's platoon. There were three of these little guns in the section. They fired high explosive ammunition as well as several other types. They could shoot to 3,000 feet away and usually were fired at targets that could not be seen from the gun. This was accomplished by computations made from maps and on a device known as a "plotting board." In those days there were no fire-control computers, and all this work was done "by hand." The squad leader carried the sight of the mortar and the plotting board and presided over its "magic" calculations. Not everyone in the company could master this process.

B Company was dead last in the regimental competition for 60 mm mortar gunnery when Corporal Lang joined the section. He became the NCO in charge of fire direction for the three-gun section. There was a sergeant section leader, but he was more than happy to let Lang fix his problem. Six months later, B Company was in the final round of the regimental gunnery competition, and Lang had been promoted to be a three stripe Sergeant. He was 18 years old. The National Guard thought he was 20. Under his leadership, the company's mortar section moved steadily upward in the regimental competition.

In early spring, the finalist mortar sections gathered at a range on an old army post near Portland. The shooting progressed uneventfully until the Number 2 gun in B Company's section suffered a misfire.

The HE mortar "bomb" slid down the tube from the muzzle, but the metallic "cough" of the gun's firing was not heard. It happened very occasionally that the cartridge in the bottom of the mortar "bombs" that caused the gun to fire failed to ignite as it struck the fixed firing pin in the bottom of the tube. If that happened, the mortar bomb then "sat" in the bottom of the tube, waiting.

There were twenty men within ten yards of the misfire. They stood rooted to the ground thinking what the result would be if the round detonated in the tube. The tube would burst, and there would be shrapnel in the air everywhere.

The manual said that if such a thing happened a certain procedure was to be followed. That began with waiting a minute for the round to "cook off."

Lang waited.

A minute passed.

No one moved.

"Oh, for Christ's sake," Lang said. He walked to the gun and kicked the tube down low with the heel of his boot. That was "Step 2" in the manual. The little gun fired. They watched the projectile fly away in a high arc. It burst down range in a puff of dirty brown smoke.

The first sergeant asked Lang to come to his hut after supper. The World War II men were gathered there. On the table was a bottle of Old Overholt rye whiskey and paper cups. Drinks were handed around.

"You will be leaving soon to go to college somewhere," Moulton said. "You will be missed."

One of the elders held up his drink. "To the last man," he said.

"… The last man," they replied.

CHAPTER TEN

Idle Hour

"Idle Hour" was a "backyard class" lobster boat. She was clinker, built by two carpenters for the work of pulling lobsters from the cold depths of coastal waters. An old Willys jeep engine ran the screw that drove her through the waves and powered the drum winch that hauled water-soaked traps from the seabed far below. She was a handsome craft and attracted tourist photography swinging at her mooring. She was painted white with a green stripe around the hull. The wheelhouse had a red roof,

The boat was strongly built so that she could "swim" in the choppy seas off Kennebunkport, Maine. There were always wind waves there, always. The ever present gales and coastal currents whipped the sea to four- and five-foot heights even when the weather forecasters might think it a calm day. To live in those waters, the little workboat was built with a high freeboard and a bluff, upturned forepeak.

She was owned by a French-Canadian named Albert Morin who was also the proprietor of a small "supermarket" in an inland town. The boat put down forty lobster "pots" in a string half a mile long. These were hauled twice a day to be emptied, re-baited, and sent down again into the depths. The traps were the traditional wooden boxes fitted with netting. These were baited with rotten fish hooked to the side of the inner chamber, the one the fisher folk called "the chamber of death." The bait was bought from the Shackford & Gootch fishing company on the town wharf at Kennebunkport on the Kennebunk River. Most of the lobsters went to Morin's grocery store. If there was a surplus, the extras were traded for bait or sold to Shackford & Gootch for the wholesale market price. That was usually about 40 cents a pound. The price varied, but not by much.

Morin had appointed his teenaged son, Raymond, to command the boat. The young man had a hired seaman to assist him most days, but his high school friend came aboard at times to help and for the sheer joy of being at sea and free of the land.

One fine day in May 1958, the friends took the boat to sea for a special harvest of the ocean's produce. They had graduated from high school the week before, and this trip would be one of their last together in "Idle Hour." Raymond would soon leave for college in Boston, and Lang looked forward to a year spent far to the south in a place unknown to him from anything but books.

The sky was bright; the sun warmed the air as it shone on the dark blue water. Clouds sailed to the land on the breeze.

The forty-foot boat began to pitch fore and aft as she crossed the bar and exited the river for the open water of the Gulf of Maine. Walker Point was on the port bow. The big frame house there was a pretty landmark. Returning fishermen were happy to see it ahead after a long day. To starboard on the other headland was a jumble of dark and foreboding buildings that were said to be a monastery of some sort.

Lang sat on the deck in the cockpit, his back braced against the transom. The sea was too rough for a seat on a gunwale bench to be comfortable.

His friend was at the wheel with the drum of the winch pressed against his knees. There was a davit and block pulley at his right elbow.

They wore wet weather gear from the boat's cabin storage forward. Spray whipped the cockpit and wet the dark red of the painted deck. The ridges of their rubber boots kept them from sliding, but only just.

"You still want to be a dentist?" Lang asked his friend.

"Yeah, I don't want the grocery store. My old man accepts that, more or less. I want to do biology at Northeastern and then dentistry somewhere in Massachusetts. I just want to make money, be comfortable, and own a nice boat."

"Maybe you could buy this one…"

Ray Morin laughed. You could just hear him above the sound of the sea and the cries of the gulls following them in hope of a handout. "No, he says he will sell her in a few months. He doesn't want her if he doesn't have me to run her. Cheap bastard, he doesn't pay me. He says college will be payment enough."

"Ah, that sounds familiar."

"You still going to that place in Virginia that I never heard of?"

"Yup. I got a letter from Tulane last week offering me a full "ride" in English for four years, but I'm not going to take it."

"Why?"

Lang struggled within himself for an answer. Morin was his friend. They had been "running" in tandem in grades and class office through the last four years. "Oh, just to torment my 'old bastard,'" he said.

"Do you still want to go in the army?"

Lang pulled the bill of his old baseball cap lower. "I think so."

"Why didn't you go to West Point?"

"My eyes aren't quite good enough. I would need a waiver that they seldom give. My eyes are good enough to be an army officer, but I would need a waiver for West Point. I think that's funny. And, I don't want to study math and engineering. The place is all about that. So, I will go to this other school. I can't say I know much about the place except it has a good reputation and Marshall went there… Maybe I should go in the navy. I like boats."

"I've noticed. Are you still dating Marguerite Lessard?"

Lang had not expected that question and felt defenseless. "No, she sent me on my way some time ago…"

"Why?"

"She said she was either going to take a job she was offered with the *corps de ballet of* some dance company in New York or study math in Boston. In either case she didn't see any place for me in the picture. Besides that, her mother doesn't like me."

"That's a shame. She's a beauty, a real beauty… Does that mean you are finished with her?"

Lang smiled. "Ah, I see. You are going to be in Boston as well…"

"But are you finished with her?"

"Don't try to be noble. It doesn't seem natural for you. I am going to be busy for a couple of years, but I will look for her eventually."

"Ah," Morin said, shaking his head a little. "Here comes our string of floats."

Lang steadied himself against the boat's motion and went to his place next to the helmsman. He leaned outboard to starboard to see the float approaching in the "chop." There was an iron handhold in the bulwark by the davit. Grasping that in his left hand, he leaned out over the side and reached down for the float. He had canvas work gloves on, but the water was cold even in May. He gripped the float just below its bulbous base. There was a multicolored stick above that, but for this operation it was just in the way. With the strength of his 18 years he lifted the float and the 80-pound weight of line, lobster pot, brick weights and lobsters off the bottom and high enough so that he could loop the line over the block on the davit and then pull in enough slack to wrap it around the drum of the winch.

Ray had the engine idling. When he saw the line around the winch, he put the hoist in gear. The old jeep engine roared in seeming joy at its task and up came the pot from the bottom.

When it broke the surface and sailed into the sunlight, Pat swung it in so that it could rest on the gunwale.

There was a large metal tank on the cockpit deck. It was half full of seawater. A smaller bait tank stood next to it and a galvanized bucket as well.

Lang opened the domed, hinged top of the trap. Seawater was still running down on the deck and over the side. The boat continued to jump up and down and to roll as well in the trough of the waves. There were three lobsters and a crab. They were beautifully colored in dark greens and brown with orange edges on the shells. He extracted them one at a time. He tossed the crab over the side along with one of the lobsters that was clearly too small. He had a pocket full of little wooden pegs and pegged the mandible of each claw behind the joint so that it could not open. Without that precaution the lobsters would clip each other's claws off. One-clawed lobsters were worthless. The pegged lobsters went into the seawater tank. He reached in the bait tank for a piece of slimy, stinking fish. The eyes of the dead fish were particularly ghastly looking. The filthier the bait the more the lobsters loved it. He closed the lid of the baited trap, glanced at Ray and then swung the "pot" out over the water. He heard the winch change gears and let go. The trap plunged back into the deep. When the line went slack, he un-wrapped the float from the drum and tossed it back into the heaving water.

Ray put the propeller in gear, and "Idle Hour" ran away to the next float. The color bands on them identified the owner. Other color patterns could be seen in the distance near the boats that were servicing "strings" of pots.

Forty traps later, the harvest tank was three quarters full, the "pots" were all back on the sea floor, baited and oozing lovely repulsive smells for the catch to come. Ray would be back the next day with his hired man.

They turned to a southwesterly course. They were about four miles offshore with no "Fish and Game" boats in sight.

Lang inspected the lobsters in the tank, measured them with the state government issued brass tool that identified lobsters legal for harvest. Lobsters could be kept if they fit a certain "bracket" in the length of the main shell from eye socket to the end of the main segment. There were cut outs on either side of the tool. When applied to the animal, they indicated whether or not it was the correct size. He found some that were too large and tossed them back into the ocean after removing the claw pegs. One big male reached around and grabbed his sleeve as soon as the peg came out. He was about a ten pounder. He could "father" a lot of baby "lobstahs."

Ray laughed as he watched Lang lean outboard to hold the lobster in the water.

Feeling its escape to be possible, the "cock" lobster let go and fell away into the dark blueness. Several more went back into the deep. All of these were too small. There were about 30 lobsters left in the tank.

Lang had kept four "hens" that were just a little too small. They had gone into the metal pail. He searched under a cockpit gunwale seat and found a small propane camping stove and a length of board that would just cover the mouth of the pail.

"Idle Hour" "steamed" along the coast with a following wind on a course that would bring them to shore in a couple of miles.

Lang seated himself on a locker top and braced the stove between his boots. He lit the tiny cooker with a match. He then put the bucket with the four lobsters and three inches of Atlantic Ocean on top. The old board topped the whole thing. He held it with one gloved hand to keep everything in place as the boat rose and fell in the following waves. After a bit the lobsters stopped thrashing around. When they were a nice red color, he put them on the deck and went forward to take the wheel.

Ray came aft with a hammer and a screwdriver. They had a clean car hubcap on board and soon it was covered with lovely lobster meat. They ate in silence. Every single piece of shell went over the side. There were heavy fines for what they had just done, but they could see five miles in every direction to seaward. The "Fish and Game" knew that fishermen fed themselves aboard the boats, but with the common sense often displayed by "Down-Easters," ignored that simple truth.

They rounded a headland into the mouth of a small river. The stream was only 70 feet wide, but they knew it was cut deep for a few hundred feet up the river. Ray throttled back while Lang filled a burlap "gunnysack" with lobsters. They crept up the little river with Lang calling depths from the bow in the clear water. There were sedge-covered mud banks to other side. The little fishing boat finally came gently to rest against one.

A car door closed somewhere close ahead. There was an invisible state highway and a bridge there.

Two young people appeared as they "waded" through the tall grass.

Lang carried the sack of lobsters to the bow and handed it across. "Don't go into Kennebunkport with these" he told one of his classmates. "Ray's dad would skin us if he knew."

"Nancy Richards asked if you would be there today for the clambake," one of the boys said to Lang.

"Your cousin?"

'Yes, we'll be on the beach at my parents' place at Wells.'

"Tell her we'll be there as soon as we can…'

The two boys on shore pushed the bow away as Ray reversed the engine. They backed slowly downstream until they could turn the boat.

As he brought the engine to a full throated roar, Ray looked at his friend. I thought you didn't like her."

"Hey man, any storm in a port."

"Yeah, you should go to sea."

CHAPTER ELEVEN

The Old Corps

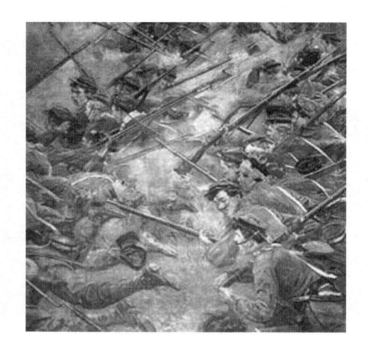

Detail of "The Charge of the Cadets"

"The healthful and pleasant abode of a crowd of honorable youths, pressing up the hill of science with noble emulation, fair specimens of citizen soldiers, attached to their native state, and ready in every time of deepest peril to vindicate her honor or defend her right."

-- JTL Preston

The Virginia Military Institute was founded in 1839. It is the third oldest college of engineering in the United States. The excuse given to the Commonwealth legislature for the creation of such a school was that state militia troops stationed in Lexington were increasingly a nuisance in the present absence of an Indian menace, and that the buildings could be used to educate engineers who would build roads, bridges, harbors, etc. This was at least in part an untruth.

In fact, the Society of the Cincinnati in Virginia, were the main actors in the effort to create VMI. Their hidden agenda was a desire to provide Virginia with a source of military leadership in a future conflict with the gathering forces of nationalism so evident in the North in the 1830s. The war they anticipated eventually came. It was catastrophic for the entire United States but even more for the South and for Virginia. In that war, VMI men fought to the death for their native states. Half the school's alumni were killed, died of wounds or of disease and neglect in prisoner of war camps. Over ninety percent served in the Confederate forces.

Pat Lang made a deliberate choice to attend this school. He had been accepted at several famous colleges and universities including Harvard and Dartmouth and had been offered scholarship money at a few. The decision to attend VMI was made in the belief that his army family background and previous service as a sergeant in the National Guard would enable him to "coast" through a school full of boys who had little knowledge of the world outside their recent high school experience. He thought that VMI would be a pleasant place to spend four years before embarking on what he thought of as "real life." He thought these would be four easy years. He was wrong.

VMI was and is a fine school in all its academic departments. Standards were high in his time, and there was very little grading "on the curve." The faculty were well-published but thought of themselves as teachers rather than researchers. The long serving faculty fully supported the VMI ideal of "a sound mind in a sound body" and was committed to the tradition of the school.

He arrived in Lexington, Virginia with the idea of majoring in physics, but a month or two in that curriculum convinced him that he did not belong there, and he moved to the English department where he prospered. A mixed curriculum in literature, history, philosophy, and languages suited him well. There were enough core curriculum courses in science and mathematics to satisfy his minimum needs. The faculty to student ratio in the English Department was so favorable that advanced level courses were really tutorials. He was usually on the Dean's List and in his last three years was declared to be distinguished in general merit. He liked wearing academic "stars" and went to a lot of trouble to be sure to qualify for them.

A VMI diploma was an excellent introduction to any graduate school in the United States. Graduates of VMI had well-developed work habits and possessed the self-discipline needed to succeed in anything.

The school required all cadets to study military or air science for four years, but most graduates did not make the military their life's work. It was expected and required that graduates accept a military commission if it was offered. but these commissions were usually in the National Guard or army reserve. Some few graduates avoided the commissioning requirement by accepting employment in the state government or public schools, but most graduates took a reserve commission, served a few years and then started their civilian careers.

Only a few men had any interest in the military as an occupation. The great majority of students at VMI accepted the role of VMI as a college that featured a military format for daily life but was not an officer "factory" in the sense that the federal service academies were designed to be.

All students were cadets of the Virginia Militia who lived the life of a soldier all the time. Nearly all the permanent teachers were also officers of the militia. There was a handful of US Army and USAF staff on hand to provide ROTC instruction.

Those few cadets who knew that they wanted to follow a military career for life were thought by most of the corps of cadets to be a little odd. The staff, faculty and student body shared a deep-seated, almost Jungian, understanding that VMI was an educational institution rather than a military training facility.

The cadet regiment lived together in the historic barracks and ate together in the cadet mess at one sitting. Two cadet rooms in the barracks had once been Stonewall Jackson's classroom.

Lang lived for his last three years with two other men who also were not native Virginians. All three were intent on military careers. Later in life, Lang thought that they would have been happier in their time in the barracks if they had found classmates who were more representative of the cadet corps.

Business, civil engineering, the law, medicine, and holy orders were much more popular destinations in life than a soldier's career. There were always a few Episcopal bishops numbered among the alumni.

Cadet life was hard. There was a great deal of physicality in obligatory exercise, intramural sports, mandatory physical education classes, running in formation and the like. Cadets were confined to the VMI post unless given specific leave to be elsewhere.

The cadet corps ran the barracks without much interference or close supervision from the staff. The result was a process in which first year students were ruthlessly vetted and "weeded out" by upper class cadets. There was a lot of hazing, some of which was quite brutal. First year cadets were referred to as "rats." Their lives were severely circumscribed. They could not walk about the barracks freely but were confined to a narrow path in which they marched at the position of attention, always silent in recognition of their status as probationary creatures unaccepted as yet. "Rats" ate in the cadet mess at a rigid position of attention with their eyes on their plates unless spoken to by an upper classman.

The rigors of this system were not evenly applied. Over half the cadets were from Virginia, and inevitably many had attended the same high schools, were related in Virginia's vast "cousinage," or came from families long embedded in VMI's history. This resulted in the existence of cliques that protected some "rats" while others were left to fend for themselves. There was a good deal of prejudice against "Yankee Rats," and that bias was acted on in harassment by Southern cadets.

Lang was not really Northern. His background was too cosmopolitan for that kind of identity to have emerged, but he sounded Northern and that was enough to cause him a lot of trouble on the basis of his speech.

There was a very developed and revered code of honor. Cadets did not "lie, cheat, steal nor tolerate those who did." This code was rigorously enforced by the cadets themselves. It was commonplace for cadets to report themselves for infractions of the Institute's regulations if they believed that not to do so would be dishonorable. A small number of cadets were expelled each year after conviction by the cadet honor court. These expulsions were made in the dead of night after an agonized ceremony conducted in the Old Barracks courtyard. For a cadet who was a native Virginian, to be expelled from VMI for failing to live honorably was a virtual sentence of social death. No VMI man would do business with him, speak his name or associate with him. The only escape from this shunning was to leave the state. When Lang taught at West Point many years after his time at VMI, he had a colleague who was also a VMI man and a native Virginian. This officer told Lang that he was haunted by a recurring dream in which he inadvertently broke the code at VMI and was "drummed out" of the corps. This captain said that, in that case, he believed he would have lost his family and his home.

This honor system created an explicit agreement between the cadets and the administration, an understanding that made life easier for all. Professors never supervised tests. Officers made status checks in the barracks in which a resident of a room who happened to be present answered "all right" to the inspectors knock on the door, and then told his returning roommates of the exact time of the check so that each could determine if he was, in fact, "all right" for his location at that moment. If he was not in an authorized place, the cadet had the responsibility for reporting himself to the cadet officer of the day. A failure to do so would be an honor code violation. This system obviated the need for numerous status checks in formation.

Doors in barracks were never locked. Money could be left in desk drawers for months without fear of pilfering.

If a cadet wrote the word "certified" on anything, the administration accepted without question that the document was a true statement.

Merchants in the town unhesitatingly sold any cadet anything he wanted on credit.

With one exception, cadets did not lie. That exception lay in the area of what was quaintly called "social honor." An example of that would be a question from a hostess if a cadet liked what had been served. The answer was always, "yes," followed by acceptance of another serving. Another example would occur in any matter that affected a woman's reputation. For example, "you escorted my cousin Caroline to the Governor's Cotillion, how was that?" In such a case the answer would always be something like, "your cousin is a lovely girl. I hope to see her again."

This honor system belonged to the cadets, not to the Institute. Non-alumni officers assigned to the ROTC departments and doing extra duty in the office of the Commandant of Cadets did not always understand this. On one occasion when the commandant, Colonel Glover Johns (an alumnus) was absent deer hunting, his deputy strayed far from the accepted limits. It was football season. A number of cadets "borrowed" a laundry truck from the Institute for a midnight expedition to the campus of VMI's arch football rival, Virginia Tech. While there, they shined the bronze equine testicles of a statue depicting the founder of Virginia Tech and his mount. They then returned the truck to its parking space at the laundry. There was a great noise about this, and the deputy commandant demanded the names of the malefactors at dinner. He was ignored. The next day, he summoned the First Class (seniors) to his office, lined them up alphabetically and asked each man in turn if he had been on the "raid" or knew anyone who had been. After the first fifty men declined to answer either question, the situation grew both threatening and dire because the deputy commandant put them all on report and said he would confine the class to barracks until graduation. At that point, the presidents of the class and the Honor Court walked to headquarters and told the Superintendent what was happening and respectfully declared that they would find it necessary to release the corps from the honor system if the questioning continued. The deputy commandant was told that if he wanted to find the names of the members of the "expeditionary force," he would have to do it in some way other than to demand the names from cadets who were honor bound to tell him the truth.

This system reflected a 19th Century belief in the existence of creatures called "gentlemen." Some have said this belief was really 18th Century because it was focused on manner of performance. Perhaps they are correct in that opinion. In accordance with that belief, the cadets lived in the barracks together in a shared atmosphere of ethical and moral certainty.

A disadvantage of the system was that they tended to forget what the outside world was like. On field trips or at "away games" cadets often lost caps and other property to people who stole and lied whenever they could.

The VMI corps of Lang's time thought of themselves as gentlemen volunteers who cooperated with the administration, but who were unwilling to be pushed beyond the limits of what they thought was reasonable regulation and discipline. The administration understood this, and a careful balance was usually maintained. From the administration's point of view, the situation was something like having a thousand half-tamed lions under "command." Since these "lions" often came from the most powerful families in the Commonwealth of Virginia, the situation was especially delicate.

High standards of dress and military ceremony were maintained. Lang calculated after graduation that he had participated in nearly 500 parades, reviews, guard mounts and the like.

At the same time, these were not "parade ground" soldiers. They liked to fight and would do so if given an excuse. Lang always remembered a football game played against George Washington University. The game was in Washington. A fleet of buses hauled the corps to an area near the stadium and then foolishly turned them loose for two hours before the game. During the contest, the well "lubricated" corps watched as GW University cheerleaders crept across the field and "stole" a small, brass saluting cannon with which VMI celebrated scoring. As the white-clad civilian students ran back across the field with their prize, the VMI Corps stood as one, flowed down the banked seats and out onto the grass in hot pursuit. The cheerleaders abandoned the gun and fled into the stands pursued by a mass of cadets. Somewhere up among the GW seats, Lang saw a George Washington student raise his hands to resist the onslaught. A cadet carefully pushed the man's date to one side with the words "excuse me, miss" and then hit the student hard enough to knock him into the next row. On the field itself the VMI football team heard the noise, stopped, turned, dropped the ball and raced back to join the action.

Such things happened from time to time. It was generally understood in the collegiate world of the era that these "beasts" should not be provoked.

The alumni encouraged the "beasts."

It would be fair to say that college girls liked the cadets.

In the course of his army career Lang was, for a time, a professor at the United States Military Academy at West Point, New York. West Point and VMI look very much the same except that West Point is much larger. Lang, then a major, had not sought the assignment. During his service at USMA he grew more and more puzzled by the differences that existed between the VMI of his college days and the West Point at which he taught.

VMI was a hard place. Punishments for violation of the Institute's regulations were swift and severe. Nevertheless, there was a kind of *insouciance*, a gaiety, and enjoyment of life in its richness that he did not find at West Point where every "sin" was treated as evidence of moral defect. There was a solemnity about West Point that had been absent from the genteel but rough world of the Virginia Military Institute. In studying the history of the two schools, he was puzzled to learn that before the War Between the States, the first superintendent at VMI had been president of the Board of Visitors at West Point for several years. After the war there was no contact, none, between the two institutions until 1900.

"Let Virginia Choose"
(Motto inscribed on the ring of the Class of 1859)

In the end he decided that the war itself and its aftermath had caused the VMI system to emerge as he had known it. The chain of events and circumstances leading to that system was not hard to understand.

The contesting parties in the Civil War were hugely mismatched in terms of available industrial resources, population and most especially potential military manpower.

After three years of attempts on both sides to achieve decisive battles of annihilation on the Napoleonic model, the war became a matter of attrition in which there could really be only one outcome, however brilliant and gallant Southern efforts might be. In the end the Confederacy was reduced to such desperate measures as the commitment of the VMI cadet battalion to decisive combat at New Market, Virginia on 15 May 1864. Their performance was a glory to be treasured, but one can only repeat the words of their commander that day. This was Major General John Breckinridge. He bowed his head and said, "Put the boys in, and may God forgive me." VMI was burned and closed by the US Army that year.

The school re-opened soon after peace returned. The military governor of what had been Virginia but was then the "1st Military District" intervened directly to make that happen. This was George H. Thomas, a native Virginian. He ordered that the cadets be given the rifles and the four artillery pieces of the cadet battery.

The reborn school was rebuilt on the ashes of its past. The faculty was recreated. Confederate veterans inevitably made up the hard core of that faculty. These tended to be very young men. They lived long lives. Some of them lived well into the 20th Century. There was no contact with the federal armed forces for many years, and the beliefs and attitudes of these men were pervasive and unchallenged for a long time. The Confederate past and the life and death struggle that they had waged were ever with them and the cadets under their care.

Forrest Pogue once told Lang the story of an occasion in which Cadet George C. Marshall asked the Commandant of Cadets if anything could be done about a disreputable character who sat daily in the Sally Port entrance to the barracks whittling, chewing and spitting on the pavement. According to Pogue, the Commandant rose behind his desk to say, "Young man, he was a sergeant in the 4th Virginia Cavalry Regiment. You are all he has left, and if he wishes, he may sit there until he dies. Good day."

The Commandant was representative of his colleagues and contemporaries. Their army had never known peace. It had never known garrison life and the politics of appropriations struggles in Congress. It had nearly always fought outnumbered and often had won against much stronger forces. These were not professionals in the sense that long-service US Army Regulars were professionals. These were citizen–soldiers whose instinctive goal was to maximize leaders and men for combat and to create leaders who were unflinching, flexible and indefatigable. Their notion of military service was a Platonic ideal of war without compromise and leaders who would possess the "will to win or die."

In retirement Lang was asked at a social event by a US Marine general if he were a West Point man. When told the truth, the general turned to another marine and said. "These are the real fighters. They don't know how to do anything else."

That heritage was born in fire, blood and desperation. In the Old Corps of Lang's time at VMI, it was still very much alive.

As Stonewall looked around him on the Brock Road at Chancellorsville, he saw the faces of his colleagues and former students, "Ah," he said, "the Institute will be heard from today."

CHAPTER TWELVE

Hiawatha

In mid-20ᵗʰ Century America all was well. The economy boomed. The after-effects of the New Deal and the Second World War "floated" nearly all boats. Even Blacks had begun to feel the effects of this era of "good feeling." There were Black officers and sergeants throughout the Army. The chance that they would rise to command the Army was distant, but change had come. Lang's father had served in an Army in which there were Black units of high quality, but they had been separated by law and custom. This had changed by 1960.

In the Army of that time, only West Point graduates automatically received commissions as lieutenants in the professional Regular Army. Everyone else, including graduates of such schools as the Virginia Military Institute, competed for the remaining Regular Army positions after West Point was served. It was the "Army Way," and Lang, raised in the Army, expected nothing less or more.

Marguerite Lessard came to the "finals" dance weekend at VMI in 1961. This was a miracle. He had been issued a box of Christmas cards in December. He struggled over addressees. He did not know many people. He had long carried the girl's image in his soul, and with one card in hand he sought to remember her address in Maine. He managed to do that, and posted the card, a scene of VMI in snow. He then went on leave with his roommate, John Cummings. When he returned in January, he was surprised to have received a letter from "the woman" as Sherlock Holmes would have called her.

An intensive correspondence followed. This unexpectedly led to Marguerite's acceptance of an invitation to a dance weekend at Lang's college in Lexington, Virginia. She arrived under the escort of Cummings' parents. She had traveled with them from New England. Without that, her mother would never have agreed.

Lang arranged for her to stay with a widow who took in girls on dance weekends. The lady's gothic revival house stood at the foot of the sloping lawn just beyond Limits Gate on Letcher Avenue. The view from the front porch was of Lee Chapel and the magnificent buildings of Washington and Lee University.

Marguerite was all that he remembered. She was a dream come to share the flower-scented paradise that is the Shenandoah Valley in springtime. The memory of this beautiful girl had come to be for him what hope he held for a personal life that might contain more than what seemed promised by his nature as a duty-bound man with little experience of personal warmth in human relations. He knew this was illogical. He hardly knew her, but in her charming person he sensed a chance for existence for that fragment of him that was not just a soldier or a coldly rational mind.

The idyllic little town with its lovely buildings and wonderfully civil citizens made a perfect courting place. The cadets of the military institute were well mannered and appreciative to a fault of feminine grace. The highland country of Virginia in May was his ally, and he pled his case well.

After the ball on the third evening of her visit, he sat with the only woman he had ever really wanted in a shadowed colonnade on the ground of Washington and Lee University. The moonlight was ethereal. She looked at that moment to be an avatar of the most handsome women of the time, of any time, "a phantom of delight." The three days had been short but somehow long enough. He persuaded her to accept custody of his precious VMI class ring while he went to Fort Bragg for ROTC summer camp. After all, he reasoned to her, it could be damaged or lost in the rough and tumble of the next months. He would retrieve it from her in the autumn. To his surprise she accepted the "trust" bestowed on her. He walked her back to the widow's house through the perfumed night where he kissed her hand and lips in farewell.

Lang traveled to Bragg with Cummings and two other cadets, one of whom was a member of an earlier class "put back" a year. He therefore had the privileges of a First Classman. One of these was to keep an automobile garaged within Rockbridge County, the location of VMI. In this man's car they drove south, stopping in Blacksburg to visit another cadet whose father was a professor at Virginia Tech.

The five young men conceived the idea of a party on an island in nearby Smith Mountain Lake. With several women from the local community, they sailed to the island in family owned canoes. That afternoon they mixed a tub of what college students of the day called "purple passion." This infernal concoction was made of vodka and purple grape juice with a few other odds and ends included. Battery powered radios provided music, and by early morning, dancing and "kanoodling" were widespread across the little island.

Lang was not interested in the girls. Like Moses, or perhaps Brigham Young, he had seen the "promised land" in the person of Marguerite Lessard, and none of the young women present at the party could distract him from her memory.

At some point in the night he decided that a maritime voyage would be a good idea. His comrades and their companions watched him drift away on a gentle current in the lake. He stood, arms outstretched in the canoe, to recite the "Song of Hiawatha."

After all, he was a literature major.

> "By the shores of Gitche Gumee,
> By the shining Big-Sea-Water,
> Stood the wigwam of Nokomis,
> Daughter of the Moon, Nokomis.
> Dark behind it rose the forest,
> Rose the black and gloomy pine-trees,

Rose the firs with cones upon them;
Bright before it beat the water,
Beat the clear and sunny water,
Beat the shining Big-Sea-Water."

The canoe began to gather speed. A distant murmuring could be heard. Lights appeared in the splendid summer houses along the lake shore. A man in a dressing gown walked to the end of his boat dock. "Hey! You damned fool! There is a dam half a mile away! Have a nice trip!"

There was a pause as Lang "considered" the words, and then continued with his favorite lines...

"Down the rivers, o'er the prairies,
Came the warriors of the nations,
Came the Delawares and Mohawks,
Came the Choctaws and Camanches,
Came the Shoshonies and Blackfeet,
Came the Pawnees and Omawhaws,
Came the Mandans and Dacotahs,
Came the Hurons and Ojibways,
All the warriors drawn together
By the signal of the Peace-Pipe,
To the Mountains of the Prairie,
To the great Red Pipe-stone Quarry."

Somehow, he fell out of the canoe, was retrieved and woke on the island in the morning cold, soaking wet and with a head "like a foot." Little was said of his adventure as the party of adventurers and their consorts gathered their scattered garments and belongings to depart the scene of their revels. The parting of these knights errant and their companions was not a scene of great romance.

By the time the "knights" arrived at Fort Bragg in pursuit of their "holy" undertaking, Lang was feeling the early symptoms of a bad cold. Within a few days his illness deepened and became annoying in its insistence for attention.

This particular Reserve Officer Training Corps summer camp brought together college students from all the northeastern states for training and evaluation. These students were under contract to the US Army while attending a few classes and drill periods during the school year at civilian universities. There were only two or three military colleges within the northeastern region. The military college cadets from these schools were quite different from the "civilians." The military college cadets lived a soldier's life every day of the school year, wore uniforms, and lived in barracks while studying for an undergraduate degree. They were accustomed to solving problems of performance in a military context on a practical day-to-day basis. They tended to have little respect for the civilian students and found their attitude toward life to be amusing and trivial.

Lang was one of the most uncompromising in his difficulty in accepting the civilian "cadets." He thought their foolish obsession with unimportant ritual to be indicative of their lack of seriousness as a group.

Thus, it was that within a few days of arrival, Lang found himself being screamed at in company ranks by one of the "civilians." This event occurred in front of the old wooden barracks in which his ROTC cadet company was housed. His company's area was one of many embedded in a wide expanse of buildings extending over many acres in the piney woods of the post.

A small blond youth from a New Jersey university was the platoon leader appointed by the ROTC staff for the day. Such positions were rotated every day. The formation of cadets was dressed in khaki short-sleeved shirts, trousers and boots. This was a meal formation. Dinner was at hand in the nearby mess hall.

The boy platoon leader had discovered that Lang had failed to button a breast pocket button. With an eye to the presence of the company "tactical officer" standing close by, this "child" was hanging on the pocket flap, tugging and shouting that he would cut off the offending flap to "teach a lesson."

Lang felt very ill. "If you do," he said in a low voice, "I will jam it and the button up your ass,"

"You can't talk to me like that," the platoon leader said.

"No?" Lang replied. "They don't do that in the 'Scabbard and Blade' or the 'Pershing Rifles?' Well, we don't do chicken shit like this where I come from."

The man took a step back and looked around for protection from the tactical officer. Lang had referred to two fraternal honors societies that the more ambitious "civilians" tended to join. Such groups were not allowed at VMI.

This captain, a Black officer named Edwards was a "tanker" who taught at a traditionally Black college. He seemed occupied with the condition of the barracks windows.

Taking his cue from that indication of intent, Lang unleashed that slice of him that remained a sergeant in an ancient combat regiment. "Actually," he hissed. "What I might do if you ever touch me again is rip your head off and piss down your neck." He probably would not have been able to remember when he had first heard that expression, but it must have been early in his Army childhood.

The little fellow moved on to other business in the platoon. He may or may not have realized at that point that he was destroyed forever as a leader in the eyes of his peers.

There were no more childish demonstrations of martinet behavior in that platoon, ever.

Two days later the tactical officer sent for Lang. "VMI," he said. "VMI." You don't sound like a Virginian."

"I wasn't, sir, but I am now."

"I see. Your file says that you are an honor student in literature?"

"Yes, sir. That is the truth."

"In what great book did you find that business about 'pissing down…?'"

"His neck,' Lang completed the sentence. He considered the possibility of making some clever remark about dualism and human nature. He looked at the captain's very earnest face and decided against it.

"I divide things up, sir. I have been thinking of applying for a commission in the Armor branch"

"Why?"

"My father was a cavalryman, a sergeant major of the 26th Regiment."

"Ah. What do you think of me?"

"It is not my place, sir." Lang knew exactly what was meant.

"My color?"

"Sir, to me you are just another officer. I was raised in the Army. It is trite to say so, but to me, you are just a darker shade of green. Actually, in my family blue would have been the right color." He realized that this could be thought to be a reference to the Union Army. "We wore blue until khaki was adopted." He knew that was not much better but at least it was not so obsequious.

Captain Edwards shut the manila file before him. "Are you well? If you don't mind my saying so, you are very white."

They smiled at that, and Lang was dismissed.

The next morning, the company formed in a cantonment street in a long line of platoons in front of eight two-and-a-half-ton trucks that waited. The trucks were from Eighteenth Airborne Corps. They were to carry them to a 300 yard "Known Distance" rifle range where they would spend a number of days qualifying with the M-1 Garand rifle.

The cadet company commander of the day was yet another product of civilian ROTC. This poor man had learned nothing but the drill field and classroom lectures from the army cadre at his college. He had to perform the task of loading the company on the trucks. He decided to march each two-squad section of cadets to the open tailgate of a truck using the "Manual for Close Order Drill." Lang knew this manual like he knew Marguerite's face. He also knew it was a completely inappropriate way to load the trucks. He was ill, but he waited with interest to see how this "evolution" would proceed. A long and complex series of commands were enunciated in a loud "command voice." At the word of execution, files of cadets began to march in various directions making right angle turns, crisscrossing each other and "marking time" in place when columns blocked each other. None reached a tailgate. Lang and the Regular Army truck drivers watched in fascination. Even as he marched in his own pain- filled space, Lang considered a way out of the farce created by this "dance."

"Mister Lang! Get over here," Captain Edwards roared.

Lang saluted when he reached the officer.

"Mr. Johnston, you are relieved as company commander! Lang! Fix this damned mess!"

Lang faced the trucks and the "mess." The chaos was still trying to march to the tailgates. "Listen up!" he shouted. "Stop that nonsense!" They stopped and looked at him. "Company formation right here facing me. First Platoon on the right! Move! Now!"

The company was soon in position and waiting. "I am sure you have seen," he began "that we are four platoons and there are eight trucks. First platoon goes on the first two trucks, etc. In the first platoon the first two squads go on the first truck, etc. We are all smart people. Does anyone not know which truck he belongs on? You, over there," he yelled at his former 'victim' from the button incident. "Yes, you! Which truck?"

"Sixth, sir."

"Don't call me that. We're just cadets. When I 'fall you out,' get on the trucks. Fall out!"

The cadets loaded themselves in a rush.

Lang walked to the cab of the first truck followed by the company guidon bearer. The staff of the little blue flag went in its boot on the side of the truck's cab. "Get in the middle," he told the cadet who had carried it.

Captain Edwards' jeep pulled up beside him. They exchanged salutes. Lang climbed into the cab next to the door.

As the jeep moved away in front of them, Lang waved the driver forward. "Roll," he said.

"Yes, sir," the soldier replied as he accelerated to catch up.

The company spent four days on the range. Divided into "firing orders," the cadets were taught to handle the weapon and then how to aim it in classes that took place behind the firing line.

They then moved forward to the line of targets 300 yards in front of the firing line. On the target line they sat in a deep concrete trench and operated a pulley and frame system by which they sent targets above the concrete trench where they could be seen. "Hits" on the six-foot square paper and cloth targets could thus be marked and reported by telephone to the firing line. Sitting in the trench on wooden benches, the detail listened to the passage of the .30 -.06 bullets overhead. Zzzsss! was the sound made by those passing to one side or other of the hearer. Craack! was the noise made by those passing directly overhead.

Rain fell steadily, interrupted from time to time by periods of steaming sunshine. Lang huddled shivering in the shelter of his rubber "poncho." His throat grew worse by the hour, and the burning, hollow sensation in his chest told him that something really bad was happening to him.

On the fourth day, his platoon was sent to the "line" to fire for record. The rain drove down in sheets. In the middle of the firing program, a deer ran out of the woods and across the range. Lang tracked it for a moment in his sights and then laughed as the animal ran away unscathed.

"No?" the sergeant who was coaching him asked. This infantryman from the 82nd Airborne Division looked interested as to why he had not shot the animal. He had seen Lang shoot enough to know that it would have been easy.

"Nah! I've killed too many of them for no good reason."

Coming off the line, Lang was informed that he had qualified as "expert" yet again. His score had been the highest in the company.

He rasped "thank you, sir" at the range officer while swaying slightly as though a gale blew across the open field.

The medics on site took his temperature, put him in an ambulance and brought him to Womack Army Hospital where a diagnosis of bronchial pneumonia was made. He received massive injections of antibiotics and was put to bed in the "contagious" ward with its complement of venereal disease infected enlisted paratroopers. By midnight, his temperature was so high that the "on duty" medical staff directed that he be placed in an ice bath to break his fever. After this he lay in bed sweating and shivering until dawn.

An Army Nurse Corps major who was in charge of the ward got him up early to have a corpsman change his soaking wet bed linen. Lang stood next to the white metal bed. He had a solid grip on the side rail. Without that he would have fallen.

The Nurse Corps major made a face. "You stink" she said. "Change that gown."

Lang had never suffered from an excess of physical modesty. He reached behind his back, undid the cloth ties, and removed the offending gown. Standing naked by the bed, he handed the lady the wet garment.

A "sucking" intake of breath could be heard across the ward.

She was careful to maintain eye contact with him. "Get him another gown and a robe," she told the hospital corpsman accompanying her, "and change his bed." With that she returned to her office at the end of the ward.

When Lang was back in bed with a nice warm blanket covering him, the corpsman shook his head while tucking him in. "I suppose you don't know that she could charge you with disrespect..."

Lang smiled. "No, Specialist, I know that very well, but she won't."

In fact, the ward nurse was careful to ensure that he was well cared for and helped him persuade a doctor to release him for duty three days later. His illness had occurred over the long Independence Day weekend, and he had only lost two days training time. He was a little shaky during the ride back to barracks but managed not to look unsteady when he reported to Captain Edwards.

"Are you sure about this?" Edwards asked. "You don't look healthy to me."

"Sir, I don't want to be 're-cycled' and have to repeat this course next summer. I have places to go and things to do."

Edwards looked at his watch. "Go tell the cooks that I want them to make you a big lunch and then go to bed until tomorrow morning. "We are going to the field for a tactical problem. Go."

Several thousand calories and 12 hours sleep later, Lang felt a lot better.

For three days the company practiced moving and preparing defensive positions. The route marches were usually 20 miles followed by a lot of digging of foxholes, command posts, and mortar positions. A lot of army shielded telephone wire was laid to establish secure communications networks that could not be intercepted. Lang was allowed to play the role of a private soldier in this "game." That was a mercy. It gave him the chance to continue to recuperate. The weather turned fair and that helped as well.

On the second night, the maneuver enemy became very aggressive towards the ROTC cadets in whose "game" they played the role of the "Aggressor Army." This was a mythical enemy who shared many characteristics of the Soviet Union. In pursuit of that impersonation, the 'Aggressors" wore special uniforms, crested helmets and fought as the Soviets were imagined to fight. The soldiers of the 82nd division were the "Aggressors" in the "war" against the cadets. They generally did not like the cadets. They imagined that these university students were scions of an imagined privileged class. In fact, most cadets were from state colleges and universities and had backgrounds very similar to those of the enlisted paratroopers. In short, the airborne soldiers were looking for a fight.

To find one, they crawled close to a number of cadet defense positions and then rushed forward seeking fistfights. These were often accompanied by salvos of full beer cans. Several cadets were injured. Confusion was general as to how to respond.

Lang understood how to discourage this behavior. He organized his collegiate comrades so that when the "Aggressors" attacked the next night, they were waiting. Paratroopers were dragged into foxholes where they were beaten with steel helmets and kicked unmercifully. The retreating enemy was pelted with rocks piled up in advance as ammunition.

The Airborne Division complained of this uncivilized behavior.

At a company meeting Captain Edwards, who was not enamored of paratroops, demanded to know who had committed such "crimes." There was no answer although he could see many looking at Lang for a cue.

"Well?" he asked stern faced while concealing his true feeling. "Well? Lang, I know you won't lie to me. Well?"

Lang looked up from the floor and rose to his feet. "They should keep their distance, sir."

Edwards nodded after a moment. "I will pass that on. Indeed I will. At least you won the fight…"

Several weeks later, Lang and his college roommate, John Cummings, met on a weekend afternoon at the Tennis Annex of the Fort Bragg Officer's Club. Seated in this wooden building next to the swimming pools and courts, they spent the day drinking whiskey sours and talking about the grand adventure on which they were embarked.

"These guys," Lang said, (meaning the cadets from civilian colleges) "live like pigs as soon as the barracks stop being inspected on weekends."

"They sure do," Cummings replied. "I'll bet they are glad that we're not in charge all the time."

Lang noticed that the 18th Airborne Corps commander, Lieutenant General Trapnell sat at a nearby table in tennis "togs." Trapnell had been captured in the Philippines while serving in Lang's father's old regiment and survived captivity in the hands of the Japanese. For one mad, drunken moment Lang thought of asking him if he knew of the fate of Chaplain McDonnell, the priest who had baptized Lang and who had died as a prisoner. Some measure of sanity intervened to prevent such a question.

After some indeterminate number of drinks, the two friends wandered off in the hope of walking the two miles to their barrack area. This proved to be difficult. They decided to "take a break" and lay down on a grassy bank by the road alongside part of the golf course to continue their discussion on the state of the universe. The sky was blue. The air was pleasantly warm, and they soon dozed off.

After a bit, a car stopped by them in the road. A familiar voice enquired as to their wellbeing. In the car, dressed in tennis whites, was an Army lieutenant colonel assigned to the ROTC office at VMI. A graduate of West Point in the class of 1945, he was a much-admired figure for both young men. Chagrin filled their souls when the reality of their condition became clear in slurred speech and poor physical coordination. The colonel loaded them into his family station wagon and took them back to the ROTC area. They thanked him and wandered off hoping that they had not too badly damaged his opinion of them.

From Lang's youthful point of view, he could only judge his performance at summer camp as a mixed "picture." Would he be considered a fit and competitive candidate for a Regular Army commission? He did not know, and the thought of his father's possible reaction to failure was too much to envision.

Feeling low, he called Marguerite to tell her of his illness and much else on his mind. She sent him back into the fight and said she looked forward to seeing him.

Summer camp reached a culmination for Lang a couple of weeks before graduation from the course.

One of the final exercises was a tank-infantry company task team attack on a fixed position. This meant that Lang's cadet company would have a platoon of five M-48 Patton tanks attached to it and would make a live fire attack on a simulated "Aggressor" position while artillery support was pretended in the form of buried high explosive and smoke munitions.

Lang was scheduled to be a platoon leader. At the appointed time he got his forty-odd men up to the "line of departure." The other parts of the task team stretched away to right and left. The five "main battle tanks" arrived and took their places in the line. Their engines idled as they waited. They made a pleasant "animal" sound.

Captain Edwards stood behind a tank along with the cadet company commander for the day, the tank platoon leader and a range safety officer who had the "role" of an artillery forward observer.

Time passed and nothing happened.

Lang began to listen to what was being said behind the command tank. He suddenly realized that the cadet in charge was making a "hash" of the situation and the mission. This young man was clearly overwhelmed.

"What do you mean?" Edwards said in a voice heard up and down the line. "You want to do what? Send out three-man hunter-killer teams to reconnoiter the hill? Where did you learn that, in GI Joe comics?"

The Army lieutenants laughed.

This was something that Edwards would not endure. The confused cadet was from the college where Edwards was assigned. He looked around. "Lang! Come here!"

He trotted over to report.

"Take charge of the attack. Sort it out and take it in. Any questions?"

"No sir."

Edwards walked away with the other cadet after Lang took several handheld pyrotechnics from him.

Lang had a silver colored whistle that he had bought in the Post Exchange. He blew it for attention and then shouted to platoon leaders. "Orders group, on me, right here, now!" He looked at the tank lieutenant. "Would you join us, sir," he asked.

The officer nodded.

"This is easy," Lang said. "Spread your platoons across the rear of the tanks and between them. Each of you hug the back of a tank and stay on the hull telephone with the commander." He looked at the range safety officer. "I will tell you when to start 'firing' your simulated fires. When that starts, I will fire a white star cluster." He looked at the tank platoon leader. "You will then start forward. The infantry will go with you. I'll fire a red star cluster," he told the range officer, "when I want you to stop setting off charges."

"We will assault over the hill and consolidate on the military crest. There will surely be a counter-attack from our 82nd 'friends' once the live fire is shut off. Any questions? No? You have five minutes. Go back to your troops."

And thus, it was, a perfect textbook attack.

Just before graduation, there was a board of evaluation that rendered its verdict on each cadet. The board told Lang that he was named a "Distinguished Military Student." That meant that if he graduated from VMI the following year, he would be a regular officer if he wished.

Captain Edwards waited outside the old gymnasium in which the board had met. "Thanks for saving my ass a couple of times," he said. "I hope you go Armor. We are going to need people like you."

Pat Lang and Marguerite were engaged at Christmas. She had kept his ring safe from danger.

CHAPTER THIRTEEN

Touch Me Not

2nd US Infantry Regiment

Walter Patrick Lang was commissioned into the infantry of the US Army in June 1962. His date of commission was three days after that of the West Point class of that year. His father told him that this was a little graduation present given each year by the West Point alumni who ran the army to their younger "brothers." The three days advantage meant that every member of the class at USMA would have seniority over officers of that year group who came from other places. Lang did not care about this. He considered graduation from college as an escape, an opportunity to return to real military life, a life devoid of professors and tactical officers, and a life like the one he had "sampled" in the National Guard.

He enjoyed a month's graduation leave in Maine with Marguerite Lessard and her mother and then reported to the 2nd Battalion, 2nd Infantry Regiment at Fort Devens, Massachusetts. This unit was part of a brigade of the 5th Mechanized Division. It was stationed at Fort Devens in central Massachusetts while the rest of the division "lived" in Colorado. There were five thousand infantrymen and 60 tanks in the brigade. The rest of the division was seldom seen, and then only on the occasion of large-scale maneuvers conducted somewhere in the mountain and desert west. This happened infrequently, and the brigade lived alone at Fort Devens. This was the sole Regular Army combat force posted in the northeastern United States.

Marguerite was forty miles away in Boston in her final year of university. That was the reason Lang had sought this assignment. A "plum" job in the legendary 82nd Airborne Division had been offered, but the 82nd was in North Carolina and Marguerite was in Massachusetts. The choice was easily made. The decision was certain to be costly in his career. Performance ratings from seniors in the two divisions would not be thought equally valuable by the Army. He knew that.

Fort Devens was the place of Lang's birth. This post was too small to be the home of a brigade of infantry. Such a unit requires a great deal of space to do the maneuver training needed to keep it in readiness for combat. As a result, the units of the brigade traveled to faraway places in the mountains of New Hampshire, the arctic wilderness of Alaska and many other environments that resembled the scenarios of contingency plans in which it was a "player."

Lang had a bad start in his new "home." He arrived on post late one evening and signed in with the brigade "Officer of the Day" at headquarters. There he was told that he would be assigned to B Company of the 2nd

Battalion, 2nd Infantry. The OD directed him to the billeting office where he was given a room in the Bachelor Officers' Quarters. He thought that he would get some sleep and go around to his unit when he woke.

Instead, he was awakened by someone knocking on his door. Waiting outside his room was a compact blonde man wearing the silver bar of a first lieutenant. He was the adjutant of Lang's new battalion. He had been notified of the arrival of a new lieutenant and came looking for him. It was eight o'clock in the morning. While Lang shaved and dressed in Class A uniform, this dignitary sat in the "parlor" of the two-room suite and commented on the virtues of punctuality and the responsibility of an officer to inform himself of the day's duty schedule.

At battalion headquarters, Lang was introduced to the staff and then reported first to the Executive Officer and then to the battalion CO in his office.

The XO, Major Hiram Henderson, was a World War II veteran who had been badly wounded at Anzio where he lost a sizable piece of his skull. His hair looked odd. Lang later learned that he wore a toupee to cover the scarred skin over the silver plate. He stuttered a good bit and had little to say other than to add a further exhortation to punctuality. The junior officers in the battalion called him "Old Fur Head." They did not know that the man had spent two years in hospital and thus had fallen hopelessly behind his fellows in the contest for promotion.

The CO was a Puerto Rican lieutenant colonel named Jaime Castro who was from Ponce on the south shore of the island. He was a round little man, not fat, but "pudgy." He and his wife were from the island's upper class, the *gente decente.* His manners were suited to his upbringing. He had spent his career assigned to various embassy and Washington posts concerned with Latin America, but he was an infantry officer and schemed successfully to get command of this battalion. It was a career necessity. He always looked uncomfortable in the field and was excitable in a fluttery, arm-waving kind of way. As he got to know Castro and his wife better, Lang was touched to see that Maria Castro took a great interest in the welfare and personal situation of the families of the thirty-odd officers of the battalion. She referred to the wives as her "leetle cheeckens" in a way that reflected her constant concern and protection. An experienced Army Wife of the old school, she relied on the battalion command sergeant major and his spouse to tell her if some problem existed among the enlisted troops that needed her intervention.

Castro told Lang at their first meeting that there was presently no company commander in B Company, and that he would be the only officer for a couple of weeks. For a new second lieutenant this was a worrisome thought even though the yearly training cycle was finished, and the unit was minimally involved in support work for the summer.

The company lived in a modern three-story brick building with six men in a room. On the first floor there was an arms room where the weapons were secured. There was also a recreational "dayroom" with a pool table, Ping-Pong, television and racks full of largely ignored magazines and newspapers. At opposite ends of the building were the company mess and the plain offices where the captain and lieutenants worked when not in the field.

Next to these spaces was the "Orderly Room," the large workplace occupied by the first sergeant and his clerks. The "first soldier" of B Company was another World War II veteran. Leroy E. Moore had served in the 9th Infantry Division in the European campaign of 1944-1945. He was a large man who greatly resembled an aging Burt Lancaster. He was not quick, but he was strong and experienced. He had spent a lot of time in Germany and France after the war and was married to a French woman he had met at Orleans while stationed there. He was friendly but reserved. It was easy to understand that he had every right to be cautious about newly commissioned officers. Lang knew how callow and inconsiderate they often were. He knew that he would either make the first sergeant an ally or face a greatly increased chance of failure in the company.

Moore told him that the brigade staff intelligence officer wanted to talk to him as soon as possible. A jeep came to collect him, and he went to learn what was wanted. The S-2 officer was a lieutenant from the previous year's "crop." He had a nice little office in the white painted wooden headquarters. Its walls were finished in the blowtorched and varnished plywood imitation of knotty pine favored by field units. A collection of meaningless certificates and letters of appreciation covered the walls, but the arrangement was tasteful. The S-2 had hair so blond that it seemed white. He seemed pleased with himself for having obtained such a soft job. In a peacetime, garrison situation, the S2 had little responsibility. He talked down to Lang for half an hour while explaining the army to him. He eventually tired of the lack of appreciative response to these revelations and came to the point.

"Your new company commander, Captain Kenneth McKeon, will report in two weeks. His security clearance has been suspended while he is under investigation. You will not be able to give him access to the safe in his office until this is cleared up."

"Why?"

"The brigade's Signal Operating Instructions are classified, Confidential, and he can't have access to them."

"What did he do?"

"Not your business…"

"Yes, it is. I need to know what I am dealing with."

That level of self-assurance had not been expected.

"He is coming from Vietnam where he was adviser to a Vietnamese infantry battalion. He was relieved for cause and charged by the Vietnamese Army with plotting to assassinate the battalion commander. This charge was supported by his American superior."

"Why is he allowed to take command in this situation?"

There was a moment's pause.

"Someone's son?"

"More or less; he's a ring knocker."

"Ah… I see. 'Duty, Honor, Country,' OK. I'll deal with it. I am going to the Infantry School in two months for courses. I can hardly wait."

In the hallway, he encountered the brigade commander,

Colonel Hume Kingsley was a "tanker" who had served in Patton's Third Army. He had the expansive personality traits of a horse soldier. Boldness, initiative, operational flexibility and velocity; these were the tradition of the mounted arm. Kingsley wore armored force insignia by choice and spent a lot of time with the tank battalion that existed as a minority in his command.

"You must be the new lieutenant," he said smiling. "Come see me some time so that we can visit. B Company, 2nd of the 2nd, isn't it?" He frowned. "There is… this problem with Captain McKeon…. Well, tell Colonel Castro and me if things get too hard to deal with." With that he disappeared into his office.

There was an ROTC summer camp in session at the post. Lang's battalion was detailed to support the training. His company had the task of running several ranges for the cadets, and as the only officer in the company he could choose the ones he wanted to supervise. He spent quite a lot of time on the 81 mm mortar range because he knew a lot about that. He also passed a few days on a range where they were teaching the cadets to deal with the 106 mm recoilless rifle.

This was a very large anti-tank weapon mounted on a tripod that rode in the back of a jeep. The ammunition fired would defeat any tank then in existence, and it was recoilless because the force of the gunpowder went out the back of the gun after it "kicked" the warhead out the muzzle. This meant that if you stood behind the gun when it was fired you would be killed, burnt to a crisp.

The big gun had a .50 caliber "spotter" rifle mounted parallel to the cannon. This was used with red, burning tracer ammunition to point the cannon at the target. When that happened, the main gun was fired, and the shell went straight to the enemy tank.

One fine summer New England day when firing was complete, Lang walked down the line of jeep mounted recoilless guns to check that they were all unloaded before they were returned to his company's arms room. From his National Guard time as an NCO, he knew how important this inspection was and asked a sergeant to accompany him to double check. That precaution saved his career because the next morning when the guns were being loaded back onto the jeeps, the front wheel of one dropped six inches from the loading dock to the jeep deck and the impact fired a .50 caliber round that was in the spotter rifle. The big bullet flew away over the post and into the civilian hinterland of the state of Massachusetts. No damage or casualties were reported from its arrival.

There was an investigation of course. The investigating officer concluded that "person or persons unknown" had found an unfired round ejected by a cadet, had loaded the weapon, and had then been unable to unload it. It was a close thing. But for the sergeant witness to the investigation, Lang would have been finished in the army before he had begun.

Because the 1st Battalion of the 2nd Infantry Regiment was also in the brigade, the regimental museum and its burden of artifacts was also present on post. One day, Lang walked a few blocks to the old wooden barracks that housed the museum. The 2nd Infantry was one of two or three oldest units of the Regular Army. For someone with historical interests, the museum was a "garden of delights." Among the exhibits were the two broken pieces of the mace of office that the drum major had broken over the head of a Mexican grenadier on the walls of Chapultepec Castle. The keys of the city of Metz in Lorraine were there, presented by the *maire* when the regiment liberated the city in 1944, only 18 years before. Most interesting of all were a silver punchbowl and cups made in Mexico in 1847. There was a cup engraved with every officer's name from that time. The name that leapt off the engraved surface to lodge in the mind was that of Lieutenant George Pickett. At the back of the room was a large wooden shield painted with the "arms" of the regiment. Among the armorial symbols was the Saint Andrew's cross, there to commemorate their greatest enemy, their Confederate countrymen. Less importantly, there were a variety of other heraldic devices; a quiver of arrows for the endless Indian Wars, a cactus for Arizona and the blood soaked struggle with the Apache, a bolo knife for the Philippine Insurrection and Moro War, a Maltese cross for their Army Corps insignia in the Civil War where they had always stood and fought whether the Volunteers ran or not.

At the bottom of the escutcheon was the motto, "Noli Me Tangere." This was as Jesus said at Emmaus, "Touch me not."

A sergeant custodian guided him through the exhibits.

It was the essence of Lang's trade to have men follow him to whatever end might come. The museum might help him in preparing them for that. He would bring new men assigned to this holy place so that they would know what sort of tradition owned them. He knew that Bonaparte had written the truth, "Brave men die for legends, for imagined truth, for scraps of ribbon and for tin stars."

He returned from a weekend in Maine with Marguerite and her mother to find that Captain McKeon had arrived and begun to inhabit the brick ranch style house that Lang had arranged and to which his rank entitled him.

Kenneth McKeon looked mad. The expression in his eyes was that which Lang later came to associate with schizophrenia. Lang's mother had eyes like that in later life as she descended into insanity.

McKeon had evidently been told not to expect access to his office safe. He did not mention the problem at all. What he wanted to talk about was his "hold baggage." This consisted of several footlockers that had arrived by railroad freight. He sent Lang to collect these trunks. He took a jeep and trailer to the freight office in town. The soldier driver looked puzzled about what they were doing. Commercial delivery of the baggage would have been the normal thing. When they arrived at the captain's quarters on post, they found him and his wife waiting. She was an attractive, well-built brunette who spoke with the same Irish American, New York City voice and style as her husband. It was 11 o'clock in the morning. Her name was Teresa. She smelled of gin and wore a lacy *negligee*. The McKeons' three children circulated in the background, running in and out of the house.

McKeon sent the soldier outside to wait and opened his trunks. Lying on top of a folded blanket in the first was an M-1 Carbine. McKeon unloaded it while his "honey" fidgeted, evidently unhappy with Lang's presence. She seemed to find that presence to be an obstacle to whatever it was that she wanted to do.

The rest of the first trunk held: uniforms, a bloody VC flag, several blocks of TNT, some blasting caps, two fragmentation High Explosive hand grenades and an M-1911-A1 .45 automatic pistol. The pistol was loaded as well. There was a round in the chamber. The two firearms were probably government property. Shipping explosives and ammunition this way was undoubtedly a violation of the law and of army regulations.

Lang excused himself and left. Looking back from the door he saw that Teresa McKeon was watching. She smiled when her husband's back was turned.

Regular Army commissioned officers of that period were famously conservative people. They were middle class, churchgoing people who shunned anything that might be described as "adventurous" in their way of living. People who wanted to live "bohemian" lives were not attracted to the army as a career.

McKeon and his "lady" were aberrations. This situation presented a new lieutenant with a variety of problems. If he reported the "shipment" to battalion headquarters, there would be a military police "raid" on McKeon's house. The man was already under investigation for conspiracy to commit murder. Such an event might eliminate this dangerously unstable character from the scene, but if that failed, Lang would find himself in a desperate situation with a commander who hated him. He was scheduled to leave for the Infantry School in Georgia in a few weeks. He would be gone six months while attending several courses. Perhaps someone would eliminate McKeon as a problem while he was gone. He decided to "hold his tongue" in this matter. It was a bad decision, and one that he would regret.

The Infantry Officer Basic Course, the Basic Airborne Course, and the Ranger Course were interesting experiences.

Lang's ROTC instructors at VMI had been concerned about scores and grades in the Basic Infantry Course. Several graduates had done poorly recently. The teachers wanted their "products" to score high. The curriculum for this course was available to them through army "channels." The course documents contained detailed lesson plans for everything taught including diagrams and maps of the field exercises. The ROTC staff included several West Point graduates. They asked friends there if they "taught to the course material," and when told they did, proceeded to do the same. They built scale model sand table mock-ups of all the field problems and taught these to the cadets. They did the same with the written classroom material.

Lang was particularly good on the sand-tables. He had an instinct for terrain and its uses that never failed him. This was a "gift" from his father who liked to discuss passing topography from the military point of view. Pat Lang had participated in that "game" from early childhood.

Sitting in the bleachers at Fort Benning and listening to an instructor discuss the first field problem in the Basic Course, he looked out over the man's head at the rolling ground, wooded hills and small streams. It came into focus, and he realized he knew every wrinkle in both the seen and the invisible ground for a mile to the front. He suppressed a smile when asked to command a team in this exercise. His lieutenant classmates, nearly all West Point graduates from that year's class, were apprehensive when he did not consult a map during the attack problem. They relaxed when they finished the exercise exactly in the right place, at the right time and with half a dozen "Aggressor" prisoners taken in a pillbox that Lang had miraculously predicted would be on one particular hill. Evidently, the teachers at West Point had not paid enough attention to the "script" for the course. Lang was not surprised when his course grade placed him second of two hundred at graduation. That put him just behind the man who had been cadet brigade commander that year at West Point. It was an obvious "set-up," but he knew the army and expected that result.

Ranger School and the Airborne Course were mere endurance tests; several months of field work in the mountains and swamps of Georgia and west Florida as well as the endless physical conditioning of the parachute school. Getting through these "schools" was just a matter of acceptance of the effort involved. To that end, he was careful to eat everything offered at meals. Extra rations were provided, and the calories were sorely needed to cope with the cold and a lot heavy exertion. He passed both courses.

In October, the Cuban Missile Crisis interrupted training for a week or so. Not surprisingly he had not been watching television news, and it was a shock when his training company was assembled at the Harmony Church sub-post to be told of the presence of Soviet IRBMs and troops in Cuba. The student officers absorbed that in silence. They were told that they would be sent to the 2ⁿᵈ Infantry Division and other units as supernumerary officers for the invasion. The 2ⁿᵈ Division was garrisoned at Fort Benning.

Lang reported to the 1st Battle Group, 23rd Infantry Regiment where he was consigned to one of the five rifle companies. The company commander said that according to the invasion plan, the 2nd Division would land on several beaches twenty miles east of Havana. The 23rd and another regiment would be the assault echelon for the division and significant resistance was expected on the beach line. A USMC force would land west of Havana and the 82nd Airborne would jump in an hour early to seal off the city. Once ashore, the 23rd Regiment, would pivot right and advance to the west astride the coast highway until link-up with the paratroops occurred on the outskirts of the capital city. An extra platoon leader was being assigned to each assault platoon in the hope that at least one of the officers would survive in command. That seemed a reasonable precaution to Lang.

That night he called Marguerite and asked her to marry him in a "proxy" ceremony, something allowed in the Catholic Church. She said no, explaining that she did not see any benefit in the possibility of becoming a twenty-year-old widow. If he survived, she would marry him at their earliest convenience. That also seemed reasonable to Lang. He told her to go home to Maine. Boston would be a target in a nuclear war. She agreed to leave.

The 23rd Regiment spent the next days briefing and "loading out" on railroad trains bound for the port of embarkation at Tampa. Similar trains were moving all across the United States as units went to the ports along the Gulf Coast. The first trains belonging to the 23rd had arrived at the port when the word was passed that the US and USSR had come to an agreement and that there would be no war. The regiment's quartering and loading parties returned and Lang went back to school. It had been a close thing.

He returned to Fort Devens and his company in the dead of winter. McKeon was still there, having survived a brush with destiny when a neighbor complained that he and his wife had locked their children out of the house in the middle of the afternoon in cold weather. "First things first," seemed to be McKeon's motto.

First Sergeant Moore no longer spoke to the company commander except to answer questions.

An annual Inspector General's visit to the company happened in February. Everyone went "all out" to prepare. It was a matter of professional pride. The company worked around the clock with McKeon "riding" them hard. The night before the inspection McKeon walked into the orderly room where the first sergeant was re-making all his office papers into copies that bore no trace of "strike overs" or other blemishes. The captain walked to the first sergeant's desk and peered over his shoulder to see what Moore was doing. He reached down and picked up a stack of freshly re-made "morning reports" and said, "What the hell are you doing this for?"

The first sergeant took them from his hand, tore them up and dropped them in a wastepaper can beside his desk. "I see that I was doing it for no good reason," Leroy Moore replied. "We will stand inspection with my working copies."

McKeon left the room quietly and did not appear again until the IG arrived with his party. As part of the inspection. the IG was required to ask if anyone wanted a private meeting with him. None of the officers responded to that. Nor did the first sergeant, but several other sergeants and enlisted men saw him privately.

The company was rated combat ready. The company commander was summoned to brigade headquarters for counseling. The nature of this 'therapy" was unknown, but he returned from this meeting red-faced and somewhat subdued. Curiosity as to what Colonel Kingsley might have said to him was overwhelming but impossible to satisfy.

Lang waited to see if the man would now be gone, but he was not.

The company now had a full complement of six officers, all of whom were senior to Lang by rank or date of rank. This meant that so long as he stayed in that unit, he would lead one of the rifle platoons. He thought of asking for a transfer to seek escape from McKeon's presence as well as other assignment possibilities but decided against it. He preferred to stay with the men he had begun to know well.

The platoon had forty-four men divided into eleven-man rifle squads and a weapons squad. Each rifle squad was led by a senior sergeant and was further divided in two fire teams of five men each. This allowed the squad to maneuver with one fire team supporting the other. The weapons squad was armed with two M-60 machine guns and two 3.5-inch anti-tank "bazookas."

In 1962, the major Civil Rights laws of that decade had not yet been passed. Three of the squad leaders were blacks married to European women. To live in the South with their white wives was to accept virtual imprisonment on army posts. For that reason, they had asked to be stationed in the North and the army had understood their problem.

The weapons squad leader was a White Mountain Apache who also had married a European.

The platoon sergeant was a Kansan named Joseph O'Connor who had spent most of his service life in Korea in the Eighth Army. He had three Silver Stars, several Purple Hearts and had been in the last company-strength bayonet charge in US Army history. This occurred in the spring of 1951 in the 27th Infantry Regiment, "The Wolfhounds."

He was the best enlisted soldier Lang ever met. He had twice won the Eighth Army tactical competition as best rifle platoon leader in Korea. This happened because US forces in Korea were perennially short of junior officers. Nobody wanted to go there. O'Connor knew everything there was to know about small unit infantry leadership and saw himself as a teacher. He was a closeted homosexual who was careful to live his personal life outside army circles. Lang did not know that about him for quite a long time. Then one day a casual question about O'Connor's love life elicited an explanation from one of the other sergeants. O'Connor's inclinations did not interfere with his performance of duty, and that was all that Lang cared about.

The soldiers in the ranks of the platoon were typical of the mixed force created by "Selective Service" after the Korean War. They tended to represent the working class in American society. Their families frequently felt a deep responsibility for service in the armed forces. The men often came from relative poverty and had been hardened by life before they were summoned to military service. Many were from rural backgrounds and possessed skills needed for life in the field. There were a few immigrants to the United States. One of them was a stocky, curly haired Albanian Muslim named Ali who had served in his native country's army. He was a willing soldier and a fine shot with every weapon in the platoon. There were several soldiers from Puerto Rico who spoke little English. They were under instruction in English, and it was necessary to forbid them the use of Spanish during duty hours in order to help them learn English.

A few of the men were from the bottom of the "spectrum" of mental capacity accepted by the army under the draft. Lieutenant Lang first realized this when one of the squad leaders asked him to come to the company "dayroom" where they interviewed a very young draftee. The man was seated beneath a display of photographs of the chain of command of the army descending in order of authority from the president to the captain commanding the company. This display was centered above the television set.

"Tell me, Jones," the Apache sergeant asked calmly. "Who is the president of the United States?"

The sandy haired, skinny, teenager looked puzzled. "Roozvelt?" he offered.

"No. Try again."

"Truman?" he said after a moment.

"Kennedy?" the sergeant asked.

After a moment, the boy soldier said that he did not think so.

He was dismissed without comment.

"Are there many like that?" Lang asked.

"Half a dozen, sir, maybe more, maybe more. I got a call from his mother last week. She said that his father is the father of an infant that this man Jones thinks is his child."

Lang could speak the language of the barracks when he chose to do so. "His father fucked his wife?"

The mission-schooled reservation Apache looked surprised and then nodded.

"He is an ammo bearer in your machine gun section? Yes? Good, keep him there."

On the other hand, there were several college graduates in Lang's platoon. These men had chosen to serve in the infantry when it would have been easy to evade the draft or obtain an "easy" service position.

The most striking example of such a man was a pudgy little soldier named Shapiro who held a master's degree in criminology from New York University.

Lang interviewed every member of the platoon with each man's squad leader present. After listening, Lang asked Shapiro if he would like to be his radio operator.

Shapiro smiled. "Why me? I am a New York Jew, and you, personally, are something I have never seen before."

"Because you will understand what he says," the black sergeant sitting next to him replied.

"And I can watch you when you are near me," Lang added.

"I accept."

A few days later, Lang walked Shapiro and a few other new men through the regimental museum, explaining as he went.

"What am I supposed to get out of this?" Shapiro asked.

"Everything, or nothing," Lang replied. "It's up to you. It's a kind of church, or synagogue. These men suffered for nothing more than their duty for the last one hundred and sixty years. It's up to you all."

In the spring of 1963, it became clear that the US Army was preparing for action against an insurgent guerrilla enemy somewhere. Training programs changed. New reading lists were suggested for officers. Kennedy was president, and he seemed to be eager for a fight somewhere against what was seen as the spreading menace of communism in the vast areas of the world abandoned by the colonial powers. Lang was good at "reading between the lines." Both Latin America and Indochina seemed likely to be in his future.

He began to train his platoon in all the counter-guerrilla techniques that he could find in army suggested readings or in the post library. Mao, Guevara, Vo Nguyen Giap, Trinquier, Paul Aussarresses, Bernard Fall; these were all writers that Lang read intensively.

Lang decided that his new "charges" would require certain, and indeed, loving hands to raise them collectively to the level of a fine instrument of violence in the service of "The Republic." To that end, he spent a lot of time talking to them in a variety of settings. He explained the bond between the army and the Constitution. He led them in physical training that was more difficult for him than for many of them. He taught them about insurgency and counterinsurgency. Most importantly he taught them to fight guerrillas. He taught them patrolling techniques, ambush formations, and immediate action drills so that they would respond to his silver whistle's measured blasts with specific responses. They drilled these things together in the dark, cold, wet, New England woods....

Having done that and having completed all the training that available time would allow, Lang found it necessary to take his platoon through the standard test for proficiency in conventional combat. Under the tutelage of O'Connor, the platoon won the brigade competition for best rifle platoon. Captain McKeon's claim to a brigade of superior training in his company was fulsome in the true meaning of the word.

Lang's platoon gradually became the counter-guerrilla training model for the 5th Mechanized Division. Sadly, the more this became true, the more

Captain McKeon showed his displeasure and a kind of jealousy that Lang had often known at home and in schools.

Field training was usually conducted under the supervision of an "umpire group" of officers and NCOs who were present to ensure neutrality and reasonably fair evaluations. These were Lang's salvation. On several occasions, McKeon attempted to divert attention from his own failures in the field by shifting blame to one of his subordinates, usually Lang.

Among the various instances were:

The evening when McKeon lost his way in the dark and took a wrong road into an artillery impact area. In doing this, he led half the company into the target zone for the battalion's 4.2-inch mortar platoon. The mortars were present that night to fire "for record" with high explosive ammunition. This mortar was as powerful as a howitzer and the platoon had four guns. The rifle platoon leader who was third in the order of march that night stopped in confusion when he reached the point on the road where McKeon had turned left at a crossroad to go into the impact area. The platoon leader sent a runner back down the line of march for Lang. They checked the map and realized what had happened.

Lang called McKeon on the radio to tell him he was in the wrong place. After the usual screaming and cursing on the company radio net for all and sundry to hear, McKeon subsided enough to ask what Lang meant.

"My God!" Shapiro, the NYU-graduate radio operator murmured. "I thought West Point did better than this...."

The other lieutenant was a West Point graduate. He said nothing. What could he say?

Just then, a series of bright yellow lights illuminated the night sky over the impact area.

The range safety officer had ordered a "sheaf" of parachute flares to be fired over the target zone to double check before the mortar platoon opened fire with high explosive shells. Half the company was displayed in stark, flickering silhouette. They were standing on a sandy road among the targets. Several of the leaders began to jump up and down waving their arms. A red star cluster pyrotechnic rose over the company, and a voice was heard on the radio shouting, "Cease Fire! Cease fire! For God's sake, cease fire!"

McKeon had climbed over the chain barrier across the road that blocked entry into the impact area and had ordered the men to do the same in spite of the objections of his officers and sergeants.

He tried to blame one of the lieutenants, but everyone knew the truth.

On another occasion, two of McKeon's command post entourage, both New York City men, fell on a mountain trail in the dark. They became entangled and blocked the path. Lang's platoon was just behind, and by the time he could get past them, McKeon and the rest of the company had disappeared in the blackness. He sent a runner forward to find the company. The man returned and shook his head. Lang broke radio silence to ask McKeon to stop moving so that half his company could find him.

"It's your damned fault! You are trying to make me look bad as usual."

"Not hard to do," a voice nearby said in the dark.

"Silence in the ranks!" roared Platoon Sergeant O'Connor. "I know who said that." He probably did not, but they did not want to risk his wrath.

"Sir, your radio men are right here," Lang said in as calm a voice as he could manage.

Heavy snow began to fall in the New Hampshire wilderness. You could hear the big, quarter dollar size crystals settle on the trees and ground. This was a sound Lang knew well. The peaceful music steadied him.

"No, they're not, you damned liar!"

"Garcia, come here. Talk to the captain."

After that conversation, McKeon shut up so that Lang could find him in the dark.

Two days later, Lang was called to brigade headquarters for a talk with Colonel Kingsley, Lieutenant Colonel Castro and Major Henderson.

The old wooden building smelled of decades of varnish and floor wax. The three men were dressed in winter field pants and Olive Drab wool shirts.

"We all heard it on the radio the other night," Kingsley began. "Disgraceful. Disgraceful..."

"Are you sure you are not provoking him?" Major Henderson asked.

After a moment of concentration on the mask he needed to wear to answer that, Lang said he did not believe he was doing that.

"Would you like a transfer to another company," Castro asked.

"Or out of the battalion?" Henderson added.

That would not have been mentioned if it had not been discussed.

"I prefer to stay with my men. I am not the only officer he dislikes."

Kingsley nodded almost imperceptibly.

"You may do so," Castro replied."

"He claims to like you," Henderson said. "He says you are his best lieutenant. We are "keeping book" on all this against the day when he gets to rate you."

In March of 1963, the brigade went to counter-guerrilla training at Camp Edwards. This was an old, nearly abandoned World War II post located in the "shank" of Cape Cod. Much of the reservation was below sea level. The land appeared to be hilly, but the low ground lay in "sink holes" that were below the level of the surrounding ocean. The terrain was largely covered with stunted hardwood forests of maple and oak trees about five feet tall. The branches locked together in a wooden embrace that bruised flesh and tore clothing from bodies. It was still winter on Cape Cod. and the sea to north and south "fed" the winds with water that was deposited on the land as rain, sleet or snow.

A Massachusetts National Guard brigade was called to active duty to act as the "enemy" for the extended training.

The exercise built to a climax in a brigade level maneuver that was "fought" across half of Cape Cod.

In one of the early phases, Lang's platoon broke out of an ambush by assaulting into the line of the ambush position. When asked his opinion of the ambush at a "hot wash" critique, he said it should have been "L" shaped. He said that such an ambush would have defeated him. There were frowns around the room. "Smart ass!" was the comment of one of the captains. Major Henderson frowned at him.

The next day, Henderson caught him looking at the floor while Henderson was briefing something. He sent Lang to stand in the back of the room.

McKeon smirked as he walked past.

"He's nuts, literally nuts," one of the battalion's captains told Lang outside. "Don't let him bother you. He's like McKeon. He's certifiable from that head wound. He shouldn't be here. I have asked for you for my company. We need a trainer like you."

The public insult hurt.

Lang's platoon continued to perform so well that his men began to see themselves as elite and to see him as the "force" that made them that. This sentiment showed in many ways, some large and some small.

On one sunny day in the Cape Cod forest, it was necessary to distribute several cases of "C Rations" dropped to them by helicopter. This was a routine task. These self-contained canned meat and "sundry" rations were packed with a variety of menus. Some were more desired than others. It was the custom in the US Army that commanders always ate last in the field and therefore had the last choice of menu. Lang followed this custom scrupulously and as a result had eaten many cans of pork and beans, often cold.

This custom among the officers of eating last was followed even during an administrative stay in the field. On such occasions, the company mess team either cooked in the field on gasoline stoves or brought hot rations in insulated containers from which each soldier was served in his folding mess kit. The officers were served on folding wooden tables with real linen; aluminum serving vessels, cups and saucers and flat wear. All this appeared from a large OD box that contained the "Officers Field Mess Kit."

This included bud vases that inevitably were filled with a rose on each table. The men sat around the officers on stumps, logs or on the ground eating the same food and listening to the conversation. They did not interject themselves in the officers' talk unless asked to do so. In this company, a place was always set for First Sergeant Moore if he was in the field, but he usually chose to sit on the ground with the men.

Lang's NYU-graduate radio operator sat close where he could monitor the radio and hear the talk. "I did not expect that they would be this intelligent," he told his boss.

"You don't know enough of them yet," Lang replied. "These guys are so Regular Army that it is painful to watch… My dad used to say that I should remember that 'in the Regular Army we cut off whatever sticks out.' It is true, but they are my people."

"I thought *we* were your people," the radio operator responded…

In light of these customs, Lang was surprised on that particular day in the Cape Cod woods that a circle of his men insisted he choose first among the meals.

"Are you sure?" he asked. "It is not our way." He looked around the group at the earnest faces.

They were wearing pile caps. These made them look strangely foreign. "It is sometimes this platoon's custom, sometimes," one of them said.

Sergeant First Class O'Connor walked away into the wood line where he stood watching something in the trees… Later that night, when he and Lang and Shapiro huddled in a crevice among granite boulders listening to the wind, howl, he had more to say.

"We had two company commanders in my Wolfhounds time in Korea. This was in E Company. One was a strange man named Millett who led us in the bayonet charge down on the Imjin River in South Korea. We all went mad together there, him most of all.

The other was before him when we were up on the Yalu River in North Korea. His name was Reginald Desiderio. He was our peacetime company commander from Japan, from the occupation…"

The three soldiers had a candle burning in the upturned cavity of a steel helmet. A rubber poncho stretched over their little hole. The temperature inside their shelter was a pleasant fifty degrees Fahrenheit.

The rest of the platoon were scattered in similar holes across a stony, wooded hilltop. A few men were rotated every hour to listening posts to guard against a surprise. The heavy weapons "sat" outside the granite holes well covered against the weather. That protection and the arctic lubricant they had been "dressed" with would keep them in order.

Lang waited for O'Connor to start again. It was going to be a long night. "Desiderio?" he prompted.

"We were on a low rise. We looked down across a half mile of frozen, open ground to the river. Manchuria was on the other side. The ground was solid. We dug all day to get holes not as deep as this. The regimental command post was right behind us, maybe two hundred meters." O'Connor leaned forward staring into the small yellow flame.

Light danced on the grey, lichen-encrusted rock around them.

One of the squad leaders stuck his head in under the poncho to say that the outposts had been relieved. Shapiro called the company command post on the sound powered telephone line to report this.

"And?" Lang asked.

"About midnight, a wave of infiltrators came right into our holes. They crawled most of the way from the river. There were hundreds of them. I mean it, hundreds. We fought them in every hole and outside the holes. Gun butts, entrenching tools, fists; we started throwing chunks of frozen dirt at them before it was over. We lost a third of the company in the first attack, but they kept coming back. They must have attacked a dozen times. After every attack, the Old Man came around to each position. He was hurt bad, but he came to ask us to hold on, to ask us not to give up. After a while he was crawling to our holes, asking, begging for the same thing.

When the sun came up, we saw we were 'buried' in the bodies of big yellow men in quilted blue uniforms. Their two-humped camels were down the slope where they left them. We collected them to use for pack animals and to sling stretchers between. The Chinese had entered the war and these guys were from Mongolia. We found the Old Man with a couple of these blue men lying across him. His .45 was in his hand. He had bled and frozen to death... His face was stuck to the ground. We poured warm water on his face to free it. He got the Medal of Honor. Twelve years now, twelve years. The company loved him. I loved him. That is why it was so hard for Millett to take over when we got back to below the 38ᵗʰ parallel."

O'Connor got up and went to check the position.

The next day on a twenty-mile route march back to the Camp Edwards cantonment, Lang told a man in his weapons squad to change loads with him. He would carry the M-60 machine gun for a while, and the soldier could carry his rifle. It was his habit to do this on long marches.

The man tried to refuse. "No. It is mine to carry," he said. "We don't want you to carry our loads anymore, sir."

"You heard what the Old Man said," the Apache called out. "Do what you are told!"

This was the first time he had heard them call him that. It was an old army tradition that a valued commander was called that. For a twenty-two-year-old, this was heady stuff.

He fell asleep standing up in the shower that afternoon and woke to find another lieutenant shaking him as he leaned into the corner in the warm water.

Two nights later in a driving, freezing rain mixed with sleet, he heard a conditional sentence of death pronounced on McKeon.

The captain had the unpleasant habit of having his overly large headquarters section dig him a shelter complete with log and sod roof every night. He told Lang that this was something like a Roman marching camp. "But, then," he said, "you wouldn't know what that was."

Lang said nothing.

His platoon sergeant and radio operator stood listening. That was what McKeon wanted.

Several hours later, McKeon called for an orders group meeting at his dugout. McKeon read his order from the shelter of his command post while his subordinates stood in the rain and attempted to take notes.

Lang watched as the ink ran off the pages of his notebook. He did not need to take notes but had always done so in the interest of harmony. On this occasion, he stopped writing.

"Too good for this?" McKeon asked.

"I know what you said," Lang replied. His patience was wearing thin. He was not good at tolerating fools.

"Tell me what I said," McKeon replied.

Lang recited the order verbatim.

"You think you're clever, don't you? I was raised in the Bronx. I made my own way. You god damned Southern gentlemen think you are better than the rest of us. Dismissed."

He was obviously drunk.

As Lang and the other platoon leaders walked away to return to their sodden, freezing men, the temperature dropped suddenly, and snow began to fall in vertical sheets.

Shapiro pulled up his collar and said, *"Gallia est omnis divisa in partes tres."*

"Divisa est," completed O'Connor. "The brothers made me learn that, and you?"

"Prep school."

"Joe," Lang began. Cold water was soaking the back of his shirt. "I can stand on my head and stack BBs in peace time, but we are going to war soon…"

"Shapiro, double out there fifty feet, and pretend not to hear."

When the radioman was gone, O'Connor said that the senior sergeants in the company had come to an agreement that if they had to go to war with Captain McKeon, they would deal with him. "We can't afford him in combat."

Lang thought about that. "Did you say something?" he finally asked.

"No, sir" O'Connor answered.

Lang knew that his duty called him to report this conspiracy to commit murder, but he knew that he would not do that. He felt crushed by the knowledge that he was no better than McKeon. The captain had done something similar in Viet Nam.

By the time they reached the platoon area, the ground and roads were frozen and slippery. A voice on the radio announced that the wide-spread small units of the brigade would have to shelter in place until dawn when they could be retrieved more safely. Two feet of snow were expected by morning.

Lang and O'Connor decided to "bury" the men. They had done this before. The platoon gathered a large pile of wood. It was dry, having stood a long time after the trees died. They built a huge fire and then each man blew up his rubber air mattress. These were placed on the ground like the spokes of a wheel with the foot end nearest to the fire. Everyone had a cup of hot cocoa or coffee and then turned in for the night. Sleeping bags went on top of the mattresses. The soldiers took their boots and overshoes off. These went into the foot end of the bags to be kept warm. The men slid inside the bags and zipped them up.

O'Connor and Lang sat up until dawn wrapped in their "bags." They took turns building up the fire from the wood pile.

The radio could be heard sputtering from inside Shapiro's bag.

O'Connor treated this as a chance to further "mentor" his protégé.

Many of the men lay in their sleeping bags and listened. They were comfortable.

O'Connor and Lang were not. As the snow grew deeper, the leaders used entrenching tools to heap it on the sleeping bags. The dry snow was an excellent insulator. The men carried hand towels in their rucksacks. They had spread these over their faces. Their faces were the only part of their bodies exposed to the elements.

The sun rose cold but bright over a "winter wonderland." Three two-and-a-half-ton trucks arrived with the sunlight. A snowplow mounted on a tank retriever cleared the road for them. When they arrived at Camp Edwards, breakfast, a shave and a hot shower waited for them. Within an hour, they were asleep once again.

While they slept, Lang and a virtual "army" of rifle platoon leaders were briefed at battalion and then at brigade that nightfall would bring a mission to "attack" a number of counterinsurgent bases.

Lang was given the job of attacking the opposing National Guard brigade headquarters post. He was shown a route on the operations map that indicated how he should approach the "enemy." The concept was that he would advance mounted in trucks and then dismount to draw near the defense line on foot. He took careful note of the exact map coordinates for the dismount point.

Glancing at Major Henderson and Captain McKeon, he saw that they looked satisfied, perhaps even content. Lang knew a trap when he saw one. When the briefing was done, he, O'Connor and the squad leaders discussed what they would do if Lang's suspicions proved correct.

After dark, the platoon climbed into the trucks and rolled down state roads to a point at which a forest track turned towards the objective. Down that snow-covered dirt road was the spot on the map at which they had been directed to descend from the trucks.

A kilometer short of that point, Lang took his men off the vehicles. He sent one man forward to lead the trucks forward in a foot of snow. The troops followed the last truck as it crept along in the dim light provided by its small "cats eye" tactical lights.

Someone in front of the lead truck "challenged" the presence of the vehicles in a loud voice. The little convoy halted as the "line crosser" walked forward into a bright beam that suddenly lit up the scene.

"I don' know." The "prisoner" yelled in the night. "Lang is crazy. He's a dam' fool. They never got on the 'deuce and a halfs.' They're still back at camp for all ah know. Crazy dam' Yankee! He's allus doin' some fool thing. Y'all got any coffee?"

Lang turned and waved an arm toward the rear. The platoon walked away followed by a five man "fire team." This team had tree branches with which they swept footprints away in the heavily falling snow. A hundred yards on the back trail, Lang patted the fire team leader on the back and turned off into the snow with the rest.

The sweepers continued on their way. According to plan, they would walk back to Camp Edwards if they could not find a civilian ride on the state road ahead of them.

The platoon line went fifty yards into the brush and stopped to wait. They were dressed in winter "overwhites." These garments were worn over the usual combat uniform. In the dim light of a forest night, the camouflage clothing made the wearer hard to see. The platoon stood quietly to listen in the night. Snow continued to fall, but not so heavily...

Voices were heard approaching on the road they had left. The voices grew louder. The possessors of the voices stopped at the point at which the platoon had left the roads

"What do you think?" someone said. "Should we go further? The prisoner insists that they are way out to the north circling around us. That's the kind of thing he would do."

"I don't know," someone else said. "Maybe this is far enough, wait here a minute, I have to take a leak." Sticks began to snap as this man walked into the brush in the direction of the platoon.

As one man they sank to the ground and lay face down with their weapons beneath them...

The oncoming man stopped six feet from Lang to unbutton. The sound of his urine streaming onto the snow was loud. "Lang is a real character," he commented. "He might do anything, anything." He turned and walked back to the road. He and his companion strolled back up the road towards the trucks.

Did he see them lying motionless in the snow? Who could tell?

When they were far enough away, the platoon moved farther into the wood. The map said that there was a woodland creek there. On the bank of the stream, the map was consulted under a poncho and a compass azimuth chosen that would lead cross country to a different road a half mile away, a road that also pointed straight into the place on the map at which Lang and O'Connor believed the "enemy command post" should be located.

Every man carried a ten-foot length of rope in his rucksack. He and O'Connor watched as they tied themselves together like a line of kindergarten children out for a stroll on the street under the supervision of school staff. That done, the column moved off through the woods. They waded across the stream. It was ice cold and thigh deep but not a word was said in protest. By the time the head of the column reached the new road, the snow had stopped, and a full moon shone down. The kindergarten ropes came off.

Lang put his best rifleman in the lead. It was the Albanian. The second man would count paces and knot every hundredth pace on a cord tied to his harness. This man's pace length was precisely known. Lang and Shapiro were next, then the two M-60 machine guns slung for marching fire. Each gun had a hundred rounds loaded in a box magazine with another two hundred rounds carried just behind the gun. Next in the column were the three rifle squads less the five-man fire team that had disguised their move away from the first road. Last in the column was Joe O'Connor, positioned to make sure there were no stragglers.

At 2335, they moved forward. They stopped twice so that Lang could check the distance covered under the poncho using a dim, tactical flashlight. After the second halt, he told the point man that he was sure they were within several hundred yards of their objective.

As if on cue, a yellow light appeared for a moment not far ahead as someone carelessly opened a tent flap. Standing quietly, they began to hear faint generator noise, and then voices.

"They must have the generator in a pit," the point man murmured, "or it would be louder."

"Make sure you don't fall in the hole," Lang replied. He fished around in a pocket until he found his whistle. He held it up in the moonlight. Men waved back at the familiar, reassuring sight. He hung it around his neck on its nylon lanyard and then rotated his right arm in a full circle from the shoulder ending with the hand pointing at the objective. He told the point man, "You may advance." He smiled in the moonlight. This was what Stonewall Jackson had told Robert Rodes at Chancellorsville.

They moved rapidly forward. The moon was now so bright that detection was likely before they reached the enemy outpost line.

"Halt!" A challenge rang out in the night. "Stop, or we'll open fire!"

Lang could see the outposts now. They were on either side of the road. There was no barbed wire to be seen. The generator noise was louder, and light began to show behind the outposts.

Lang put the whistle in his mouth and blew three loud, piercing blasts. This was the signal for the "action front" battle drill. At this sound, the point men opened fire. All the weapons were fitted with blank adapters and functioned fully. The machine gunners ran to left and right to take their places to either side of the platoon leader. The rifle squads fanned out to the flanks to form a line of fire and assault. Lang blew the whistle four times. The assault swept forward with every weapon firing, and the men screaming their lungs out.

From the viewpoint of the "defenders" the shock, suddenness, unexpected direction and volume of fire of the attack were stunning. National Guardsmen stood up in their holes with their hands in the air.

"Get down. Get down!" Lang's men yelled at them. The plastic "wads" in blank ammunition could kill at this rapidly shrinking range. The line swept by the outposts and suddenly found itself in a "square" framed by tents and vehicles.

Lights came on everywhere. "Cease fire! Cease fire!" voices shouted.

"Platoon halt! Cease fire!" Lang ordered.

They stopped as one man. The ragged line was only thirty yards long. Gun barrels were hot. The machine gun barrels smoked and glowed. They stood quietly, but their breath was ragged in the cold air. Many shook with emotion from the moment that had just passed.

O'Connor came forward to talk the men "down" from the adrenaline "high" and to ensure that weapons were unloaded.

Lang was too busy to deal with that.

McKeon had rushed out of a big command post tent. "God damn it! What are you doing here? You're supposed to be…" He stopped when he realized what he was saying.

Major Henderson was beside him. "You could have killed them! Do you understand that?"

"Yes, sir, we would have killed them all and you as well if you were in that tent…"

Henderson and McKeon were red in the face and about to "say" more.

"Lieutenant Lang, come in here please," a voice commanded. It was the brigade commander speaking from the doorway of the tent

Castro could be seen behind him.

Lang was told to sit and took his place across a table from Colonel Kingsley. Castro sat next to Kingsley.

All others sat or stood in places around the tent wall.

A gasoline stove hissed pleasantly in the background.

Hot coffee in a brown mess hall Bakelite cup was put on the table in front of him. It steamed and smelled wonderful.

He ignored it.

"Tell me how you evaded the trap that I have now learned was set for you," the colonel asked.

Lang told him.

"Who taught you to do all that?"

"Sergeant First Class O'Connor has been a great help, sir."

"Ah, the Wolfhound man," Kingsley said.

"Don't believe it, sir," O'Connor said from just beyond the wall of the tent. "Don't believe it. He taught us all."

"You don't want your coffee?" the colonel asked. He smiled and nodded. "Captain Jones, go see that the lieutenant's men have coffee."

The conversation in the tent turned to training methods for small infantry units. When satisfied, slurping, clinking noises grew loud outside, Lang picked up the cup.

When he had finished, Kingsley told him that hot chow would be waiting at the camp. "Take your pack of wolves to their den," he said. "You may go, lieutenant. Well done...."

Lang stepped outside to look at them.

Someone turned up his head and began to howl. In a minute they were all howling at the cold, silvery moon.

"I'll put a stop to that," McKeon said inside the tent.

"No, you won't," Kingsley replied. "Let him do his work... I wanted to talk to you about General Hammes. I saw him at Fort Jay last week. We talked about your future."

When the men had been fed and tucked into the double bunks that filled their barracks, Lang began to think of rest. The big space they slept in was warm. A potbellied stove glowed at one end of the room. The sergeants had rooms at the end of the squad bay.

He turned off the lights and walked down the center aisle headed for the door.

"Goodnight, sir," someone said.

"Goodnight," he said.

"Goodnight, Pat," another someone said. This was repeated around the room...

He turned off all but the red fire watch light and walked into the night.

His room was in the next building. He rolled his sleeping bag out on a steel framed bunk, put his folded poncho under the head end, slid in, zipped it up and was instantly asleep.

CHAPTER FOURTEEN

Red Diamond

5th US Infantry Division

So long as specific military units exist, they carry a burden of group memory, legend and shared identity that transforms the consciousness of their members. These influences shape those who serve. For many, the effect is forever.

The Regular United States Army of the period between the two world wars was allowed less than 300,000 men by Congress. That number had to include: cadets at West Point, the Army Air Corps, officers serving on senior staffs, service school instructors, the army medical service, ROTC instructors, recruiters, post administrative garrisons, National Guard advisers and inspectors, soldiers at arsenals, etc. In reality, the army was not able to keep its strength at 300,000 men. The Harding, Coolidge, and Hoover Administrations were all intent on saving money, and the possibility of another foreign war was not taken seriously by civilians for a long time. The National Guard was theoretically allowed almost half a million troops but never came close to maintaining those numbers.

Nevertheless, with the resources available, the Regular Army managed to sustain five infantry divisions in the active force at various levels of strength. There was also a horse mounted cavalry division and several separate regiments like the "Old Guard" ceremonial troops at Arlington National Cemetery. The divisions should each have had seventeen thousand men but were never fully manned. The great strength of the five regular infantry divisions lay in the many professional officers and sergeants who had served in these units for decades. They were superbly trained and imbued with the traditions of service and discipline that prevailed in these units.

By the end of World War II in 1945, the army had ninety divisions. These varied widely in quality. Some of these were infantry and some armored. The cavalry division still existed, but without horses. The best of the new infantry divisions were the paratroop units. These had been raised from a population of athletic volunteers and given many of the best younger Regular Army officers available. Some of the new divisions were of great value, and a few were simply terrible. Most notable among the terrible, was the division that surrendered *en masse* to the *Wehrmacht* during the Battle of the Bulge.

The five pre-war Regular Army divisions that were "topped off" with reservists and draftees before Pearl Harbor, were intensively trained and then were sent to the European Theater of Operations early in the war. Europe had been judged by the Allies to be the main "arena" until Germany was defeated, and the logic prevailed that the best should be sent there. These five divisions proved to be all that had been expected.

The 5th Division landed across Utah Beach in Normandy a month after the invasion. The three fighting infantry regiments in the division were the 2nd, Tenth, and Eleventh. They quickly moved up to a position in the front line and soon began a relentless process of efficient and dependable forward motion that carried the 5th Division into the heart of Germany eleven months later. This progress across France was remarkably free of adverse incidents and reversals although there were many heavy engagements. In the autumn, the division liberated the city of Metz in the Lorraine. An initial attempt by the 10th Infantry Regiment to seize the city in an unrehearsed *coup de main* failed. After a few days' preparation for major action in a metropolis, the 2nd Infantry Regiment drove the Germans from the city. A few months later, the 5th Division pushed through the fortified Siegfried Line and was the first American force across the Rhine River.

By that time the highly competent Germans had long referred to the 5th as the "Red Devil" division. This was a reference to the small, red, diamond that was the divisional shoulder insignia. One German Army commander recorded in his diary that with such a division he could have held back the Allied advance. Never "flashy," always reliable, the division justified all hopes for its performance. In the Vietnam War, the division sent one mechanized brigade to the war. Once again, their performance was impeccable and fully within their tradition.

Lieutenant Walter Lang joined the 5th Division (Mechanized) eighteen years after the seizure of Metz. From childhood, he had been widely read in the military arts and history. He had been lucky to have a family deeply involved in military service. His father served in the army for thirty-two years and had an encyclopedic knowledge of everything imaginable about world affairs and military history. Two of his uncles had been career navy men. They talked continuously of naval subjects. From all this exposure, Lang began early in life to form clear ideas regarding the nature of war, the theory of strategy and tactics, logistics and the key role played by a sense of unit identity and tradition in making soldiers into effective fighters.

When he came on active duty, he read all there was about his regiment and the division of which it was a part. Having satisfied himself that he understood the past, he began to build better soldiers by indoctrinating his men with the example of those who had gone before them in these organizations.

This practice paid rich dividends in the performance of his forty-four men. As time passed, he found that he was more and more invited to lecture to the soldiers of other units of the 5th Division brigade that was stationed at Fort Devens. This became so much a part of his duties that he developed standard lesson plans that included 35mm slide shows, rich with period photographs and maps. He found that the soldiers and sergeants in his audiences were indifferent at first, but as he developed stories of the courage, loyalty and team spirit of their predecessors, they became more and more engaged and willing to ask detailed questions that filled lacunae in his prepared talks.

After watching the reaction of their men, commanders usually asked him to return. The word spread through the brigade and these talks became a major part of his duties.

A few of his men always came along to help with the apparatus of the talks and to act as "shills" if the audience was slow in responding.

Lang spent a lot of time preparing his lectures and thinking over the implications of all he knew of the performance of various fighting units through the millennia. In the course of this meditation he came to believe that as Bonaparte had written, "In war the moral is to the physical as three to one." That meant that the material factors involved in the creation of units with high combat potential was not as important as all the non-material factors; leadership, training, tradition, experience expertise, political motivation and so forth. He never forgot that self-taught lesson.

Throughout a career that progressed from combat arms service to tactical intelligence to an eventual role as a significant figure in the national intelligence community, Lang always insisted that military units are distinct entities, each one different from the next, and that they have an "organic" life of their own that persists so long as memory persists.

The 5th Division had been de-activated after World War II but it had been such a memorable experience for its members that an active "alumni" society was available in the decade of the 1960s. These men were eager to teach the division's lore and story to those who served. Lang was surprised and gratified to learn that the "spirit" of the division was easily implanted from one generation to another.

CHAPTER FIFTEEN

Lieutenant of Infantry

Company B, 2nd US Infantry Regiment

In April of 1963, Lieutenant Lang learned that the Fort Devens brigade of the 5th Division would travel to Washington State in late May to join the rest of the division in a major maneuver run by US Strike Command. In this maneuver the "friendly" force would be portrayed by the 4th Infantry Division, while the assembled 5th Division would play the role of the forces of "Aggressor land," the US Army's carefully created maneuver enemy. The "Aggressor" enemy was a close reflection of the Warsaw Pact.

The 4th Division was based in the northwestern United States at Fort Lewis, Washington. The maneuver was to be in the high desert country of central Washington State. This vast and nearly empty land could be easily reached from Fort Lewis by road. For most of the opposing 5th Division, the travel to the maneuver involved a short trip by air from Fort Carson, Colorado, but the 2nd Brigade of the Fifth "lived" in Massachusetts, and for that third of the division to join the "game," a transcontinental airlift was needed.

Captain Kenneth McKeon informed Lang that he would oversee the preparation and transportation of the battalion's vehicles and other "impedimenta" to the maneuver assembly area at Larson Air Force Base at Moses Lake, Washington. The majority of the soldiers in the battalion would be flown to Moses Lake in contracted airliners but Lang's "charges" would go in Air Force transports.

The maneuver was meant to demonstrate that the air force could bring the 5th Division together near the main battlefield so that it could quickly and decisively be committed to the fight. From Lang's point of view, this meant that he had the major job for the battalion in this exercise. Logically, the battalion logistics staff officer, the S-4, should have done this job, but after a talk with him, in which the man voiced his frustration, Lang knew that this man had been deprived of his normal function so that Lang could be given it. The young lieutenant knew nothing of the intricate business of planning the air movement of so much equipment and so many vehicles, and it soon became clear that there was not going to be any sort of special instruction for this task.

He assumed that this was yet another opportunity to fail presented by Captain McKeon and Major Henderson.

The airlift would be from Westover Air Force Base in western Massachusetts. Lang called there and after several false starts found the airlift office in base operations. The staff there expressed disbelief that he was to do the planning for this movement more or less single-handed. They offered to help. He drove a hundred miles to visit and to receive instruction from those with whom he would have to work. They gave him a "mountain" of material to study. He read that in a few days and returned to spend several days with air force "loadmasters" who explained to him exactly how the trucks and palletized loads of cargo were to be put together. The next step was to learn what the tonnage and cubic measurement would be for the battalion "load out" without most of its men. He sat in his little office with reams of chart paper and constructed an aircraft by aircraft graphic plan. That done, he drafted instructions to each company sized unit in the battalion telling them what they had to do, when it had to be done, and where the "serials" of vehicles would assemble for movement to Westover AFB.

McKeon went with him to battalion headquarters to review the plan for approval. Castro and Henderson listened as he briefed for an hour. Henderson and McKeon said nothing, asked nothing. Castro asked a few questions and then approved the work. It would be sent to brigade for approval and then to the air force. Castro said that he hoped brigade did not "manage" to lose the plan after so much work had been done. He said they were known to do things like that.

"I have a copy in my office safe, Colonel," Lang responded. "You needn't worry."

"Good. Good," Castro replied.

"Is there an allowance in this for broken down aircraft?" Henderson asked.

"The Air Force said that they will add extra aircraft in their plan once they have ours."

"You talked to the Air Force? Who authorized you to talk to the Air Force?" Henderson asked.

"The battalion S-4, Captain Miller," Lang replied.

"I didn't know that," McKeon bleated.

"You told me I could go to Westover for a few days...." McKeon had not cared what he was going to do there.

"You may go, lieutenant," Castro said.

Brigade approved the plan without amendment. On the appointed day in mid-May, trucks appeared from all over the battalion as well as a few from other brigade units to form in columns on a large parking lot. Loads were inspected and chalk marks were made on trucks to identify them in the column.

Castro and Kingsley came to inspect and left satisfied.

The long convoy drove out the South Gate of the post and onto Massachusetts Route 2. This was a four-lane highway that led directly to Westover AFB.

The brigade's armored battalion's M-60 tanks had left for Colorado by train a week before.

Two evenings before the road march, Lang had driven in the same gate in his little red VW Beetle. He had been in Boston all that day with his fiancée.

At the Military Police outpost, the MP on duty saluted and waved him through.

He was not focused on the soldier. His head was still filled with the day and the girl. The late spring foliage was lovely. The air was warm. The windows of the car were open. https://www.shutterstock.com/image-photo/legendary-us-army-handgun-colt-1911a1-93415852

Twenty yards past the glass and aluminum hut he heard a shot. Backing up, he could see no one in the little structure. He pried the door open and found the MP writhing on the floor in a pool of blood. His white cap and military police jacket were stained red. He had shot himself in the head with his .45 caliber sidearm. Lang reached into the MP hut for the telephone. A phone number was taped to the base. The MP desk sergeant answered. "This is Lieutenant Patrick Lang. I am at South Gate. Your sentinel here has shot himself." He felt for a pulse. "Actually, he has died. I will wait here."

The provost marshal arrived with an ambulance. "Why didn't you help him?"

"And what would I have done, sir? He put the muzzle in his mouth and pulled the trigger."

"Did you know this man?

"Colonel, I don't fraternize with your enlisted men."

"So, you drove past the outpost, and then he shot himself..."

"That's right."

"Can you come to the provost marshal's office to make a statement?"

"Of course."

Maddeningly, this incident persisted as a recurring subject of curiosity on the part of Criminal Investigation Division investigators who insisted on interviewing Lang half a dozen times as they tried to decide why this MP had shot himself at the moment that Lang had passed.

Throughout this period, the US Army experienced a steady "trickle" of suicides in its ranks. Nearly all of those who killed themselves were draftees, many of whom were simply unable to adapt to military life.

At Westover AFB, the aircraft were gathered for the lift to Moses Lake. The aircraft were variously C-133 Cargomasters, C-124 Globemasters and C-130 Hercules. Lang put his hundred-man quartering party on the first three aircraft with a few trucks full of supplies and sent them on their way. A senior sergeant had the diagrams for erection of the "tent city" in which the battalion would live while at Moses Lake. The next aircraft were filled with tents, generator sets and kitchens. Finally, the dozens of vehicles, water and fuel trailers, wrecker trucks and artillery pieces were loaded. A steady stream of aircraft disappeared into the blue sky.

Lang boarded a Globemaster, went forward to say hello to the flight deck crew and then stretched out on the webbing troop seats along the side of the fuselage and slept. The massive truck tethered to the deck next to him seemed a reassuring presence, something like a friendly elephant. The loadmaster sergeant woke him for an in-flight meal and coffee. An hour later they landed at Moses Lake.

He went around the camp to see if everything had arrived. Tents were going up, and all were in the right places. A mess team had food in preparation, and air force trucks were parked by the kitchen tents delivering more food from their "ration break down" facilities. The same was true of fuel. Everything seemed well in hand. The airdrome next to the camp was that of Larson Air Force Base. Base operations there told him that the first leased airliners carrying the troops would arrive the following day. The operations people were wrong. Someone had changed the "flow plan" for the leased aircraft.

In the belief that there would be ten or twelve hours before the first of these arrived, Lang arranged the guides and reception parties at the airfield into shifts, left a sergeant in charge of the first shift and lay down in his company's Command Post tent for three hours sleep.

Mckeon woke him screaming that he would "have your ass for neglect of duty." He had arrived at the airfield and not found Lang. That was an opportunity that he would not overlook.

Lang had been asleep in his sleeping bag.

Mckeon had rushed into the big tent, seized the bag and lifted it off the ground. He shook it up and down bellowing his rage.

Lang was face down in the bag and feeling claustrophobic.

"Put him down!" First Sergeant Moore yelled at Mckeon. "Put him down!"

When finally dropped on the earth from the level of McKeon's waist, Lang came out of the bag and started across the tent in the captain's direction.

Moore stepped between them.

"Come on, damn you," McKeon screamed. "Let's have it out now! I'll see you court-martialed yet."

It was a scene from a John Ford movie.

Lang was aggressive by instinct, and at that moment, all he could see was McKeon's red face.

"Come on, Pat," someone said from beside him. "Back off, he'll ruin you if you don't." The speaker was the company executive officer. "That's what he wants."

Life came back into focus. "Is the 'company street' laid out to your satisfaction, sir?" Lang asked.

McKeon turned away.

Lang went to the battalion CP to enquire if the "tent city" was to Castro's liking. "Yes, absolutely… What was all that noise?"

"Captain McKeon was expressing himself. It must have been a long flight."

Castro nodded

"You did a good job in this, lieutenant," Major Henderson said from a chair beside the briefing map, "a remarkable job. Sit down and tell us about it before you go back out into that damned wind, remarkable. Coffee?"

The S-4 officer nodded his agreement. "I didn't know what the hell I would find here. I am glad to see that you came through this so well." He was looking at Henderson's back while he said that.

When Lang rose to leave, the battalion commander followed him out into the "street." "You are getting married soon," Castro said. "You have known her long?"

"Since high school."

"Ah, good, good. May Maria and I come to your wedding?"

"Of course, you are on the invitation list. The wedding is in August in Maine."

"We will look forward to it. I hope you will invite Captain McKeon…"

"As you wish, colonel."

For three days, the rifle elements of the brigade took part in live fire exercises on government owned ground around Moses Lake and the air base. These were conducted by 5th Division headquarters. The division wanted to know if these soldiers of the 2nd Brigade were as well trained as their commander claimed them to be.

In one of these live fire drills, Lang and his friend and fellow platoon leader, Larry Clarkson, were called on to conduct a two-platoon attack against a low, grass covered ridge near the base. Clarkson was a 1962 graduate of West Point. He was from Montana, a Westerner and a cowboy through and through. A life spent in the mountains and plains of his native state had given him field skills that matched Lang's. Before he came to the 2nd Infantry Regiment, Clarkson had no experience at all with enlisted men. He watched Lang, more and more admiringly as he saw that Lang could forge bonds with troops that were beyond anything that he had thought possible. He watched as Lang disciplined men for infractions of discipline but did it without leaving emotional "scars." Clarkson had a difficult time reconciling the "war band chief" model of junior leadership with the "Prussian" drillmaster concept in the tradition of von Steuben that he had thought proper. On one occasion, he heard a soldier, who was a constituent of Congressman Adam Clayton Powell, say something that a Montanan might interpret as racist against whites. When he rebuked this man, there was an impudent reply. Clarkson, who was no mean physical specimen, grabbed the man by the scruff of the neck and belt and threw him over a fence onto a grassy space. Once there himself, he ordered the soldier to do "push-ups" until told to stop. He joined the man in this activity and outdid him.

When this confrontation was done, the soldier screamed, "I'll have your ass, you cracker,"

Clarkson walked away.

Lang asked the man aside to talk. He had one of his black squad leaders as witness. "Am I against you because of race?" he asked.

The soldier looked at the sergeant.

"I am told that you are not."

"Neither is Lieutenant Clarkson. He just doesn't know what to say or do with you. You are not innocent in this either. You set out to goad him. How about giving him a break, and not writing to Powell?"

"Can I talk to you when I need to?"

"Yes, what are you called?"

"They call me the 'banana man.'"

When Clarkson and Lang were faced with the need to assault the ridgeline, their long association and mutual understanding dictated what they would do. The two platoons fanned out into the lines needed to bring maximum firepower to the front.

They began to advance by "fire and movement" against the objective. The four machine guns supported the advance and moved forward by bounds. Rifle squads did the same with their five-man fire teams. The wave of orchestrated mayhem rolled up the slope with never a reduction in fire. As they reached the crest, the umpires called a halt.

"Who taught you gentlemen to do that," the senior judge, a lieutenant colonel asked the two officers.

"We taught each other," Clarkson answered.

The umpire nodded. "You may go back to camp. Load your men on the trucks. Well done."

The next day, the brigade was loaded into an armada of C-130 Hercules transports for a tactical air movement into a reserve position just behind the rest of the division. Two dirt airstrips had been bulldozed and graded. The stream of aircraft seemed never ending. Tail ramps dropped on unloading areas just off the "runways." Vehicles and troops poured off as "serials" of trucks formed for departure to an assembly area just behind the existing "line of contact" with the Blue "enemy" forces. Until this sudden reinforcement, the Blue force had enjoyed a great numerical superiority. Suddenly the situation was reversed.

The 5th Division "Red/Aggressor" force was resplendent in dark green uniforms topped by crested helmets emblazoned with the "triangle in a circle" emblem of the Circle Trigon Party. Five hours after the Fort Devens brigade closed into the assembly area, the division attacked into the Saddle Mountains with Lang's brigade passing through one of those online and moving forward at twenty miles an hour with priority of fires given them, as well as all available air support. Within half a day the Blue force had been pushed back ten miles, and Lang's battalion of the 2nd Regiment was established on a bare peak a thousand feet above the surrounding country.

Lang may have been the whitest man in North America. His skin needed protection from extremes of sun and wind. He could tan, but that required gradual exposure. The high desert burned his ears to a blistered, crusty mess. The medics wanted to evacuate him, but he ignored them and started wearing an Olive Drab towel as a neck and ear covering.

An hour or so before sundown on the day they took the bare peak, McKeon's company was told that it would conduct a raid that night to another peak a few thousand yards away on which a substantial Blue force was lodged.

A company strength night raid across this mountain and desert ground was a major undertaking. The company's officers gathered to look out across the terrain in the fading light. Castro and an umpire listened. McKeon told Lang that he would personally take the majority of the company down a large terrain finger that ran from their position to the valley floor. There they would go across the low ground to another finger that led up to the enemy position high above. Lang would go down the finger part way and then make his way to a different ascending finger and climb to near the top where they would wait for McKeon's group to open fire. This would be the signal to create a diversion by firing into the enemy position.

"Let's see your ears," the umpire asked Lang.

"You don't have to do this," Castro said after looking at them.

The umpire made a note.

"I'll be fine, sir. I wouldn't miss this for the world."

The umpire made another note.

Lang discussed the evening's planned "festivities" with his sergeants and then brought the platoon up to a place outside the company position where they could see the route and the objective. He told them what they were going to do.

"What's going to happen, sir?" someone finally asked.

"We are going to do our thing," he told them. "My guess is that the captain will get lost in that tangle of arroyos and stream beds at the bottom and we will end by making the attack on that peak over there. If there is barbed wire, we will back off after shooting the place up. I don't want to see any of you ripped up by razor wire or impaled on pickets. Understood? OK. No helmets, wear pile caps. No canteen cups either, nothing that will rattle."

As dark fell on the mountain, he inspected them, walking up and down the line, having them jump up and down to listen for noise, looking at the camouflage darkening on their faces. Even the blacks wore this. Their skins shone in the dark like everyone else.

"Challenge and countersign?" he asked. The answers were satisfactory.

After the sun set, they filed into position behind McKeon's "main body" and automatically roped themselves together as per platoon policy.

McKeon watched this, shook his head, and walked away.

Lang put Ali the Albanian soldier and his support man, a Cuban American, first as "point." Next in line were a compass man and a second compass man, just to be sure. After that, in the line of march was the "pace" man who would count for distance. Lang and Shapiro were next. The Strike Command umpire, a captain who had listened to the platoon meeting, said he would stay close to Lang. Following the little command group were the two M-60 machine gun teams, then the three rifle squads. O'Connor brought up the rear as always. As Lang had said, this was "their thing," and long practiced.

The wind howled and rattled the half-frozen canvas on the company's trucks. There was a new moon.

The platoon followed what they thought of as McKeon's "army" of sacrificial lambs out through the perimeter and down the finger.

The company weapons platoon would hold the perimeter until they returned.

About three quarters of the way down, they reached a large boulder that Lang had picked as a marker. There, they turned to a new directional azimuth. The pace count was right, and Lang was sure they were on course. They left two men to man this rally point. They went down the side of the finger, picking their way through the mesquite and shale. At the bottom they slowed, as numerous dissected stream beds and cottonwood tree lines interfered with their progress. After another mile on the same azimuth, they reached the upward finger. A conference under a poncho confirmed their position, and they started up having left two more men at this rally point. Halfway to the top, they saw that someone had broken light discipline in McKeon's column. Flashlights could be seen down in the maze of streambeds. This was followed by a lot of muzzle blast from defenders on the mountain top. A mortar coughed from the top of the mountain. As one man, the platoon lay flat with their faces to the ground. The parachute flare burned out. They rose and continued up the finger.

When they reached another large rock that Lang had picked as the objective rally point, they took a five-minute break, left two more and started again. Lang told them that they would be attacking because McKeon was as lost as they had expected. They un-roped and went into line across the finger when the pace count told them they were close. There was no barbed wire.

They penetrated the Blue perimeter in a hurricane of blank cartridge fire. Once inside, they grabbed two prisoners, tied their hands behind them and started back down the mountain in the wind, dark and cold. At the objective rally point Lang did a "head count" to make sure he had not "misplaced" someone. They were all present. They had achieved a complete surprise. Not a shot had been fired on the other side.

As the sun rose cold and frosty over their own battalion's mountain, Lang and his "boys" were eating breakfast among the mess trucks behind the peak. Scrambled eggs, cubed bacon, fried potatoes and onions were traditional. Light snow was falling into mess kits and down necks.

Kenneth McKeon came stumbling into the position after a night spent wandering in the wilderness. Men from his group had straggled in for hours. Once he had been given coffee, the army's panacea for everything, he was introduced by Lieutenant Colonel Castro to Lang's prisoners.

"You didn't have to tie us up," a 4th Division warrant officer growled. His fellow captive, a sergeant, agreed.

"Sorry, just being careful," Lang said, smiling the while.

Standing next to him was Sergeant James Caldwell, the self-described "banana man." He had asked for a transfer to Lang's platoon. Lang had caused him to be made a fire team leader.

Caldwell jumped up and down and thumped his arms across his body. "It's sure enough cold. The hawk's out this mo'nin lootenant, the hawk's out."

"Yup, I just saw him fly over."

The maneuver ended. The brigade motored back to Larson Air Force Base. They were to spend two days there and then be flown back to New England. The first night back in camp, Lang and his buddy, Larry Clarkson decided to go onto the base to have a meal at the officer's club. They took a jeep in, had a couple of drinks in the bar, devoured steaks and then watched the circus on the dance floor where officers from the brigade were having a good time hustling the wives of SAC officers gone on mission. McKeon was out there steering a blond around. She looked like an airline flight attendant. The two lieutenants decided to return to the tent city. They went to the club lobby. There was a long coat closet with sliding panel doors painted white. The lobby was built and decorated in the modernist déclassé style favored by the air force. Clarkson slid open a door to retrieve their caps from a shelf and revealed McKeon, their company commander, standing among the coats with his pants down around his ankles having sex with the blond. She was obviously and messily drunk. Clarkson said, "Excuse me, sir," retrieved the caps and shut the door. Nothing was said on the way "home." The disgrace was too great to be spoken of.

Clarkson and Lang lay outside their shared shelter tent for hours, looking at the stars and listening to a radio. A Japanese tune named "Sukiyaki" was the rage of the day, and they heard that a number of times on a local station.

Early in the morning, they watched a pickup truck come down the company street. The blue revolving light told them that it was the property of the air force security police at the base. It stopped in front of the command post tent. The lieutenants rose to learn what might be happening.

First Sergeant Moore came out of the tent.

The air police lowered the tail gate and dragged out the sodden, nearly unconscious body of his captain.

"Is this yours?" an air force man asked. The mockery in his voice was clear.

"No! No!" Moore said. "Not mine! When I think of my ... no." He went back into the tent.

Clarkson stepped forward. He and McKeon were West Point graduates.

"No," Lang said. "You don't have to do this. I am an officer," he told the air policeman. "I will sign for him."

"Is this how army officers act?" the policeman asked.

"I didn't ask for any of your lip," Lang said. The sergeant in him had floated to the surface. "Do you think we are not ashamed?"

"I'm sorry, sir"

"Just go away."

Lang and Clarkson dragged the drunk into the tent and draped him over the first sergeant's field desk so that he would not drown in his own vomit.

"You all right, top?" Clarkson asked.

"Thank you both," was the answer from inside Moore's sleeping bag.

McKeon was relieved of command "for cause" two days later. The air force complained to the Army Chief of Staff in Washington and that was the end of him. They did not complain because of the episode with the air force man's wife. The complaint was that he was a public disgrace.

This was a great convenience for Lang. An officer relieved of duty for cause could not rate his subordinates. In his place, Castro and Henderson rated Lang, and they were generous. Given a chance to do so, McKeon could have done a lot of damage to whatever Lang's prospects might be. McKeon hung around in the army in various unimportant jobs for several years but was never allowed to command troops again. In the mid 60s the system finally caught up with him and a medical board put him out of the service for bipolar disorder. Along the way to that end, he suffered many indignities at the hands of people he encountered in bars and in the field. Lang met one such, a former enlisted marine, who, when he heard McKeon's name said that in an officer's club in Germany, he had beaten McKeon senseless in a bathroom. When asked why he had done that, he shrugged. "Too much mouth," was all he would add.

McKeon left his mark on the company that he had abused in the 2nd Infantry. Every officer who served under him in the company resigned his commission as soon as he could. Lang was the sole exception.

Marguerite expressed disbelief when she saw Lang's ears. These appendages were then still more like tattered cauliflower than anything else.

Lang had been home at Fort Devens two weeks when he was told that his battalion would conduct summer training at Camp Drum, New York for all the Army Reserve and Army National Guard troops in the First US Army's area. This consisted of New England, New York and New Jersey. He was told that as the best teacher in the battalion, he would be the sole lecturer for demonstrations of squad- and platoon-strength live fire attack exercises through which all the infantry troops that came to Camp Drum would pass that summer. His own platoon would go to Camp Drum for the summer to do demonstrations for the Guard and Reserve troops. At the same time, he would be the headquarters commandant for the 2nd Regiment training team and would run the barracks, the mess, arms room and motor pool.

A first lieutenant from a previous class whom he had distantly known at VMI would supervise the training effort, and Castro would be in overall command. Lang wondered what the several officers from the battalion who would be going on this summertime expedition would be doing to fill up their days.

Little concern was expressed for personal commitments. Lang went to Camp Drum at the time Marguerite was graduated from college in Boston. When he later learned from his wife that this had happened, Castro rebuked Lang for not asking for permission to stay behind while the unit went to Camp Drum. Given the level of backbiting hostility that he had experienced in the battalion, Lang would never have asked for such a favor, and Marguerite did not think that he should.

The troops that his unit trained that summer varied widely in quality and level of training. Some of the National Guard units were superb in the quality of their people and the traditions that drove them to excel. There were some units that Lang would never forget.

One of these was the 102nd Infantry Regiment from western Connecticut. In the period of the draft, lawyers, Wall Street brokers, teachers, accountants and the like sought places in the reserve forces in order to avoid conscription into the Regular Army. Such men performed very well in the 102nd Infantry Regiment. It was not hard to understand why that would be. There were many others queued behind these men waiting for a place if the incumbents should be thought unworthy. As a result, that National Guard brigade was almost absurdly easy to teach. They listened closely to instruction and then executed instructions as well as the 2nd Infantry's soldiers. It was not necessary to tell them anything more than once.

The most amusing group Lang met that summer were a "society' battalion of the 69th Infantry Regiment from New York City. The officers of this battalion lived in handmade English tents and had their meals catered from Delmonico's restaurant in New York City. Two cooks from the restaurant had accompanied them to summer training. Lang enjoyed their hospitality on several occasions. They seemed to enjoy his company.

In general, the National Guard units were of higher quality than those of the Army Reserve. The 50th Armored Division (Jersey Blues) and the 26th Infantry Division (Yankee Division) from the National Guard were particularly good and could have been trained to Regular Army standards in a short time.

The worst Army Reserve unit seen that summer was the 77th Division from the New York City region. This division was filled with people who seemed to have emerged from a criminal past to infest the division. While at Camp Drum that summer, men of the division were required to guard the post ammunition dump. This task always requires solid discipline with regard to smoking and all other possible sources of ignition. Within a week of the division's arrival, half the post's ammunition dump blew up one night with a roar that shook the countryside for miles. Such a thing never occurs in the armed forces of a developed country. Three men were killed.

The investigation concluded that these three were probably responsible. After the 77th's departure, a newly turned patch of dirt was noticed in the forest. Under several feet of dirt were two new jeeps carefully wrapped in plastic sheeting. The apparent intention was to return and retrieve them. The military police traced the serial numbers on the jeeps, and the FBI arrested the culprits in Brooklyn. In later years the army wisely decided that large combat units could not be maintained in the Army Reserve where they lacked the oversight of the state adjutants general and the governors. For that reason, nearly all Army Reserve units became focused on logistical support. Hospitals, heavy engineer construction, transportation; these functions became the principal focus of the Army Reserve.

The wedding was to be in late August. Lang went to Marguerite on weekends whenever he could. The distance to be traveled was about four hundred miles.

He always needed to be back at Camp Drum for duty on Monday morning. The temptation to wait until the last minute to leave Maine was overwhelming. One night in July while driving in the mountains of western Massachusetts, he fell asleep at the wheel in his VW "bug." He hit a guard rail, bounced across the road and struck a rock "face." The little car slid out into the road. Lang applied the brakes. The engine was still running. The headlights were lit. Lang thought that the damage might not be too bad. He tried to put the "Beetle" in first gear and realized that the gearshift lever was broken off in his hand. At the same time, he felt wetness spreading over the right side of his face and chest. He raised his hand and felt a cut that went through his right brow ridge. His fingers touched his skull. In his cheek he felt a long cut.

He reached through and touched his teeth. His mouth was full of blood. He turned off the engine and got out of the car. There was a round hole in the windshield where his head had gone through, removing the rear-view mirror from the glass on the way. "Oh, shit," he said to himself. "Marguerite will not be happy with this." He remembered a farmhouse back down the road and walked toward it. It was probably a mile distant. Keep moving, he thought. Don't pass out from loss of blood. He held the brow together with one hand.

The road seemed endless. Two cars passed but would not stop. Finally, after what seemed an endless walk, the lights of the farm could be seen at the end of a long gravel drive. Lang walked to the porch where he knocked on the screen door. A woman came to see. He stood in the dark and asked her not to turn on the porch light. "I've been, hurt, ma'am. Please get your husband."

When the light was turned on, the husband cried out in horror and came down the steps to help him into the house. Lang asked them to telephone for help and to let him lie on the kitchen floor. They insisted, over his objection, that he lie on the couch in the living room.

The county sheriff arrived. He had been called by some of the people who would not stop. The sheriff took him to the home of a doctor in North Adams. The local hospital was so small that the emergency room was unmanned at night. The doctor was in pajamas, bathrobe and slippers.

They put Lang on a long trestle table in the kitchen.

The doctor looked at his wounds and at his haircut. "You are mighty calm, young fellah, mighty calm. What do you do fer a livin'?"

"Army, sir."

"Ah, I was in the ahmy in the big wah, No'mandy to Bavaria in the Yankee Division, I was a battalion suhjun... Whut do you do in the ahmy?"

"Doctor, I am a lieutenant of infantry."

"Ah. I thought as much. Well. Well. George, shut up, you ah makin' me nehvus."

This was to the sheriff who was blubbering on the wall phone about Lang's "terrible" injuries.

"I haven't done this kind'a thing for a while. I used to do it on a door laid across two sawhorses. Tell you what, son," he said to Lang. "You have three bad lacerations. One is in your cheek, one in the eyebrow. That's the worst. The muscles are cut all the way through there. The third is in your ear where the cartilage is cut. I have bad news. I have Novocain enough for two of them. Take your pick."

"What would you choose, sir?"

"The eah will huht the most, and the eyebrow will take a lot of stitches."

"OK doc, I'll go with your opinion."

"It's awful, he's sewin' him up without an anesthetic."

"Come on, George," Lang said to the sheriff. "Now you're making me nervous."

The doctor chuckled as he went to work. Before he started on the cheek, the doctor asked if he would like a shot of whiskey.

"Absolutely, maybe two, thank you, sir."

The doctor's needlework hurt like hell.

They checked him into a small hospital. The country doctor came to see him the next morning to pump him full of antibiotics and something to hold the lockjaw at bay.

One of his company's officers arrived in the afternoon to collect him.

"Jesus, Walt, what are you trying to do to yourself? I thought you wanted to get married."

"Don't make me laugh, it hurts too much. Let's go look at the car."

They met an insurance adjuster at the junkyard. "That's a gonner," the man said of Lang's car. "We'll send you a check."

They stopped at the farmhouse on the way out of town. Lang asked them to let him pay for the mess he had made in their house. They would not hear of it.

Lang returned to his work at Camp Drum.

Odd, challenging and sometimes wonderful things continued to happen that summer:

His old unit in the Maine National Guard came to train. He invited several of his high school friends to dinner at Alexandria Bay on Lake Ontario. They said that all the old World War II veterans were gone from the company. The former executive officer had gotten command. He was a highly ambitious lawyer who cared for nobody, and the old timers had left rather than endure him. His friends wanted to know what it was like to be an officer. "Same old crap," he said. "There's always somebody out to screw you."

On a Monday morning after a weekend of heavy rain, Lang drove to a range to observe training by Massachusetts troops on a squad live-fire attack exercise. This range had been carefully built for safety.

An M-60 machine gun on a tripod was mounted to one side on a concrete slab with two vertical pieces of reinforcing iron bar that limited the left and right movement of the gun barrel. The drill was that the squad would make its attack against a ridge pock marked with sandbagged pits in which were electrically fired blocks of TNT and smoke grenades that simulated artillery support. In the space that extended from the "start line" to the objective, there was a line of red stakes that marked the point at which the machine gun would cease fire. This point was well short of the point at which they could be hit by bullets from the machine gun.

Water was still dripping off the trees, and the clay in the soil underfoot was slick.

The Bay Staters had put several squads through the exercise when Lang arrived at the range. A "break" was announced, and Lang's men provided the National Guardsmen with hot coffee and doughnuts from their own mess hall kitchen. The exercise resumed in a few minutes.

The next squad went forward advancing by bounds. One fire team supported the other as it moved. Halfway to the objective, the squad rose to assault the ridge using marching fire.

At that moment Lang saw red tracer bullets pass between two men on the right side of the line.

The rain had softened the clay mound on which the machine gun platform sat, and the whole thing had slid two inches and rotated toward the squad.

Lang asked the National Guard leaders why they had not called a cease fire themselves before he arrived.

"We thought it was part of the training," they said, "very realistic."

On another Monday morning Lang rode a two-and-a-half-ton truck to another squad range. His jeep followed behind the truck. He was in the cab of the truck. His weapons squad leader sat next to the driver. The driver was a big man of limited intelligence. Lang rode in the truck because he wanted to talk to his sergeant about a member of the platoon who had gotten in trouble in Watertown, New York while off duty. Watertown was a decrepit wreck of a city that looked fearful of enjoying the summer. The prospect of the next nearly arctic winter always seemed foremost in the townspeople's minds. Soldiers from Camp Drum were welcome in Watertown, but only for their money.

They drove along a dirt training area road while Lang and the sergeant talked about the soldier they had in jail in town. The road was on a high "berm" and was raised above deep ditches to either side. Lang noticed that the driver seemed fixated on something on the right and was driving a long trajectory toward the left side of the road. He shoved his sergeant to make him look. After a moment, the Apache grabbed the wheel and tried to wrestle it from the control of the driver. The man was locked to the wheel with his eyes fixed. Lang leaned across and added his strength. The truck ran across the road and toppled into the ditch on its left side. When it stopped moving, Lang could hear the engine running. He reached down and turned everything off. The other two men were below him in the cab. He climbed over their various limbs, stood on them and opened the right door. This was now above him as though it were a hatch in a submarine. Levering himself out, he stepped onto the empty road, and walked to the back of the truck to learn how many men he had lost... Jumping down into the ditch, he looked into the "bed." The troops had been asleep. And as he watched, they untangled themselves, cursing the while and climbed out with their weapons to form up on the road. They were all there, and there were no injuries. It seemed a miracle.

"What the hell, sir," one of them said. "You don't love us anymore?"

A tank retriever arrived, and after a calculation of the geometry of the situation anchored the ditched truck to a tree to its front and then dragged it out of the ditch.

The truck was wrecked beyond repair. There was a "Report of Survey" investigation to determine financial responsibility. The vehicle was determined to be worth $20,000. Lang was potentially liable as the responsible officer. His finances would be devastated by a judgment against him. He remembered that his father, when a cavalry trooper, had accidentally shot a ten-year-old troop horse in the head on a riding pistol range. The father had been found "pecuniarily liable" and made to pay for the residual value of the horse at so much a month collected from his pay.

The investigating officer was a captain from the Camp Drum permanent garrison and therefore clearly not from the "top of the deck." He interviewed everyone involved and then after letting Lang "sweat" for a week, announced that the accident had been caused by the driver's inattention, but that the man had suffered some sort of mental lapse and should not pay for the truck. This was a deep relief for all concerned.

Lang's face looked a lot like the proverbial "train wreck" for weeks after his automobile accident. Several dozen black suture ends hung from his various wounds and the right side of his face was badly swollen. While narrating the platoon demonstration one day for a large audience his helmet liner blew off. The wreckage of his eyebrow and ear was revealed, and the New Yorkers in the bleachers made a collective noise that revealed their shock.

Lang retrieved his headgear and said, "That's what happens to you when you don't follow instructions."

At lunch in the field that day, Lang sat around the table with three other Fort Devens officers and chatted while the enlisted troops listened nearby.

"How long have you known this girl you are marrying," Lang's boss, a first lieutenant asked.

"I don't know, maybe seven or eight years."

"Must be like screwing your sister."

"You have no idea, or maybe you do."

The troops roared with laughter.

Lang's parents and sister arrived from the west coast by automobile. His sister was thirteen. She would be a bridesmaid. His mother had "sold" the idea of such a trip on the basis of a chance to visit her relatives in Maine.

His parents were at Camp Drum for several days. The plan was for Lang to "convoy" with them to the wedding in Marguerite's hometown.

After his parents had been at Drum for a few days, one of Lang's sergeants told him that his father was circulating among them, seeking to elicit comments as to his defects as an officer, soldier and man.

"It's not right, sir. It's not right," one of them said. "Where I come from no father would talk of his son like this. The men are unhappy. He does not know what we have done... He does not know what you have done for us. He does not listen."

"Don't worry about it, Ali," Lang said. "He doesn't like me very much. He did the same thing at my graduation from college. It's enough to have friends like you."

In Maine, his mother competed with his future mother-in-law in describing the disadvantages to any young woman in marrying her son. In one such exchange: "He is such a dry, humorless thing, no personality at all," his mother said.

"And he is a child of the ruling class..." Marguerite's mother added. This last did not find favor with Lang's mother who had worked in a textile mill before she met his father.

"Do you still want to do this?" Lang asked the woman in his life when told of these comments.

"There is no doubt," she said.

The wedding party assembled.

There was a bachelor's party at a family cabin on the shore of a lake. The little building was somehow, oddly, built to resemble a Chinese pagoda. At three in the morning, the groomsmen threw him off the dock and into the lake. They fished him out, dressed him in Army Blue and took him to the church in time for the ceremony.

Marguerite wore a dress of *peau de soie*. Her mother had made it. Lang had been the driver for a trip from Maine to Boston when the material was bought. He had watched in wonderment as they bought Belgian lace for the veil. She looked incredible the day of the wedding.

A "society" photographer from Boston was hired. He hovered in the background throughout the wondrous events. The pictures were marvelous.

Lang had a minor skirmish with a curate at the parish church during the rehearsal. The young priest could not refrain from staring at the bride and began to address the groom, as "general." To put a stop to this, Lang took a hundred dollars from his pocket and handed it to the man. "We look forward to seeing you at the ceremony tomorrow, father," he said.

The reception was at the local businessman's luncheon club on the top floor of a brick building that dominated the town's central square. Everything of value in the town: the textile mill, this club, the country club, the library, and the hospital, were the products of the enterprise and beneficence of the English family who had founded the mills 150 years before. A statue of the founder looked down from his pedestal on the square below the club windows.

The wedding and reception were replete with the trappings of army life. The requisite arch of swords was a feature of departure from the church. The battalion colors were present, crossed behind the wedding party's table. The blue battalion color was heavy with the regiment's honors. The next time Lang would see these flags, they would be caked with the red laterite dust of Vietnam. The battalion commander and his lady were present as well. In

US Army custom, this twofold witness to the marriage made Marguerite a daughter of the regiment, and part of the living tradition.

The groomsmen were handsome in blue. They enjoyed the occasion and the bridesmaids' company on the dance floor. The girls were all close friends of Marguerite from college. Lang's sister was the welcome exception.

McKeon and his wife were not present. The bride had declined to invite them.

The Langs left the party when a decent interval had passed. Like all newlyweds, they wanted to be alone. Oddly, but typically for them, they went on a weeklong driving visit to Civil War battlefields in Virginia, Maryland and Pennsylvania. The bride listened with apparent interest to endless talk about these places and events. It was a lovely trip, something to be cherished in memory. They returned to Fort Devens to begin their new life together. The army provided them with a small, red brick ranch style house adequate to their need. A search for furniture began all over eastern Massachusetts.

A new company commander arrived in September. He was a stolid, honorable man with a growing family. He told Lang that he had been briefed on the antics that had characterized McKeon's "reign of terror." "I think that you would be sitting in this chair if you were a few years older," he said. "I hope that you will give me the help that you tried to give McKeon."

"It will be my pleasure to do so, captain."

In October, the brigade traveled to the amphibious warfare training center at Little Creek, Virginia. For a week they practiced loading ships with their equipment, supplies and men. They learned to plan assault loading of ships. In this difficult drill, the ships were loaded so that things that would be needed first were available first. This wasted a great deal of space in the ship's holds but was necessary. Next, they learned to administratively load ships so that all available space was used. After this logistical training, the brigade began to make landings on Atlantic beaches near North Carolina. These grew in size from company to battalion and then to a culmination in a brigade landing from ships offshore in which Colonel Kingsley defied the marine trainers who were supposedly in charge of the exercise to put ten M-60 tanks in the first assault wave. The tanks charged up the beach with the infantry behind them. They picked up the barbed wire obstacles as a continuous band and dragged it inland. The tanks chased the marine maneuver enemy for a quarter mile until they trapped them against a lagoon. There was a "scene" in which a marine officer tried to upbraid Kingsley in public. Kingsley turned his back, climbed on a tank and ignored the man. The armor rolled away leaving the marine spluttering on the beach.

At Little Creek, Lang experienced his only "skirmish" with the new company commander. This happened when Lang asked him in an "orders group" what they should do if the navy did not put them ashore in front of their objective. Experience thus far showed that the navy never landed them in front of their objective.

"How about you let me run the company, Lieutenant." the captain asked.

"Just asking you what I should do, sir."

Outside the building, a number of sergeants gathered around Lang in silent support while they talked about everything but this moment.

The captain later told Lang that he had seen that group form. "Jesus, how do you do that? If you could bottle it..."

"I do not want to bottle it, sir. I don't do anything to encourage this. They know I care. That is all. I don't want them to do anything for me. They should do what they do for their country, or the regiment. I am not Desiderio..."

"Who?"

There could be no answer to that.

"Yes, you care, and they do sense that. Maybe you care too much. What will you do when they die? What will they do when you die?" The captain shook his head and walked away.

They had no further problems while Lang was in the company. He was grateful for the fine effectiveness report that this captain gave him and was saddened many years later to hear of the man's death in the Pentagon of a heart attack while serving on the Army General Staff.

Lieutenant Colonel Castro and Maria came to dinner with the Langs in November. The four sat on the flimsy furniture the Langs could afford. After an excellent dinner served on wedding gift china and sterling flatware, Castro told Lang that the brigade had selected him to go to the Northern Warfare Training Center at Fort Greely at Big Delta, Alaska to become a qualified instructor in arctic warfare and mountain operations.

Marguerite went home to her mother. This became a customary solution for his absences.

In Alaska Lang learned to survive, prosper, and operate at temperatures far below zero.

He was seated in the bar in the Fort Greely officer's club with Larry Clarkson when the black and white TV set over the bar announced that Kennedy had been shot in Dallas. They were eating reindeer burgers when this was announced by Cronkite. Lang continued eating while consternation swept the bar.

"Don't you care?" the civilian barman asked.

"What can I do about it," Lang replied. "Bring me another beer."

The next day, Lang was summoned to the post headquarter and handed an order promoting him to first lieutenant. The garrison commander pinned on his new insignia.

"You don't look excited by this," the officer said.

"Thank you, colonel," Lang replied. "I am not. I am not. Words fail me." He saluted and left.

The following day, there was a memorial service held for John Kennedy. The sun shone in a pale sky. The temperature was 50 degrees below zero Fahrenheit. The garrison of the post gathered on skis and in arctic gear on the parade ground. The post commander spoke, eulogizing the fallen commander in chief. A bugler blew Taps. At the right phrase, he introduced the *sanglot*, the "sob" that was a part of military mourning for the US Army. Cannon fired, beginning the long salute for the dead president. The report of the gun shocked the moisture-laden air and precipitated an Arctic Fog. In an instant, the field was so hidden that Lang could not see the tips of his skis. He was happy for this. He could weep in peace without being watched.

Training resumed the next day. The graduation exercise was a 100-mile tactical ski march with a variety of field problems along the way. The role of "enemy" in this maneuver was played by an Eskimo Scout company of the Alaska National Guard. Along the way, Lang was on guard one night and skiing a circle around his company's arctic tents. He skied clockwise while another man skied counterclockwise. What they were looking for were tracks that broke their trail. The temperature was about 60 below zero. Within a few moments, the moisture in Lang's nose froze into hard little crystals. Just in front of him, an American Buffalo walked out of the pines and into the circle of white tents. The big animal stopped to look at him and then walked on. Close behind it, paced two white arctic wolves. Lang was astonished. From the tip of the tail to the nose, they looked about six feet long. They watched him for a few seconds and then turned away to follow the bison across the camp.

Lang returned to the brigade to head cold weather and mountain training for two weeks in the White Mountains. He was thought by many to be too junior for that level of responsibility, but Colonel Kingsley said that he would have no other to head the training committee.

Christmas came and went. The Langs settled comfortably into their little house on El Caney Road.

One day in February, Lang went to the post library to spend a quiet hour reading alone. The library was a large, old, wooden building from the era of World War II.

A civilian woman who was librarian approached. "What are you doing here, lieutenant during the duty day?"

Lang was seated on an aluminum framed green plastic upholstered settee. "Are you going to report my pursuit of knowledge?" he asked playfully. "I'll give you the company's phone number."

She was grey-haired, but handsome. "Don't fool with me," she said. "You know I will not do that."

"You are an army wife?"

"Widow."

He rose. "Ah, how may I help you, ma'am?" he said. He was always a "sucker" for a good-looking woman who carried herself well and was a member of his tribe.

"I run the post testing center as well. Come with me. I will give you some tests."

He followed docilely to her office. She administered a number of tests. They meant nothing to him. He wanted to make her feel fulfilled in her job.

"You have remarkable results," she said after an hour.

"Thank you, ma'am," he said and left.

Unknown to him she sent the results to the Department of the Army in Washington. He thought no more of it. Two weeks later the phone rang. On the other end was a military bureaucrat from army personnel... "Hey, we are really impressed with your perfect score on the language aptitude test."

"You are? What are you offering?"

"How about the 8th Special Forces Group in Panama?"

"My record is that bad? You hate those people."

There was a pause. "Why didn't you take the job in the 82nd?"

"Love."

"What am I supposed to say?"

"What if they want me to stay where I am?"

"Let us know."

"I'll take your offer."

Two weeks later, a "request for orders" arrived at Devens. The orders from Department of the Army would send him to the Special Forces School at Fort Bragg, then to Spanish language school and on to join the "damned." It seemed a natural destination for him.

He was summoned to brigade headquarters where he met yet again with Kingsley and Henderson. "Fur head" had succeeded Castro in command of Lang's battalion.

"You don't want to stay with us?" Henderson asked.

"What is there here for me, colonel? I have commanded the same rifle platoon for two years."

"You are very young," Henderson said.

"You have done well throughout your apprenticeship," Kingsley said... "We want to give you a company."

"A rifle company?"

"There are many captains available," Henderson remarked. "We have in mind Headquarters Company of the battalion."

"I thank you both for the offer. I believe that it is time that I should be on my way...."

Marguerite was glad to go, as was he.

The battalion transferred to the 1st Infantry Division when that division went to Vietnam. A year and a half later, the "banana man," then a rifle squad leader, crawled out into a firebreak in the Michelin Rubber Plantation in Binh Duong Province to try to drag his wounded white platoon leader back out of North Vietnamese machine gun fire. They died there together. Sergeant First Class Caldwell held his leader close...

Touch them not.

CHAPTER SIXTEEN

Aaron Bank's Children

Colonel Aaron Bank, US Army

"Captain Lang, I understand you are in charge of this training project?"

"I am, General Alger, I am indeed. I have been in charge of this for six months, although that is not my primary duty."

The "US Army South" commanding general looked appraisingly at the SF colonel who had come with Lang to this meeting at Fort Amador on the Pacific side of the Panama Canal Zone. The two Special Forces officers were seated around the mahogany table in the conference room next door to Alger's office.

Several members of Alger's staff sat farther down the table.

The SF colonel realized that he was expected to speak. "The operations section would usually run something like this, but they are so busy with our training missions in so many Latin countries that Colonel Simons gave this to the intelligence section to do. I continued that when I took over, and they have done well...."

"Your sergeant was arrested as a vagrant by the Canal Zone police in Cristobal at five in the morning yesterday, even though he had forty dollars in his pocket." Alger said reading the report before him. "He identified himself, said he was on a training mission and was on his way back to Fort Gulick." The general looked at the papers in his hand again. "The police report says that he was in rags and looked like a hobo." He looked up.

"If I may continue, General?" Lang asked.

Alger nodded.

"Staff Sergeant Wilkinson was telling the truth. He had volunteered for a two-day training exercise that we call 'Isthmian Adventure.' We posted a notice offering our Special Forces soldiers the chance to participate. We have had a hundred volunteers so far and have sent six men on these missions."

"Just Special Forces men? You did not include soldiers from the attachments, the engineers, AIS people, etc.?"

"No, sir, we really did not think...."

Alger nodded. "Continue."

"We notified men the day they were to go on mission, briefed them, gave them the clothes they were to wear, a pocketknife, and took them out to France Field for the airlift."

"What was the mission?"

Lang took a breath. He knew how badly this discussion might end. "We flew them to the old Rio Hato camp up near Costa Rica on this side."

Alger waited. He looked neutral. That was good.

"We flew them up there in a U-10 Heliocourier. Each man was instructed to make his way back to Fort Gulick in less than two days. The jump was always at night. There was a drop zone safety party, but they hid after the man exited the aircraft. The "player" had a sealed envelope that he was told had emergency money in it. They were told that they were not to open it unless there was an emergency. All of them opened the envelope as soon as they were on the ground. We expected that."

There was a restless sound among the USARSO staff officers.

"And?" Alger asked.

"In the envelope was a Confederate bank note."

There was more restlessness in the staff. One officer raised a hand and was recognized by the general. "Why did you expect them to do that? They were told not to do that."

"Because of what they are…"

"So, he got home or almost home in less than 24 hours," Alger said. "He was dressed like that, with no papers, and with the Guardia Nacional and our MPs hunting him." He looked at Lang who nodded, "He had no money. "No, wait. He had forty dollars U.S. on him when apprehended for vagrancy."

Alger looked at Lang waiting for an explanation.

"He talked a merchant in Panama City into 'breaking" the counterfeit Confederate hundred-dollar bill. We will reimburse the Panamanian."

Alger smiled. "Of course, of course, what do you mean when you said, 'what they are?'"

"They are Bank's children. We are all his children."

Colonel Aaron Bank was born on 23 November 1902 in New York City. His parents were immigrants from Russia. His father died the year after he was born. Bank lived with his maternal grandfather as a child. The grandfather was an insurance broker in the city, presumably in the Jewish community since the grandfather spoke little English. As a child and young man, Bank had little taste for formal schooling. He left home early for a life of adventure. He was an athlete throughout his long life and made an early career of work as a swimming instructor and personal trainer. When he was 29, he married a woman 14 years his senior who was one of the wealthiest people in California. She was a widely accomplished person. Bank was the third of her four husbands. They traveled together on several continents. Bank acquired language and social skills appropriate to her position in life. For some period in the 1930s, they resided In Biarritz where Bank is said to have been the head lifeguard at a hotel. In 1939, war began in Europe, and the Banks returned to the United States to live in Dade County, Florida where he worked in real estate, specializing in the sale of large residential properties. In the middle of 1942, he was drafted and volunteered for Officer Candidate School. At graduation he found that the army's ground combat forces did not want him because of his age. He was forty-one years old. Unwilling to accept a largely meaningless training job in the United States, he asked to be

assigned to the "Office of Strategic Services," a group formed in imitation of the British "Special Operations Executive." The British organization had been created at Churchill's urging by amateur enthusiasts from the British upper classes. Many of these people were university professors, journalists, country gentry and part-time soldiers from the yeomanry. The belief was then prevalent that German successes in the first year of the war were due in large part to expert "leveraging" of the shock action and disproportionate effect of small groups of soldiers inserted by parachute or other means into their enemy's rear area where they spread havoc through sabotage, propaganda and guerilla warfare.

Bank volunteered to participate in an effort to assist and enable French resistance groups in German occupied territory. After a year of training in the US and Britain, he parachuted into southern France as a member of a three man "Jedburgh" team. Their function was to train and supply the French Maquis in the area around Nimes and Arles. He fought with the resistance until relieved of this duty by the advance of American forces from their landing beaches on the Riviera in Operation Dragoon. Bank sought a follow-on mission behind German lines in Austria, but the war ended before that could occur. He was next sent to China, but the Japanese surrendered before he could get back in the fight.

Following the end of the war, Bank presided over a variety of counterintelligence and intelligence activities in Europe in the Counter Intelligence Corps. This was a good refuge for him because the CIC was largely manned with officers who, like him, lacked the educational background wanted by the Army in peacetime.

The Cold War began within a few years. The Warsaw Pact came into being and was understood to be an offensive force that could overrun much of Western Europe if war began between that alliance and NATO.

In 1951, Bank was in Korea serving with airborne troops. He was surprised and somewhat dismayed to be summoned to Washington to work in the Army General Staff in a section engaged in a process of introspection on the related subjects of psychological warfare and assistance to guerrillas in occupied Europe in any future war.

The CIA had been busy from 1950 onwards in weapons cache building across Soviet occupied Europe. It was expected that as Soviet and other communist forces advanced westward in a war with NATO, the subject peoples behind their lines would rise to act against them just as the peoples of Western Europe had acted against the Germans in World War II.

As this notion clarified in the collective mind of the US Government, it was decided that the CIA could not play the role that the Office of Strategic Services had in that war. OSS was essentially a military organization under the command *of the Joint Chiefs of Staff, and as such it had coordinated its activities closely with overall military plans. As an Army manned group, OSS had received the full support of the US military establishment. The CIA was a civilian agency that lacked the skills needed to organize, train and hopefully lead guerrilla armies behind Soviet lines.*

After a prolonged internal debate, the Chief of Staff of the US Army decided to establish a group for the resistance assistance mission and at the same time to provide 2,500 military personnel authorizations with which to make that possible. These personnel "pay billets" were conveniently made available by another army decision to disband the Ranger light infantry raiding companies that had existed in the Far Eastern command. These soldiers had carried out patrols behind Chinese and North Korean lines; reconnaissance and the like. The army had decided that they were too much of a drain on leadership manpower that ought to be in line units, and so they were disbanded, to be reborn twenty years later.

At the same time a decision was made, largely at Bank's urging, to base the guerrilla assistance force's methods on the OSS's effort in occupied Europe. This meant that the emphasis would be on recruiting well-educated, language skilled and highly flexible soldiers who would train, advise, and coordinate the actions of foreign guerrillas. These guerrillas would be commanded by their own leaders rather than Americans. Such work would demand a subtlety of mind that might be hard to find. Aaron Bank had done precisely this kind of work in France.

From the point of view of the Regular Army establishment, Bank was an interesting and capable officer but still someone thought of as "Christmas Help." Bank was not a general's son-in-law or nephew. The careers of sons-in law had to be protected from the craziness of ventures such as this. Promotion boards were certain to scratch their heads and not wish to promote people who volunteered for this kind of "foolishness." Officers who brought to mind Clint Eastwood's character in "Where Eagles Dare," or anyone in "The Guns of Navarone," would not be favored by selection boards. Bank was an obvious choice to organize and train what he insisted should be called Special Forces and also to establish its doctrine for operations. When he was appointed, he was pleased to learn that he would have a free hand in creating the group unless he wanted too much for his "band of thieves."

He began to recruit. The first commissioned officers in Special Forces were nearly all former OSS men with combat experience in Europe. Like Bank, they had somehow survived in the army. They felt they had been reborn.

He decided that the enlisted soldiers should be very special. The first hundred were recruited by him from the draftee stream by looking for athletes who were second generation Americans whose parents came from the European areas where the mission would be focused. Superior intellect was greatly desired. This was determined by interview and test. Such men were easily recruited from among the draftees by the prospect of adventure and an outdoor life.

Bank next searched the US Army and the world at large for very skilled and experienced combat soldiers. Europe was then filled with veterans of the world war and the colonial wars of the post war period. Few among them were U.S. citizens. The law barred their enlistment in peacetime in the US Army. At the Pentagon's request, the Congress passed the Lodge Act. This law made it possible for Bank to offer U.S. citizenship to those whom he wanted and who would join him. Among the possible candidates were many veterans of the German Army, or their allies, the Finnish Jaeger Commandos.

There were Spanish Republicans and Nationalists from the Spanish Civil War and the Spanish Foreign Legion. There were many exiles from the armies of the communist regimes of Eastern Europe. There were Germans who had served in the Wehrmacht, then the French Foreign Legion in Vietnam. and who yearned to come to America. There were quite a few from the Panzer Grenadier Division Grossdeutschland, the premier fighting formation of the German armed forces. The "word" had gone around the division "alumni" that Bank was hiring. Such foreign soldiers knew everything there was to know about soldiering that was worth knowing... They were an endless resource, and once given asylum they responded with the loyalty that marks their kind. Many of these "foreigners" are buried at Fayetteville, North Carolina near Fort Bragg.

Another group of US soldiers brought into Special Forces at the beginning were Rangers who had lost their army "home" when the Ranger companies had been disbanded. Either from a sense of guilt for causing that or because of internal army politics, Bank welcomed many of these assault infantrymen into Special Forces. These men and their spiritual descendants rarely relished the sophistication *of the OSS Europe model for the new kind of unit. They remained dedicated to commando operations carried out by American soldiers, as well as to extreme standards of physical fitness. Most of them never embraced the idea of working through foreign irregulars and simply hoped for "better days."*

The last major group of volunteers to be Special Forces soldiers was made up of old paratroop sergeants, many of whom had served in the airborne force in World War II. These men were glad to embrace Bank's vision and were among his most devoted followers. Bank hand-picked all these people.

In the matter of organization and specialization, Bank decided that the capabilities of both the OSS Jedburgh three-man teams and the larger 30-man OSS Operational Groups should be found in the new force.

To do that, he created 12-man "A" detachments as the basic units in Special Forces. In each of these there would be a captain and a lieutenant of some experience, a master sergeant operations planner, a sergeant first class intelligence planner, a light weapons specialist (rifles, machine guns etc.), a heavy weapons specialist (mortars, artillery, tanks, etc.), two demolitions specialists, two medical specialists, and two communications specialists.

Bank believed that these detachments could be split in half if necessary and would then resemble the capability of a Jedburgh team. He believed that a half "A detachment" could train and support a fifteen-hundred-man guerrilla regiment. Alternatively, several "A detachments" could be combined to resemble the OSS Operational Groups.

Bank judged the skills combined in the "A Detachment" to be those necessary for the resistance assistance job. The training he required for these skills was formidable. Special training programs were created at army service schools. The training was extensive and prolonged. The longest of the programs was that for the medical specialists. This lasted over a year and involved a lengthy "practicum" in hospital work. The medics were taught surgery, pharmacology, preventive medicine, orthopedics, obstetrics (guerrillas have women and children). These Special Forces medical personnel were not "medics" in the sense of the Geneva Conventions. They were combat men, fighters who happened to know a lot of medicine. They did not claim the often-meaningless protection given to medical personnel by those treaties.

Bank insisted that having completed specialty training, the team members begin to cross-train each other.

Field training across the world was continuous. The government immediately found these soldiers useful and they were often "loaned" to CIA for missions that the CIA was wise enough to know exceeded their own ability.

The men were gone from their home stations much of the time. It became a joke in Special Forces to say that a typical SF sergeant was someone who passed through Fort Bragg every few months with "a Rolex watch, a bag of dirty laundry and an erection."

First Lieutenant Walter Lang chose to join this "circus menagerie" in 1964; eleven years after the founding of what became the Special Forces Regiment. He had already experienced some minimal contact with Special Forces officers before he joined. They impressed him as odd but committed to their unusual task if only because some of them had nowhere else to go.

Lang saw in this unit an opportunity to "soldier" as he understood the profession and simply accepted the fact that this choice would reduce the possibilities for his army career. He discussed this with his beautiful, intelligent, educated wife and they accepted the assignment while understanding that the decision might "kill" his career.

They shipped what furniture they owned to Fort Bragg, gave back the little house the government had "loaned" them at Fort Devens and drove south along the coast on a bright spring day. It was a kind of vacation. The world was blooming. The air was warm. More and more flowering trees appeared along the roadsides as they moved steadily away from New England's frigid climate.

They arrived at the northern end of the 23-mile-long Chesapeake Bay Bridge-Tunnel on the day it opened for business. There were hundreds of cars waiting in line for the gate to rise. Many had brought picnic lunches. It was a festive moment. When the barriers were removed traffic flowed forward. The salt breeze from the bay was intoxicating. The only unpleasantness in the day was the sight of many dead birds scattered along the elevated roadway of the bridge. These creatures had not yet learned that they no longer owned the bridge.

They stayed overnight in Williamsburg, Virginia and walked the streets of the colonial town in the moonlight.

Lang reported to the Special Warfare School, and was told to come back in a few days when his courses would start.

The young couple inspected the local newspaper and drove around Fayetteville looking at the possibilities for housing. After a few false starts they found a new, one story brick row of apartments built in a colonial style. The buildings looked clean. The landscaping was neat and the location was just a few miles from Fort Bragg on the main road from the post to the city of Fayetteville. The owners lived in a pretty house next to the apartments

Lang sat in the car for a few minutes and watched people come and go from the apartments. "Come on, honey," he finally said. "We are going to walk up the stairs to the office together."

The owners were a family of middle aged, middle class, North Carolinians who came to the door, inspected them, invited them in, served lemonade and leased them a furnished apartment for the period of his training. "You are what we are looking for, lieutenant," the wife said. It was clear that Marguerite herself had been a major feature in their decision to rent them the apartment. Their one-bedroom flat was immaculate and plainly but tastefully furnished. They enjoyed the place immensely. The army would keep their furniture in storage while they were in North Carolina.

Lang was at Fort Bragg to study and be trained at the US Army Special Warfare Center. This institution had been created by Aaron Bank twelve years earlier as a "refuge" for odd military skills like psychological warfare as well as the achievement of a capability to interact with foreign soldiers and civilians in behind-the-lines work.

General Maxwell Taylor was a man much admired by the Kennedy brothers. He had played a significant role in the decision by the army to create the Special Forces. President Kennedy recalled Taylor from retirement to be Chairman of the Joint Chiefs of Staff. Taylor had written a famous book which baldly stated that Eisenhower's reliance on the air forces for national defense against communism was a mistake. Taylor believed that the army in general and the Special Forces in particular should be made larger and thought of as mainstays of Kennedy's foreign policy. Johnson's succession to power in the United States after the assassination had not diminished Taylor's role at all.

The main non-nuclear threat from the USSR and newly communist China in 1964 was the possibility that these countries might launch massive attacks in Europe or Asia for the purpose of adding more territory and people to the still-growing "world" of Marxism-Leninism. To deal with that danger the armed forces were massively augmented throughout the Kennedy period.

In addition to this growth in the conventional and nuclear forces, the Kennedy Administration developed more exotic interests. The foreign policy "fad" of the day was the notion that the "Wars of National Liberation" being waged by Third World peoples against European colonizers were being "hijacked" by communist infiltration as a secret weapon that was as dangerous as the chance of naked attack by the big communist states. Nikita Khrushchev presented this idea at a Soviet Communist Party congress by claiming that all such wars were instruments to be used by "Worker's Movements" across the world... Foreign policy specialists seized on this claim to develop a virtual cottage industry of theses and books that developed the theme. General Taylor may or may not have encouraged this idea in the Kennedy group, but whether he did or not, they and their intellectual circle of friends were fascinated by the thought. This fascination was somewhat akin to the largely illusory World War II era belief in German Fifth Column successes that had called forth both the British Special Operations Executive and the American OSS.

Kennedy asked Taylor what could be done about this danger. The answer given was in the form of a discussion concerning the tiny, underfunded psychological warfare school at Fort Bragg and specifically about the handful of Special Forces there and in Bavaria.

Kennedy went to visit and was enraptured by the romance of the thing, the carefully staged demonstrations, the more or less multi-lingual soldiers, and the obvious and fearsome reality of these warriors. He asked the Fort Bragg commander of Special Forces, Lieutenant General William Yarborough if these enablers of guerrilla warfare would be effective in training native soldiers to fight against guerrillas. The president suggested that they ought to be good at either task. This question from the commander in chief could only be answered in the affirmative... Thus was born a second major mission for both Special Forces and the schools at Fort Bragg where they were trained.

Lang's first course at Bragg was called "Counterinsurgency Staff Officer." This was principally an auditorium-based lecture series on a wide variety of topics. There were officers in the course who were not destined for Special Forces. They were on their way to jobs as training advisers overseas, staff officers in various commands, and they were nearly all senior to Lang and were a lot older. There were quite a few exercises in the course in which plans for action were prepared in different scenarios. Lang knew that a group of majors did not want to be "led" by a twenty-four year-old "kid." He habitually waited until an impasse of some kind had been reached, and then, if asked would offer an opinion. Even that effort at modesty attracted some hostility.

The history, anthropology, psychology, economics, and geography of probable areas of insurgent activity were subjects explored in lectures by leading academic writers and teachers. French and British writers and experts on counterinsurgency appeared to speak of their theories and experience of counter guerrilla warfare. The school was skilled in attracting excellent lecturers. Robert Thompson, David Galula, Roger Trinquier, Paul Aussaresses, and Bernard Fall were among the instructors that Lang heard lecture in the auditorium of the school. The amount of material crammed into six weeks was impressive. Lang had always been deeply interested in cultural differences and their intersections with the history of warfare. The quality of the teaching in this course brought a great deal of knowledge acquired over the years into sharp focus in such a way that he saw why his efforts at troop leadership at the platoon level had been so fruitful. It was apparent on reflection that human relations were, as Napoleon had written, the most important factor in any kind of warfare. This understanding had profound implications for the rest of Lang's government service. It was something he carried forward with him into the world of intelligence. He had already decided for himself that human societies developed in a continuum of events and beliefs that extended from the past, stretched through a moment in the present and persisted far into the future. These realizations and a mind that catalogued and stored facts like a machine created a powerful tool kit. The most important moment in this course for Lang was the day Bernard Fall stood on a stage and wrote on a blackboard the words, "Counterinsurgency = economic development + political action + counter-guerrilla operations." Fall stepped back, looked at what he had written and turned to the class. "That's it," he said. "That sums it up... Remember this. If you can persuade the US government to sponsor such actions you can beat any insurgency, but you have to have all three elements in your program. You have to make the targeted population prosperous. You have to make them believe that they are not oppressed. You have to fight the guerrillas, the agitprop teams and the terrorists. It won't be easy to do..." Fall was a former French officer. "We failed in Indo-china. We succeeded in Algeria and Tunisia, but our government gave up. That may happen to you." He shrugged in a very French way. "No matter, remember you must know the people. The war is for control of the minds of the people. You must know them."

The counterinsurgency class ended with the sort of ridiculous graduation ceremony and fancy certificate that the army found necessary for every sort of study whether it was for a five-day Jumpmaster course or the War College.

Lang had read the books of most of the lecturers long before and found the pace of the curriculum easy. It left time for nights spent in leisurely dinners with his wife in Fayetteville and weekends shopping in nearby North Carolina cities.

The lectures were useful "glue" with which to bind together all the lessons in counterinsurgency that he had taught himself. In later years, he found it sadly amusing that hyper-ambitious generals claimed that they invented counterinsurgency during the Iraq War...

After a week's break in training while waiting for a Special Forces Officer course to begin, Lang reported to the branch of the school that trained Special Forces men. He asked the warrant officer who processed him in if there would be a PT test before the course began. He expected that there would be such a test. In his experience there always was. He had been running and doing calisthenics.

The crusty old paratrooper smiled and said there would not unless he wanted one. Warrant officers and senior sergeants in that era were often veterans of the airborne force in the big war. There was a limit to how much deference they would show to those they judged to be callow lieutenants.

Lang knew the drill. He waited.

The warrant finally sighed and said, "Lieutenant, this isn't the 82nd or the 101st. They won't give you a PT test. They think that is undignified. What they will do is load you up and see if you can carry the weight cross-country and still do your job when you arrive. That's what they will do..."

He was correct. That is what they did. A common practice in the field during the course was for an umpire/trainer to declare an "emergency" caused by approaching "enemy" troops. This "emergency" always required a quick shift of position to another campsite some miles away. In that move those who happened to be in camp at the time would shoulder their own gear and that of someone absent and move off across the hills. This was a far more effective proof of physical capacity than any test could be.

Lang found the whole Special Forces Officers course to be in that spirit. Officer candidates for the Prefix "3" designator for their Military Occupational Specialty identification code were grouped in their own course to be trained separately from the enlisted men. They were organized in training detachments. Each numbered fifteen officers. The detachments were named for famous guerrilla leaders in American history: Mosby, Rogers, Cochise, etc. There were many foreign officers in the course. France, Italy, Britain, Australia, Canada, Greece and the Republic of Vietnam were all represented among the students. All these officers came from, or were destined for, units analogous to US Army Special Forces. Many had a great deal of combat experience. The Vietnamese were often veterans of the French colonial paratroops in the first Indochina War. Several had been captured at Dien Bien Phu and had spent years in POW camps in North Viet Nam. They hated their communist countrymen.

The course was designed to produce leaders for the behind-the-lines mission in Eastern Europe. The classroom work concentrated on the history and theory of resistance warfare with many case studies of particular campaigns. Theorists like T.E. Lawrence, Mao, Guevara and the like were studied as well as the practices of such groups as SOE, Special Air Service, EOKA (the Cypriot Resistance to British Rule), the Zionist resistance to the British, and resistance groups in the Balkans in World War II. It was an exhaustive process of reading and analysis. There were many map exercises in which the process of establishing, controlling and sustaining new resistance efforts behind Soviet lines, or indeed, any lines were planned.

Clandestine political warfare against the occupying power was taught as were: propaganda operations of various kinds, sabotage and the rudiments of recruiting and "running" espionage agents. Activities that in another day and cause would be called terrorism were included to be used as necessary. Assassination techniques were an integral part of the training. It was clearly expressed in the training program that terrorism and assassination were to be employed against occupation forces and collaborators. A lot of time was spent learning the right way to plan guerrilla operations, how to approach and strike the enemy's rear, and then escape to fight again. It was stressed that guerrillas could not be "spent" in operations that lost a lot of men or even just a few. If that happened, people would not want to join the movement. The theoretical work was quite thorough.

After that, activity shifted to more "hands-on" fieldwork. This was preceded by opportunities to demonstrate various abilities.

Swimming was done in a big indoor pool. After that test, Lang's detachment was escorted to a field behind the pool where there was a long trench filled with water. The student officers were in field uniform. They had been told to wear their most worn clothing and boots. Each was given a pack loaded with bricks and an old rifle to sling across his back. The student was then told to jump into the trench at the near end and proceed the thirty yards to the far end where a ladder waited.

When it was his turn Lang jumped in and let himself sink the eight feet to the bottom. He walked and hopped along the muddy bottom, popping up every few yards for a breath of air, exhaling going up and inhaling before he sank again beneath the water. He had been intensively trained in survival swimming at VMI and he could "bob" like this all day long. At the far end he climbed the ladder and was rebuked for not swimming. "You did not say I had to swim," he said. The instructors conferred and decided he was right. He passed.

The course required that he renew his acquaintanceship with parachutes and parachute rigging for personnel parachutes and "door bundles." This required a few days in the parachute school at Fort Bragg. He passed.

Land navigation was easily demonstrated in the piney woods surrounding Fort Bragg. He had always been good at that. The little red chigger bugs that infested these woods were a nuisance, and the number of poisonous snakes that hissed at him in the night was worrisome but, he passed easily.

There was no PT test.

In fact, there was no harassment of any kind. Instructors never raised their voices. The belief was strong in Special Forces at that time that one must learn to deal with people calmly. Guerrillas were armed civilians. The point was often stressed that if such people were angered, they would become unreliable and dangerous.

There was specialized training:

Demolitions were an important subject. Various standard explosives were studied and employed as well as infernal mixtures that could be created in the field from available materials. The application of these materials to the destruction of a variety of structures was taught. Bridges were a matter of particular interest. Diamond shaped charges, shaped charges, Special Atomic Demolition Munitions for big bridge destruction were trained on (without the foreigners present), as well as booby traps. The list of techniques taught and practiced was impressive.

Communications from the field to distant bases was an important feature of the training. This was done using a manual Morse HF radio called AN/GRC-109 with antennae cut to frequency lengths and oriented toward the receiver. This low power radio could communicate over several thousand miles. The use of this radio was a constant menace because of the threat of triangulation, so the radio had to be quickly moved after each use. Codes and ciphers were an indispensable part of the communications training.

Several weeks were spent in an abbreviated version of what the enlisted SF medics were taught. Even so, a great deal of medical and field surgical technique was imparted. Later in life, Lang took part in the amputation of limbs in the field when there were a lot of casualties and not enough hands. In retirement from the army, he was often asked by doctors how he knew so much of their business. He hesitated to tell them the extent of his experience.

A lot of time was spent in familiarization with light and heavy weapons. The student officers practiced assembly and disassembly, marksmanship training, and employment of such weapons in a variety of settings. Most of the training was done on foreign weapons: submachine guns such as the British Sten and Sterling guns, The Swedish K, the Danish Madsen, the Soviet PPSH and many others. Warsaw Pact-made machine guns and mortars were particularly appreciated for training purposes since they would presumably be available from casualties inflicted on enemy forces in Soviet rear areas.

Concurrently, tactical and operational training began with a series of practice raids that began in each case with a night parachute jump into the objective area or nearby. In some cases, there would be a link-up with troops or local civilians playing the role of guerrillas. The guerillas provided additional firepower in the actual assault and guides to and from the objective. The "guerrillas" and students usually lit a grassy landing strip with hooded flashlights for an aircraft to land and retrieve the student raiding party. World War II airplanes like the C-47 Dakota added to the cinematic illusion of the thing. At times Lang expected to see a Lysander emerge from the darkness to pick him up with his friends. It would not have surprised him to see Sir Ralph Richardson leaning out the cockpit window. After a flight back to Pope Air Force Base, the ritual was to have breakfast before dawn at the officer's field ration mess on Smoke Bomb Hill at Fort Bragg, where the cooks on duty around the clock produced wondrous, hearty meals. The option offered was to eat American food or dishes from any of a dozen other countries. Home by 7 AM, Lang would shower and crawl into bed beside Marguerite.

Some of these practice operations developed into memorable situations. There was one dark night in which Lang exited the aircraft loaded up with his weapon, ammunition, water, a radio and a 40-pound Personal Ammunition and Equipment (PAE) bag hung under his reserve parachute. The jump was onto Camp McCall, an abandoned sub-post of Fort Bragg forty miles to the west.

The airplane, a Curtis Commando C-46, bucked and jumped all over the sky. He stumbled on the way to his exit from the aircraft and bounced off the trailing edge of the door as he fell into the darkness. His helmet scraped along the fuselage before it went under the tail with the rest of him. He tipped his head back as the airplane noise lessened and watched his canopy open. Two nylon compartments in the canopy were blown into flapping shreds by the force of the opening. The additional turbulence through which the plane flew that night did its best to tear his parachute to bits. This loss of supporting nylon in the canopy meant that he would be falling faster than normal. The normal speed of landing was equivalent to the experience of jumping off a two-story building. Additional speed was not welcome. The night was very dark. There were no lights at all visible on the ground. Lang dropped his PAE bag to the end of its 30-foot tether. This was very important. If it was still hung on him when he landed there would be broken bones. He sensed the approach of the ground and looked straight out to the front. If he watched the ground during landing, he would inevitably tense and would probably be injured.

The PAE bag went into the basement of a disassembled building. It hung halfway down the wall. He hit the ground hard just outside the basement. The canopy of the parachute was still inflated. It lay down on the ground for a few seconds. The ground wind increased slightly. The canopy inflated and dragged him away from the hole in the ground. The wind then decreased, and the forty-pound bag dragged him back to the edge of the basement. He could not see down into the void and had no idea what might be down there. The canopy dragged him back from the edge. This cycle was repeated several times before he could draw his jump knife and saw through the PAE bag lanyard with the serrated edge. When he arrived at his home the next day, Marguerite was curious as to how he had gotten so scraped and bruised.

The "graduation exercise" in this course was a two-week guerilla army generation "problem" in the Uwharrie National Forest in western North Carolina. This was called "Cherokee Trail." The "Aggressor" enemy would be played by two battalions of the 82nd Airborne Division. The guerrillas, subject population and underground resistance to 82nd Airborne "tyranny," would be played by the local North Carolina mountaineers with their stills, guns, missing teeth and all. After intensive preparation and briefing, he and his student detachment were parachuted from a C-123 Provider into a cornfield inside the national forest.

With the "stick" still in the air and descending with their cargo "bundles," automobile headlights came on all around the cornfield. The mountaineers had turned out *en masse* to welcome their "liberators." Lang could hardly pick himself up out of the corn before he was mobbed by several teenagers who wanted to carry his gear off the Drop Zone. The team departed the area quickly in pickup trucks. It would not do to be trapped by the 82nd so early in the "fight."

Several days passed in training guerrilla recruits, scouting operational targets and establishing radio communications to headquarters at Fort Bragg. Attacks and ambushes then began against the forces of the aggressors. These were always conducted with the mountaineer guerrillas playing the major role, and the Special Forces men coaching and accompanying them.

Several of these operations were fixed in Lang's memory. He was the lead SF man in a night raid on a bridge that carried the enemy's main supply route. After an approach march through the forest, his party found the guerrillas "staking out" the bridge. There were no guards. Dummy demolitions charges were set under the bridge. Lang remembered that he put his bare hand through the wall of a wasp's nest and stood quietly while the bugs crawled up and down his arm.

A few nights later, the SF trainee officers brought a hundred guerrillas together to attack the command post of the 2nd Battalion, 504th Parachute Infantry Regiment. The guerrillas captured the CO of the battalion. This enraged the paratroops who stepped up their patrolling in the mountains where they "lost" yet more men to ambushes.

For Lang, the climax of the exercise came in the middle of the second week. On that night. he was in charge of several of his detachment comrades for the purpose of meeting with a guerrilla leader at the man's farmhouse. The SF students rode to the meeting in the back of an old truck. They were covered with a dirty piece of canvas. On the forest roads, the civilian guerrilla driver drove so fast that the old truck began to "float" on its springs and wobble back and forth across the dirt road. Lang knocked on the back window of the cab and yelled, "Slow down!"

The driver stopped the vehicle. He and an SF major from the school who was an umpire got out of the cab. The civilian walked to Lang and started screaming. "Who do you think you are? I'm not a soldier! To hell with you! You are just a god damned kid. Screw you! Get lost! You're not riding in my truck!"

Ah, Lang thought. *The umpire put him up to this.* "OK. Calm down," he told the bearded man in bib front overhauls.

"To hell with you, you skinny little Yankee runt!" the country man yelled. He stepped forward and poked Lang in the chest. That was a mistake.

Lang saw this as an existential threat to his authority. His rifle muzzle came up and was lodged in the man's throat. "How would you like to die here tonight?" he asked the driver.

The man fell silent.

The umpire stepped around the farmer to ask what they would do with the body.

"We'll say the 82nd did it at an ambush site when we find one," Lang said. "There are several right around here."

"And what about me?" the major asked"

"That depends on you, sir," one of the men behind Lang said. "That depends on you and what we think of you."

The major made a few notes. "All right," he said. "I told him to do all this... Get back in the truck."

Lang took the muzzle away from the man's neck. "Anything else?" he asked.

The driver shook his head and turned away. "Would he have shot me?" he was heard to ask the major.

Lang expected to be expelled from the course and perhaps the army itself, but two days later, he was told that a board had decided that he would qualify and that he would command the detachment from that time until graduation a few weeks later.

There was no graduation ceremony.

The Langs moved on to Washington for six months where they studied Spanish together in a contract language school on 14th Street at New York Avenue. This was two blocks from the White House. They were gifted linguistically and soaked up Spanish like sponges. It is an easy language to learn. The grammar is regular, the lexicon is not large. The six months passed quickly and pleasantly. They lived in a one-bedroom apartment in Fairfax County, Virginia just across the Potomac. Three other officers destined for the 8th SF Group in Panama were in their small class. They had a lot of trouble with the language.

In April they left Washington. There was a shortage of army housing in the Canal Zone. This had been caused by the increased garrison brought together to execute the Kennedy Administration's counterinsurgency and development policy in Latin America. As a result, he would have to go to Panama without his wife until he could find housing for her. They visited her mother for a week and then drove to Quebec City, passing by the Rangeley Lakes in western Maine. Marguerite's mother protested the trip. She had lived in Canada for much of her early life and explained that near arctic conditions would still prevail at Quebec City at that time of the year. She was right! The province of Quebec was a giant icebox. The St. Lawrence was frozen. They crossed from the east bank on a car ferry that was also an icebreaker.

A few days in Quebec City was more than enough. There were a few early colonial buildings to visit, but the weather was so bad that the Langs huddled together in their hotel. One evening they dined in a small café evocative of a Paris bistro. Marguerite could speak both metropolitan and Canadian French with equal fluency. In the land of her ancestors, she spoke their language. Lang spoke good French but at that point in his life he had a pronounced accent and it was the accent of a native English speaker. He noticed after a while that he was being watched with some hostility from neighboring tables. *Ah, a good-looking French-Canadian girl with an Anglo,* he thought. He looked around the room and announced that he was American, not Canadian and that his mother was French Canadian. The atmosphere in the room warmed immediately, and a bottle of wine was sent to their table. They visited Montreal, found it boring and as cold as Quebec. They went home.

He left his wife in Maine with her mother and drove to Charleston, South Carolina where he shipped his sad little car to Cristobal, C.Z. In his baggage was the .357 Colt Python revolver that he had bought as a side arm. He flew to the Canal Zone by charter air. By the time he was halfway there, he missed her.

He reported to the 8th Special Forces Group with his classmates from Spanish school. The adjutant, a Military Police major from the group's MP detachment, announced at their joint interview that the other three would be assigned to the two Special Forces companies in the 8th SF Group, and Lang would be the Executive officer of Headquarters Company of the Group. The adjutant told the other three that they should prepare for immediate deployment to Mobile Training Teams at work in Central and South America. They left the room.

Lang waited.

"Yes?" the adjutant asked.

"Why me?"

"Don't you think you should just accept it?" was the answer. The major was not an SF man. He was a member of one of the attached technical support units needed to do training in South America. That made the situation worse from Lang's point of view.

Colonel Arthur Simons, the 8th Group commander, came out of his office. This was behind the adjutant's anteroom.

Lang recognized "The Bull" immediately. The big, slope-shouldered body and the massive grizzled head were unmistakable. Lang came to the position of attention.

The adjutant looked startled.

The sergeant major put his head out of his office to know what was happening.

Simons held out his hand.

The adjutant put a file in it.

"VMI," the colonel said after a moment. "Regular Army, they were impressed with you at Bragg. You chose to join us." This was not a question.

"Yes, colonel."

"Tell him," Simons said and went back into his room.

"Headquarters Company has the only mess in the group," the major began. "Our soldiers contribute to an imprest fund with which we hire Cuna Indians from the San Blas Islands. These Indians do the kitchen police work that the soldiers would normally be required to do, washing dishes, pots and pans...."

"Yes, major, I have done KP. The grease trap is my favorite duty."

The adjutant looked at the file.

"I was not always an officer," Lang said.

Simons laughed beyond the wall.

"The Indians speak no English," the adjutant continued. "You speak the best Spanish by test of any Anglo officer in the group."

"Ah," Lang said. "There are problems in the kitchen?"

"Yes, and a few others that have nothing to do with the mess..."

"Go fix this, lieutenant," the unseen Simons said.

"Yes, Colonel." He saluted the adjutant and left.

"Have you ever known any VMI people?" Simons asked the adjutant after Lang had departed for Headquarter Company. "No? This one is typical, duty bound, but unwilling to take horseshit from anyone. Ray Gallagher's managerial problems will end. If this guy has to work day and night, that is what he will do."

Captain Gallagher was a skinny little Irishman from the streets of South Boston. He was what his own people call a "skin job." He looked a bit like the early film actor Barry Fitzgerald. He was middle-aged, minimally educated and a veteran of twenty years in the Airborne Force. His friends knew that he was not "up to the job" for any kind of training work in Latin America. A high level of leadership quality in Headquarters Company was essential to the well-being of the 8th Special Forces and its collection of attached units. These units were often referred to by the SF men as "the Peace Corps."

Headquarters Company housed and fed a variety of people, as well as performing the administrative tasks needed for all. The troop mess was important, but so were operation of the motor pool, a mailroom that sorted and forwarded deliveries to men deployed across Latin America. The company had control of all foreign equipment and arms storage facilities as well as housing for a variety of enlisted soldiers. The most numerous of these were to be found in a parachute rigging platoon that packed and inspected all items of air equipment used in the 8th SF Group. These soldiers were Quartermaster Corps men, distinguished for their red baseball caps and low collective IQ.

Captain Gallagher greeted Lang with enthusiasm. He said that he had been told that Lang would clear up the difficulties left by the last XO. That officer had not seemed able to deal with the army cooks in the kitchen. Gallagher looked at Lang closely to see if he "bought" that story.

The first sergeant was an old SF man named Freitag. He, too, looked at Lang, then at Gallagher, and held out his hand. "Welcome," was all he said. Lang judged both Freitag and Gallagher to be ineffective. If they had not been, they would have "fixed" the company's many problems.

The first two or three nights in the Bachelor Officer's Quarters, he was awakened in the middle of the night by "whooping and hollering" in a hallway. He assumed correctly that someone was drunk and celebrating. He went out one night into the corridor to find a tall, undernourished looking man knocking a trash can around the hallway with a bullwhip. Lang held out a hand. "Pat Lang, I just showed up."

"Shelton; people call me 'pappy' cause ah'm older. Where you gonna be in this lash-up?"

"I got stuck with a shit job in HHC, for now."

"Ah see. Ah'll go outside fuh practice."

"Thanks," Lang laughed. "Let's go out and get lit some night."

Soon after Lang reported to the 8th Group, the Panamanian *"Partido Del Pueblo"* re-started the anti-American riots of the previous year. Several thousand nationalists and communists marched in the main streets of Colon. They tried to break into the Central Bank of Panama branch in Colon, the Panamanian city on the Caribbean coast. They approached the Canal Zone border.

There had been similar but larger riots the previous year. Four soldiers from the 10th Infantry Regiment had been killed by snipers in a parking lot that was located between Cristobal, the Canal Zone town, and Colon. A general break down in Panama-US relations followed that was not easily overcome.

Since those "troubles," the US and Panamanian governments had thought about what would happen if a Panamanian mob invaded the Canal Zone and decided to prevent a recurrence.

As soon as the rioters appeared, Colonel Simons was directed to take charge of border defense on the Atlantic side of the isthmus.... 8th Group was always short of men in Panama. Most people were absent on training missions. Simons took all the SF men he could find to the border. This included Captain Gallagher, Lieutenant Lang and Freitag, the First Sergeant of Headquarters Company. There were perhaps thirty SF men in all.

Before they moved to the border, Lang went to the group arms room, a facility for which he was responsible, and signed out an M-14 sniper rifle with a telescopic sight. The gun was kept zeroed for 300 yards in a special "ready rack."

About ten in the morning, Lang was standing behind Simons in a parking lot on the Cristobal-Colon border when a shooter on a roof top in the distance fired a round that skipped off a car roof.

Simons said, "Don't point." He looked around and saw Lang. "Do you see him?"

Lang nodded, "Yes, Colonel"

"Are you any good with that thing?" he asked, meaning the rifle carried in the crook of Lang's arm as he always carried rifles.

"Yes. I can hit him."

Simons nodded.

Lang and Freitag retired around the corner of a building. They looked at a one-to-five-thousand scale town plan and decided the range was a little over three hundred yards.

"What would you say the 'drop' is?" Lang asked.

"About six inches at this distance, would you like me to take the shot?" the first sergeant asked.

Lang looked at him.

"Sorry, sir."

Lang wrapped the sling around his arm to stabilize the rifle and leaned against the corner of the building. He found a sight picture that placed the aiming point just above the distant head visible over the building's wall. He took a breath, released half, and squeezed his whole hand while concentrating on sight alignment. He was careful not to anticipate the instant of the shot. He thought of Marguerite's body to avoid that. The rifle leapt unexpectedly in his embrace. He watched the armor piercing, black-tipped bullet chop through the masonry wall as the man was knocked backward in the moment of death.

"Damn fine shot," Freitag commented.

Several sergeants congratulated.

"First man?' Simons asked.

"Yes, Colonel."

"Where did you learn to shoot like that?" Simons asked.

The sergeants and Gallagher waited for an answer.

"'Been shooting a long time, Colonel, a long time, started at twelve up in Maine, taught by an uncle..."

"Captain Gallagher, Lieutenant Lang will be in charge of our sharpshooters..." He departed to deal with other problems.

Later that day, a car full of Panamanians who may have had a drink or two, drove hell bent toward a sand-bagged position on the border that had five SF men in it, including Colonel Simons. Warning shots were fired, one of which went through the radiator. The car sped on with the Panamanians cheering and firing out the windows.

Simons waved his hand dismissively, and a LAW anti-tank round struck the driver's side of the car's windshield followed by a volley of rifle fire that killed everyone in the car. The vehicle decelerated and stopped. An incendiary rifle grenade set it afire. The car burned in the road in a gathering silence.

The June 1965 riots were over.

Lang rode back to Fort Gulick in the back of a truck with his snipers.

He and Freitag sat on a bench facing the parade ground and handed a fifth of rye back and forth between them. He had killed two men that day, the first of many. Freitag was not Lang's idea of a really good NCO, but at that moment he wanted the man's company.

He went into Cristobal the next night to visit the Canal Company telephone and telegraph office. He needed to talk to Marguerite. Their relationship was so deeply and intensely intellectual, spiritual and sexual that he needed frequent contact with her. This was a weakness in him that was reflected in his career. He sometimes occasionally declined assignments that would deprive him of her presence. That hurt his promotion prospects.

"I heard there was trouble," she said.

"Not to worry," he said. "Not to worry. I am looking for a house."

With the "entertainment" of the riots behind him, Lang began repairing Gallagher's problems.

The mess account was overdrawn a thousand rations from the USARSO ration breakdown office.

The imprest fund for the Indian KPs had five thousand dollars in it. Not more than a thousand dollars was needed for a month's payroll. The USARSO regulation that governed such funds specified that not more than two months payroll could be held in the fund. An excess in funds in this amount would immediately be thought by the Inspector General to be an indication of intent to embezzle.

"I understand that your cooks like to slap these Indians around. Is that true?" Lang asked the mess sergeant at a meeting called to discuss the kitchen.

"No sir. They wouldn't do that." The mess sergeant was a middle-aged man who was badly overweight. He would not look Lang in the eye.

"No? That's good, because they are all black, and it would grieve me to think that there was something racial in the way they treat these Indians…"

The mess sergeant was silent.

Captain Gallagher hovered in the background but said nothing.

Lang opened a door into a hallway outside the mess hall kitchen. Half a dozen of the Indians filed in accompanied by their *cacique*.

"Diga me la historia de sus vidas aquí. Diga me otra vez," Lang told the Indians.

What emerged from their mouths was a sorry tale of physical and sexual abuse, of extortion of money using physical force and of forced participation in theft of rations and kitchen equipment.

"Anything to say?" Lang asked the mess sergeant. "No? How far are you from retirement?"

"A year... sir"

"Well, the three men named here will receive Non-Judicial Punishment from the company commander. As you can see, he is present and has heard the statements. If the unholy three wish to reject that punishment, the CO will recommend Special Courts-Martial to Group headquarters. I have often been "trial counsel" for such courts, and I can pretty much predict six months confinement at hard labor and reduction to the lowest enlisted grade as the result if there are trials. And you can be added to the list if you feel some great loyalty..." Lang looked hopeful. "No? So be it."

When the Indians had gone, a new topic was introduced. "With regard to the missing and overdrawn rations, I do not believe that this has been a problem of portion control. I am now Mess Officer. What I should do is call in the Criminal Investigation Division of the MPs in order to protect myself from liability. I hereby declare an intention to do this... I will write a memorandum for the record to that effect. I will submit it in two months. In the meantime, I will continue to investigate the details. If, at the end of two months, it appears that the accounting was mistaken, and my ration account was not actually over-drawn, I will drop the matter. Understood?"

Lang watched Gallagher visibly relax in his corner seat. That confirmed a suspicion he had held concerning the CO.

"I will eat in the mess every day to check the quality and quantity of the food. Are we clear?"

In two months, the mess account was in balance.

Lang dealt with the excess funds in the KP account by declaring a contribution "holiday" for several months.

The parachute rigger platoon that was lodged in Headquarters Company was completely out of control. They were much more interested in whoring and fighting in Colon than in their duty. Lang talked to the Rigger platoon leader and got no satisfaction. The officer was no better than his men. Lang told Captain Gallagher that he wanted to charge the Rigger platoon leader and several of the soldiers with various instances of misbehavior and public drunkenness.

Gallagher decided to bestir himself and said that he would take action without legal intervention.

A few days later, Lang heard Gallagher's high-pitched voice as he bellowed, "Get your damned paw off my desk!"

Lang and Sergeant Freitag found the captain on his feet and screaming at a Rigger who was too drunk to stand up. The man had come into the office to ask Freitag for his liberty pass so that he could go into Colon. Freitag refused to give it to him, and the soldier had then gone into Gallagher's adjoining office where he made the mistake of leaning on the company commander's desk. In the Army of that time, to do this was a "mortal sin," something akin to spitting on the captain's mother's grave.

"Goddamn you! Stand up straight!" the captain cried out. He reached into a desk drawer and retrieved a .38 caliber Snub-nosed revolver and four sets of handcuffs.

The Rigger was marched up concrete stairs into a squad bay where a number of men were sleeping or talking. Gallagher tipped the mattress off the drunken rigger's steel bunk and chained the man to the bunk facing down into the metal springs. "You are all responsible for him," Gallagher told the stunned audience. "If he drowns in his puke…"

Back in his office, Gallagher put the .38 back in a drawer of the desk, put his jump boots up on his desk and asked if Lang thought that would do with regard to the Rigger platoon. Rigger behavior improved markedly.

The mailroom was a subject of great interest. There were many complaints from men in the field who had not received bills and payments mailed to them months before. Lang crawled around in the small space on the ground floor of Headquarters Company that housed the mailroom until he found a dozen hidden sacks of mail that the relatively senior mail clerk had not bothered to forward.

"What have you been using?" he asked the big, blond, good-looking clerk. "Is it Marijuana, Cocaine or just liquor?"

"No."

"No?'"

"Sir."

"That's better. The first sergeant will take you to the hospital to see if that is true..."

"It is true, sir.

"That's too bad, because if it is true, you are a lazy shit who doesn't care about other people."

The man looked up.

"Want a piece of me?" Lang asked. "We can do that. I'll 'strip my blouse' like they say in the movies. No?"

"No, sir. I heard."

"You heard what?"

"About Colon, people who were there say you looked like you didn't give a damn..."

"OK. You will work every day from dawn to dusk under my personal supervision until this is cleared up, and then I will fire you, understood? I would charge you, but there are others involved."

"Yes, sir."

The 8ᵗʰ Group arms room was a big problem. This facility held all the small arms in the unit that were not U.S. standard issue. Two sub-machine guns were missing.

"You have a week to get them back with the right serial numbers or the CID and FBI will be informed," he told the sergeant armorer.

"Well, Lieutenant, maybe I can and maybe I can't," the man began.

"Don't give me that crap, you stupid asshole. You'll have these guns back here, or you'll be the most popular white man in the Disciplinary Barracks at Leavenworth. Understand?"

"Yes, sir."

"You have a week, and if you get any funny ideas, I am generally armed and will come for you."

"Understood, sir."

The two weapons were returned within the week. The sergeants' "grapevine" soon "reported" that the armorer had sold them to the Panamanian *Guardia Nacional* and had taken several of his pals to visit the *Guardia* and retrieve them.

While Lang was in the midst of purging this *Augean Stable*, a captain from the Group Intelligence staff office, the S-2 shop, stopped by his office to visit. This man, John Carlson, was about Lang's age, a graduate of The Citadel and a native of South Carolina. They chatted for a few minutes. Lang was pleased. He knew few officers in the Group and hoped to have some friends among his peers. This officer seemed to feel some sense of kinship with Lang as well as sympathy for the "messes" he had been left with.

"Your wife is not with you?" Carlson asked.

"Waiting for quarters," Lang said with more than a hint of sadness in his voice.

"Ah," Carlson said. "We can fix that. Canal Company employees go on leave to the states and sub-let their houses."

Lang was instantly attentive.

"Come to dinner at our place tomorrow, Sandy would like to meet you, and we will do some research about a house by then."

"Sandy?"

"My wife, she heard about what you did."

"Ah, I will be pleased...."

Carlson's wife was a delightful Southern lady. Dinner was delicious. The couple's beagle adopted Lang and sat by his feet throughout the evening. Best of all, the Carlsons had found a notice on a Canal Zone bulletin board that advertised a house that sat on a low ridge above Gatun Lock.

Lang and Carlson drove to Gatun the next day. The house was beautiful; the view of the lock was superb. There was a Costa Rican maid, two green parrots and a marmoset that lived in a big wire cage in the garden. The cage contained a little house in which the marmoset could take shelter against the rain. It had its own little blanket therein and could often be seen wrapped in it and contemplating the world through the little door.

The householders were nice country people from Appalachia. After a couple of visits, a bargain was struck, and Lang sent for Marguerite. She arrived within two weeks, just a day after he saw the householders off on a Canal Company steamer bound for New Orleans.

To his surprise, she quickly became attached to the animals at the house, especially the marmoset. Her mother feared domestic animals, and Marguerite had never had any. He often arrived home to find her sitting in the garden talking to the marmoset through the chicken wire. Very soon the little black and white beast would come and sit next to her on a perch in the cage. It made amusing faces at her and chattered in response to her whispers. She fed it bits of fruit and one day as he watched, the marmoset sat close to the wire and licked her fingertips. "Whatever you do," he told her, "don't let it out. It will leave and these people will never forgive me."

One weekend afternoon, they sat on the terrace listening to the trade winds blow gently through the palms while Marguerite talked to her "baby." Lang looked down into the lock and saw an American aircraft carrier in transit to the Pacific. The deck was crowded with "cocooned" helicopters and soldiers lying in deck chairs. There was an extra yellow flag at the ship's yardarm. This meant that the troops on board were part of the 1st Cavalry Division en route to Vietnam. Lang waved.

Marguerite stood and shaded her eyes to see.

Lang was still in uniform from the morning's work and a US flag flew on the terrace.

The troops rose to waive back and to cheer her beauty.

The ship sounded its horn in tribute.

A band practicing on the flight deck struck up "Garryowen."

"Our hearts so stout have got no fame
For soon 'tis known from whence we came
Where'er we go they fear the name
Of Garryowen in glory."

And then, "The Girl I Left Behind Me."

"Though many a name our banner bore
Of former deeds of daring
But they were of the days of yore
With the old ones fate entwines me,
Sweet girl I left behind me."

"Wish you were with them?" she asked.

"Soon enough." he said. "I'll see them again. Let us enjoy this."

The mechanical "mules" pulled the ship through the far lock doors, and the carrier steamed through Gatun Lake toward the Pacific Ocean. The music faded in volume as the vessel moved away but it played on…

"Around her neck she wore a yellow ribbon
She wore it in the winter
And in the month of May
And when I asked her, Why the yellow ribbon?
She said, It's for my lover who is far, far away
Far away, far away, far away, far away
She said, It's for my lover who is far, far away
Far away, far away, far away, far away
She said, It's for my lover who is in the cavalry."

The Langs and the Carlsons grew close. The two couples shared many interests, and the level of education was a close match.

Marguerite began to absorb Southern culture from Sandy Carlson, her new friend. New dishes appeared at the Lang table and immensely valuable lore was transmitted on the fine art of managing a household in an environment filled with servants, street vendors and the like. Sandy was a master of the manner and behavior needed to have servants do what was required without resenting the situation.

Lang loved dogs, and the beagle loved him.

"It's an animal thing," Marguerite explained.

Carlson owned a sailboat berthed at the Panama Canal Yacht club in Cristobal. Lang knew nothing of sailing, but wished to learn. The boat was a locally built thirty-foot sloop constructed of inch thick mahogany. It was a keelboat with ballast built up of cannon balls from the old Spanish forts around Limon Bay. The boat was so heavy and wide in the beam that it was remarkably forgiving. After a few trips in this craft Carlson offered to sell Lang a half interest in the boat. He gratefully accepted and, as a bonus, was eligible to be a Flag Member of the Panama Canal Yacht club for the princely sum of two dollars a month. Neither Marguerite nor Sandy much liked the sloop and the two men spent a lot of time together sailing and drinking local beer.

Captain Gallagher departed into retirement. He had been lucky to escape unscathed without some penalty for the poor job he had done as CO. He thanked Lang for saving him, and Lang's "report card" reflected that. Because of the big war in Asia, he was recalled to active duty and sent to the war. Lang met him there. They were still friends, two paratroopers.

The new company commander, Ellison Gilbert, was nothing like Gallagher. He was an intelligent, well-mannered, kindly man who had been raised from the ranks in the Corps of Engineers. He was a widower whose mother lived with him to care for his three orphaned children. As an Oklahoman, he had a folksy quality and a disciplined spirit that endeared him to all. He was Colonel Simons' personal friend. He was grateful to Lang for sorting out the chaos in his company's administration before his arrival.

Lang haunted the USARSO housing office, and within a month of Marguerite's arrival, they were scheduled to move into a furnished three-story stucco house on Fort Gulick. They went to look at it from outside. The house had five-foot overhangs above the windows. They were built to shade the house from the sun and to keep tropical rains away from the walls. Marguerite loved it.

Carlson eventually told Lang there was an empty position in the intelligence section in Group headquarters. The job was designated as requiring "fill" by a captain, but the Group S-2 major, Carlson himself, and Colonel Simons were agreed that he could have it if he wished.

Marguerite said, "That means you won't be traveling all the time?"

"Yes, not so much."

"Then, I am for it."

Captain Gilbert said he would be sorry not to have Lang's company every day, but that Colonel Simons had spoken to him about the change. "I would have objected if you had been in this job less than six months. That would have looked like you were fired. You have my blessing. You know we will be neighbors when you are in your new house?"

"Yes, sir, right across the back fence if there was a back fence."

A year later, a newly promoted Major Gilbert was ordered to Vietnam. A delegation of enlisted men from Headquarters Company came to the S-2 "shop" to ask Captain Lang to take possession of a collection of money that the men had gathered and to use it for a "going away" present for Gilbert. "The new XO won't do it," one of them said. "He says it is against army regulations."

Lang held his hand out for the money. "I'll do it if you let me contribute…"

Carlson said he was a damned fool. To take or give such a gift was a punishable offense. Carlson then added some money to the "pot."

They went to the Canal Zone "Rod and Gun Club" and bought a Smith and Wesson Combat Masterpiece revolver and had it engraved, "Lest We Forget."

On the appointed day, the company mustered on the basketball court behind the barracks. One of the men came forward to give the revolver to Gilbert. He choked up when he saw the sentiment. The soldiers came forward to shake his hand and wish him good luck.

Lang's new job in the intelligence section of the staff was one for which he was qualified by nature and accumulated learning.

The S-2 was an infantry major.

There were two captains.

One was John Carlson, and the other was now Lang.

Carlson was an officer of the new Army Intelligence and Security branch. He had been head of the counter-intelligence detachment of the 82nd Airborne Division, had never been anything but an intelligence officer and knew the work thoroughly. Carlson was the real manager of the section.

The major concentrated on golfing and politicking at USARSO Headquarters at Fort Amador on the Pacific side of the isthmus.

The senior NCO was a master sergeant of long service who was a native of Guatemala. While Lang was still a college student, this sergeant had been deeply involved in the training of the Cuban "Bay of Pigs Brigade" while seconded to the CIA. In 1965, many senior SF sergeants held reserve commissions given to them in preparation for a future wartime enlargement of the army. This man was a reserve lieutenant. He was called to active duty in that rank a few months after Lang joined the section.

There were five enlisted analysts who were not qualified SF soldiers but good at what they did. One of them was a "stumpy" little man who was Brazilian by birth, had been a journalist before he joined the American army and was an endless store of knowledge about his native country. He and the other enlisted analysts specialized in de-briefing returned mobile training teams and converting the fruits of their observation into Intelligence Information Reports that were sent to a long list of recipients by classified mail or wire.

Lang's principal daily job was to supervise the analysts in their almost "industrial" task of producing an endless stream of reports to feed Washington's appetite for information. He edited their reports, gave them guidance and briefed teams departing to the field on current political and insurgent situations in the areas they were destined for.

Late in his tenure in this job, he out-briefed Major "Pappy" Shelton and his team for a mission they had in Bolivia. Their orders were to train a Bolivian Army counterinsurgency infantry battalion for the pursuit of Che Guevara's Indian guerrillas. Lang presented all the available evidence and suggested to Shelton that Guevara would be found in the eastern half of the country where the many jungle-covered valleys would provide shelter. There were other 8th SF Group teams working in Bolivia in a variety of medical, engineering and intelligence training roles, but it was understood that Shelton was to coordinate all of them through a communications team in La Paz.

A couple of months later, an SF sergeant treating villagers at a medical "fair" near Cochabamba, was told "the man you seek is nearby."

Shelton moved quickly, but by the time his Bolivian battalion arrived, Guevara and his men had fled. Shelton chased them cross-country for hours in a process that could have only one ending. Bolivian peasants were perpetually under-nourished and accustomed to living with hunger dulled with coca leaves. Shelton fed his Indians three thousand calories a day for months in preparation for this pursuit. His troops simply ran Guevara's men into the ground and took many prisoners, including Che. Shelton called from Cochabamba to pass the news.

8th SF Group quickly arranged transportation for the prisoner to the Canal Zone only to be told that the Bolivian commander of the Bolivian battalion had summarily executed him.

Shelton visited Guevara the afternoon before the killing. The guerrilla chief laughed when he saw the Green Berets. "Yes, I thought so," he said.

At the time he started the S-2 work, Carlson told Lang that he would be expected to serve as the 8th Group repository of collective knowledge of Latin America. To that end, Lang read everything in the considerable library of the intelligence section, read all the operational reports of the last years and then crossed the isthmus to read in the holdings of USARSO and US Southern Command Headquarters.

While there, he encountered Colonel Jaime Castro, his first battalion commander in the army. Castro was a great help in Lang's researches. Marguerite was pleased to hear that her old friend Maria Castro was at

Quarry Heights, the headquarters post on the Pacific side of the isthmus. The Langs were invited to dinner with the Castros and accepted. It was much like a family reunion.

As part of his self-prescribed learning program on Latin America, Lang enrolled for off duty study in the Canal Zone campus programs of Florida State University. At nearby Fort Davis, he studied Latin American history, economics, politics and anthropology. He was enrolled in these courses for over a year.

At the same time, his wife took courses intended to give her a teaching credential. Officer's wives had a hard time finding work near the husband's duty station. Employers knew that the husband would inevitably be transferred and hesitated to hire them. While in this process she succeeded in competing for a job in the high school equivalency program for soldiers. She taught mathematics at night to GIs and was obviously someone of great interest to them. One of them asked if she was married to the mean looking SF lieutenant who they saw occasionally at Fort Gulick. When they were assured that she was, they lost interest in anything but the algebra she was trying to teach them.

The production level of valuable reports generated by Lang's analysts rose steadily. Under his sympathetic guidance, the analysts knew that their work was appreciated. He sought promotion for them and in several cases succeeded in getting it.

The work was too routine for his taste, but fortunately its placement in a Special Forces group situated overseas provided many chances for diversion from that routine.

Lang found time to attend the Jungle Operations course at Fort Sherman on the other side of Limon Bay and the canal. This two-week program put him in the field with the troops of an infantry brigade preparing to deploy to Vietnam. He enjoyed being back with enlisted soldiers under these conditions and because of his skill in small unit tactics was frequently asked to lead.

All Special Forces soldiers were parachute qualified and paid a monthly bonus as such. The payment required them to jump regularly into various kinds of terrain. At the beginning of his time in the 8th SF Group, Lang was in the habit of volunteering to act as "wind dummy" for a mass jump. This meant that he would not steer his parachute during descent so that the Drop Zone safety party could judge the direction the winds blew. On several jumps he ended his trip to the ground hung in an eighty- or a hundred-foot tree in the jungle surrounding the DZ where he waited for a helicopter to "grab" the apex of his canopy and pull him from the tree. He stopped volunteering for this hazard when a seasoned master sergeant took him aside and told him to stop. "We get it, sir," the sergeant said. "You're 'in'. Knock it off before one of us has to go tell that beautiful girl the bad news."

The 8th Group had a mission to rescue downed astronauts in Latin America wherever they might descend in an emergency. To be ready for that, the rescue team with Lang among them practiced making night jumps in "smoke jumper suits" into heavy forest and into Gatun Lake itself. The suits were one-piece coveralls with helmets like those worn by fencers. This was dangerous business.

Panama itself offered many chances for an adventurous outdoor life. Lang went several times to the San Blas Islands far down the Caribbean coast towards Columbia. His Cuna Indian KPs had come from there. The Cuna lived there in splendid separation from the world. They were farmers and fishermen. Lang was well thought of among them for having defended them from the cooks. On one occasion he traveled there with Marguerite in an old C-47 Dakota, owned by an American expatriate drunk who flew tourists in and out of an abandoned fighter airstrip near the islands. When he handed his wife down out of the airplane, he looked around in dismay at the surrounding triple canopy jungle and the pierced steel planking of the runway. Grass and bushes two and three feet tall were growing through the openings. The group boated out to the islands in motorized dugout canoes. The American officers' ladies were enchanted.

Marguerite walked through the narrow streets among the straw buildings following a group of Indian women who wanted to show her how they lived. Not many could speak Spanish, and one of his KPs translated for her from the Cuna language into Spanish. It was a glorious sunny day under a southern sky.

Lang and Carlson returned to the waters near the islands a few months later when they voyaged in a friend's sailboat to Nombre de Dios and Puerto Bello on the pirate coast. The trip to the east was easy with a following breeze and favorable current. They anchored off Henry Morgan's old base to spearfish for a couple of days. Lang long remembered hammerhead shark grilled on a white sand beach with wind sighing in coconut palms. There were fish and shrimp glowing in the water everywhere at night.

The trip home was not so much fun. The wind was adverse and the current running steadily against them. To make a mile of headway to the west, they sailed long traverses to seaward and then toward the land. They had a small auxiliary motor, a long shaft "British Seagull." It flooded several times. Night found them off a Panamanian village glowing onshore. They could hear a generator running and music from a radio in the local cantina. The adventurers anchored the sloop outside the surf line. The owner stayed aboard while Carlson and Lang shot in through the breakers in the dinghy. The local *Guardia* sergeant waited with a pistol. The villagers stood ready with shovels and axes to support him. They had thought that the shadowy vessel offshore carried Cuban infiltrators come to spread their revolution in Panama. A telephone call brought the wives from the Canal Zone for a rescue.

Lang's reputation as a briefer and teacher spread throughout the US forces in Panama, and he was frequently invited to lecture on the context of the effort being made by the United States to create social progress in Latin America. Unfortunately for him, he believed less and less in the efficacy of these efforts, however well intentioned. He travelled extensively in both Central America and the Southern continent. The more he saw for himself, the more he believed that the vested interest of the landowner *latifundista* class would not allow the kind of beneficial transformation that counterinsurgency doctrine sought. He could do nothing about the US policy, but frustration grew.

Lang sought chances to spend time outside the office. US Air Force South conducted a SERE School for aircrews. The acronym stood for "Survival, Escape, Resistance and Evasion." This training was designed to prepare aircrews for the struggle to survive when shot down behind enemy lines or in remote wilderness. USAFSO routinely asked 8th SFGA to provide a couple of Green Berets to go into the field with the air force trainees. What was desired was for the SF men to make sure that the air force people did not perish out in the jungle. Lang went through one of these cycles. The field craft needed was elementary to him. He could survive forever with the equipment a "downed" airman would have in his survival kit, but the really interesting

feature of this training was the time spent with the Choco Indians in the deep, inaccessible jungle near the Colombian border. These Indians were the kind seen in the Amazonian forests. They filed their teeth, cut their hair in the familiar bowl shape and fished and hunted for a living while the women cultivated small plots in clearings that they burned in the forests. They were very different from the Cuna of the Atlantic Islands who were highly organized socially and lived in large villages. The Choco lived in small settlements under the leader of a chief who was the absolute ruler. Lang found them fascinating. Like the Cuna, the Choco seemed to like Lang. He returned often to spend a few days with them and learn their ways. This experience served him well with tribesmen across the world.

The S-2 section continued to play a major role in designing and conducting training projects within the 8th SFGA.

Resistance to interrogation was taught in a "Prisoner of War" camp that the 8th Group ran at Battery Sherman across Limon Bay. The "commandant" of the PW camp was a major assigned to 8th Group who had been a prisoner of the Chinese in Korea. He reproduced his experience in the training that he conducted. Most of the training was conducted for SF men flown in from Fort Bragg, North Carolina. There were various kinds of; confinement enclosures, sleep deprivation, and harassment with sound played at all hours of the day and night. The sound was generally discordant music, or the cries of animals being slaughtered. Prisoners were kept naked and given items of their own clothing as rewards for cooperation. It was grim business, and it lasted several days at a time. Lang and John Carlson were the principal interrogators in this training. After a few iterations of these endless sessions of intimidation, undermining of confidence and mockery, Lang came to hate this duty and always apologized to the trainees when the ordeal had ended.

The 8th SFG had a contingency mission to infiltrate Cuba if war occurred. This was for the classic mission of organizing guerrilla resistance. They practiced for that mission in quarterly exercises that were elaborate, time consuming and dangerous. The procedure was to isolate an "Operational Detachment A" at an old coast artillery fort near France Field on the Atlantic side of the isthmus. Once confined there and cut off from communication with the outside world, the A Team was barraged with a mass of information that indicated a degenerating political situation between Cuba and the United States. An actual Cuban exile was introduced to the preparation as an "asset" exfiltrated from Cuba to help them prepare, re-enter with them, and "broker" the link-up with his guerrilla band. The "theater" involved in all this was comprehensive and thorough. It convinced the team that they were going to war.

At the end, they were issued live ammunition and demolitions, were loaded on an old USAF transport and flown across the Caribbean to what they thought was Cuba. The navigator kept a chart on his table where they could see it indicated flight to a DZ a hundred miles west of Guantanamo Bay. The navigator did his real work on a chart in the cockpit that showed the true course to a DZ east of Ponce in Puerto Rico where the exercise would be conducted. Lang acted as jumpmaster on several of these flights. The air force flew low across the water as the afternoon faded into night. The door was always open, and the aircraft was so far down "on the deck" that it would have been possible to fish out the door. Five miles out from the coast, the heavily burdened team stood to prepare to jump. Once they were inspected and hooked to the anchor line cable, Lang would take a "bull horn" and announce that this was an exercise and require that each man indicate that he understood. "Stand in the door," came next and then, "Go!" with a slap on the butt for the first man.

Lang would go out last to help assemble them in the sugar cane field below for the "war game." This system worked well until another jumpmaster in another exercise forgot to tell the team that this was an exercise before they jumped. To compound the problem, the air force dropped this team into a cane field distant from the desired one, and contact was lost with them. There followed a frantic search for the team. They were on "radio silence." Fortunately, they sat up on a hill and watched traffic the next day and decided they could not be in Cuba. Procedure was changed to prevent a recurrence.

The biggest exercise Lang and Carlson played in was a USARSO game in which the US Army "line" brigade stationed in the Canal Zone was required to clear a large, forested area of supposed guerrillas. The brigade had three battalions of infantry, one of which was mechanized, a tank battalion, a towed artillery battalion and the usual assortment of logistical and other support units. All in all, the brigade had about three thousand officers and men. USARSO designed the exercise so that the brigade was to move forward along two dirt roads in the jungle for about 15 miles. There were no people living in the maneuver area. 150 Latin American cadets from the School of the Americas would be the "Aggressor" opponents to the brigade under their teachers. USARSO ordered that the 8th SF should provide a few people to introduce a note of Unconventional Warfare realism in the "game." The brigade objected to this but was overruled by USARSO. Major General Alger suggested that the people who had run the Rio Hato "Adventure Training" be given the job.

Carlson and Lang were told to take charge of this. They asked the School of the Americas for 20 cadets in civilian clothes as helpers. They thought about the average American GIs that they had seen in the Canal Zone in training, and decided that these soldiers, unlike the SF men, were frightened by the forest and the animals in it. To make use of that, they designed and executed a psychological warfare program in which they printed leaflets and sponsored radio broadcasts that announced that the deadly Bushmaster snake was about to come into its breeding season. This creature was black in color, 10 to 15 feet long and was indeed venomous and aggressive. The Bushmaster was the only snake in the world that frequently stalked and attacked humans. Lang and Carlson made lunchtime visits to PX snack bars in the brigade's area where they could be heard discussing the Bushmaster menace. They then approached the management of an American Legion post located on the "start line" of the exercise. The Legion post readily agreed to let the SF men use their facility as a safe house from which to observe the brigade's motor movements. A manual morse radio team was installed in the attic. Carlson announced that he would run this end of the operation. Sandwiches and beer were major features of the Legion post's hospitality.

Lang got the job of taking his "guerrillas" and several SF men into the forest to wreck the brigade's attack. He took his men way back in the woods a couple of kilometers from each of the two axes of advance. Then he used the cadets to improve two old tracks just to a state that was just good enough for the movement of military vehicles.

As the exercise began, the brigade moved forward along the two routes while pushing the main body of School of the Americas cadets before them.

Carlson passed strengths and spacing to Lang over the HF keyed radio. Lang passed this data over low power voice radio to the two SF sergeants waiting with "guerrillas" near the routes of advance. They let all the fighting forces pass by and then began systematically to halt and seize logistics and communications vehicles as they came by. The guerrillas drove the vehicles back into the "motor pool" that Lang began to assemble under camouflage in the deep jungle.

This loss of vehicles was soon noticed by the brigade. They sent a company of troops back to clear the roadblocks. By the time they reached the ambush areas, they had passed many posters placed on trees that "spoke" of the snake danger. The SF men faded back into the woods and watched the infantry's futile search of the area near the road. They were clearly afraid to go deep into the woods.

New tracks were prepared from the "motor pool" to the routes of advance, and the process of dismounting and starving the brigade of fuel, food and water continued.

An unexpected development was the desire of a number of brigade drivers to volunteer into the guerrilla force. Lang accepted them, and "swore" them to loyalty to the: Circle Trigon Cause. Everyone enjoyed that. There was a lot of food in the trucks, but Lang's desperados also received a helicopter delivery of sandwiches from the American Legion kitchen.

By the third day, the brigade was immobilized. They were out of fuel. They could not advance. They could not withdraw. Their troops were afraid of the snakes. The men were hungry. The brigade had been defeated by half a dozen SF men and twenty Latino cadets.

The brigade commander then threw the SF men out of the exercise.

Major General Alger, the USARSO CG, sent his congratulations to the Green Berets.

Lang began to think of what the future should hold for the Langs. He found he liked the potential in the intelligence work that he was doing.

The army's project to create a unified corps of professional intelligence officers was progressing, and the name of the branch had been changed to Military Intelligence. It was unclear what this new branch would be in the end, but at that point the possibilities were attractive.

Lang sent a letter to Washington to ask if he would be wanted in the new corps of officers. His answer was a telephone call in which a colonel told him they would be happy to get him and would seek his release from the infantry. The colonel said that he could have his choice of specialty within the branch so long as he understood that his first duty after training would be in Vietnam. That was inevitable, and he agreed.

A month later, the Langs went home to the United States, and a new phase in their lifelong journey together.

CHAPTER SEVENTEEN

"Ahoy, the Tigrone!"

USS Tigrone

Walter Lang did not like schools. That was strange. Schools liked him. He was an "easy study." He had a retentive memory, and a mind that was both analytic and synthetic.

The father of a college friend told him that was true after considering him for a year or so. The father was a former war correspondent who became a newspaper's managing editor after World War II. He had known Hemingway and Pyle in Europe. Lang foolishly assumed the man must possess some secret store of wisdom derived from association with these writers. Lang's parents lived in Oregon. They were too far away to visit much. Invitations from the parents of classmates to stay over holidays were deeply appreciated. He could do that or stay in the cadet barracks at VMI with the housekeeping staff while his friends went on vacations. Lang was repeatedly invited to the newspaperman's home. He and the editor frequently sat and talked in the kitchen of the man's 18th century farmhouse. They talked for hours of the drive across France and Germany into Austria. The Vermont winters were usually bitter when Lang arrived with the man's son for skiing. The son had little interest in their discussions and usually went out to chop wood, throw snowballs at squirrels, or just walk around in the snowy forest.

The editor delighted in asking Lang questions about obscure details of history, literature, geography and the like. He frequently made notes so that he did not repeat the questions. One night after he had worked his way through two packs of Camels and half a bottle of single malt, he asked Lang what his IQ was.

The twenty year-old sat back for a moment to consider the enquiry. This was not a question that he welcomed. Experience told him that the truth would bring rejection.

The low ceiling held the smoke to table level. Wood had evidently been expensive in the 18th century. The big house was filled with small rooms, rooms in which white beams had to be remembered and avoided. There were doors everywhere.

Lang's classmate and a younger brother were in another room watching television.

He gave the editor the number.

"Ah, I thought so. Why do you go to school at all? You can't like it. It must be terribly boring. All you need is a library and a chance to learn from living."

"You must be 'credentialed,'" The college-boy replied. "Without that you are stuck in a box with very high walls. You can try to climb out over the walls, but the odds are against you. I would rather wait for the door in the side of the box to open so that I can walk out with my pieces of paper in hand. I imagine that I will then be allowed… something. I'm not sure what."

"Why don't you come to work for my newspaper when the door opens? There will be a job for you there so long as I am managing editor. It is a place to start. Who knows where it might lead.…" He looked quite earnest. The cigarettes and the whisky might kill him soon, but he seemed serious in this offer. This was a considerable offer. The newspaper was a bastion of liberal thought with a high international reputation for quality.

"Let me think it over," the boy answered. "I have another year and a half…" In his heart he knew he would not take the proffered job. Deep in his guts, he could already hear the beating of the drums that so many of his ancestors had followed. He would be a soldier if anyone would have him.

The editor knew this as well. You could see the disappointment in his face.

Captain Walter Lang and his lady returned to the United States from the Panama Canal Zone in the spring of 1967. He had successfully applied for and received a branch transfer from the infantry to military intelligence. He had never experienced any formal intelligence training, and his new "owners" in Washington required that he be trained at a level appropriate to his rank. After that, he would be on his way to the steadily intensifying war in South East Asia. The army intelligence school was then in Baltimore, Maryland at Fort Holabird, an  installation located in the industrial quarter of the city. The army had owned this small post since World War II. On one side of the post was a General Motors factory from which vehicles had been received and shipped overseas during the war. On the other side of the fort was a Proctor and Gamble soap factory. On yet a third side, there was a brewery. The buildings were grimy commercial structures fitted inside with flimsy partitions. The noise of sheet metal machines could be heard from the GM plant throughout the day even as the aroma of brewer's yeast infiltrated air conditioning systems. Fort Holabird and the factories were surrounded by gritty working-class neighborhoods in which blue collar bars served as community centers. These bars provided a pleasant, beery environment for liverwurst sandwiches at lunchtime. The bars were usually filled with steel workers from the nearby Sparrows Point steel plant. They and the soldiers were congenial and seemed to like each other.

The relative status of the new military intelligence branch could be guessed from the appearance and location of the branch school. On the other hand, the location of the school within a major metropolitan area provided an excellent training area. The city of Baltimore itself was a fine "training aid" for teaching the skills needed to operate in European countries. The army intelligence school trained officers and soldiers to be counterintelligence agents as well as case officers for the business of espionage against foreign target countries. Signals intelligence personnel and photo-interpreters were trained elsewhere. The intelligence branch was also required to provide mid-career military education for its officers. That happened at Holabird as well.

After a visit to the post, Lang decided that he wanted to live as far away from the place as he could manage within the context of a daily commute to class. Fort Holabird was in the southeastern corner of Baltimore. There was a peripheral four lane beltway road around the city. Lang drove around that to the northwest corner of the city and then further to the northwest into the farther suburbs. In a little town called Owings Mills, he saw a roadside sign for new flats. They were pleasant three level brick buildings. He leased a two-bedroom apartment. He reckoned that Marguerite could use the extra bedroom for storage and sewing and his mother-in-law was bound to visit. Pleased with himself, he rolled out his ever-present sleeping bag on the living room floor and settled while waiting for Marguerite and the furniture to arrive. The neighbors were friendly. The Langs were soon well installed in this bucolic Maryland town. Farther up the highway to the northwest was agricultural Maryland at its finest, and down the highway towards Baltimore's center was a wonderland of urban distraction and cultural events.

Military Intelligence Branch required that he acquire a school trained "hard skill" in one of the branch's basic functional collection activities. The branch had been "cobbled" together over the previous few years from people and units that had little in common other than an interest in information as a commodity in the decision process.

The Army Security Agency had long been in the business of signals intelligence. It worked closely with the National Security Agency and was the most powerful of the factions merged into the new branch of service.

The Counterintelligence Corps (CIC) was the next largest group. This was essentially an army version of the FBI. These people investigated complaints and conducted operations against adversary intelligence organizations overseas. They carried badges and thought themselves a kind of police force. Lang had known a lot of them in Panama where the 470th MI Group had been instrumental in keeping Panamanian mobs out of the Canal Zone.

Another population was a fairly small collection of officers who were specialists in commanding units that did interpretation of air photographs.

Yet another group was made up of people who had made a career of serving as the staff intelligence officer for combat units or higher headquarters. Lang had been one of these in Panama.

Lastly, there existed a small, clubby group of officers and their enlisted helpers who did what the CIA did but thought they did it better. Careful to maintain their anonymity, this fraternity had recruited and "run" foreign espionage agents across the world since the world war. Hidden from public acknowledgement, these men and women lived under cover wherever they were stationed and were hardly known even to the other soldiers of army intelligence. To say that the CIA disliked and feared this competition would be a massive understatement. This was ironic because many of the most senior people in the Directorate of Operations at CIA throughout the late 20th Century began their careers as enlisted operatives in army and air force intelligence in Europe. CIA recruited them away when their talent was observed. With a lemming's talent for self-destruction, Lang chose to become a member of this obscure and esoteric department.

In the mid-sixties, when all seemed possible, it appeared that some merger of these skill areas would be productive. Lang thought that was true and so had the Army General Staff when it ordered the fusion, but in the end, the strongest group, the SIGINTERs of the Army Security Agency seized control of the branch in the post-Vietnam period and imposed their tradition of bureaucratic and rigid organization on all the others. In 1967, this was only a dimly perceived possibility. There was a huge war to fight. That need surpassed all other needs.

Lang's training in the murky art of understanding and using human nature began soon after his arrival at Fort Holabird. The instructors in this course were all veterans of the Cold War struggle against the Soviet Union and the Warsaw Pact. They were middle-aged men and women who had lived for decades in Germany and were well adapted to European life and culture. The details of what they called "operational data" concerning trains, hotels and language were instinctive to them. They wore trevira suits in a businessman's "cut." They wore European shoes, and their hair was trimmed to European standards. They had "run" agents in East Germany, Poland, Czechoslovakia and Hungary for so long that they could hardly remember doing anything else. They had come home to teach a new generation. They knew very little about the Far East, but that mattered little. Their talent was a portable skill for it was concerned with essential human nature.

The course was five months long. It trained military and civilian intelligence people from all parts of the Department of Defense. Many of the students were under cover throughout the course, and their true identities were not known to their classmates.

The training began with field exercises that seemed "holdovers" from bygone days when agent handlers cut their way through barbed wire to reach the Soviet Zone of Germany or rowed ashore from boats in the Baltic Sea. Thinking back on these seemingly outdated "drills," Lang eventually perceived that they were designed to test the physical ability of candidates in this kind of training as well as the willingness to endure privation. Aesthetes who feared the dark, the water, or the wild places of the earth would not be suitable for the job of controlling other people by force of character.

In one of these "drills" conducted at night, Lang and two others paddled ashore in Baltimore Harbor in blackface camouflage and rough clothes. Once on a tiny beach in an old coast defense battery, they proceeded to cut their way through a couple of rows of concertina wire so as to reach a "reception party" waiting in a parking lot a hundred yards inland.

On the way home to Owings Mills, Lang was stopped by a Maryland state policeman for speeding. He might have been 20 miles an hour over the speed limit. It was four in the morning. The state cop escorted him to a nearby Baltimore County police station. The giant, impassive state trooper stood by while Lang handed the desk sergeant his identification and license.

The police sergeant looked up. "You are an officer in the army?"

Lang was a muddy, ragged mess.

"I am. I'm at Holabird for training. I spent the evening crawling around in the mud at Fort Howard. That's why I look like this..."

"Why would you do that?" the sergeant asked.

"I was practicing landing in the Soviet Union from a submarine."

The two policemen looked at each other.

The state trooper escorted Lang back to his car, opened the door for him, saluted and said good night.

Throughout the course, there was classroom lecturing on what was called the "operational cycle." After the lectures there were practical exercises in application.

Clandestine intelligence collection is, by definition, a quest for secret information, information that cannot be obtained in other ways. The desired information usually concerns enemy intentions. Clandestine collection seeks this information by recruiting foreign people who are trusted by their own governments to protect the information.

In the operational cycle, the clandestine unit receives requirements from above, identifies people who may have access to the information, and then recruits these people as tools with which to obtain the information.

This activity is always illegal in the targeted country or army. Detection in the act of illegally taking the information inevitably leads to severe punishment. The punishment is often imprisonment or death. Because of these penalties, this work must be invisible to the world and especially to the security services of the target country.

The psychological process of convincing someone to spy against his own people is an art form to be practiced only by a select few who have a deep understanding of human nature. This art form requires deeply felt empathy, patience and persistence. What is sought in this process is a state of mind in which the targeted person decides to make a transfer of loyalty, obedience and often even identity. In achieving this, the recruiter seeks to establish an imagined identity of interests with the prospective recruit, a shared emotion so strong that the target eventually responds positively to a request for cooperation. This sounds easier to do than it is. In reality, the difficulties inherent in persuading someone to defect in place and work for his country's opponents are daunting. Training for this must be extensive and lengthy. A constant evaluation must be made by trainers with regard to the suitability of each candidate for the job of agent handler and recruiter.

The method used for training was that of role playing in lengthy practice of every phase of the operational cycle. The course possessed a small theater complete with a stage and proscenium arch. In the business of the course, a scenario would be presented with target somewhere in Eastern Europe. Based on that scenario, the students developed plans and implemented them on stage in interviews and confrontations with role players. Some of these "playlets" continued for weeks with students relieving each other on stage to "drive" the "operation" forward.

In US Military Intelligence, motivation for the recruitment of foreign agents is sought in something greater than money. Nevertheless, money is usually provided in such operations. In fact, the acceptance of money is often insisted on by the recruiter in order to "seal the deal," but payment should not be the principal basis of a relationship. Recruitment made solely on the basis of money or intimidation is typically unstable and undependable. In general, patriotism found in action against an oppressor, or a desire to find a new life in the United States is a much better motivation than mere money.

The process of approaching a potential source, conducting the recruitment itself, and then training and communicating with a recruited agent requires great discretion and skill in masking the existence of the bond from people outside the relationship. This skill is found in what is called "tradecraft."

Clandestine activities are frequently detected and destroyed through defects in the communications built into the operations themselves. To avoid such sad endings, clandestine units spend a lot of time doing things that are intended to protect those communications. Dead and live drops for messages are devised to enable the delivery of messages without detection. Concealment devices are used, signaling marks are made on trees, rocks, mailboxes, etc. Photography and miniaturization of documents is necessary but always dangerous because of the existence of physical proof of "crime." Personal meetings must be held from time to time. These are also quite dangerous because the association of agent handler and agent is visible in the period of the meeting. To minimize this danger both surveillance and counter-surveillance tactics are taught and practiced until they are instinctive.

Some of the training for these "routines" could be dangerous. On one occasion Lang was chased down a darkened Washington street by drug dealers who thought he was a policeman. On another he was almost crushed by a delivery truck when he escaped from pursuers by going out the back door of a department store in Baltimore directly into the path of the truck as it backed up to a loading dock.

Clandestine operations must be conducted with great rigor to avoid fraud committed against the United States by foreign agents, counterintelligence penetration or provocation. To that end, documentation is extensive and lengthy. Reports of contact with potential and actual sources are detailed and are reviewed by commanders and headquarters staffs. Contrary to popular imagination, espionage involves a lot of very routine paperwork that must synthesize data that is continuously screened, checked, and cross-checked.

The writing of well-made "product" reports on the information collected is a critical feature of activity. Lang was a person of some literary achievement. He was surprised to find himself in classes conducted by an elderly civilian widow who taught all field operatives to write voluminous, detailed, and accurate reports. Obedient to her guidance, he visited the Alexandria, Virginia

classification yard of the R.F. & P Railroad, the Sparrows Point complex owned by Bethlehem Steel and a massive Westinghouse plant in Baltimore. The resulting descriptive reports took days to write and were all more than twenty pages long. The months, weeks, days and nights were filled with seemingly never-ending training and activity.

This intensive and transformative course would end in a "graduation exercise." Training tests of that sort were analogous to final examinations in civilian education and were dear to army tradition. An ambitious and worldwide exercise was scheduled that would test students' knowledge of all the many aspects of their new skill.

The "game" would be played in the context of a scenario in which the United States had been conquered by the forces of the "Aggressor Empire" and was now occupied and ruled by the Circle Trigon Party and a vast array of American collaborator police and government officials. In this scenario, authentic U.S. forces and a government in exile still occupied island bases in the Caribbean from which they planned to "liberate" America. This was a great convenience for the test because the task in the exercise was to infiltrate occupied America for the purpose of establishing intelligence collection networks that would be useful in the liberation campaign. In the course of doing this, the students would be expected to demonstrate their skill in all the stages of the espionage operational cycle: mission analysis, analysis of the task, spotting possible assets, recruitment, training, tasking, de-briefing, re-briefing, dispatch and report writing. Most of these activities would be carried out in a highly realistic field environment in which the FBI, local police, and army counterintelligence would all be participants in the "game" for the purpose of providing difficulties that would mirror real life. In other words, they would hunt the students in the same way that an agent handler would be hunted in a country like East Germany. Surveillance of targets, counter-surveillance against the police, resistance to interrogation when questioned with regard to cover stories, the use of concealment devices; all these things would play a role. Students would carry a full set of "occupation" government documents. These would include: an identity card, ration card, driver's license, work permit, internal passport and the like. To make the "play" yet more challenging, the student would be required to have a separate, second cover identity complete with a different "legend" and different documents. Such a thing would never be done in reality. This would be a feature of the exercise for the purpose of illustrating the impossibility of remembering the details in a second "story" when under pressure. The student would need to conceal the second set of documents and switch identities in the middle of his "trial by fire."

The first phase of the exercise would consist of planning in detail while still at the school at Fort Holabird. Each student acted as agent handler for another and planned the mission to be undertaken by that student. In return, someone else performed the same service for him. The students would be deployed to areas across the continental United States, as well as Alaska, Hawaii, Puerto Rico and Okinawa.

On the appointed day, Lang and six others were flown to the US Navy submarine base at New London, Connecticut. In the game, this base was supposedly offshore in unoccupied territory. They boarded a World War II era diesel-electric "boat" for the voyage to the "hostile shore." The ship was USS Tigrone. She was a veteran of ten patrols against Japanese shipping. The Tigrone was still in service because of her usefulness as a sonar research platform.

The students were dressed in "spy clothes," jeans, turtle necked sweaters and Wellington boots. Black was the preferred color. It would be harder to see at night.

Lang found himself bunking in the forward torpedo room with several sailors. One of them asked if he were a marine. He told the man that he was an army captain. "Oh well, that's all right then," the sailor responded. "Welcome aboard."

They sailed about Long Island Sound for several days and nights, diving and surfacing and training for the movement to the beach. There was a large inflatable rubber boat lashed to the deck. They practiced inflating it from an

air hose and then paddling it around the ship to show their proficiency. In the midst of one of these circumnavigations, the helmsman raised his paddle and called to the watch in the conning tower, "Ahoy, the Tigrone, have yuh seen the white whale?"

The response was instantaneous. "Ay, we saw him two days ago off Tahiti. God luck to yuh!"

The voyage was great fun. The submarine's little wardroom seated ten around a square table. Lang thought the food was quite good, but he had an infantryman's lack of sensitivity in such matters.

At 11 PM one night, they inflated their boat and paddled away into the darkness. The sea was flat. This was a blessing because the distance to the beach was much longer than might have been expected. The distance was about a mile. There was no escort boat. They would either reach the beach on their own, or their bodies would wash up somewhere in Connecticut or Long Island. A hooded red flashlight on the shore guided them to their landing. A "reception party" watched them bury the rubber boat and then drove them to a "safe house" where they changed into old clothes and assumed their cover identities. They boarded a commuter train in a nearby town. This train carried them through the New York suburbs to airports and railroad stations.

Lang's colleagues were *en route* to destinations all over the eastern United States. Lang himself was on his way to Syracuse, New York. At La Guardia airport, he was stopped by several plainclothes policemen, taken into a private room and questioned closely about his business. His documents were inspected carefully, and his minimal baggage searched. He had built a concealment device by disassembling a can of shaving cream. He had placed his alternate identity documents inside and then re-assembled it complete with gas pressure and shaving cream. A policeman went through his shaving kit, looked at the can and pressed the button. It worked.

In Syracuse, he registered at the Onondaga Hotel as he had been directed by planners. This was a great convenience for the police since they would always know where to look for him. Once in his room, he disassembled the medicine cabinet in the bathroom and hid his extra papers in its structure. Within an hour, the FBI showed up and ran him through the interrogation process while they searched his person and the room looking for the other papers. They failed and went away disgruntled.

For several days, he wandered the streets looking like a minor character from "The Death of a Salesman." There was "art" in this appearance. He had learned from his teachers that a shabby looking man is not closely watched by the authorities. There is a psychological reaction in nearly all that makes humans disregard the poor and unsuccessful. Workmen are not interesting. Men in good suits are watched and are expected to be in a hurry. If they loiter, they are thought to be up to no good. As an illustration of that phenomenon Lang saw a classmate arrested as he sat on the rim of the wall around a public fountain reading a newspaper. Lang watched from a park bench across the square. The classmate was in a business suit. Lang wore clothing of the sort that a house painter might wear. The police stood near Lang to watch and discuss the classmate and then crossed the street to pick him up. They hardly looked at Lang. The classmate went into the "drunk tank" overnight where he had to defend himself from the inhabitants.

The days were filled with planned activities. At night he returned to the hotel for rest hoping that the "hounds" would allow him a few hours sleep.

The evening of the third day he entered the lobby, weary and footsore and walked steadily toward the grimy brass elevator doors.

Two large, curly haired men rose from cracked leather club chairs and entered the elevator with him. When he reached for the floor selection button one of them stopped him.

"No, you are coming to the penthouse," the man growled. "The boss wants to talk to you."

Lang nodded. "Sure, why not?" he said.

His escorts looked Italian. They wore loud, Hawaiian looking shirts. A good deal of curly black hair showed at the neck. Gold chains glimmered in the hair.

The picture of the situation he was in grew clearer to Lang by the minute. At the top of the building, the doors opened into a marble floored hallway. They marched down the corridor. Lang was flanked by the two new "friends." The art on the walls was just trash, but expensive trash. At the end of the hallway, a man sat behind a reproduction French desk that dripped with *ormolu* and fraud. This man was an older, and even more sinister, version of Lang's new acquaintances.

Lang stood erect across the table from the "don." He was acutely conscious of his shoddy appearance.

"We've been watching you," the man said. "We don't like the FBI coming in our place."

Lang silently cursed the fool who put him in this hotel.

"Empty your pockets on my desk!"

Lang obeyed.

The goons leaned forward to see. You could imagine them licking their lips at the prospect of prey.

Lang arranged his pocket litter on the desk with the real documents to one side, and the exercise documents on the other.

The "boss" pawed through everything. He looked up. "You're a spy."

"Yes, sir," Lang said, "but I am a US Army spy in training."

The "don" looked at his real ID card. "Captain?" the man asked.

Lang nodded. He was not entirely sure how this interview might end.

"Guido," or whatever his name was, smiled. "Me and my brother were in the CIC in Italy during the war. Sit down, Captain Lang. Sit down and tell us all about it."

Lang decided that this was not a time to hold back information or seem coy, so he told "Guido" whatever he wanted to know. Espresso was sent for. An hour passed.

The two goons seemed even more interested than their boss.

When Lang finished telling his story, his host smiled broadly displaying gold teeth in the process. "We'll fix the local and state police," he said "and I have one or two people I can ask for a favor with the FBI, but I can't do anything with Army intelligence. I didn't really know they were here. We move in different circles you could say, but when you are in here, nobody will bother you, right boys?"

The heads dipped in agreement.

"Now let's eat. You like steaks? Good! We'll start with some carbonara."

The rest of the exercise was stress-free. Lang watched for days as his classmates were "trashed" by the police. Nobody touched him, not even the Army CI people.

At the "exercise critique," when the "game" had ended, the FBI agent in charge told Lang privately that "Guido" had "squeezed" every cop in town to get the desired effect. "Are you Sicilian?" he asked.

"Hardly, but I wouldn't mind taking a couple of these guys with me to Vietnam."

Lang graduated with honors.

Three months later, two students drowned in the surf on a Puerto Rican beach, and the era of boat landings in this course was over.

Captains in the US Army were then required to complete a mid-career management course in order to be considered "branch qualified" by promotion and selection boards. These courses were generally referred to by officers as "the advanced course." Military Intelligence as an officer career branch was no different. The MI course was also at Fort Holabird. The course had its own building. This was a converted wooden theater. All students had security clearances above Top Secret, and much of the instruction was at that level of classification. The building had its own MP force and was essentially a large "safe" in which open storage for classified material was allowed.

There were nearly a hundred officers in the course. All but a few were captains, and the rest were majors. These more senior people had somehow been prevented from attending earlier in their service. There was one woman officer, a major, who was a Soviet specialist and whose normal duty was to "run" the US-Soviet military "hot-line" in Washington. She was Southern. as was a male major who was the class commander. One day in class, vulgar language was used by a lecturer. The class leader protested on the basis that a lady was present. The vulgarian said that she was not a lady. She was an officer in the army. She picked up her purse, walked out the door and called the major general on the army general staff who was chief of intelligence. The lecturer disappeared from the school.

Fully eighty percent of the class had recently returned from a combat tour of duty in Vietnam. The army was critically "short" of experienced combat intelligence officers. Everyone in the class knew that graduation would be followed by return to the war. Everyone knew that the army would not accept their resignations until the crisis had passed. That meant eventual death or mutilation for many of them. Some of them had been in very heavy fighting. Lang's "seat mate" was a SIGINT officer who had taken a voice intercept detachment into Landing Zone X-Ray in the Ia Drang Valley. He shot an NVA infantryman within ten feet of the helicopter in which he arrived and then fought for three days with the famous 1st Battalion, 7th Cavalry Regiment. Most of the students were reserve officers on extended active duty. This meant that they were truly "Christmas help" and that the army could end their active duty administratively whenever it wished to do so; and in many cases, they would have to go back to the "ranks" in order to serve long enough to retire. They knew this would probably happen as soon as the war ended, and it did. All of this resulted in a great spirit of independence in these people, a spirit whose motto might have been, "what are you going to do to us, send us back to Vietnam?"

Instructors soon feared them. This was, of course, what they wanted. Various amusing incidents occurred.

The faculty developed a routine in which the teachers would assemble Friday afternoons for comments by them and the students on the material taught. Some of these teachers were truly terrible pedagogues. A "wag" in the class had a teakwood statue of a naked man bent over so far that his head disappeared in his own anus. All personnel in the class and faculty had a purple stripe running down one side of their photo badges. This was a convenience for the MPs in checking people into the building. The owner of the statue painted a purple stripe around the vertical axis of the statue. At the next Friday "preening," the class took a vote as to who was its least favorite instructor. The "winner" was presented the statue and told he could keep it for a week. The school put up with that for some time and then stopped holding the Friday critiques.

A guest instructor stood on the stage one day to explain the general superiority of the CIA in a demeaning tone. After listening for a while, a student who had once been a sergeant said, "This guy used to be an E-4 in my unit before CIA recruited him." A document destruction bag circulated and was filled with ashtray detritus, scraps of food, old cross word puzzles, etc. When it reached the front of the room, it was addressed to the man on stage, stapled shut and tossed up to land at his feet.

On another occasion, the Chemical Corps staff of the school brought a white rabbit onto the stage in a big wire cage.

The rabbit twitched its nose and regarded the audience calmly while seeming to wonder what was happening. The class knew that the white-coated combat boot-wearing characters on stage were going to kill the rabbit with a drop of VX nerve gas. This was a demonstration that they clearly loved doing for the purpose of showing how important they were. They staged this demonstration at every service school and in every course. Everyone in the class had seen the rabbits die before. As a colonel of the chemical corps approached the cage with his vial of death, the MI student class leader stood to say that they all knew that VX would kill a rabbit and that this death was unnecessary. The colonel told him to sit down and continued his advance towards the rabbit's destiny. The intended victim was oblivious. The class stood as one man and an animal sound went round the room. The chemical colonel hesitated. "We have to kill it," he blurted. "We don't have anywhere to keep it." A student captain spoke to say that his children would love the rabbit. With that he walked up the stairs and onto the stage and retrieved the rabbit before returning to his desk where he stood holding the white creature in his arms. The colonel ranted and raved and threatened all manner of retaliation.

Someone in the class held up the purple striped statue of disgrace. The colonel fell silent.

A great deal of valuable information was imparted in this long course, and Lang, with his sponge-like ability to absorb facts, did well. He was the Honor Graduate in the class.

The MI School was glad to see them all go.

Three weeks later, Lang arrived at San Francisco International Airport on a flight from Boston. He had left Marguerite behind. She was brave as a lioness and dry-eyed as she saw him off for what could easily be the last time. She would shelter with her mother against the day of his return.

A thirty-mile bus ride was necessary from the civilian airport to Travis Air Force Base for the airlift to Vietnam.

Lang picked up his bag and walked out of the front doors to wait under a marquee for the shuttle bus. A marine gunnery sergeant stood waiting with him. Across the parking lot, the door of a rusty, battered VW "bug" opened, and a fat, slatternly young woman emerged. She wore a flowered *muumuu*.

As she approached, Lang automatically said, "Good afternoon, ma'am."

She looked at the marine's chevrons, then at Lang's bars. She spat on Lang. Her spittle ran down the front of his khaki shirt.

"Do you do that often?" he asked her.

She nodded.

"You have a roster at the house so that you know whose turn it is on a given day?"

She nodded again.

"Do you know that I could hit you hard enough to put you in a hospital?"

Fear showed in her face.

The marine sergeant put his hand on Lang's arm. That was surprising. Marine sergeants did not touch officers in those days.

"Don't worry, Gunny. I won't hit her."

They rode the bus together to Travis.

CHAPTER EIGHTEEN

"Worthy of Our Steel"

525th Military Intelligence Group

"Respect was mingled with surprise
And the stern joy that warriors feel
In foemen worthy of our steel."
Sir Walter Scott

Captain Walter Lang arrived in the Republic of Vietnam in May 1968 on board a civilian Boeing 707 airliner. The troop airlift to south East Asia was so large by that time that it far exceeded the capacity of the US Air Force to carry so many to and from the wars. Major airlines and companies created solely for the purpose of the airlift made a lot of money in this trade. The airlift was well funded, and the charters were required to feed the passengers a steak every five hours. These were all cooked "well done" and cut from a mysterious unknown animal that apparently had nothing but muscle tissue in its body. The meat was uniformly dense and without fat or connective tissue. By the time the aircraft reached Honolulu and paused to refuel, everyone on board was thoroughly constipated. One hundred and fifty men stood in patient ranks in the terminal bar listening to Hawaiian music on the Muzak system and bought three drinks apiece from carts that waitresses pushed through the crowd. No one cared what was in these drinks so long as they were strong and effective. By the time the aircraft left the ground, nearly all on board were asleep.

The flight from California had seemed endless. Daylight persisted for an unnaturally long time as the plane hurried westward racing the sun. Sometime in the night, Lang searched in his carry-on bag and found the new Buck knife that he had bought in Boston. It was a broad bladed hunting knife. The blade was of a moderate length, and he intended to carry it as a general-purpose field knife. It had the Buck Company's characteristic black grip. He had a pair of Arkansas stones and a can of oil in the bag as well. The stones were in a wooden box. One was "soft" and the other, much harder. He arranged his instruments on the tray table attached to the seat in front of him and went to work on the knife edge. The blade was semi-hollow ground. Lang did not want that. He wanted something as sharp as a straight razor. He had all night to work on the blade and set to work, first with the soft stone and then the grey-blue hard one. After a couple of hours, he looked around to see that half a dozen people had gathered to watch him work including one of the stewardesses.

Among them was a Special Forces sergeant. "You know what you are doing, captain," he said. "You must be one of us."

"I am indeed," he told the man.

By the time the 707 arrived at Tan Son Nhut airport and airbase on the outskirts of Saigon, the passengers would have killed to be the first out the door and into the blazing sunlight, heat and humidity. There were half a dozen airlift transports unloading into army buses that waited alongside the aircraft. The civilian terminal was visible in the distance. Military aircraft parked in hardened revetments were everywhere. The smell and noise of a Far-Eastern city drifted across the parking ramp.

Artillery could be heard in the distance. They had arrived in the midst of the second phase of the *Tet* Offensive of 1968. A bus carried Lang to a replacement depot where a clerk checked his orders and put him on another shuttle bus that took him to a facility where newly arrived officers of the 525th Military Intelligence Group were housed until sent on to their final destinations within the group. This was an old French boarding school. There were walls surrounding the two-story buildings. He was housed on the second floor of what had been a dormitory for Vietnamese girls. The room was both pleasant and plain in design and furnishing. The school's mahogany furniture was still used, and the outline of a crucifix that had hung above the bed was a comfort. The building backed onto a city street. He opened the window and looked down on a scene filled with mopeds, Vespa scooters and old cars that seemed to be burning as much oil as gasoline. Young women in beautiful *ao-dai* dresses were everywhere. One waved to him from the pillion seat of a scooter. The din was overwhelming.

In the fading light of his first day "in-country," he sat on the veranda outside his door and considered the school and its beautiful buildings. They surrounded its central courtyard. There were giant flame trees and purple bougainvillea everywhere in the courtyard. The bougainvillea covered the pillars of the veranda. The scent of tropical flowers filled the darkness as it fell over the city. *I am not surprised that the French fought so hard to keep this place*, he thought. With that conviction lodged in his head, he staggered inside and to bed. It had been a long trip from home.

The next morning, buses from the 525th MI Group came to take the new arrivals to the US Army Vietnam centralized personnel facility for the inevitable "processing." This operation was housed in a large warehouse formerly the property of a colonial enterprise of some sort. The interior was huge. The ceiling was far, far above. Birds circled and perched among the beams and rafters. It was typically pre-war French. Lang half-expected to see *Commissaire Jules Maigret* wandering about, pipe in hand. The structure stood on the bank of the Saigon River. The river was a hundred yards wide, with palm trees visible on the other bank. Lang looked out one of the large, open windows at sampan traffic and people walking on what seemed a road on the other bank. The floor of the warehouse was covered with standard US Army desks, filing cabinets and chairs. The furniture was made of gray steel. He sat with a clerk who looked like all the other clerks. Close cut hair, glasses, clean and pressed tropical field uniform, jungle boots; they all looked the same. The young man typed purposefully at a long list of forms concerning Lang's pay and status in the Vietnam Theater of War. His M-16 rifle leaned against a tan-colored concrete wall.

Suddenly, there was gunfire in the sunlit world outside the windows. Bullets zipped across the big room. The characteristic "Zzzzzzzzzz!" was unmistakable. The personnel warrant officer in charge of the facility asked his "clients" to lie on the floor. The clerks put on their helmets and body armor, picked up their rifles and went to defense posts. Those on the riverside began to fire at targets on the other bank. The "clients" lay on the concrete floor, smoking and joking. None of them had yet been issued a weapon. After a few minutes, a pair of helicopters arrived and began shooting into the distant vegetation. One of the clerks yelled, "There they go. They're running across that rice paddy!"

The helicopter noise grew fainter, and the clerks returned to their desks.

"Does this happen often?" Lang asked.

"Only in the last couple of weeks, sir. Let's see, I was filling out your allotments…"

Lang was having lunch that day when a staff car arrived to take him to group headquarters. He soon found himself in the conference room of the group operations staff. He was told that they had an offer to make him that he would not be able to refuse.

Little did they know.…

With an organization chart at hand, the operations officer, a lieutenant colonel, explained that the 525th Group presently had four combat support battalions deployed across South Vietnam to mirror South Vietnamese military boundaries, a fifth battalion that conducted country-wide operations and a little known sixth battalion that conducted operations outside South Vietnam that had North Vietnam as the focus of their activity.

That mission made sense. Agents must be recruited where they are found, and they are found in odd places. This sixth battalion had detachments in Paris, Phnom Penh, Bangkok, Hong Kong and Macau.

Lang waited.

The operations officer frowned. "You are not interested?"

"What are you offering me, Colonel?"

"The Macau detachment, you and your wife are good at languages and you come well recommended by the school at Holabird. We asked them to suggest someone."

"My wife?"

"Yes, if you will stay in Macau for three years, she can join you there…"

"Thank you for the offer, but I came here to go to the field."

Back at "the school" that evening, Lang went to the small bar attached to the mess and had a couple of stiff drinks.

The next day, another bus arrived to pick up Lang and a half dozen other officers assigned to the 3rd Battalion of the MI Group. This bus was painted in the familiar olive drab palette. It looked as though it had received harder use than the army buses he had seen thus far in Saigon. The driver was a skinny little private first class who chattered without pause while waiting for his passengers. He insisted that they should leave quickly because it was a long drive, and he had a big date that night with his Vietnamese girlfriend.

Lang finally told him to shut up. He told the driver that they would leave when the senior passenger, a major said he was ready.

The driver fell into a sullen silence.

The headquarters of the 3rd Battalion was in the city of Bien Hoa, thirty miles from Saigon. The US had built a four-lane divided highway between the two to carry massive civilian commercial traffic. This highway was "outposted" by the 12th MP Brigade. Their armored cars were distributed along the shoulders of the road.

The bus rolled along the highway for a few miles in heavy traffic, and then without a word, the driver turned off on a secondary country road. "What are you doing?" the major asked.

"Just taking a shortcut, sir, just taking a shortcut."

They drove through rice fields and villages filled with churches, ruined churches. There were many shell holes and damaged structures in every town, although the streets were filled with women going to market and children at play. The driver announced that these villages were inhabited by Catholic North Vietnamese who had been refugees from the North after the French war ended in 1954. The communist Vietcong had given these towns very special treatment over the previous month.

Beyond one of these towns, the road ran on an earthen causeway with rice fields on both sides. A tree line was nearby to the right. There was a classic iron girder bridge with a round top above the roadway. The bus ran up a low grade to the bridge.

A machine gun fired from the tree line. Unexpectedly, there were new holes in the sheet metal sides of the bus, holes filled with sunshine.

Lang went prone on the floor of the bus with the other passengers.

The machine gun hammered on, drilling holes up and down the bus, more and more holes.

The driver stalled the engine and took shelter on the floor.

The major crawled up to him and took his sidearm. "You get in that seat, or I will shoot you and drive it myself," he said above the noise.

It was just a matter of time before the machine gun killed everyone in the bus.

The kid started the engine and drove across the bridge.

When they arrived at the compound of the 3rd Battalion in Bien Hoa, Lang counted over a hundred holes in the vehicle. He told the driver to go hide somewhere before he decided to punish him and do it personally.

The battalion commander heard this and said, "You must be Lang. Group called. They think you are nuts, and so do I, but things are a mess in Song Be. Make it right, and I will support you."

It was not a good beginning.

The 3rd Battalion, 525th Military Intelligence Group was engaged in providing counterintelligence and espionage support to US armed forces units operating in the 3rd Corps Tactical Zone of the South Vietnamese Army. This area was generally made up of the provinces around Saigon and north to the Cambodian border.

There had previously been separate MI Groups for counterintelligence work and for espionage. They had been merged within the previous few months. This had caused mismatches in skills that were worrisome. The outgoing battalion commander who had thought Lang, "nuts" was a CI man, essentially a cop with little understanding of espionage work and an instinctive distrust of espionage operators like Lang. Lang's Special Forces background was even more dubious in the eyes of this man.

Nevertheless, Lang was given command of 3/525th MIG's Detachment "A" which was in the process of establishing itself in Phuoc Long and Binh Long Provinces north of Saigon on the border with Cambodia. These two provinces were held throughout by the forces of the Communist Viet Cong and their North Vietnamese allies and masters. The two provinces were heavily jungled and hilly in the eastern parts. The population was Vietnamese in the scattered small towns and villages and Montagnard in the countryside. The Republic of Viet Nam government held the towns with small garrisons; the communists held everything else, and the U.S. Army operated across this countryside as forces were available. Lang's area of responsibility also extended into Cambodia if he could drive his operations that far.

The Sergeant Major of 3/525 MIG announced his opinion of Lang's operating area when they first met. "Well," he said, "At least you won't have far to walk to Cambodia when you're captured."

The towns in Lang's area were all besieged and under more or less continual attacks by fire with mortars, rockets and the occasional artillery strike from somewhere out in the jungle. There were also ground probes that from time to time became really serious.

Mobile U.S. forces came and went, but a permanent network of civil and military advisory teams, corps level artillery firebases, and Special Forces camps provided an ongoing presence.

Lang flew to Song Be, the capital of Phuoc Long Province in a C-45 twin engine Beechcraft transport. Song Be was 20 miles from the Cambodian border. Air America, the CIA airline had a contract to provide scheduled transportation service for the efforts of the Civil Operations and Revolutionary Development (CORDS) counterinsurgency effort country-wide. CORDS was in the process of becoming the major focus of US strategy in Vietnam. CORDS advisory teams were present at every level of Vietnamese government and in every ministry, province and district. There were many thousands of people involved, and their activities penetrated all aspects of Vietnamese life. CORDS was the vehicle through which American money funded the Republic of Vietnam government. Major U.S. forces in this period were transitioning to the role of support and protection for CORDS.

The job of Lang's detachment was to insinuate itself into the available "cover" provided by the activities of CORDS and to find indigenous or European persons brave enough to repeatedly penetrate enemy units and bases outside the towns to obtain good information.

What he discovered when he arrived in Song Be was a shambles, dignified with the term, "detachment." His predecessor was a CI captain who had made no effort at all to conceal his men within the CORDS organization. He preferred to keep them grouped around him in a little Vietnamese apartment that was part of a row of such apartments. They all wore uniforms unlike most of the CORDS civilians and had little plausible explanation for their presence other than a vague claim to be a supplement of some kind for the large CORDS presence in the town.

He also discovered that his predecessor had acquired the next-door neighbor's wife as a mistress and had been making "progress" with her teen-aged daughter as "reinforcement" for her mother's efforts. The father of this girl was a Vietnamese Army sergeant who lived on the property and who was "paid off" in American Post Exchange supplies that would sell well on the black market. The predecessor also had established the charming custom of what he called the "Friday Night Follies," in which local Vietnamese ladies were invited in for "community activity" once a week.

Lang had carefully read the roster of American personnel assigned to his detachment. There was one missing from his sight. This was a lieutenant who he had known at Ft. Holabird in the agent handler course. He was a tall, blond young fellow from the mid-west. Lang and Marguerite had met his wife on several occasions. The predecessor told Lang that this officer was on "detached duty" and living in a Montagnard village a few miles outside Song

Be. A visit revealed this fellow dressed in a native sarong with teeth stained black from chewing betel nut and co-habiting with a 12-year-old girl who he described as his "Pocahontas." When asked if he had learned anything as yet, he replied that he understood that the bare-breasted Montagnard girls "hit their prime" at 14.

Completing the picture was the evident inability of the group to recruit any agents or collect a scrap of information. They were held in contempt by both the local CIA and the CORDS advisory team.

After a few days' investigation, Lang called Bien Hoa and requested a helicopter to fly him and the two refugees from "The Heart of Darkness" to headquarters. He delivered them, then flew back to the mountains where he explained to the remaining enlisted men that a new beginning had come, and that if they gave him the slightest excuse, they would be sent to the worst possible duty that he could discover.

He visited the CORDS province senior adviser. This was a retired army colonel who had been in the 82nd Airborne Division at the time of the Normandy invasion. He had jumped into St. Mere Eglise as a "pathfinder." After an hour's conversation, the province senior advisor said, "Ah, you are something quite different. Welcome. We have some extra living space in our residential compound. Can I offer you one of our trailers? Yes? Good. We could use a few more guns around here at night. As for cover positions, I have a number of empty "slots," but you will have to go talk to my boss, John Vann in Bien Hoa about that."

A meeting with John Paul Vann led to an agreement in which Lang would fill unoccupied CORDS jobs with his men covered as either military or civilian employees, and that these "spooks" would do CORDS work during the days and Lang's secret work at night. This was a very satisfactory arrangement. Some of Lang's men became so skilled at their CORDS jobs that Vann and CORDS tried to hire them permanently when their intelligence tours of duty were ended. They were variously: education, agriculture, press, refugee and many other "species" of adviser for CORDS.

There remained one final organizational issue to deal with. In a neighboring province, Lang's detachment had a team headed by a captain only a few months junior to Lang himself. It became clear that this man resented bitterly that his commander was so near to him in age. Eventually, it became necessary to relieve him for insubordination.

Lang prepared to move his headquarters staff into the CORDS "trailer park." The little community of house trailers and prefabricated buildings was shielded by a few hip-high blast walls and a chain link fence. The buildings were placed beside the narrow runway that ran through the outskirts of Song Be. At one end of the runway was the French colonial capital building. The clock tower seemed to supervise the city as a reminder of bygone days. The other end of the runway ended in an abrupt drop to the valley of the Song Be River far below. Beyond that valley rose the peak of *Nui Ba Ra*, "Black Dragon Mountain."

Across the runway from the CORDS compound was a line of militia positions that secured that edge of the Song Be plateau. The compound was essentially undefended and under constant observation from VC positions on the mountain. One morning while shaving in his trailer, Lang heard a distant report from a large weapon. This was followed by a clanging noise on the runway. From the front porch of the main CORDS building, Lang could see a great commotion in the USAF revetted enclosure where the Forward Air Controller light aircraft were kept. There was another explosion on the crest of the mountain, and as Lang watched, a large caliber shell from a recoilless rifle struck the runway near the CORDS compound and "skipped" up the runway to strike the revetments around the airplanes. After a moment, 105 mm howitzers began to fire from South Vietnamese artillery positions. Shells struck the mountain and enemy fire ceased. The only casualty had been the pet dog of the air force men in the revetments. It had been killed instantly by the first round fired at the airplanes.

The possibility of sudden death from shelling and other enemy fires was always present in Song Be. A few weeks after Lang arrived, he had been working in a building at the south end of town when a Rocket Propelled Grenade fired from outside the perimeter ripped through the front wall of the structure. The shaped charge warhead passed between Lang and another man. It looked like a white-hot energy core. This was followed by the tail fin assembly. The fins on the tail made a "whup, whup" sound as the piece of flying "junk" crossed the room to bury itself like a hatchet in a wall. Things like that happened frequently in Song Be.

A new battalion commander arrived in Bien Hoa. Lieutenant Colonel Paul Landon had been an adviser to the Vietnamese in Song Be during a previous tour of duty. He understood how difficult Lang's task was in the jungle-covered mountains and did everything he could to support. With Landon's assumption of command, the overall situation changed for the better. First class people began to arrive to bolster the detachment's ranks.

Over the course of that year, the detachment grew to twenty or so American intelligence personnel and a hundred Vietnamese, Montagnard and European agents. These last were recruited from among the staff of the French-owned rubber plantations that dotted the region. They were recruited personally by Lang after meetings in the better restaurants found in Saigon. In one instance, the French Consulate General in Saigon contacted 525th MI Group to offer the services of a large informant network run by the rubber plantations in Binh Long Province. The several hundred workers in this apparatus were a welcome addition to the detachment's capabilities. A French intelligence officer continued to run the network under Lang's supervision.

The detachment operated from a half dozen surrounding hilltop towns. Song Be, Bo Duc, and eventually Duc Phong in Phuoc Long Province, An Loc, Loc Ninh, and Chon Tanh in Binh Long Province were the names. Coverage on the ground eventually blanketed the two provinces and extended well into Cambodia.

The unending efforts of the enemy to bombard or seize these intrusive fortified locations were dangerous enough, but when the targeted efforts of the VC to identify and kill the men of the detachment were added as risks, it is not surprising that a quality of morale arose in the unit that might be described as "gallows humor." Constant danger and an insistence on high standards of performance made the detachment a destination for men who would not soldier willingly elsewhere.

The men who came to compose Detachment "A" 3/525 MIG were not everyone's "cup of tea." To begin with, MI soldiers were not average inductees of the drafted army, an institution the very existence of which Lang considered to be an abomination, an insult to the profession of arms, and constitutionally dubious in a situation short of general war. These MI men had been carefully identified by the Army through tests and interviews, and then plucked from the stream of conscripts for the work of espionage. They were case officers or clerks dedicated to the same work. Other members of the detachment were long- service sergeants, warrant officers or officers raised from the ranks in intelligence work. In civilian life, the draftees had been seminarians of lost faith, "cub" reporters, graduate students who had run out of money or CIA management trainees unwilling to hide from military service in reserve duty at CIA headquarters.

They had a distressing but amusing habit of staging casualty "pools" to wager on the magnitude of disasters experienced in operations by the South Vietnamese Army. The ineptitude and frequent cowardice of these native soldiers made the idea attractive.

One corporal from Los Angeles had been in Viet Nam for two years and had been thrown out of Tay Ninh Province the previous year at New Year for firing a thirty round "banana clip" from an M-2 Carbine into the sandbagged wall of the house trailer of the American Army colonel who was the province senior advisor. It was his idea of a joke. It must have been quite a party. Exile to Song Be was accepted by the colonel as an alternative to court-martial. In Lang's detachment, this was thought of as a youthful indiscretion. In the Third Battle of Song Be, this man was a tower of strength.

After some months of Lang's tenure of command, it came to be an accepted idea in 525th MIG that recalcitrant soldiers who, nonetheless, showed promise were to be sent to Song Be to live with Lang and his ruffians. A couple of weeks of that made "believers" out of them, and they returned to their units. A few asked to stay, an even smaller number were allowed to do so.

Lang's relationship to the CIA presence in Song Be was a "sometimes thing." There were two actual Directorate of Operations career "spooks" and four or five army sergeants seconded to "The Agency" for the purpose of running the Phoenix Program campaign in Phuoc Long Province. There were also forty Montagnard tribal fighters involved in that program who served in what was called the "Province Reconnaissance Unit." The purpose of this program was a search for underground Vietcong political cadres throughout the province. The American sergeants were supposedly there to lead the Montagnards, but it was soon evident to Lang that the pervasive presence of the enemy in the countryside so frightened these "CIA" people that they never left Song Be and instead, devoted themselves to drinking and playing cards.

In an effort to "get along," Lang went to a range in town to shoot with the head CIA man. This fellow had spent his life in Moscow and hardly knew one end of a rifle from the other. He was in his mid-fifties, grey haired and distinguished looking. He seemed friendly.

After watching Lang shoot, he asked how Lang felt about shooting individuals. The reply was that this would depend on who they were. A "star grade" Garand sniper rifle was produced along with a case of match grade ammunition. Such a rifle was marked with a stamped star on the muzzle and was an exceptional piece.

Lang soon learned from his CIA "friend" that VC agitprop teams were terrorizing villagers in various remote parts of the province by holding "people's courts" at night, convicting small landholders and shopkeepers of "social crimes," and then supervising the villagers as they were forced to kill and bury them.

"What's that to me?" Lang replied. "It's your job to stop that. My job is to use my men to find enemy troops and see to it that they are fought."

The CIA man was silent.

"Ah," Lang replied to the silence. "They won't do it, will they? These drunken clowns won't go do it, and the Montagnards can't do it alone. All right, let's make a deal. You say you are going to build a new compound for yourselves behind the house you now live in. When you move, I want the old house. I want to get my headquarters out of the CORDS "village.""

The Agency chief held out a hand in agreement.

As a result of this conversation, Lang accepted the task of a voluntary additional "night job" for CIA. When VC agitprop activities became too outrageous in contested villages, he traveled to the scene with a couple of Montagnards from the Province Reconnaissance Unit for the purpose of breaking up "people's courts" with one well-placed round. He did this half a dozen times until he learned that the VC had begun to search for an American who carried a sniper rifle. At that point he returned the rifle to the CIA, but by then he had moved into the house that he wanted.

"Try us, oh Lord,
And find the ground of our hearts..."

In the autumn of 1968, the enemy high command decided to attempt once again to bring American forces in Viet Nam to decisive battle to inflict casualties that would cause the American people to demand an end to the war. In this plan, three NVA divisions marched south from Cambodian sanctuaries. They passed around both sides of Song Be, the capital of Phuoc Long Province, slipping between and among the various locations from which Lang's detachment operated. As they passed, these divisions exerted maximum pressure to keep American intelligence and reconnaissance bottled up in the towns of Phuoc Long Province.

Ground fighting became commonplace around the Song Be defense perimeter. This defense was made up of fortified "hard points" ringing the hilltop town. This was itself surrounded on three sides by a loop of the Song Be River. A MACV Advisory Team, the RVN province headquarters, the 31st ARVN Ranger Battalion, an ARVN infantry battalion, a Special Forces "B" team fort (B-32), and various Regional and Popular Forces militia units held portions of the defense line around the hilltop. The Vietnamese town and small airfield "sheltered" within.

Six miles south of town, a U.S. corps artillery heavy battery was in position beside an airfield that had been built by the Japanese during WWII. This battery had two eight-inch howitzers and two 175 mm long rifles, as well as numerous 40 mm mobile AA guns and quad-fifty machine guns mounted on halftracks. In the battle that followed in February 1969 for the survival of the Americans in Song Be, the fires of this battery made the difference between life and death.

In the course of the passage of the three enemy divisions in December and January 1968-69, flank guard battalions of regular NVA infantry three times penetrated the perimeter of Song Be. At the time, these seemed to be maximum efforts to overrun the town, but experience of the real thing the next month showed that Lang's agents were right when they insisted that the NVA only wanted to "keep you occupied" while their force moved south toward Bien Hoa, Saigon and Long Binh.

Throughout this period, Lang's growing intelligence collection operations against the passing force continued. Air and artillery strikes harassed the massive enemy force while US ground and air forces fought them on successive lines, weakening them greatly before they reached their assembly areas to the south

In early December, Lang accompanied Company "D," 2nd Battalion, 7th Cavalry Regiment on a bomb damage assessment (BDA) mission to learn the effect of a B-52 strike (Arclight) that had been run on an enemy troop concentration about 15 kilometers northwest of Song Be. The strike was made because of the detachment's information. The mission was run out of Landing Zone "Buttons" at the Victor 241 airfield where the corps heavy battery was located.

Airborne, but standing off a few miles, the cavalry troops watched the B-52 strike. The sky and the earth shook in mutual sympathy. The company landed at the south end of the stricken area and plodded north looking for evidence of the effect. There were the usual craters, ten to fifteen feet deep in the loamy soil. Tropical hardwood trees had been thrown around like toys. It was the moon with torn green foliage everywhere. Wild animals wandered in from the edges of the strike, concussed into oblivion and unafraid of the cavalry soldiers.

Four NVA soldiers sat in one bunker in the "sweet spot" between four craters. All were dead with not a scratch on them, killed by the "overpressure." There were broken bunkers and pieces of NVA troops everywhere. The enemy had used this place as a "staging" and rest area for the major troop movement toward the south.

Lang trudged north with the company commander, his radiomen and a Kit Carson Scout. This was an enemy prisoner of war who had changed sides. On the edge of the blasted area, a terribly mutilated NVA captain was found. It was clear from his injuries that this man would live but a few hours. His legs were gone, as was one arm, and his genitalia. His viscera littered the ground. His head was still in one piece. He focused on the two American officers and whispered hoarsely. The Scout would not translate, would not look at him. He began to speak in French.

Lang knelt.

The captain pawed with a bloody hand.

"Eh, bien, mon vieux, qu'est ce que tu veux?" Lang asked.

"Grace, frere, grace," was what the man said.

Lang rose and told the cavalry commander what had been spoken.

One shot was fired.

Spinoza grieved well when he said that, "because man loves God, it does not follow that he has any right to expect that God will love him in return."

Garryowen in Glory, the 7ᵗʰ Cavalry Regiment at Ap Bu Nho

By a quirk of fate, the same company was given the chance to demonstrate the plausibility of Spinoza's despair.

A Montagnard agent reported to Lang that the 141ˢᵗ NVA Regiment was temporarily in position just to the west of the Montagnard resettlement village of Ap Bu Nho, 20 kilometers southwest of Song Be. This village, like others in Phuoc Long province, had been created in earlier years of war and migration throughout Indochina. It was perfectly rectangular, three streets wide and five hundred feet long with the long axis running east-west, with a dirt road extending to the asphalt two lane road connecting Song Be with the south. The Song Be River passed north-south to the west of the village. There was a circular patch of woods just northwest of the village. The wood was about one kilometer in diameter. The river ran along the west side of the wood. On the eastern side of the wood, was a large "field" covered with grass, hip high. The field extended along the whole northern side of the village and out to the tar road. There were three or four hundred inhabitants living in tribal style in long houses and other flimsily built shacks. These folk originally lived in the area of the French post of Camp Roland in the northeastern corner of Phuoc Long Province. They had moved or been moved during the First Indochina War. They were S'tiengan people. The agent was one of them and lived in Ap Bu Nho.

Lang drove to Landing Zone (LZ) "Buttons" near Song Be with this information to visit the command post of the 2ⁿᵈ Battalion, 7ᵗʰ Cavalry which was then operating from the landing zone. In a bunkered underground facility, he talked to the Intelligence Staff Officer of the battalion. Lang had been providing this officer with information for some weeks. An example had been the information that led to the BDA mission previously mentioned.

While the two intelligence officers were discussing the report, the lieutenant colonel commanding 2/7 Cavalry entered the command post. He was new, having arrived in country within the previous month, and having joined the battalion the week before.

In his late thirties, blond, and in his newfound dignity as a commander, he had a "lean and hungry look." The S-2 introduced Lang to him, told him how valuable the detachment's information had been in the past. The CO seemed to have a hard time understanding who Lang was. In talking to Lang, he seemed to be more interested in "showing off" for his operations staff than in listening. The idea of an intelligence officer resident in the province who had brought him information seemed more than he could handle. After a few minutes, he tired of the whole thing and asked to be shown on the map. After a glance, he asked the S-3 what "D" Company would be doing the next day. This major said that "D" was in LZ "Buttons" resting and refitting. The CO casually said "Well, put'em in there at first light." His finger indicated the big, grassy clearing in the angle between Bu Nho and the round woods to the west. The S-2 looked at Lang, opened his mouth and then said nothing.

Lang thought, *what the hell! I don't work for this man...* "Colonel," he began, "there is at least a battalion of the 141st NVA Regiment in that wood. They are the best troops in the 7th NVA Division, which is the best in their army. They have been in that wood for at least two weeks. They will be ready."

The CO was irritated. "That's all right, Captain," he said. "You are really a captain, aren't you? We'll take it from here. Most of these reports are untrue. When I was here as an adviser in the Delta, none of the stuff we got from you people was true."

The man did not believe the report and was simply looking for something for "B" Company to do. This was a delicate situation.

"I must protest, sir," Lang began. "I would be negligent..."

"That will be all!" the CO barked. "Good Day!" The sycophants on the staff bristled in the hope that their master would recognize them as the good dogs they were.

Lang drove back to Song Be and called his higher headquarters to tell them that a disaster was about to occur. The foreseeable reply from 525th MIG in Saigon was that they would not attempt to interfere with the exercise of authority by a line officer in command of troops in the field. Lang then asked for a helicopter to come to Song Be to be at his disposal the next day. This was agreed. The "Huey" showed up early, and Lang was sitting in the thing at 3,000 feet listening to the 1st Cavalry Division when the fire preparation of Ap Bu Nho commenced.

> *"They will not grow old, as we who are left grow old,*
> *Age will not weary them, nor the years condemn.*
> *At the going down of the sun, and in the mornings,*
> *We shall remember them…"*
> *Inscribed in Washington Arch at VMI*

There was a lot of fire from corps heavy artillery batteries, including the one at the Victor 241 airfield. Then there were tactical fighter strikes with bombs and rockets. Then there was a massive fire preparation by armed helicopters. The 1st Cavalry Division had many. The bombs, shells, and rockets searched the round wood and the big, grassy field.

While the armed helicopters were still working on the patch of forest, twenty odd "Huey Slicks" (transports unarmed except for a machine gun on each side), swooped onto the scene from the east, having picked up "B" Company at LZ "Buttons."

Throughout the preparation, there had not been a shot fired from the area under bombardment.

Lang could hear the cavalry division talking about it on the air. Their opinion was that this would be a "cold" LZ, and that the enemy was not present. With mixed feelings, Lang watched the assault unfold. The landing was in two columns of helicopters, perhaps fifty yards apart. There were ten helicopters in each column. The cavalry troops scrambled out of the aircraft and headed for the round wood.

The 141st NVA Infantry Regiment had held its fire throughout the preparatory bombardment. This was a remarkable display of fire discipline. As the helicopters lifted, the enemy opened fire in a roaring, ripping demonstration of just how much firepower a well-trained and disciplined light infantry force can possess.

Four "Slicks" were shot down on the LZ. All four exploded. It was not likely that anyone lived. The fire balls killed a number of "D" Company men nearby. Several more helicopters were badly damaged and departed smoking.

The NVA had organized the defense of the wood in such a way that interlocking bands of machine gun fire from log and earth bunkers crisscrossed in the open field. The guns appeared to have been laid so that the fire was about two to three feet above the ground. The inevitable dips in the ground were filled with the fires of mortars shooting from positions behind the bunker line.

A general in the War Between the States remarked on a similar occasion that "not even a chicken could live under that fire." It was thus.

The NVA were all in the round wood. The bunkers themselves, as later inspected, were solidly built with two layers of hardwood logs separated by a foot of packed earth and with another layer of earth on top. They had firing embrasures six inches high, were positioned for mutual support and were staggered in depth.

"D" Company 2/7 Cavalry was "dead meat" out in that field in the bright sunlight. They could not move forward, and to move back meant rising, which was certain death.

The fighters and armed helicopters returned to repeatedly bomb and rocket the woods. Corps artillery joined in when the aircraft withdrew. It did not help. 12.7 mm heavy machine guns and RPG-7 teams engaged the aircraft from within the NVA position. The iron grip of the 141st NVA held "D" Company fast. Everyone was pinned flat on the LZ, face to the dirt.

Additional cavalry troops were inserted into the fight. The rest of 2/7 Cav landed to the east of "D" Company, 1/5 Cav landed north of the round wood, and 2/12 Cav landed to the west of the Song Be River and west of the round wood. All these insertions were by helicopter. What they discovered, as they closed on the wood, was that the 141st had organized the position for an all-around defense. The volume of fire and the strength of the bunkers were as solid on the other sides as they were on the east. The position was so large and so well put together that it may well have contained the whole 141st Regiment.

The reinforcements got nowhere. The only difference between their situations and that of "D" Company was that they were not pinned down at close quarters. All these units took substantial losses in this fight.

Wounded from "D" Company crawled toward the eastern side of the big clearing. They crawled toward the earthen "dike" that carried the main north-south road. They could be seen from the air. As some got across the road, Medevac helicopters began landing in the fire shadow of the road to pick them up.

The warrant officer flying the 525th MIG "Huey" told Lang he would land to pick up wounded. Altogether, the strange helicopter with the blue boomerang insignia on the tail boom, made four trips from LZ "Buttons" to Ap Bu Nho carrying 2/7 Cavalry's wounded. After a while, the floor of the bird was slippery, and everyone in back was busy trying to keep some of them alive long enough to deliver them to the medics. The helicopter took a number of hits.

About four in the afternoon, the CO of 2/7 Cavalry made a fatal error. He requested a napalm strike on the round wood. December was the height of the dry season, and the wind was blowing steadily from the west. This could be seen by the direction that smoke drifted across the battlefield. The

napalm strike went in, delivered by two F-4 Phantoms. It may have done some damage to the NVA, but what it certainly did was to light a grass fire that swept toward "D" Company. The Company faced an ancient dilemma.

Lang's great-grandfather had written of the same problem in the Wilderness in 1864. The choice to be made was to lie prone and burn or stand and be shot.

According to the medics at Ap Bu Nho, most preferred to be shot.

While men were facing the necessity of choice, "D" Company's commander decided that he would not accept the choice. With his pockets full of grenades, he crawled as close as possible to the nearest machine gun bunker. With a dozen of his men firing in support, he rushed the bunker while throwing grenades. He jumped down into the position and killed all within with his pistol.

With the help of this small crack in the enemy position, "D" Company moved forward behind their captain and by nightfall had broken the outer defense perimeter of the 141st. They held half a dozen bunkers.

The sun went down. The fight ended. All night long the Cavalry Division moved forces into the area to finish the 141st the next morning.

"Good! Whenever you find a real bastard, especially a dumb bastard,
make sure you stake him down, through the heart, through the heart!"
LTC (Ret.) Walter P. Lang to his son, June 1969
"It is not a mercy to tolerate incompetence in officers,
think of the poor men…"
Robert E. Lee, thinking of Bristoe Station

In the morning, it was discovered that the enemy had gone, taking their dead and wounded with them. They had slipped out through some gap in the surrounding lines and simply vanished.

"D" Company was extracted and mustered at LZ "Buttons" that afternoon. There were 12 men in the ranks. 52 killed and over 70 wounded was the "Butcher's Bill" at Ap Bu Nho.

This may have been the single worst day's bloodletting in the 7th Cavalry since the Little Big Horn. There too, they had been commanded by a fool.

At the muster, the company commander, who was unscathed, stood dry eyed before his remnant while strong men wept, Lang among them.

Lang asked the battalion commander and the S-3 how they spelled their names and left. He would have happily killed them both with his own hand, and they seemed to know that. He sent his report of the action disguised as an intelligence report on the performance of the 141st. It went to every echelon of command above 2/7 Cavalry. Under investigation by division headquarters, the lieutenant colonel later claimed that the agent's report had been a "provocation" intended to lure him into an ambush. The Division commander was not deceived.

525th MIG saw through Lang's subterfuge, and he was admonished for responding to the operations side's attempt to scapegoat intelligence for its own failure. This was the first instance in which he saw this syndrome of the leadership of the intelligence community. He continued to see it for the rest of his government career.

The battalion CO and the S-3 were eventually relieved for cause a few days later and given jobs in which it was unlikely that they could waste men's lives. In later life, Lang treasured the belief that his report had contributed to their end.

The Huron Carol

By Jean de Brebeuf, S.J., Martyr

"Twas in the moon of wintertime, when all the birds had fled,
That God the Lord of all the earth sent angel choirs instead
Before their light the stars grew dim
and wandering hunters heard the hymn.
Within a lodge of broken bark, the tender babe was found.
A ragged robe of rabbit skin enwrapped his beauty round;
But as the hunter braves drew nigh,
the angel song rang loud and high.
The earliest moon of wintertime is not so round and fair,
As was the ring of glory on the helpless infant there.
The chiefs from far before him knelt
with gifts of fox and beaver pelt.
O, children of the forest free, the angel song is true.
The holy child of earth and heav'n is born today for you.
Come kneel before the radiant boy,
Who brings you beauty, peace and joy."

   The war went on in the central highlands. At Christmas time, Lang decided to hold a detachment party. He mentioned this to Paul Landon during a visit by him to Song Be. As they discussed this, a five-gallon water jug of homemade "hootch" bubbled happily in a corner of Lang's office under the beneficent warmth of an electric light. Pineapple juice, brewer's yeast and a daily "feeding" of sugar were creating something within that obviously was alive. The application of sugar invariably produced a tempest in the bottle. The men began to think of it as a pet.

Landon ignored the bottle. "Are you going to leave someone to man each station?" he asked. "That's all right then," he said when assured. "Let's not tell Group. They already think you and I are nuts."

Lang bought cases of Mumm's Cordon Rouge champagne and other goodies in Saigon, and on the appointed day mysterious personages began to arrive from all over the border on Air America's scheduled service. There were about twenty partygoers. The province senior advisor, LTC Hernando Guzman and the local CIA boss attended. There was much singing of Christmas carols, as well as a ham, a turkey and such delicacies cooked by the kitchen in Special Forces camp B-32 in town.

In preparation for the party, the men decorated the house. An evergreen tree was found on the slopes of the mountain, and holly was retrieved from an abandoned school a few miles away.

"For every boot that tramped in battle,
every cloak rolled in blood,
will be burned as fuel for flames.
For a child is born to us, a son is given..."
Isaiah, 9:1-3, 5-6

At midnight, celebration was interrupted by the sound of machine gun fire in the distance. The revelers trooped outside to see if they were going to have to fight on Christmas Eve. There were hard words concerning the ancestry of the enemy. Across the wire, across the outpost line, across the valley of no-man's land were the crests occupied habitually by the "opposition." From these heights there rose a stream of green, Soviet-made "tracer." The celebrants contemplated this for a minute, and then Guzman suggested a reply. An M-60 machine gun emerged from the house, and while one man fired red tracer into the air, another held the bipod above his head, and another fed the gun its belted ammunition. The streams of bullets crossed in the black, star filled sky. The VC gun fell silent, as did the American. There was a hush as warriors waited for some sign that the hope of common humanity yet lived. The VC fire resumed. Now there were three guns shooting green stars into the blackness. The MI men's guns chattered merrily, spilling a river of shell casings into the street. Red and green filled the night.

"You understand, I could shoot you where you sit..."

Just after the New Year arrived, Lang decided to expand the detachment's operational zone into Duck Phuong District to the east of Song Be. After some thought, he picked one of the most experienced men in the group to go. This fellow had been a newspaperman in Boston and, along with one remaining case officer, had been in Song Be when Lang arrived. With no expectation of a problem, Lang told the man, a sergeant covered as a warrant officer, what the plan was. The soldier, who was named Tom, said no, he would not go. When asked why, he said that he liked it in Song Be. Lang repeated himself with regard to Tom's future address. The response was the same. Lang said,

"OK, I'll give you two days to think it over, and if you feel the same way, I'll return you to battalion. They can do what they want. I will recommend trial by General Court-Martial for disobedience of a lawful order." Tom left.

The next day, the other soldier who pre-dated Lang, and who was Tom's buddy, showed up, plunked himself down, and after trying to talk the CO out of Tom's transfer, said that perhaps Lang should be careful because officers who did things like this sometimes had "bad things" happen to them. The detachment clerk was sitting within earshot. Lang asked him if he had heard. He had and was sent out of the building. Lang retrieved his sidearm from a desk drawer and laid it on the desk. "Let me explain to you the niceties of military law," he began. "You are armed and have, before a witness, mutinously threatened your commanding officer under combat conditions. I could shoot you where you sit and get away with it. Perhaps I will... Take your pistol out of the holster carefully and lay it on the floor." He did so. "Let me give you a message for anyone who thinks like you," Lang said. "If any of you think it would be profitable to "frag" me, know that if you do not succeed, I will kill anyone I suspect of complicity. There will be no trials and no mercy. Do you understand? Yes? Good, get out! You are forbidden to carry a weapon until further notice." He left.

The next day he was back to ask if Tom could still go to Duk Phuong and if Lang would accept his own apology. The answer to both questions was yes. Tom left for Duk Phuong the following day where he did a splendid job.

The "mutineer" was transferred at Lang's request to clerical duties at battalion headquarters a week later.

"At least no one from Group comes to bother us..."
Joe Hole

At about this time, the detachment received an unexpected visit from a staff officer at battalion headquarters in Bien Hoa. This was a Major Gerald McGinnis, a tall blond man, graduated from West Point, who had been in and out of the army a couple of times and who had come back in specifically to volunteer for service in Viet Nam. He was operations officer (S-3) of the battalion and had been harmless from Lang's point of view since Lang normally conducted his business with the battalion commander, Paul Landon. After a few minutes' conversation, McGinnis announced that he had come to confiscate all unauthorized weapons. The manning and equipping documents of the 525th MIG had been written for a European environment. The only weapons authorized were .38 caliber snub-nosed revolvers. In the border war setting, these were toys for children. After learning that this was not a joke, Lang protested and reminded McGinnis that he, McGinnis, always carried an M-16 rifle and .45 automatic pistol, indeed, he had them with him now. McGinnis said that his orders from 525th MIG were to confiscate all such "illegal" weapons, and that he would do so. If Lang refused to accept this, he would be relieved for cause. Clearly, Landon had sent this loser to do something that he was required to do, but for which he had no taste. Lang told McGinnis that they would give him the weapons, but that if anyone died in Song Be as a result, his friends would remember. McGinnis blanched and asked if that was a threat. "No, only an observation," was the answer. McGinnis left and never returned. This was wise.

Five minutes after his departure, Lang left for the SF camp and the advisory team compound where the detachment was issued new weapons by those who relied on the fighting spirit of the MI men to help them stay alive. The new weapons were actually better than the old ones.

As their divisions continued to march south from Cambodia toward the South Vietnamese capital region, the enemy increased his efforts to press US and RVN forces back inside the perimeters of the scattered hill towns.

In late January, Lang's operations discovered the presence of a battalion-sized VC force in a Catholic re-settlement village named Long Dien. This settlement was a few miles west of the V-241 airfield. The village was perfectly square. The streets were laid out in a grid. The gravel roads were crowned. There were several thousand inhabitants. A white church stood in the central square. The houses were solidly built of white stucco and all had red tile roofs. Lang had maintained an agent in the town for months. It was clear to him that the parish priest ran the town.

Lang passed this intelligence to the U.S. adviser of the ARVN 31 Ranger Battalion in Song Be. The Vietnamese commander decided to visit *Long Dien* with his men. Lang was asked by the American to "tag along." The battalion slipped out of Song Be late one night and marched through the jungle to the outskirts of the objective village. They arrived in midafternoon. The distance covered was about fifteen miles. With troops on three parallel streets, the battalion moved toward the church. Halfway there they were halted in their tracks by snipers firing from houses and crew-served machine guns firing down the axes of the streets from the front and the flanks. There were ditches along the streets. The Rangers took shelter in these ditches. Lang, the American adviser, his radio operator and the Vietnamese battalion commander were all pinned down together in one section of ditch with streams of machine gun bullets passing overhead. An impromptu conference took pace in which the possibility of calling for artillery or tactical air bombing of the pretty little town was discussed. With no dissent from the Americans, the Ranger battalion CO decided that they would not destroy the town. They would wait for darkness and then slip away, leaving the same way they had come. When night had come, the ARVN officer announced to Lang and the other two Americans that a messenger had arrived at the head of his column to summon him to a meeting in the church. After some time, he returned. In the church he had met with the priest and the commander of the enemy force. The enemy commander, a major, had wanted to know why the town had not been subjected to bombardment. When told of the collective decision, he had said that he did not want to see the town wrecked and would withdraw before dawn. The Ranger said that the VC commander had asked if any of the Americans carried a rifle with a telescopic sight.

A messenger would necessarily go back to the church with the agreement of all concerned. Before a lieutenant crawled forward with the message, Lang asked him to tell the enemy major not to stand in firelight too long.

When the man came back, he said to Lang that the enemy officer had laughed and said that he looked forward to an early meeting.

In the morning these "foemen worthy of our steel" were gone.

CHAPTER NINETEEN

Doc Lap! Doc Lap!

"They believed that we had simply replaced the French as a colonial power,
And we saw Vietnam as an element of the Cold War."
Robert S. McNamara

In the first week of January, Lang was called to a meeting in Bien Hoa at battalion headquarters. It was a routine quarterly meeting of commanders and staff to review performance and requirements. He had a number of ways to travel to and from Song Be in Phuoc Long Province: Air America, 525th MIG helicopter, a passing Forward Air controller, Air Viet Nam, or a space available ride on a USAF cargo carrier hauling freight to Song Be. The roads were not an option for anyone who did not want to sample the hospitality of the Viet Cong or North Vietnamese Army.

On this occasion, he chose to "hitch" a ride on a USAF C-130 "Hercules" flying to the Victor 241 airfield south of Song Be. The four big artillery pieces located at the airfield were continuously supplied by air with ammunition and replacement barrels for the guns. This aircraft would have a cargo of "tubes" for the battery.

At the scheduled time for the arrival of the four-engine cargo plane, Lang waited on the small, pierced steel planking "apron" at the airfield. One of his men had driven him from town. They sat smoking and chatting in a jeep. Both were in uniform.

The looming peak of the Nui Ba Ra Mountain seemed to hang over them to the east, a brooding green presence that could never be avoided.

Montagnards trudged past on the old French colonial road. They peered at the Americans. Their woven baskets seemed heavy. They were on their way to sell their produce in the marketplace in Song Be. Two children walked up to the jeep and held out a hand. Their copper colored bodies exuded the smell of wood smoke and dried amniotic fluid still on them from the time of their births. Lang's driver found a couple of candy bars for the kids. Their mother came to collect them. Her withered breasts, teeth stained black with betel nut and filed to points were an unappetizing sight. She was probably about twenty years old.

The laterite soil of central Vietnam was everywhere. Red earth and steamy green jungle dominated.

There was an air force aerial port detachment located at the airfield. There were half a dozen airmen. They lived with the artillery and handled loading and unloading of cargo. For this purpose, they had forklifts and heavy trucks. Wooden pallets from previous cargo were stacked to one side of the apron.

A very young air force enlisted man sat on a forklift. He pointed at the horizon to the south. "Here she comes," he called out. "Here she comes."

Lang smiled. There was a strangely comedic element in the scene somewhat like the opening of a popular TV show of the 80s in which a dwarf in a white tropical suit pointed at the sky to shout, "Da plane! Da plane!"

The C-130 was low over the trees beyond the end of the runway. The big plane had its wheels and flaps down. As it crossed the end of the runway a recoilless rifle fired from the tree line to Lang's right. The aircraft was twenty feet in the air when the shell hit it below the wing root. Machine gun fire bored through the flight deck. The aircraft hit the ground hard and burst

into an enormous fireball. The flaming wreckage slid toward Lang's jeep. Mortar "bombs" began to fall on the apron. Lang and his driver rolled out of the jeep and under it. The VC put twenty rounds of what seemed to be 82 mm mortar fire into the apron. The burning airplane came to a halt out on the runway. The heat was intense. The mortar fire ended, and Lang concentrated on screaming from nearby. The sound pierced his skull.

On his feet next to the jeep he saw the air force forklift operator rolling from side to side on the steel planking. This man, a boy really, had been caught by the mortar fire while seated high in the air on his machine. Several pieces of ragged steel had penetrated his back and side.

Lang picked him up and cradled him in his arms.

"No. No," the boy said. "No." And with that he died.

Lang thought, *to hell with it,* and called his battalion to say that he would not be coming to the meeting.

Lang's life in the border region involved frequent collaboration with the US Air Force. He had formed the habit of flying with the Forward Air Controllers (FAC) who maintained a small "fleet" of Cessna Bird Dog aircraft at Song Be for the purpose of guiding air strikes to enemy troops located out in the woods. Lang went on these flights to help the pilots find targets that his operations had found. These pilots had learned the technique involved in adjusting Army artillery fire and they seemed to do that as much as direct air strikes. Riding with them in the back seat of their flimsy, underpowered planes was a great adventure. Lang made it a habit to sit on his body armor jacket in the probably naïve hope that that flying metal might be kept out of his "butt." He carried an M-79 grenade launcher on these trips. The FAC aircraft were often engaged by anti-aircraft weapons on the ground. When that happened, the FAC pilot would "roll in" on the gun and fire a couple of high explosive rockets at it. They typically carried these as well as marking rockets. Lang would then kneel on the seat in the back, lean out of the cockpit and fire 40 mm grenades down at the gun. The pilots liked that because it often made the gun crew run away from their weapon. Lang's only conflict with the FAC pilots had to do with wild animals. There were standing orders from the air force in Vietnam that draft animals found untended in the jungle were to be killed so that they could not be used by the enemy. Lang loved animals and could not accept such a policy. After several heated discussions he managed to convince several of the pilots to simply ignore orders that required them to kill wild elephants with rockets.

One of the FAC pilots was a red faced, red haired man in his thirties who lived to fly and drink at night in the little club the FAC pilots kept busy in their maintenance area. Lang and he got along splendidly, and they flew together often. Unfortunately, this officer was shot down and killed on the airstrip at Song Be while Lang stood by as a helpless witness. The "Red Baron" had been on "short final" when a rifle bullet came through the fabric floor of his cockpit, sliced through his thigh and cut his femoral artery. The plane "wobbled" out of the air and onto the runway, slowed to a halt and ran off into the grass. By the time Lang and a few others reached the aircraft the man was dead in a deep pool of his own blood.

Lang received orders for a week's Rest and Recreation leave in Hawaii. Marguerite arrived before him and was waiting at the R&R reception center in Honolulu. They spent a wonderful week in a little cottage on the beach at Bellows Air Force Station on the Windward Side of Oahu. Lying in bed and listening to the music of the surf, it seemed impossible that he could return to the war, but he did.

A few days after his return, a CORDS employee came to see him in a state that could best be described as panic. This man was named Emilio Rodriguez. He was a Mexican American from El Paso, a retired army supply sergeant and one of the people in the CORDS team concerned with supply of local building projects throughout the province. He had risen at dawn that day and driven to an outlying Vietnamese village to make a delivery of building materials. Being the person who he was, he had not bothered to check with the province Tactical Operations Center (TOC) with regard to the area he was driving to that morning. If he had checked. he would have known that the village he was going to visit had changed hands during the night. In blissful ignorance he drove down the road in his USAID pick-up truck dressed as usual in jeans, an open necked shirt and cowboy boots. A six shooter rode low in a cowboy style holster.

He turned left a mile or so past the V 241 airfield and drove through an outpost.

The soldiers looked at him and did nothing.

He drove into the village square. There were no civilians on the streets.

Thirty or forty soldiers sat on the steps of the church.

Rodriguez backed his truck up to them, got out, lowered the tail gate and tried to wave the troops over to help with unloading the delivery.

They watched him and did nothing.

Their leader approached.

Rodriguez handed him his clipboard. He needed a signature in receipt of the supplies.

The leader looked at the cement, plywood, chicken wire and the like. He said something to his men, and they began to unload. He signed the receipt and wrote a note on the same piece of paper.

Rodriguez continued to babble but began to focus on the people he was with. He noticed that they all wore dark blue trousers and khaki shirts. The leader wore a pith helmet. There was a red metal star attached to the front. He suddenly understood that he was in the presence of the enemy.

As they watched him, they saw that he recognized his predicament. The VC soldiers laughed as though it was the best joke in the world. They raised his tail gate and waved as he drove away.

Rodriguez described the leader's collar insignia.

"A lieutenant," Lang said. "Show me the receipt."

The note read, *"Dit au tirailleur que nous le visiterons tôt."*

Lang smiled.

"What does it mean" Rodriguez asked. His hands were shaking.

"Ah, 'tell the rifleman that we will visit him soon.'"

Rodriguez looked blank.

"Just a joke, forget it."

The level of combat activity around Song Be rose steadily throughout the following weeks. There was something in the air that suggested an approaching climax.

On the 8th of February, Lang was promoted to major while standing behind a wall outside his detachment headquarters a few hundred feet inside the southeast perimeter of Song Be. During the ceremony, small arms fire came over the wall to strike the upper story of his headquarters. People attending the ceremony did their best to ignore this. His battalion commander, Paul Landon, had flown in for the occasion. He left immediately thereafter. He needed to get out of this place before the incoming fire got worse, or the sun went down. It was correctly feared that the helicopter he had come in would be destroyed or damaged, and that this would maroon the MI battalion staff in a place that might well be captured by the enemy.

Several weeks later, two of the detachment's agents risked their lives to make their way through enemy troops encircling Song Be to report. Both were Montagnard tribesmen. One, a S'tiengan, said that three Main Force VC battalions of infantry and a Sapper company had been ordered to capture Song Be. The assault would be that night and would be timed to coincide with a main attack on the objective of the overall countrywide campaign. This objective would be the American headquarters at Long Binh, outside Saigon. The other man, a M'nong Gar tribesman, had been conscripted to work as a porter for the VC Sapper Engineer company and had exact details on the plan to attack the MACV Advisory Team compound in Song Be with satchel charges and bangalore torpedoes. This would be followed by a general infantry assault. This agent said that the VC province committee believed that if they could kill all the Americans in the advisory team compound, then they would surely eliminate the hated intelligence team that they correctly reasoned was responsible for the deaths of so many of their men. They were mistaken. In fact, none of the detachment's men lived or worked in that compound.

With this information in hand, Lang visited his friend, Lieutenant Colonel Hernando Guzman, the senior advisor to the Vietnamese province governor. Guzman lived in a sandbagged house trailer within the advisory team compound. After listening, Guzman insisted that the enemy realized that they had lost the war in 1968 and that there would be no more serious fighting. He had last said this a week earlier at a concert played by the First Cavalry Division band in the marketplace of Song Be. By then, the combat units of the Cavalry Division had moved far to the south following the enemy's main force, but non-essentials like the band were still available to help the Vietnamese celebrate Tet. Guzman believed that the communists had given up on the idea that they could defeat the United States and that a negotiated peace would soon result. Lang asked how he explained the heavy pressure on Song Be and the massive enemy troop movements toward the south. Guzman said that the VC and NVA were positioning themselves to be able to claim a greater role in a negotiated settlement.

With these reports in hand, Lang begged him not to ignore this warning that his men had risked their lives to bring. Guzman hesitated, but finally said that because of past performance by the detachment, and because of their friendship, he would put half the Advisory Team's men in the defense line that night. This precaution saved the compound from capture in the first assault.

Having done what was needed for the local American force, the detachment reported its warning to higher headquarters, and prepared to receive the attack as best it could at detachment headquarters. Defenses were improved: letters from home burned, ammunition issued to U.S. soldiers and to the Nung guard force that the detachment shared with the CIA compound located nearby. Escape and Evasion plans and routes were reviewed and 525th MIG's aviation detachment was tasked to pick up survivors at rally points if it became necessary to exfiltrate the town. With that done, the four men of the detachment headquarters waited for midnight, the planned time of the enemy attack. They were the only people in town (other than the enemy) who believed that something serious would happen that night. For lack of something better to do, they watched television from Armed Forces Vietnam TV. "Combat," always popular with the troops, featured a gripping drama set in France that evening. Johnny Carson was as amusing as always. At 2330, they shut off the generator, and buried their Collins single sideband radio and TV set.

At 0003, the enemy's preparatory fires commenced. The American and ARVN compounds in Song Be received 500 rounds of mortar and 122 mm artillery rockets in the first 30 minutes. The fire went into the military facilities with considerable accuracy, largely missing the civilian town. Since the detachment's headquarters was on the edge of the town, only a few rounds of 122 mm landed nearby. The crescendo of fire at the other end of the plateau declined after 30 minutes, but explosions could be heard from the area of the Advisory Team compound as well as other military posts. These were followed by a roar of small arms fire from the same places. These sounds marked the enemy's execution of his plan exactly as the Montagnard agents had reported it. Bombardment had been followed by Sapper demolition attacks on the predicted facilities followed by infantry assault on the wired-in defenses. The men manning the front-line bunkers reacted well enough to break the assault as Sappers tried to blow the front gate. The Americans then killed a dozen enemy soldiers of the company sized infantry force trying to climb the double apron barbed wire barrier in front of the bunkers.

At about that time, Hernando Guzman came out of his trailer, climbed into his jeep and drove up to the gate where he blew the horn and demanded that someone unchain the gate and let him out. There were enemy infantrymen still dying in the wire. A Quartermaster Corps captain commanding the defense of these bunkers finally left his shelter to open the gate.

In 1973, Lang ran into this officer, then a major, in the PX at Fort Lee, Virginia. After a few minutes talk, this brave man broke down in tears.

Hernando turned left to approach the Vietnamese Province Chief's fortified residence, found that the gate was locked, and honked his horn to be let in. No one answered because the guards were all dead behind the gate and his counterpart was hiding in the basement of the house from Sappers searching for him. Guzman's attention was then attracted by smoke and firing around the province Tactical Operations Center, an underground facility 100 yards to his right.

He drove to the entrance to the TOC where an enemy soldier standing next to the door shot and killed him.

The TOC had been attacked with satchel charges. These had collapsed the roof, and all the Vietnamese Army people present for duty within had been killed. The three-man American watch team located deeper in the bunker had escaped through a tunnel hidden behind some paneling and had made their way underground to a concrete "paint shed" a few yards from the TOC. There, they had stood watching helplessly through slits in the steel door while Guzman died. Assaults on the military posts continued all night. At one point, the Vietnamese Regional Forces 155 mm howitzer section placed just across from the Advisory Team fired one hundred rounds of "beehive" ammunition at point blank range at attacking troops. This ammunition blasted a multitude of steel darts into an attacking force.

At about the time that Guzman was killed, the Advisory Team's operations advisors (a major and a lieutenant) left the 31ˢᵗ ARVN Rangers compound where they had been attending a promotion party. They drove into the middle of an enemy infantry unit and were killed instantly. Lang found them the next day while making his way to the Advisory Team. Three enlisted soldiers were killed as well in the first bombardment of the Advisory Team's compound. They died in their bunks.

At Lang's end of town, it was relatively quiet while this happened. And then at about 0130, there was a flurry of firing around a Popular Forces (PF) militia post 300 yards away from Lang's house on the perimeter of the town. This suddenly stopped, but a few minutes later, Lieutenant Joe Holte came from the upper story of the building to ask Lang to come upstairs. Holte and an enlisted soldier were manning an M-60 machine gun in an upstairs window. The gun was on a table with two spare barrels and was well protected by sandbags. A mountain of ammunition sat on the floor. Holte pointed through the window. Shadowy figures could be seen advancing in column toward the headquarters from the area of the PF post.

The question to be answered was whether they were friendlies withdrawing or were they the men who had just captured the PF post?

Lang called the SF Camp on a landline laid for such an emergency and asked for illumination over the oncoming troops. Three mortar parachute flares burst in a line over the scene. The light revealed a hundred enemy infantry in column. They were trotting toward the headquarters.

The machine gun opened fire in a chattering, tearing voice, ripping up one side and down the other of the column. The gunner fired a whole belt in one burst, requiring a barrel change and advice on technique. The gun fired on and on while the SF camp kept the area lit up. Lang added to the mayhem by firing 40 mm HE rifle grenades at anyone who looked like he might be a leader. Nevertheless, the very fine soldiers out in the field in front of the house "got it together." As soon as they had heard the mortars' metallic "cough" from the SF camp, the VC started to run forward, going from column into line and then advancing by "fire and movement" against the machine gun. For what seemed forever, but could only have been a minute or so, the two groups contested the moment. Then, more and more rifle fire ripped through the walls around the machine gun, and Chinese stick grenades began to bounce off the outside of the building, detonating as they fell to the ground.

Lang then ordered the evacuation of the building. It would be in enemy hands in a few minutes. The machine gun team went down the stairs and out the back door headed for the Provincial Reconnaissance Unit (PRU) camp seventy-five yards away. Lang could hear Holte yelling "Don't shoot! Don't shoot!" as they crossed the open space. Lang followed the machine gun team down the steps and after getting the Nung guards out of the house he started for the back door. As he passed his office, Lang was stopped by the voice of the fourth soldier in detachment headquarters. He was seated on the floor of the office with a radio battery between his legs and a wire in each hand. These were connected to the thermite document destruction kit locked in the detachment safe with all their records. "Now?" the man asked. The answer was yes. With a happy smile, the records clerk set off the charge that destroyed the hated paperwork. Black smoke poured from the safe. This helped cover the withdrawal from the building.

Hands reached down to help the last two MI men over the defensive berm and into the PRU camp. Inside the dirt walled fort, the PRU Montagnard mercenaries manned the ramparts, trapped within the walls for the time being with their families. The half dozen CIA trainers and advisers were glad to see the MI men. The CIA civilians asked Lang to assume control of the fight and their PRU troops. The rest of the night passed fairly uneventfully. Buildings were burning everywhere. Smoke poured out of the detachment headquarters building and part of it was badly burned. The enemy seemed confused by their losses and unable to locate the Americans in the PRU camp. The noise from the other end of town was deafening. About 0630, in the false dawn, the enemy began to pull back, frustrated in their efforts to capture the province capital and understandably worried about American air power. US Aircraft were certain to show up in the light of day. Just before the sun came up, the NVA began to ring the bells in St. Dominic's Catholic Church a few hundred yards away across the runway and near the PF position that had been destroyed in the night.

> *"Tell the bishop's daughter*
> *that I was obliged to stay with my infantry..."*
> *Major Durnford at Isandhlwana,*
> *to the soldier to whom he gave his horse. 1879*

When it was clear that the enemy had left town for the day, the team dug up a radio and antenna and after starting the CIA's generator, called 3/525 battalion headquarters in Bien Hoa, 70 miles away. After hearing Lang's report of the night's festivities, Paul Landon, the Battalion CO asked Lang what he intended to do. The answer was simple; continue to prepare the PRU compound for defense. Landon asked if Lang thought the detachment should be evacuated. Lang said that he thought this impossible if 525 MIG ever wanted to operate in Song Be again. As long as there were Americans defending Song Be, the MI soldiers had to stay with them, or leave forever.

By this time, the defenders of the PRU camp knew of the advisory team's losses. A captain with less than three years' service had succeeded to command there.

Lang said that he personally felt obliged to stay, and would be staying, but that he would get the men out if that were the decision. Lang couldn't get Durnford's last recorded words out of his head for the next few days.

Landon stopped the conversation so that he could talk to 525th MIG and called back in a few minutes to say that the Group Commander was mightily irritated, but that he grudgingly accepted Lang's opinion. The senior officers of the 525th MIG were men who had been formed in the phony war environment of NATO's protracted staring match with the Soviets. The idea of MI personnel committed to combat was impossible for them to grasp except as a kind of cosmic security violation.

Landon asked what the team needed.

They had opened a CIA arms bunker during the night to find two more M-60 machine guns, an 81 mm mortar and a 57 mm recoilless rifle as well as a couple of Starlight Scopes.

Landon was asked to find two more machine guns, illuminating rounds for the mortar, flechette ammunition for the recoilless gun, and some Claymore mines.

Patrols moved back and forth between the two ends of the town during the day. They met scattered resistance from pockets of NVA holed up in buildings in the town itself as well as in the church. These had probably missed "the word" to leave at dawn.

At around 1030 a silver, unarmed Air America Huey helicopter landed in the PRU compound carrying two crewmen in male flight attendant uniforms. They wore holstered .38 revolvers and carried M-1 Carbines. There were two passengers. One was a uniformed US Marine Lt. Col. and the other was William Colby, the Deputy head of CORDS. The helicopter left and could be seen circling in the distance.

Colby talked to his people while the marine inspected the defenses. Having done that, the marine came to talk to Lang about the fight the previous night.

Colby approached to say that he was ordering the evacuation of his men, and to say that the MI people should leave as well.

Lang asked him what he intended to do about the 40 to 50 PRU soldiers and their families.

Colby said that their safety was their problem.

Lang told him that the MI people would stay with their American and indigenous comrades, and that Colby should not plan on much of a presence on the border in III Corps while memory of this abandonment lived.

Colby said that Lang was "just trying to make us look bad," and that they "would not forget this."

The marine saluted the Army major before he got on the returned helicopter. He clearly believed Lang to be already a dead man. A marine can always respect a man who has died for duty.

Other Air America "birds" came later to take the Agency people away. This included the half dozen Nung guards. Lang's men turned their backs on the departing Americans, would not shake hands with them. The Montagnard headman of the PRU stood holding hands with Lang while they watched the helicopters fly away with his "advisors." He was a picturesque little fellow. He was dressed in a loincloth and boots. His teeth were filed to points and stained the customary black.

Around noon, MACV headquarters in Saigon flew in an Army LTC named Benson who had been unceremoniously jerked from the Saigon staff, as well as a major newly arrived in Vietnam. These officers were replacements for the seniors lost the night before. Huey Cobras plastered the area around the TOC while these two scrambled out of a "slick" and ran for the gate of the Advisory Team compound. The Huey transport took a lot of fire trying to lift off, and then limped across the town smoking and stuttering. It crash-landed in a small lake in front of SF Camp B-34. It had "cleared" the PRU camp by about fifty feet. The SF men came out to retrieve the aircrew.
They spent the rest of the battle manning weapons in the camp.

Throughout the battle for Song Be, the enemy never attacked the SF camp. The place was a miniature Gibraltar and they were simply afraid to do so. After the second day, Major Bill Helms, the camp commander, and a friend from the 8th SF Group in Panama, started making announcements over his public address loudspeakers saying in Vietnamese that the enemy commander was a cowardly incompetent for avoiding the camp. They did not rise to the bait. The SF camp provided much needed mortar fire support for the PRU camp by firing "box barrages" around it during enemy assaults.

During the afternoon, Lang got everyone busy knocking down a number of buildings that stood too close to the PRU camp. TNT, and C-4 were used to weaken the buildings and an available 3/4-ton truck then pushed the walls over. By nightfall, quite respectable fields of fire had been cleared.

In the late afternoon, LTC Landon, showed up with the requested munitions. The helicopter touched down in the compound, made the delivery and went away.

After dark, the party started up again. Mortar attacks were followed by platoon assaults against the three vulnerable walls of the camp. The fourth faced the MI house and the open space did not provide enough room for a deployment prior to an assault.

On the other three sides, the MI soldiers could see the VC coming with the Starlight Scopes. The 81 mm mortar then fired illumination to light up the scene, the machine guns chopped them up on the way in, and the 57 mm recoilless blew holes in the assault line as they approached the barbed wire outside the berm. Claymore mines threw fragments into them as they left. By about 0100 it was clear to them and to the defenders that they were not going to take the camp this way, and they stopped for the night.

The noise from the other end of town indicated that similar activities were underway.

Lang ever afterward remembered the calm courage of the three MI soldiers, and the way the PRU men took heart from that.

He also remembered that the 81 mm flare shells made an interesting noise as the base separated from the parachute flare. There would be a "pop," followed by the light and a "whup, whup, whup," noise as the base of the shell fell several hundred feet to earth striking the tin roof of a building with a "clang," or a strange earthen noise as it struck the ground. These bases weighed a couple of pounds and had fins on them. They were a hazard in themselves.

The MI men and the PRU held the camp for two days and nights. It was much the same both nights. The enemy averaged half a dozen attacks a night against the camp and seemed to be slow to learn. This may have reflected a loss of leaders. In daylight the PRU patrolled out a few hundred feet and carried messages to other parts of town. At night, the enemy renewed their attacks. By the third day this was becoming routine, but that afternoon Lang's second in command, a captain covered as a civilian, made his way with escort from the Advisory Team compound to say that one of the detachment's agents had managed to make contact with his case officer to report that the enemy had decided that the PRU camp was a severe nuisance, and that they were going to mass several hundred men against it that night. Lang thought that the enemy had probably lost fifty or so men against the camp's defenses. There were that many bodies rotting in the sun in front of the PRU camp's wired-in defenses, rotting and noisily breaking wind in the obscene flatulence of the unburied. Nevertheless, this scale of reaction was unexpected. It seemed impossible that the little fort could be held against these odds. The defenders of the PRU camp had lost four dead and a dozen wounded who were being cared for by the SF camp medics to whom those who lived long enough were delivered each morning.

After considering the situation, Lang consulted the PRU leaders. They said they wanted to leave the compound and Song Be. He asked how they proposed to do that. They said that they believed that the VC force had been disorganized by the fighting, and that they could slip out of town during the night. Lang thought about this, talked to the other Americans and found that they, too, wanted to move to one of the larger defended camps. He thought it over. *Why should these people die because I like to fight?* He thought. Maybe Colby was right... He decided to accept the wishes of the PRU leader and his men.

The Americans gave the PRU everything they wanted that they could carry. They kept the night vision gear and two of the machine guns.

In the late afternoon, Lang watched the PRU men and their families march out of the camp and into the town. Shortly after they had left, it was pointed out to him that Republic of Viet Nam flags had disappeared from the streets and that enemy flags were beginning to go up on houses. He knew that meant that the townspeople judged that the VC would rule there that night and that they accepted the idea. This changed the PRU's situation radically. Remorse filled him for his acceptance of their attempt to escape. He knew that they would lose many trying to break out of the town. The women and children would likely suffer worst. It was too late. Regret, indeed, shame, for taking the easy way, for yielding to temptation, for allowing these people to ruin themselves, would haunt him. He had failed to live by Durnford's example.

The four Americans moved at dusk to the province advisory team's compound at the northwest corner of the Song Be plateau. Lang was asked to act as principal staff officer and deputy to LTC Benson, the new Senior

Advisor. The major who had been flown in with Benson had been killed by a sniper within 24 hours of his arrival. Lang and Benson were the only surviving field grade officers in Song Be. Lang was also asked to have his men take over defense of the Number Three outside Berm Bunker in the compound's defenses.

This defense was laid out on the very edge of the plateau. The bunker and trench line followed the geographical edge, snaking around in a rough quarter-circle. Double-apron barbed wire obstacles fronted the excavated field fortifications with concertina wire piled up between the two lines of fences. Fields of fire had been cleared all the way to the bottom of the slope for about three hundred yards. The Song Be River lay there and beyond the river there were more hills. The difficulty with this terrain lay in three spurs or fingers which jutted out in front of the main position. Each of these extended forward perhaps fifty feet at the same elevation as the main line, but then broke sharply downward. As a result, the downward slope from these three fingers could not be seen from the main line. To deal with this, three fighting positions had been built outside the main entrenchments, one on each spur at the break point in the ground. The three positions were built of sandbags, steel I-beams, concrete and chicken wire. The sandbags formed the walls, rising out of the terrain. The I-beams held up the roofs. These were made of concrete and more I-beams. Chicken wire was fastened to the pyramidal top and extended to the sandbag wall where its skirt was buried. The intention was that grenades would bounce off the wire and roll to the ground where they would explode harmlessly. This worked in just that way. These positions would hold four men and two M-60 machine guns. Number Three was connected to the main fortifications by a zigzagged communications trench about six feet deep.

It was a lonely place, and it had been under more or less continuous attack each night since the battle had begun. The advisory team had been holding this exposed position with a group of Ordnance Corps motor mechanics who had done a good job, but who had reached the end of their emotional capital in doing so. LTC Benson asked for the MI men to take over, and Lang accepted.

It was the post of honor.

The enemy seemed to have decided that if they were to take the advisory team compound, they should begin with the Number Three Bunker. God only knew why. It looked just like the other two except that it stood at the extreme right of the defense. Perhaps what they really wanted was to take the Vietnamese Headquarters compound that was next in line. Number Three Bunker's machine guns covered the front of that position.

In any event, the VC had come to Song Be to kill the MI men. This would be their greatest opportunity.

There were eight members of the detachment in Song Be. Six were thought to be military by the other Americans, and two were covered as civilian members of the advisory team. One of these "civilians" was Lang's second in command, a solid fellow commissioned from the ranks. He took his place in the line with everyone else without comment. He and Lt. Joe Holte commanded the Number Three bunker. The other "civilian" was a draft induced "volunteer" from New York City who protested that his cover would be ruined by remaining in Song Be and who demanded to be evacuated with the other "civilians" as soon as possible. This was an awkward development because two of the agents run by this case officer were producing the best information concerning the ongoing battle for Song Be. Nevertheless, Lang believed that if this man was allowed to "get away" with this, then the whole detachment would disintegrate under the stress of combat. Decisive action was needed. Lang told the "civilian" case officer that he would be allowed to cower in an underground shelter with the civilians while soldiers defended them, but that if Lang heard another word from him on the subject of evacuation, he would be chained unarmed like a dog to a stake in the communications trench outside Number Three Bunker where he could serve a useful purpose as a listener and alarm raiser much as the geese had served Rome in raising an alarm at the approach of the Gauls. The classical reference was wasted on this man. He made no further trouble.

When the MI detachment took over Number Three, there was a general feeling of elation among the noble "clerks and jerks" of the advisory team. They had fought the good fight and had reached the end of their inner resources. They thought that the real killers had arrived on the scene to help. Early that first morning, the corporal who had been exiled from Tay Ninh Province for shooting up the colonel's trailer, was standing on an ammunition box in the communications trench looking over the parapet at the dead VC littering the ground when an advisory team sergeant from the main position approached to ask if it were true that Lang's men would hold this bunker. The MI clerk assured him that it was so. This man was six feet tall, twenty years old, blond, and habitually dressed in camouflage field uniforms made in Cholon for him by a Chinese tailor. The advisory sergeant said that everyone was relieved to have an "elite" unit hold this key position. Now they could all relax. Lang's man looked him in the eye and told him not to give it another thought. The sergeant wandered off happy.

More days and nights passed. During the hours of daylight, Lang ran the new TOC. This was in a bunker beneath the main headquarters building of the advisory team compound.

This compound had been the B-34 SF camp before the establishment of a CORDS team. Thereafter, the SF team had moved to the south end of town and had built their "fortress."

There were artillery and air missions to plan and request, resupply drops onto the Song Be plateau to coordinate, and endless conversations with staff officers at higher levels of command who were busy gauging the potential for resistance of the Song Be garrison in trying to allocate scarce American maneuver assets to the fighting across the III Corps Tactical Zone.

So long as it seemed that Song Be would not "go down," higher commanders could concentrate on the destruction of the enemy's main forces around Saigon and Bien Hoa. Since these were the same forces that the detachment had fought for months in their movement from Cambodia, Lang was quite willing to see them destroyed.

Lang's routine in those days was to spend the days in the staff bunker and the nights with his men in Number Three Bunker, but on the first night he was detained in the TOC by a radio conversation with the commander of the Corps artillery battery at Victor 241 airfield. In the midst of that, he was gripped by an intense need to urinate. He excused himself and ran up the concrete steps to the alleyway between two surface buildings where he unbuttoned and was in the act of relieving himself when a noise to his left attracted his attention. An enemy soldier was climbing over the fence that stood between the TOC and the Vietnamese Army compound beyond. This poor soul had a rifle in one hand, the top strand of barbed wire in the other, and was poised precariously with one leg raised to clamber over the top of the fence. On his back was something that looked like a high explosive "satchel charge."

The two men looked into each other's eyes for a second. Lang drew his .45 automatic and shot the sapper in the chest at about ten yards. The impact of the heavy bullet drove him completely off the fence. He lay in the darkness beyond without moving. After a moment, Lang went down into the bunker to get his shirt. It was time to join his men.

The first two nights passed fairly quietly. The MI men had been warned by the previous tenants of Number Three of a sniper who liked to lie at night behind a large tree about halfway down the slope in order to take "pot shots" at whoever was visible. By the second night, they determined to send this fellow on his way. To do this, they sandbagged one machine gun so that its fire would graze the tree at ground level on the left side and did the same with another machine gun for the right side. The sniper's technique was to peer out from one side of the tree, fire a shot and then look around the other side of the tree to see how well he had done. Unbeknownst to him, the MI men had watched him do this through a "Starlight Scope" night vision device. On the night in question, they held up a helmet on a stick, he fired and both machine guns ripped off twenty rounds. He hit the helmet but was not heard from again.

On that second night, the main enemy force was defeated decisively in the Long Binh area and, as a result, the enemy high command decided that they would make an all-out effort to capture Song Be, a provincial capital.

The American high command debated the totality of the enemy's defeat. Song Be was not yet high on the priority list.

The desultory mortar and rocket fire that generally harassed the compound picked up in intensity through the afternoon of that third day. By nightfall it was nearly continuous, and it was clear that something important was going to happen. At 2100 Lang insisted on going down to Number Three bunker to join his men. There were enough people in the TOC to handle the radios, and Benson was there. The detachment had seven men, three of them commissioned officers in the fighting position or just outside in the commo trench. There were two radios tuned to the advisory team command net, and a landline telephone "ran" to the TOC.

"Let us roll the iron dice once more..."
Eric von Manstein

The assault started sometime around midnight. This time the enemy did not waste men in probing attacks. They knew exactly where the American positions were. They abstained from an effort to take the camp from the plateau side. Because of buildings, and friendly units, there was not enough room there to deploy a force big enough to carry the defenses around the main gate.

They came right up the hill from the river valley. There were several hundred of them deployed in what looked like squad teams. They were armed with rifles, machine guns, grenades, and RPG-7 rocket-propelled shaped-charge "bazookas." These last were intended for use against the fighting bunkers. As they came on, enemy mortar fire worked back and forth along the line of entrenchments.

The US heavy battery at V 241 fired continuously. Its shells thundered down to burst catastrophically among the advancing lines. The SF Camp fired its 4.2-inch mortars into them as well. The three forward bunkers tore at them with everything available, and as they came farther up the slope, the fires of the weapons in the main position reached them as well. After a while they fell back to the bottom of the hill where there was some cover from everything but the artillery. These same troops assaulted three more times. In memory, the attacks could not be separated as distinct events. They were much the same, all except the first and the last. They must have continued to receive reinforcements from across the river, because the numbers did not seem to diminish.

Sometime in the early morning, they evidently made up their minds to have one more grand "try" and to put everything they had into this trial by fire. This time there were a lot more men in the assault. They came up the slope like avenging angels. They screamed, "Doc Lap! Doc Lap!" (Independence! Independence!) The charge closed to hand grenade range, and soon grenades bounced off the chicken wire of Number Three.

The detachment screamed at its enemies.

"You little bastards! It's us! It's us you want! You want to kill us? Come here, you little motherfuckers! Come here! God damn you all!"

Grenades sailed over the wire into the communications trench, but because of the excellent zigzag construction, the defenders dodged behind the corners of traverses to avoid the blast and fragments.

Climbing over the barbed wire obstacles was tried with poor results. Along the forward-face of the wire they began to cut their way through.

The two machine guns in Number Three were completely occupied in firing across the face of the slope to enfilade the main force. The crews had no other thought.

The three remaining MI men in the communication trench had to deal with the VC who were desperately trying to get through the wire. At this point the range was about ten yards. Lang later remembered firing all the M-16 ammunition he had at them, and then shooting at them with his pistol.

An AC-47 gunship arrived on the scene. This was a C-47 cargo plane equipped with three door-mounted 7.62 mm electrically-driven Gatling guns. The Gatling guns had a rate of fire of four thousand rounds a minute. These "Rube Goldberg" creatures were nicknamed "Spooky" and were deeply loved by the ground troops. This one circled and dropped big parachute flares that lit up the countryside with a yellow light brighter than day.

In this light, Lang could see that he and his men had killed twenty or so enemy soldiers, but there were at least fifty more intent on getting through the barbed wire barriers, and yet more were arriving at the wire, having run the gauntlet of fire while coming from below. The land-line phone rang from the Tactical Operations Center. LTC Benson wanted to know how bad it was. When informed, he told Lang to talk to the "Spooky" pilot on the radio. The ensuing conversation went something like this:

"Spooky two-niner, this is Number Three Bunker, over..."

"This is Spooky two-niner, pop smoke so I can see where you are."

"This is Number Three popping red; do you see it?"

"I see you. Jesus they're all over the left side of that trench, is that you waving?"

"Roger, Spooky. How many do you count?"

"Looks like ants to me all the way to the bottom, to the river..."

"Shoot into'em, Spooky! Shoot now! Shoot into the wire."

"I can't do that! They're too close! Seventh Air Force policy... Is that a pistol I hear?"

"Roger, Spooky. Shoot, damn it! They'll be in here with us in a minute! Please..."

Pause....

"OK, soldier. When I say down, get everybody flat."

"Roger, Spooky."

Five minutes later.

"This is Spooky two-niner, anybody hit?"

"Not us, just them. They're finished. They're all dead in front of us. We can see some running at the bottom. Thanks. Thanks a lot..."

"My pleasure, soldier, we'll hang around for a while in case they come back."

The back of the VC effort to capture Song Be was broken. The survivors would probably hide in the heavy growth along and beyond the river while trying to reorganize.

Lang did not know it at the time, but the central point of his life had passed that night. His father had said that an unfortunate by-product of a fighting soldier's life was that the logical climax of existence would come before you were through living. For his father, it had come when he was seventeen, in Mexico, when his regiment made a mounted attack against a walled hacienda called "Ojos Azules." For his great-grandfather, it had come in the stand of the Sixth Army Corps in the town cemetery of Middletown, Virginia during the Battle of Cedar Creek.

As the sun came up, Lang and his men huddled together in the trench behind Number Three bunker wondering if they could do this again anytime soon. No one had anything to say. The seven men were closer to each other in that moment than living flesh can expect to be. In a real sense, they had "died to the world" together. Nothing would ever be the same for them again. It seemed terribly cold. Mist drifted over the surface of the river below. There were small fires all over the hillside lit by high explosives and "tracer" ammunition. The enemy's wounded made pitiful sounds, but no one thought to do anything for them. Their friends might return at any time. Smoke hung over the dead; some of the bodies were on fire...

Lang was grateful for the warmth of his body armor.

Emissaries came from the main defense position to console, comfort, and congratulate. They were surprised at the level of sullen indifference, bordering on hostility that greeted them. LTC Benson was among them. He said that the advisory team owed the seven men their lives.

Fuck your lives, was in Lang's mind.

After an awkward silence, Benson said that he would leave them alone for a while.

Just after dawn, the soldier listening to the radio asked who Garryowen Six would be. Lang was too sleepy to answer, but his second in command said that this would be the 1st Cavalry Division's Commanding General and asked why. The soldier said that Garryowen Six had just told the TOC that he was "inbound" ten minutes out. When this news soaked in, Lang knew that the high command had decided that the time had come to "save" Song Be and that he and his men would probably live a while longer.

A pair of "Cobras" with crossed sabers and "1/9 Cavalry" on the nose arrived and circled overhead followed by a "slick" Huey that deposited three men on the medevac helipad inside the entrenched position. LTC Benson met them there and led them around the post, beginning with Number Three bunker. There were MG George I. Forsythe, Colonel John Strongbow, commanding 2nd Brigade of the Cavalry Division, and a captain *aide de camp*. The captain was the officer who had commanded "B" 2/5 Cav at Ap Bu Nho.

Forsythe, a fighting soldier's general, looked down the hill at the enemy dead, and congratulated Lang on the fight that they had made. He said, "Major, I want to commend you on your defense of this position." It meant a lot. He shook hands with Lang's men, all six of them. One of the sergeants began to weep quietly while holding Forsythe's hand, released suddenly from the murderous dream in which they had been living. Forsythe hugged this warrior for a minute. Lang was grateful.

Strongbow and the *aide de camp* stared at the carnage.

Lang always remembered one VC soldier who hung on the wire with a strand supporting his chin. His open, dead, black eyes examined the Americans, asking a question that for Lang would never be answered.

The question was - why? Why had this happened? Why were Americans condemned to fight these brave men so far from home? These were men who shouted "Independence!" as they attacked. What "threatened" American interest was worth this? It was true that the Vietnamese Communists had succeeded in taking over the Viet Minh and Viet Cong movements, but Lang ever after felt that the NVA and VC were better people than the policy "wonks" and ideologues on both sides who caused young men to fight each other in the jungles, mountains and swamps of Viet Nam.

Forsythe asked Lang for a briefing on the enemy situation as he understood it. The party moved to the briefing room. This stood above ground over the hidden TOC bunker. The sliding map boards were shredded in many places, cut with sharp edged slits in others. There were several large holes in the roof and walls.

Lang hoped that neither he nor his second in command would die while giving a briefing.

Forsythe and Strongbow seemed unconcerned by the amount of destruction that the building had suffered. Forsythe confirmed that the cavalry division had been ordered by General Abrams to ensure the retention in friendly hands of the Song Be area.

Lang's second in command briefed on the detachment's ongoing operations, which he had been running, and Lang briefed on the tactical situation.

When he finished, Forsythe asked him to show on the map where he thought the survivors of the D211, D212, and L168 battalions were located. Lang pointed to the wooded river bottoms that surrounded the Song Be plateau and said that they had taken shelter there after their defeat the night before and were probably afraid to cross the open space beyond because of American aircraft. The two Cobras could be heard outside. Forsythe nodded, and asked what the enemy was going to do next. Lang gave him three possible courses of action for the enemy.

Forsythe stopped him. "I am going to have to commit my maneuver reserve to this battle tomorrow morning," he said, "and you are going to commit with me. What are they going to do?"

Lang never forgot that moment. It guided his work for the rest of his career in the government. He told the general what the NVA would do. Forsythe nodded, and asked, "What should we do?"

Lang looked at the captain of Ap Bu Nho.

The blond, crew cut officer was looking at the floor.

"Kill them," was Lang's answer, "all of them..."

Forsythe and Strongbow glanced at each other.

Forsythe asked if Lang would serve as the S-2 (Intelligence officer) of the Task Force with which the 2nd Brigade would fight at Song Be. Strongbow would command, employing all of his brigade and a variety of other assets. The captain of Ap Bu Nho would be the Task Force S-3 operations officer.

Lang said that 525th MIG would have to approve. Forsythe said he would deal with them, and that was settled.

The day passed in organizing the Task Force's offensive planned for dawn the following morning. The enemy force tried to move away several times during the day but was forced back by air action. The same thing would continue during the night under a sky made deadly clear by parachute flares.

Requiescat in Pace...

In the following night, Lang developed a need for something to drink while working in the TOC. The mess hall building was across a small courtyard, and someone said there was orange juice in the walk-in refrigerator there. There were two doors in the mess hall kitchen. One opened into the refrigerator, the other into a walk-in freezer. It was dark. Lang had a flashlight. He opened a door, went in and closed the door behind him. He switched on the flashlight. The advisory team's dead were stacked among the cases of steaks and five-gallon containers of ice cream. Hernando Guzman was on top of one stack. "Rank hath its privilege in the Army." His men had kept moving him to the top of the stack as others were brought in. His eyes were closed, and his hands were folded on his chest. There was frost on his face. The others were all there. The operations officer major and his lieutenant assistant who had been killed the first night, the major who had been flown in with Benson, the dozen enlisted men killed thus far, they were all there, covered in hoar frost.

Lang knelt on the cold floor to pray for Hernando, to pray for the repose of his dead friend's soul. It was a moment which marked the beginning of another phase of a long journey toward God, a god he hoped to know.

Payback is a Bitch...

At first light, the cavalry division began to lift its troopers into the Song Be battle. The 5th Battalion, 7th Cavalry Regiment landed on the Song Be plateau and relieved in place the battered collection of support troops who had survived the previous days in the bunker line. 1/5 Cav., 2/5 Cav., 2/12 Cav., and the ARVN 31st Ranger Battalion were all lifted into landing zones several kilometers in front of the Song Be defenses. A troop of the 1st Squadron, 9th Cavalry Regiment, the division reconnaissance, was also committed to the task force. This unit was entirely helicopter mounted and packed a fearsome punch in its helicopter gunships. The airmobile rifle battalions drove inward toward the Song Be position supported by swarms of armed helicopters. As they advanced, the cavalry wrecked what was left of the enemy force.

It was payment in full for Ap Bu Nho.

At the end of the second day, the lines met when 2/12 Cav. forded the Song Be River below the advisory team compound and walked up the slope over which the enemy had made their attacks three nights earlier.

It was over, finished. Detachment A, 3/525 MIG had not lost a man. This was a miracle. Lang estimated that the three enemy battalions involved in the eight days of fighting had been destroyed as organizations. Their losses must have been more than five hundred dead, with corresponding numbers of wounded. The count of dead bodies was over four hundred. Song Be stank to high heaven. The number of prisoners was small, less than fifty.

"On 31 January 1969, the COSVN had issued Directive No. 71 ordering that an offensive be undertaken on 22 February 1969. The directive prescribed that the primary target would be United States forces. The resulting actions were not an all-out attack, as at Tet of 1968, but the fighting did surpass in intensity the feeble efforts of May and August of 1968. The enemy, largely Main and Local Forces with a heavy NVA flavor, attacked over 125 targets with small scale sapper attacks and shelled 400 others. There were two attacks by regimental-size units and sixteen battalion size assaults. All were easily repulsed."

> *Philip Davidson, MG, U.S. Army (Ret.)*
> *J-2 MACV 1968-1969*
> *"Vietnam at War" pp. 590-591*

If what had happened at Song Be had been "easily repulsed," the scale of the "butcher's bill" did not reflect the effort involved. The prisoners taken said that the three battalions involved had been shattered.

Many years later Lang dined in New York City with a retired general who had served in Song Be as an adviser the year after Lang was there.

"It was real quiet, Pat," he said. "Real quiet, and we knew why. You gents killed them all, damned near every VC in the province. It took years for them to re-build."

"Yes, we killed them all..."

In the aftermath of the battle, several disturbing things happened:

First, a colonel of Intelligence arrived from MACV Headquarters in Saigon. He was appalled by the local scenery and seemed to be on the verge of nausea from the stench. He insisted that only one enemy battalion had been engaged at Song Be and that, therefore, the numbers of enemy soldiers present and enemy casualties reported could not be accurate. The cavalry people still on hand laughed at him and walked away in disgust. LTC Benson had a screaming match with him over his insistence that he knew what had happened and those who had lived through it did not.

Lang was still Task Force S-2 for the 1st Cavalry Division, and in that capacity was the custodian of the prisoners who had been taken. He lined up VC from all three battalions and then questioned them in the presence of this colonel. He asked them for their unit identity and the name of their commanding officer. It was clear from the answers that there had been three battalions. The colonel insisted that they were lying, and insinuated that Lang was distorting what they had said. He left, to the relief of all concerned, but MACV continued to insist on the correctness of his opinion, and 525 MIG changed its order of battle for VC Military Region Ten to conform to this nonsense. Eventually, Lang learned that MACV was downplaying the numbers of the enemy across the country, because that was what the Johnson Administration wanted. The reason for this was simple. If the numbers of the enemy were as high as Intelligence in the field was reporting, then no progress was being made in the war.

A CIA analyst named Samuel Adams "blew the whistle" on this fraud at the expense of his career. He paid a visit to Song Be a few weeks after the battle. He and Lang discussed the deceit in detail. Adams said that because of the perceived need to maintain the falsehood involved in the "numbers game," the fight at Song Be would undoubtedly be played down, and he was right.

Second, the 5/7 Cav. continued to operate in the immediate neighborhood of Song Be for a couple of weeks following the end of the battle. One day, Lang happened to be on hand when one of their patrols came back from the bush with a prisoner, a lieutenant. The battalion CO of 5/7 Cav was there, and when the prisoner would not answer questions to his satisfaction, he had the man taken up to ten feet in a helicopter and shoved out the door with his hands tied behind him. The lieutenant still did not perform satisfactorily, was taken up to twenty feet and pushed out. At that point Lang approached the battalion commander, a lieutenant colonel, and said that if he did it again, Lang would be obliged to charge him under military law with abuse of a prisoner of war. A tense moment followed in which the battalion's staff officers looked to their chieftain for a cue. He finally said something like, "I thought you were one of us…," and walked away leaving the prisoner in a heap on the ground.

The irony of this situation was that Lang cared nothing for this enemy soldier, nothing at all. His protest to the 5/7 Cav commander was just something that had to be done. Lang had not made the Army his life to be molded into someone who cared nothing for the most elementary principles of civilized life. He came from a tradition in which soldiers respected themselves, and their profession, too much to abet such conduct. So long as this enemy lieutenant was under arms and free, he would have been a valid target for hostile action, but bound and in our protection as a noncombatant, he was only an object for compassion. Lang left him on the ground, got into his jeep and drove away.

Third, the Deputy Commander of 525 MIG came to visit. In preparation for this grand occasion, the SF Camp kitchen made doughnuts, a great heap of frosted doughnuts. The briefings for the visit were delivered in the much shot-up detachment headquarters building in which repairs were underway. After listening to the account of the unit's operations, this rather large, rather pompous colonel opined that he did not like the security situation in Song Be. He proceeded to recount a tale of horror in which some years before, a team of MI spooks in Kassel, Germany had been murdered in their beds supposedly by Czech Intelligence. He asked rhetorically if security here were not equally as bad as that which had prevailed in the fleshpots of Kassel. The criticism was clear.

One of the clerks replied that he agreed that this was an intolerable situation. "Why just two weeks ago," he said, "the bad people tried to murder us all." He pointed out the open window and told the colonel that in self-defense he had been forced to kill about twenty of them out in the field beyond. The colonel blanched, and left shortly thereafter, still muttering about shoddy security.

Fourth, 525 MIG continued to insist that participation of the detachment in the battle had been unwise and unjustified, and that MACV J-2 had established that there had not been anything like the number of enemy troops engaged as the detachment had reported. This was believed in 525 MIG Headquarters. Accordingly, there was no possibility that 525 MIG would accept award recommendations for valor for anyone in the detachment. This was a crushing blow for Lang. Almost every one of his officers and men should have received the Silver Star. Lang's contempt for the MI establishment of the Army was born in this incident.

Lastly, the G-2 staff at 1st US Infantry Division accused Lang of fabricating his reporting. The basis for their accusation was that his information was too accurate to have been produced by clandestine HUMINT collection. The principal officers in this staff at the First Infantry Division were all something other than clandestine HUMINT people and they seem to have felt that the quality of Lang's reporting was a reproach to whatever it was that they believed should be the true basis of intelligence analysis.

In any case, they had been clever enough to obtain staff jobs. How could the "buffoons" in Song Be have done so well? Lang's response was to request a formal Court of Enquiry. This was his right under military law. As soon as he did that, the commanding general of the First Division told his staff to shut up. He had no choice. There was no evidence of Lang's supposed crime.

The Task Force was disestablished, and the VC prisoners from the destroyed battalions were readied to be transferred to a PW camp in the Saigon area.

Before they left, Lang went to talk to them one last time. One of his "boys" drove him to the PW "Cage." He asked the prisoners if any had been at Long Dien the night the "deal" was struck that saved the town.

A sergeant stood to say that he had been there.

"And what has happened to the major, the officer who was in the church?" Lang asked through an interpreter."

"You killed him the night of the last attack here. It was machine gun fire. He was in command."

Lang nodded and turned to walk away.

"*Et vous êtes le tirailleur?*" The sergeant asked. He repeated the question in Vietnamese. The prisoners came to stand at the wire to listen.

"*Non, il est mort aussi, mort au même combat. Bonne chance à tous.*" Lang had not meant to say this, but the emotion of the moment overcame him.

"What was said?" he was asked as they drove away leaving the VC looking out at them through the barbed wire.

"He wanted to know if I am the rifleman. I told him that I am not. I told him that the rifleman died in the same fight as his boss. There was some truth in that."

His driver looked at him for a moment and then away.

The months until May passed quietly for Phuoc Long and Binh Long Provinces. Men "rotated" home. New people arrived. By the time Lang's replacement arrived, there were only a few men left of those who had survived February and March. The new detachment CO happened to be another VMI graduate. This officer, who had no prior combat experience, was extremely concerned about security in Song Be.

Soon after Lang's departure this man moved the detachment into a rebuilt, relocated MACV advisory team compound where they were safer but had little or no access to people who could be recruited as agents. In six months, production of intelligence declined to nothing, and before a year had passed, the detachment was withdrawn from the border.

When he heard this had happened, Lang was sure that 525 MIG was happier with the "security situation"

"If you don't mind, I would like to spend a little time alone with my men..."
This was the request of a former Union Army officer
At Sharpsburg many years after that war.

When speaking of his men, Lang always had a hard time explaining to people why he never tried to stay in touch with them.

One reason for this self-imposed isolation was that he knew the war in Indochina was so traumatic an experience that it would not help them to be forced to remember.

In fact, in the main it was because he did not believe that he had any right to think that he had any meaning for them. He believed that what mattered was for soldiers to do their duty to the Army and to the Republic. He did not accept the idea that these men should have suffered and in some cases died for him personally. It was a repulsive thought. The officers and men of Detachment "A," 3/525 MIG were wonderful, cheerful, sardonic, brave and healthy young men with whom it was a pleasure to live and serve. They would always be for him "dear hearts across the seas," forever young and filled with hope.

The detachment had a kind of domestic life. Isolated in the mountains, they chose to build for themselves amenities that symbolized their collective resolve to improve their daily existence. They were highly accomplished "scroungers." They quickly learned that the USAF air bases on the coastal plain were an endless source of "trade" for the wealth the air force possessed in machinery and vehicles. The airmen also seemed to have an unlimited hunger for "combat souvenirs" that could be carried home to America in proof of their heroism. The available supply of blood-stained VC flags, helmets, etc. was not sufficient to sustain their commerce, so the men contracted with several Chinese and Vietnamese women for the manufacture of suitable "barter goods" appropriately stained with dried chicken or hog blood. These could be traded for generators, fuel bladders that could be made into water reservoirs, pumps, vehicles and anything else that was needed. With this trade underway, a complete electrical system, running water and a flush toilet had appeared at the Song Be house. The Chinese woman who was the landlord objected until she learned that all this would be left behind.

"You killed him. You killed him, you heartless bastard!"
One of Whitey's friends to his "murderer."

They had a lot of fun together. Illustrative of the "family life" of the detachment is the saga of "Whitey the Rat." In the detachment headquarters house in Song Be, there was a large room that served as a lounge. There was a bar in one end, and behind the bar an ancient refrigerator to keep beer cold. A television set sat on the bar. AFNVN TV came in clear with the TV antenna seated atop the team's 100-foot radio mast. Comfortable chairs arranged in a semicircle faced the bar. Along one wall next to the bar was a day bed the men had "scrounged" somewhere. An electrical "knife" switch was placed on the wall that enabled the TV audience to kill the generator, and the lights, when firing started outside the house. In the evenings, Lang, in his capacity as "Laird of the Manor," would take his ease upon this couch while they all watched television. They dressed in black "VC" pajamas and sandals made by the enemy from airplane tires. The dress was required on the theory that if it became necessary to fight their way out of the town, then they would seem less obvious in the dark. Rifles, pistols, hand grenades and other weaponry occupied every corner of the room.

The house was inhabited by a tribe of rats, large, healthy, furry brown rats. For some time, the detachment experimented with methods of killing off these unwanted neighbors, but after a while it had become clear that this was a pointless and counterproductive effort for a number of reasons: The house was in the Vietnamese town. The town was overrun with rats. The more you killed, the more their relatives moved in.

Dead rats smell bad.

There was a neighbor cat who was a friend of the house. The men were afraid of poisoning the cat.

The rats were so well fed that they did not seem interested in the team's possessions and they did not bite. Based on this analysis, the troops decided at a "family meeting" that they wanted to leave the rats alone. That was all right with Lang. He had no wish to participate in unnecessary killing.

Because of this decision, the team developed personal relations with a number of these rats. Among them was "Whitey." This robust specimen of masculine rathood must have weighed at least two pounds. He had one white foreleg, and so the name. The rest of him was an attractive medium brown. He seemed to take particular pride in his magnificent white whiskers. Over some months he learned that he was accepted, indeed he seemed to believe that he was part of the household. He would walk around at night on the ceiling beams in Lang's bedroom, peering down from time to time to see what was going on.

A game developed between Whitey and one of the men. This soldier sawed off the barrel of an M-1 Carbine, pried the bullets out of some ammunition, poured out most of the gunpowder and filled the cartridge cases with soap. Whitey had the nightly habit of tiptoeing along the wall next to Lang's couch, sticking his whiskers out at the foot to check for clear running, and then making a dash across the space between the bar and the wall. His "playmate" would wait patiently until one of his "mates" said, "I see his nose." Then, when the rat made his run the sniper would fire, plastering the wall with soap while Whitey "scooted" to safety to the accompaniment of cheers from all on hand. Lang would plug his ears with his fingers to block out the report of the Carbine while the "boys" played with the rat.

The inevitable happened one night. The soldier got the "lead" right and hit Whitey with the whole load of soap. Lang took his fingers out of his ears and joined them all where they stood in a semicircle looking down at the rat's motionless body. It lay on its back, next to the wall, four feet in the air, plastered with pink soap. The other soldiers reacted with fury. "You hit him! What the hell is the matter with you! You killed Whitey! You weren't supposed to hit him! You dumb bastard." These were among the milder rebukes.

Lang kept quiet, but his opinion was not much different. They stood there grieving for a moment while the "killer" tried to tell them how sorry he was. These were the same men who had stood "in the breach" and done serious work in fighting a brigade of infantry to a standstill. After a few minutes, Whitey responded to being poked solicitously with a finger. His whiskers began to twitch, a leg quivered. Smiles broke out as he staggered to his feet and wandered off behind the bar. The next night the game was resumed, but he was never hit again.

"That man killed my division."
Major General George Pickett to a friend
upon emerging from an unhappy meeting with Robert E. Lee, June 1865

As the time for him to leave approached, Lang was asked by several groups if he would stay in Vietnam another six months or a year. As an inducement he was offered what could only be called "plum" jobs. One of these was to be the regimental S-2 (intelligence officer) of the 11th Armored Cavalry Regiment. Colonel George S. Patton IV commanded the regiment and personally offered Lang the assignment. Another was command of the Hong Kong office of the 6th Battalion. A third was the chance to run a highly classified clandestine collection program under command of the 5th Special Forces Group. He would have wanted all of these jobs, but home beckoned and Marguerite waited. It had been a long year. He told all his "suitors" that he would decide before he left the country.

In May, Lang turned over command of the team and went to the coast to spend two weeks at battalion headquarters writing reports, being debriefed, and deciding if he wanted any of the positions that he had been offered enough to stay in Vietnam.

After a few days of this he was utterly bored and volunteered to fly as "door gunner" on the battalion's utility "Huey" helicopter. That provided amusement for some time while he thought about his future. One day the helicopter landed at a re-fueling base in the Mekong Delta. Lang hopped down from his seat in the flank of the aircraft and went to the pilot's hatch. He opened this and slid back the ceramic armor panel alongside the seat so that the aviator could get out of the "bird" if for some reason it caught fire. That done, he stood chatting with the pilot. A soldier came from the control tower to learn what air unit this was.

He tapped on Lang's back.

Lang turned and the man saw the gold oak leaf on his collar. "What is it?" Lang asked.

"Nothing, sir, nothing. If this "bird" has a major for a door gunner, I don't want to know anything about it."

For want of something better to do, he went to dinner one night at a brand-new Chinese restaurant located as a concession on the big U.S. Army post at Long Binh. There were four MI people at Lang's table, and nearby, several junior officers from the 101st Airborne Division were eating at another table. Among them was a young captain wearing the faded, worn uniform in which he had come in from the field. He had the haggard, sunburned look that came with living in the outdoors. He had the look that in the French Army is called "Christ descended from the cross." During the meal, the restaurant door opened and in came MG Melvin Zais, the 101st's CG and his aide.

A week or so before, the 101st had repeatedly assaulted a hill in the central highlands, the hill that came to be known as "Hamburger Hill." They assaulted it nine or ten times from the bottom up instead of landing on the top and fighting their way down. This did not make a lot of sense given the number of helicopters in the division. Rumor had it that Zais had ordered the attack to be made in this way to demonstrate to the American command and to the NVA that the 101st was still as fine a fighting organization as it had been when he had served in it in World War II. It had been a difficult fight. A lot of men died. They took the hill.

The young-old captain put down his chopsticks and placed his sun-cracked hands on the edge of the table to watch General Zais.

Zais ignored him, although the aide whispered something. Tension grew in the restaurant.

The captain's friends talked to him. One of them put his hand on the man's forearm. The young man struggled to his feet despite the restraining hands that tried to drag him back into his seat. "Blackjack!" he roared across the restaurant, shaking his fist as he did so.

Blackjack was Zais' radio call sign.

"Blackjack! Damn you! You killed my company! Damn you! Are you happy now? Are you happy? You killed my company..."

Zais never looked at him. He stood up and walked out the door trailing his aide.

The captain sat down, put his elbows on the table, and covered his eyes with his hands.

"What do you think?" one of the MI men asked as they left the restaurant.

"That's it for me," Lang said. At the end of the month, he went home to his beloved wife.

He had "seen the elephant."

CHAPTER TWENTY

Murder Is Murder

26ᵗʰ US Cavalry Regiment (PS)

After Lang's first Vietnam year, he and his wife spent three years together overseas. He was assigned to the United States Army Special Security Group (the SSO Group) first at Frankfurt, Germany as the second in command of a detachment of that Army General Staff activity, and then as detachment commander at Izmir, Turkey.

Before he left Vietnam, Lang decided to take what he thought of as an easy job in the Special Security Group. He received a message directing him to visit the big US Army post at Long Binh. This was thirty miles from Saigon. A specific unit was named as the destination for his visit.

After some searching of the post, he discovered that this group was housed in several sandbagged Quonset huts surrounded by masses of barbed wire. There was no sign identifying the facility. He had passed it several times. An MP at the gate summoned a sergeant from within.

"Ah, Major Lang," the man said. "We can't invite you in. You are not cleared yet, but you were cleared in school?" he asked.

"Yes, I see. I did not actually know what you did here."

"Right. How do you want to go Europe?"

Lang suspected a weak attempt at humor. He was not in the mood. "I was thinking of driving," he said.

The sergeant laughed and then understood that he stood on the edge of a precipice with a sign labeled "Ass Chewing Ahead" in clear view. He looked closely at this apparently exhausted combat officer and decided that he should be careful. "You can go by air or by ship, sir," he said.

Lang had gone to Europe by ship when he was a child. This sounded intriguing. "What ship?" he asked.

The sergeant looked at the message form on his clipboard. "The SS United States."

"I'll take that option." He gave the man his wife's address. She would receive the paperwork for their trip. The sergeant disappeared into the hut and reappeared with a captain who apologized for their inability to invite him in for coffee. This was correct Army custom. Lang asked if the captain had heard of the "problem" he had experienced with the SSO Group's office at 1st Infantry Division.

The answer was that this had been investigated. "It was obvious that you had no access to Special Intelligence. The whole thing was crazy. When Group looked at your record in Washington, they decided they wanted you. That is why you are here."

They shook hands, and Lang drove off through the red dust of Vietnam. The sound of helicopters was everywhere. Black, acrid smoke filled the horizon. The metal tubs filled with excrement from hundreds of latrines were "burned out" with gasoline every day. It seemed impossible that he would soon be on his way to Germany with Marguerite.

He visited relatives in California, and then went home to her in New England. On the appointed day they, boarded the ship in New York with their little dog. The animal took up residence in the ship's kennel for the trip. His rank caused them to be assigned a first-class cabin. He had been instructed to bring Mess Dress on the trip. They had their meals at the First Engineer's table. Everyone dressed for dinner. Black tie and gowns were the custom. The Duke and Duchess of Windsor were at the Captain's table next to that of the Langs. There was dancing in the nightclub every evening after dinner. All too soon the ship arrived. After a port call at Southampton, the military passengers were delivered to Le Havre. A US Army railroad train waited on the pier. The ride across France and Germany seemed interminable. The train would end its run in Berlin.

Lang was thankful when he and Marguerite were deposited in the cavernous, echoing *Hauptbahnhof* in Frankfurt. Waiting for them was the commander of the SSO Group detachment at 5th US Army Corps headquarters in the city. This lieutenant colonel took them, the dog and their baggage to their beautifully furnished apartment in what had once been the housing facility of the American High Commissioner for Germany, the military governor of the American Zone of Occupation. Because of the valued services provided by the SSO Detachment, the best available housing was provided to its members. At the apartment, the refrigerator and pantry were full, as was a case of German beer. Lang asked his new boss how much he owed him. The answer was that the only thing expected was that the next man to arrive in the detachment would be treated the same way regardless of rank.

The detachment commander departed a few weeks later, and a friend who was a year senior to him in rank as a major arrived to take command. Germany was lovely, but after Song Be and combat command, it was not acceptable to complacently sit as a peacetime deputy for another major. The duty in Frankfurt was easy. There were entertaining social events, *Oktoberfest, Fasching* and the like. At an *Oktoberfest* celebration staged in a big tent by the American Consulate General, Lang found himself drinking just a few too many steins of beer followed by several shots of *Jaegermeister*. When he awoke the next day in a bath tub at home, Marguerite explained to him that at one point he had staggered out of the tent to view a line of unconscious drunks lying on the grass. She said he had wandered over to them and solicitously enquired as to how many of them were dead and how many wounded. At this point he was four months removed from combat. It must have seemed a reasonable question. She did not seem to agree.

The Langs spent that Christmas at Garmisch-Partenkirchen. This Bavarian alpine city was the location of a major US armed forces recreation center. There were half a dozen US forces hotels and guesthouses for generals. The generals made an annual pilgrimage to this place and to Berchtesgaden as well. They arrived in their "command trains." These were carefully sized according to the rank and command of the "owner." Lang went to Garmisch to set up and run a temporary SSO station in a garrison communications station. He did this for two hours a day and then skied the rest of the time with his wife. At night they dined and danced at the "Casa Carioca," a restaurant that featured a central ice rink and show as well as a roof that rolled back for dining under an alpine moon.

In the midst of this moment in paradise, Mu'amar Qathafi overthrew the king of Libya. Lang's circuit chattered wildly with messages from the USAF commander of Wheelus, AFB in Tripoli, Libya. Colonel "Chappie" James wanted action to crush Qathafi. He reported that Qathafi had no more than two hundred men. Lang watched while the senior generals in Garmisch met at *Haus Flora* to deliberate. In the end they recommended to President Nixon that the paratroop brigade at Mainz be flown into Tripoli to restore King Idris' rule. A major general among them was chosen to lead the expedition. He asked if Lang could bring his team to support from the Wheelus air base. Lang said that they could be ready in a couple of hours. In the end Nixon decided to allow Qathafi's coup to succeed, and a great opportunity was lost.

As a year in Germany passed, Lang increasingly realized that he would not be able to endure several more years in Frankfurt as another major's deputy. He had experienced too much responsibility and indeed excitement in

Vietnam for that to be an acceptable future. Life in Germany was exceedingly pleasant. His boss was a good friend, but he needed something more. For these reasons Lang solicited command of a detachment of his own and received a transfer to Izmir, Turkey where he would be the boss.

The detachment he was joining supported two major NATO headquarters. These were Allied Land Forces South East Europe and 4th Allied Tactical Air Force. These headquarters were charged with command of all NATO ground and air forces in Greece and Turkey in the event of war with the Soviet Union. Both of these commands were headed by American officers, and Lang's job would be to ensure that they were provided with the best of information and personal communications.

The trip to Turkey was an adventure in itself. The Langs drove to Venice where they boarded a very modern French built motor ferry for a three-day trip to Izmir across the Mediterranean. The sea was blue, their stateroom was pleasant, and the cuisine in the first-class dining room was splendid.

At Izmir, he made the acquaintance of a truly memorable "Old Army" character. This was Major General John K. Boles, the Chief of Staff of Land Southeast. This crusty old buzzard was a true "diamond in the rough." He was from the Class of 1939 at West Point and had fought his way across northern Europe in the 3rd Armored Division. His whole family was cavalry all the way back to the 1830s, when an ancestor had been a founding member of the 1st Dragoons, the very first US regular mounted regiment.

Lang first met the man when he reported in the general's office in Izmir. Boles was filling his pipe from a large wooden humidor. The tobacco looked and smelled like Burley. This was hopeful. A*t least he's not altogether a Yankee...* Lang thought.

Boles' "blouse" was open and in closing the drawer of his desk, he caught the skirt of it. He looked down and said, "Well, good thing I had my pants on...." He then looked up and began to question Lang's provenance in the closed world of Army society. "You look like Old Army to me," he said. "Just the way you stand there... You're not afraid of me. Are you Steve Lang's son? No? Are you the nephew of the Lang girls in Baltimore?" He asked if Lang were related to this Lang or that, and finally said, "Well, who the hell are you, Lang?"

Lang was angry. He looked Boles in the eye and said, "Sir, I am Sergeant Major Lang's son." This was not strictly true as the father had retired as a lieutenant colonel, but he had been a sergeant major at one point.

Boles considered that and then asked, "Which regiment?"

Lang ransacked his memory and chose the best one. "26th Cavalry," he replied.

This was the Philippine Scouts cavalry regiment.

Boles now really looked at him. "My father commanded the regiment in the 20s," he said. "I was born at Camp John Hay. We lived there for twelve years. I remember a sergeant named Lang in "G" Troop..."

"That was my father," Lang answered in astonishment.

"Your father taught me to ride. Sit down. Is your father still living? Yes? Please pass him my regards." the general said.

After a half hour of conversation, Boles asked if he knew what happened to the horses.

"The regiment's horses?"

"Yes."

"They shot them when ordered to surrender on Bataan. They killed them to save them from the Japanese. Each trooper shot his own mount. My father still cannot speak of it."

Boles lowered his bald old head and nodded.

Sergeant Major Lang's son had found a friend. He and General Boles became boar hunting and SCUBA diving companions. Friendship is not too strong a word for the relationship that emerged.

The countryside around Izmir was beautiful and reminiscent of the California Coast near Santa Barbara. There were many archeological remains and the SCUBA diving and fishing were wonderful.

On one occasion during the trial of Lieutenant William Calley for the massacre at My Lai, Boles invited Lang to lunch at his quarters. He sometimes did when he wanted company at meals. The two men sat across from each other in the center of an elegant room filled with Chinese antiques. During the meal, the general's Filipino houseman was summoned to the table. While the houseman stood at the end looking down the table at the two officers, Boles asked Lang what he thought of the My Lai case.

This was an awkward thing. Many in the Army were confused over issues of loyalty, and resentment was strong toward the press for the general savagery of their attacks.

Lang did not want to lose Boles' esteem which he valued, but there was no choice in what had to be said. At VMI, he had learned that decent men must stand up for what they believe to be the truth, win or lose. The Confederate ancestors of all VMI men had done that no matter what the cost. Lang told the Filipino that what had happened was murder and should be punished accordingly.

Boles asked if there could be extenuating circumstances.

Lang replied that there could not. Murder was murder.

Boles looked at the Filipino and said, "You see, Manuel, I told you so. *I told you he would say this...*"

The man left.

Lang was touched. His opinion had been sought in a matter touching on the honor of the Army. Somehow Boles accepted him as someone who should have an opinion on the state of the Army's soul.

Lang happened to be present on the diving trip when John Boles army career came to an end. They had been down in thirty feet of Aegean seawater when Boles saw a Spotted Moray eel whose head just protruded from a hole in a cliff wall. The general shot the eel through the body with an arrow and then, with one fin on either side of the hole proceeded to try to drag the beast from its lair. It was a big, strong eel. Boles would pull a foot or two of it out and then the animal would drag him back toward the cave.

Boles' *aide de camp* was along on the dive. He was a captain whose personality did not match that of his master.

The general waved the captain forward.

The man did not respond so Lang drew his diving knife and sawed through the spinal column. The eel proved to be six feet long and a foot wide in the middle.

The next day, the general had the head in an ice filled cooler in his office where it was much admired by the Turks and Greeks.

He and Lang were chatting of the dive when Boles face "clouded" and he hesitantly asked if Lang thought his aide-de-camp had been... afraid.

Lang knew what the answer must be, and he assured the general that the man had simply been concerned for Boles' welfare. That saved the officer's career for at least another day.

Unfortunately, Boles had suffered a massive "silent" heart attack in the incident and within a few weeks was gone into retirement at Killeen, Texas where he ran a huge motel for many years with great success.

In a sad way, the loss of his friend was a blessing for Lang. He had discovered that he no longer had any taste for hunting and Boles' absence made it possible for him to stop killing animals for sport. He had hunted boar with the general a number of times. He was such a good shot that even an animal that ran as fast as a horse and had ten-inch teeth was not much of a challenge. Small game—birds, rabbits and the like—sickened him at heart. He never hunted again.

The Langs knew many splendid people at Izmir. The two four-star general commanders-in-chief were wonderfully different. The first was Ben Harrell. He had been Lucian Truscott's operations officer at Anzio and in the drive up the Italian peninsula. He discovered that Lang knew a lot about World War II and delighted in sitting in his big office talking for hours with the young major of such things as the capture of the Gustav Line. Harrell was a very smart man who held his cards close to his chest and seldom made errors. He was from Oregon. His wife, Harriet, was his high school sweetheart. She was a lovely, unpretentious woman and representative of the best in the American middle class. Lang spent so much time at their quarters on business that she seemed to come to think him numbered among her several soldier sons.

On one occasion, he lent one of her sons a blue uniform when he came to visit unprepared for a formal party. On another day, Lang was standing in the general's parlor when Harriet came into the room looking for her husband. They were in a hurry to depart for some social event and she needed the hooks in the back of the neck of her dress done up. Lang was finishing doing this when her husband entered the room. He laughed. "Well that's a first. I guess that settles where you are in the social order here."

Harrell's successor was altogether different. This was Frank Mildren. While Harrell was "all brains," Mildren was all guts and instinct. He was a cowboy from Nevada. It had taken him five years to get through West Point. Mathematics was nearly the undoing of him. He had earned seven Silver stars in Europe as an infantry battalion commander. He and Lang shared a passion for old Oriental rugs, and as a result, they spent a lot of time together in bazaars. His wife's name was Audrey. She was an elegant, statuesque lady who had been raised on various army posts in the Southwest. She was a gracious hostess. Like Lang and Boles, she was Old Army through and through. Her husband was not. One summer day, Lang and Mildren's Turkish ADC, Kemal, were sitting with "the old man" in his back garden, sipping tea, when a workman on an adjoining building site threw a brick that just missed the general. Mildren was nearly sixty but he gave chase across fences and back gardens with Lang, the Turkish officer and a couple of guards right behind him. He captured the miscreant and was in the process of fighting the man with his fists when Lang and Kemal dragged the workman away. They handed him to the guards who proceeded to knock him about themselves.

The most interesting person Lang met in Turkey was Colonel Bill Harris. He was the chief logistician in the headquarters and someone whom Lang briefed every day. This man was a college dropout from St. Louis, Missouri who had joined to army in 1939 and by war's end had been a major and the operations officer of the 505th Parachute Infantry Regiment in the 82nd Airborne Division. He had made all four of the division's jumps. He was an ingenious, witty, delightful person. He was married to a young woman who was exactly Marguerite's age. She seemed older than he. After knowing Bill Harris for a while, Marguerite said to her husband that she knew he would never be a general. "You and Bill are like peas in a pod" she said. "If they did not promote him, they won't promote you."

In Turkey, Lang made a decision to become an area specialist in the Arab World. There was a program for this. It involved graduate school, language study, and travel in the designated area followed by repeated assignment to duties involved with this area. It was also understood that an officer who volunteered for this kind of career was accepting the fact that he probably would not rise higher in rank than lieutenant colonel or just possibly colonel. The Army knew it needed such people but was certain that they should not command anything important. Lang had never wanted to be a general, had always thought that soldiering was its own reward, so this was not much of a psychic cost. He was selected for the program.

Training would have to wait until he returned from another tour of duty in Viet Nam. It was his turn in the barrel.

One day in 1971, the phone rang in Izmir. It was an assignments officer in Washington who said he had a requisition in Viet Nam that he wanted to fill with Lang. It was for an MI officer who was Special Forces qualified and experienced in South East Asia, was an experienced clandestine case officer with service in combat in Viet Nam, and who had been decorated for valor. "Ah, SOG," Lang commented.

"Yes," the voice said. "USMACVSOG."

"Well, sign me up," Lang replied. "Sign me up."

When this call came, the Langs were in the midst of a production of the musical comedy, "The Fantastiks." This was being staged at the US Information Service theater in the city. The play was "running" to packed houses. Marguerite had choreographed the show and danced in it, and Lang played the role of "Mortimer the Indian." When the production closed, they prepared to leave. She would go to her mother as she had during his first Vietnam tour of duty.

One evening he went to the Officer's Club to close out his account.

While he was standing in the lobby, Frank and Audrey Mildren came in dressed for a party. The general was in blue mess dress, and his wife was as lovely as ever.

She saw Lang across the room and came to kiss him goodbye.

"Keep your head down," she whispered in his ear. "Keep your head down."

"Thank you, ma'am" was all that he could manage. He would never forget the moment.

CHAPTER TWENTY-ONE

The City of the Trojans

In the early summer of 1972, Major Walter Lang flew to Danang in the Republic of Vietnam with his new commanding officer. They flew north from Saigon to supervise the launching of reconnaissance patrols into Laos. Their small Army airplane took hours to reach the Marble Mountain airfield just south of the city.

After they arrived. the colonel was briefed on the day's activities. Several patrols had been landed by helicopter across the Laos border that morning. The man in charge, a lieutenant colonel, explained that the number of North Vietnamese Army troops in the targeted area of Laos was so impressive that C-130 Hercules cargo aircraft carrying fuel-air explosive "Daisy Cutters" had been used to blow cleared spaces in the heavy jungle in places where it was hoped the NVA were not. Despite this, one of the patrols had been met with fire on two successive attempts to land in freshly created clearings.

"Where is the team?" the colonel asked.

"Over there," the briefer said and pointed to a small group seated with their backs to a hangar wall. They were smoking and taking advantage of the shade provided by the building. It was a blazingly hot day.

"What now?" the colonel asked.

"They want to try again in a couple of hours…"

The colonel walked across the "apron" to the team.

They stood and waited for the two officers to arrive. Their leader, a senior Special Forces sergeant saluted.

"What's up?" the colonel asked.

"We had a little trouble this morning," the man said, "but we'll get in this next time."

There were seven of them. They were dressed in camouflage clothing made somewhere in Europe. They carried a variety of firearms. Many of these were not of US manufacture. There were three Americans and four native soldiers. Each man had his blood type neatly embroidered on his left breast pocket where a medic could find it. Two had bandages on superficial wounds.

The colonel walked away from the team so that he and Lang could speak privately. "Is this one important?" he asked.

Lang had a folding map board with him. He opened it and pointed at the place in Laos. "No, no, sir. This is Quebec-79. We accepted this one from the staff at MACV as a compromise on some other recon targets. We had no idea it would be this hot. We need to put some Arclight cells on it. The B-52s will have a field day."

"Go get that truck," the colonel told Lang while pointing at a two-and-a-half-ton vehicle parked by their plane.

Lang returned with it as well as the lieutenant colonel.

"Sergeant," the colonel said. "You are through for today. Put your men on the truck and go back to camp. I don't want you trying to get into that area again."

"Sir, that's our target,' the sergeant said, "The little bastards are not going to keep us out of it."

His men waited. They looked eager to follow the pack leader.

"Lang, help me lower the tail gate," the colonel said. Having done that, he turned back to the sergeant. "This is an order. Put your men on the truck."

He and Lang watched the vehicle depart.

Having been temporarily relieved of their burden of duty, the team began to sing and laugh as they rode away.

"What do you think?" the colonel asked.

Lang spoke after a moment:

> *"I carry two sorts of destiny toward the day of my death.*
> *If I stay here and fight beside the city of the Trojans,*
> *my return home is gone, but my glory shall be everlasting."*

"What's that from?"

"The Iliad, sir. It's from the Iliad."

"Military Assistance Command Viet Nam Studies and Observations Group" (MACVSOG) is a name that should be carved deeply on the memory of anyone who wishes to grasp the heights of glory and the depths of incompetence that have been reached by the armed forces of the United States. SOG, as it was usually called, organized and conducted all military cross-border reconnaissance and raiding in Cambodia and Laos as well as all military black propaganda aimed at North Viet Nam. It possessed 10,000 native troops recruited from ethnic minorities of the region, several specialized American and Vietnamese air units, and a fleet of high speed patrol boats, numerous installations, and an unlimited budget. The existence of this organization was a well-kept secret because of the cross-border operations it conducted against North Vietnamese Army supply dumps, the "Ho Chi Minh Trail," and enemy headquarters. US servicemen serving in South East Asia heard rumors of the existence of such a group, but they knew next to nothing about it. Men lost across the borders were reported to their next of kin as having died in South Viet Nam. The native troop units subordinate to this headquarters were led by U. S. Army Special Forces officers and men.

These Green Berets were a self-conscious elite, an elite recruited from an elite for duties that defied comprehension by civilians and most other soldiers.

The SF men in MACVSOG were hand selected from volunteers in the larger SF organization. They were the finest soldiers that Lang would ever know. Their courage was, in Arthur Fremantle's phrase, "simply beyond praise." He was speaking of the infantry of the Army of Northern Virginia, but the comparison is apt. Self-fulfillment was a psychobabble gibberish term of the late twentieth century, but it described the inner motivations of these men. They were born for this task. If they had not accepted it, and their fate, they would have denied themselves.

"We are what the rest of the Army would like to believe it is. It is for this that they hate us… Do not expect to be loved." (Special Forces Credo)

For most of the war these troops operated only outside South Viet Nam in Cambodia, Laos and southern North Viet Nam. For reasons satisfactory to the US Government, they were not allowed to try to bring down the North Vietnamese government, but they were always allowed to fight, bleed, and die in support of the futile strategy of attrition followed in South Viet Nam. In some years, the American casualties in SOG were over 100%. How could that be? Many people were hit more than once. In the field, they were divided functionally between the Recon men, and the Hatchet Company men. The recon men spent their time in missions "across the fence." They were sent there by Military Assistance Command Vietnam (MACV) headquarters to investigate enemy activities and locations. There usually were six to eight men on these missions. Often, over half the men on a reconnaissance mission were indigenous soldiers. These were usually Montagnards or tribal Chinese Nungs. Helicopter insertions were the rule until late in the war when parachute drops began to be frequent because of an ever- increasing shortage of helicopters. Such reconnaissance missions were very dangerous, and they became yet more hazardous, as the enemy reacted to SOG's activities by stationing over 200,000 men across the borders hoping to halt SOG intrusions into what for them was their rear base area. The NVA's sensitivity to this activity was stimulated in part by the fact that they lost a lot of men whenever they stumbled into SOG recon teams.

The Hatchet Forces were members of company- and battalion-sized units that were kept in readiness as "backing" for the recon teams. Their task was to fight actions too big for the recon teams to handle. A call for help by a team in action quickly brought the presence of several hundred Hatchet men.

This work had begun in 1962 as a CIA project staffed with SF men "borrowed" to do the dangerous work. The US armed forces seized control of the group as the military buildup began in Viet Nam. The "new management" built on the CIA project office in creating a headquarters that was always cursed by a lack of personnel qualified by experience or temperament to direct the work performed so well by the troops in the field.

Throughout the last several years of its existence, SOG suffered from a massive security problem that killed its men and often destroyed its units. It became clear throughout that time that somehow the enemy knew of SOG operations in advance and was often waiting for the recon teams at the points of insertion. Casualties went up and up. High Altitude Low Opening (HALO) parachute operations were tried with some success, but US signal intercepts indicated that enemy headquarters in Hanoi knew of these too, and were providing their units in Laos with detailed information of the composition, names, objectives, landing sites and plans of the teams.

In late 1971, the colonel commanding SOG ordered an exhaustive security survey to include polygraph examinations of all hands. This investigation was about three years overdue by the time it was conducted, but no significant action was taken when it ended.

Lang arrived in Saigon in 1972 just as SOG as such was beginning to be de-activated as part of the "Vietnamization" and withdrawal program that was being followed by the Nixon government.

By 1972 there was only one replacement depot left in Vietnam. When he had left the country in 1969 there were many. They had all been very busy processing officers and men in and out of the country. The remaining facility was located at MACV headquarters at the Saigon air base. It had well-built buildings and seemed more like a hotel than a military camp. He expected to go to SOG immediately after arrival but found that the personnel people were firmly in control and doing their own version of "welcome to Vietnam." He was required to participate in a lot of silly meetings about drugs, racism, atrocities, press relations etc. The most entertaining of these was a seminar led by a couple of ex-convicts from the California penal system who told the group what a bad thing using narcotics was. They had both been convicted as heroin merchants and armed robbers.

Lang asked them how much they were being paid for this nonsense.

That caused him to be counseled by the Adjutant General's Corps "paper shuffler" who ran the replacement center.

"Listen, Colonel," Lang said. "Spare me the programmed idiocy and let me go to my unit."

After that dialogue, he was sent to see General Creighton Abrams' aide-de-camp. The "command suite" was the site of the interview. It was beautifully furnished and carpeted, although Lang thought the rooms were overly air-conditioned. The temperature resembled that of a meat locker. The well- groomed, well-tailored colonel who carried Abrams' briefcase for a living smiled and said that he thought Lang should become Abrams' French translator. Abrams was overall commander in Vietnam and was then involved with the Cambodian Army in some sort of negotiation. None of the Cambodians spoke English.

"Would General Abrams rate me personally?" he asked the ADC.

The colonel sat back and seemed distracted as though listening for a telephone to ring. "Well, no. He doesn't like to rate people as junior as you."

"Well then, I don't want the job."

"We could make you take the job."

"Yes, you could, but you won't."

As soon as this talk was over, Lang found a telephone in an outer office and called the number that he had been given for SOG Headquarters. There were no telephones in the replacement depot. A voice at the other end said that "they" had been looking for him and that he should be at the gate in an hour.

At exactly that time a small, white, automobile arrived. It was driven by a blonde man in civilian clothes.

Lang ignored the protestations of the MP on duty and walked out the gate with his bags while the confused young soldier called someone on the phone to report this catastrophe.

Major Lang rode away with the sergeant who had come to pick him up. When they reached "home base," the sergeant handed him the keys. "This is your car, sir," he said. "I just drove it to pick you up."

The adjutant told him that he had already made a call to the replacement depot to tell them to "mind their own business." SOG managed to escape censure and punishment for such behavior because only they could and would do what they did.

Throughout its life, USMACVSOG had been both a US direct action group as well as an advisory team for a Vietnamese Army counterpart unit called the "Strategic Technical Directorate."

It was planned that STD would continue to exist after SOG's demise. For this reason, a decision was made somewhere "on high" to provide continuing advisory and logistical support, and for that reason a "rump" SOG would continue to exist for some time. This was called the "Strategic Technical Directorate Assistance Team 158," or STDAT-158.

It was headquartered in the old MACV-2 headquarters buildings on Pasteur Street in Saigon next to the Italian Embassy. This was the same compound and buildings which had been used by SOG headquarters. The people working there had all been SOG people; the filing cabinets were full of SOG papers. The facilities around town and all over the country were all SOG facilities, and the funding was all SOG funding. It was SOG under a different name. They had stopped "taking in" in non-SOG people the month before Lang arrived. Lang was treated as an exception because he had been specifically requisitioned, *by name*, by SOG.

It had been expected by Washington and Honolulu that STDAT-158 would confine itself to advising and supporting STD, but that did not happen. STDAT-158 continued to command an American led Montagnard mercenary force located at Pleiku in the central highlands. This unit had about five hundred men. They were the distilled essence of the whole body of Special Commando Unit (SCU) troops with which SOG had fought its war. This was called the "Special Mission Force" (SMF). It was led by a major whom Lang had first known in Panama in the 8th SF Group. This fellow was a walking muscle and not much else, but he was quite adequate to the job given him. The official mission of the SMF was to provide capability to react to intelligence reports that "spoke" of the location of American POWs. They were never allowed to perform this mission because the American government was terribly afraid that POWs might be killed or wounded in the course of a rescue operation. It was clear that the end of the war was approaching, and nobody wanted to see anything like that happen.

It should not have been a surprise that the existence of the SMF proved to be a temptation too strong to be overcome by MACV headquarters. Very soon after the creation of STDAT-158, they were often in action in a variety of combat missions close to the Lao border in the mountain area of 2nd ARVN Corps. At times, they found themselves, by error or design, on the other side of the border where they were not "allowed" to be. Lang accompanied the SMF on several such operations for the purpose of learning exactly what they were doing. In the assembly area for the first of these, he was introduced to the Montagnard "officer" who would command the native troops in this foray into the woods....

This "captain" was in his forties and had served with the French *Groupements des Commandos Mixtes Aeroportees* (GCMAs). These French units had been very like SOG. When he understood who Lang was, and after they talked a while, the camouflage clad Montagnard held up his twisted, crippled right hand for Lang's inspection. He had been shot through the hand

the year before while hanging onto the harness of a US SOG officer during an emergency helicopter extraction from Laos. He had not let go, but the American had still died of his wounds. *"Mong Comangdangt! Tu mort! Moi mort!"* the native officer said to Lang. The meaning was clear. Some of the people left behind in Vietnam when SOG closed up shop were showing a lot of "wear and tear" by the time Lang arrived. In the intelligence section of headquarters, were several MI officers who were not Special Forces men. They resented Lang and the easy way he had with the handful of SF soldiers remaining in the headquarters. Lang's habit of "escaping" to the field to participate in operations seemed to be particularly unacceptable to them.

This "boiled" to the surface one night in a Saigon Chinese restaurant. There were five people at table. Three were "leg" (non-airborne) intelligence officers. One of them was Lang's immediate superior, a major. Another was a skinny little man from the Bronx in New York City. He was a captain and a West Point graduate. There was an Army nurse at the table. She was the New Yorker's mistress. He was married, but for the captain that meant little so far from home. He and Lang's boss were photo-interpreters, or rather, managers of photo-interpreters.

Lang had been raised to be polite to women, and he addressed various pleasantries to the nurse throughout dinner. This got to be more than the Bronx-born lover could bear. This reaction was encouraged in the man when the nurse began to react to the attention.

"You're lucky I am older now," the captain said.

Lang ignored him.

"A year ago, I would have done something about you," the man said.

"Don't hold back," Lang said with a smile. "I'd be glad to accommodate you."

The captain's face turned red. His muscles tensed under the uniform.

Lang put his chopsticks on the table. His body began to speak to him. He could feel what he would do. There would be a sudden smash to the man's nose. This would be a blow with the heel of the hand. This would break bone and cartilage. This would be followed by a sudden, hard, pull on the khaki shirt. That would bring the angry man across to Lang's side of the table where more bones could be broken. Lang sat looking at the captain.

The nurse stood up and backed away from the table. "Jimmy, shut up," she said. "He was just being nice."

Jimmy looked fearful. He left the room, taking his "dolly" with him.

Lang "deflated," and went back to eating.

"Thanks, for not doing it," the boss said. "What would have happened?"

"Hospital, then court-martial I suppose. You should get a muzzle and leash for your dog."

"He's had a lot of trouble here with people like you..."

"I would imagine so..."

The captain was sent to the United States the next week.

The nurse lieutenant called after "Jimmy" left. She seemed displeased that he was not interested.

The Saigon Chinese seemed to anticipate an enemy victory and a coming need to flee. They began to sell their family possessions. There were several Chinese shops on the road to Tan Son Nhut airfield. Lang frequented these and bought a variety of lovely things. He had a particular inclination towards the Ming Dynasty and brought a small collection home when he left the country.

MACV headquarters was at the airfield. He often combined shopping with necessary liaison visits there. On one particularly memorable day, Lang was seated in the MACV headquarters dining facility, lunching with someone from the intelligence section when a European looking civilian woman approached the table. Lang's lunch companion knew her, and she sat. She was a New Zealander employed by an international charity. She was in her thirties and looked a bit "down at the heels." She was at the headquarters for a charitable projects meeting. They bought her lunch. Lang asked if she needed a ride back to the city. Everyone in SOG headquarters had some sort of little Japanese car. Lang particularly liked the white Datsun that he drove.

There was a long, straight, four lane road from the airport to Saigon. There was a lot of traffic: cars, trucks, motorbikes, military vehicles. White uniformed Vietnamese National Police directed traffic. American GIs generally referred to them as "white mice." There were traffic lights at major intersections. The "mice" controlled them with manual switches.

Lang chatted with the woman as they drove through the engine exhaust and noise. She worked for some group involved with orphans, or whales, or saving the Montagnards, or maybe preserving Vietnamese embroidery or something like that. He began to look forward to dropping her off somewhere. Anywhere would do.

A red light stopped him. He waited for the policeman to change it to green. His left elbow was on the sill of the open car window and his left hand gripped the roof.

A young man hopped off the back of a motorbike and ran to Lang's car. He grabbed the case of Lang's Rolex Submariner with both hands and leapt up to put both feet on the door. He leaned back and pulled hard, hoping to break the steel band. That effort failed and he was left hanging on the door like a monkey. He looked in the window and found himself nose to nose with the watch's owner. The owner initially thought to shoot him, but he was left-handed, and this would have involved an awkward draw of the .45 in his right side shoulder holster since this "kid" was on the left side of the car.

While the thief stared at him from a distance of about a foot, Lang reached out and grabbed the front of his short-sleeved shirt. At about this time, he became aware that the "do-gooder" woman was screaming. Yanking on the shirt he smashed the thief's face into the roof of the Datsun. The traffic light went green. He let up on the clutch and sped off down the street dragging the Rolex admirer alongside the car. At fifty miles an hour he let go and watched the fellow bounce a few times. A mile or so down the street he asked the New Zealander where she wanted to go.

"Are you always like that?" she asked.

"Like what?"

"That calm."

"Only when I haven't had enough to drink..."

"The Caravelle Hotel," she said in a whisper.

The STDAT-158 Vietnamese counterpart unit, "Strategic Technical Directorate" had a lot of troops. These were all Vietnamese paratroopers recruited out of the Army of the Republic of Vietnam's (ARVN) Airborne Division.

As the months of STDAT-158's life slipped past, MACV J-2 staff (intelligence) began to task STDAT-158 to use STD's troops in cross-border reconnaissance in Cambodia. Recon teams were inserted overland or by parachute at night. Losses were high. This sometimes resulted from clumsiness on the part of the American planners and advisers. The operations section of STDAT-158 (OPS-30) was full of Regular Army infantry officers (many fresh from the faculty at USMA) who had served one or more combat tours in Viet Nam. They were brave, dutiful men, but they knew next to nothing of special operations and did not seem to want to learn. They appeared to be intent on "riding out" the rest of the war in a nice, safe, staff billet (with "jump" pay). They did foolish things, things that common sense should have prevented. One of the worst involved a reconnaissance mission in the "Parrots Beak" area of Cambodia to the west of Tay Ninh Province of the Republic of Vietnam. The objective to be scouted was a rest camp for enemy troops about 15 kilometers inside Cambodia. The eight-man STD Vietnamese team was inserted by parachute by the USAF 90th Special Operations Squadron who flew in from Okinawa for the operation. The team disappeared without a trace after having reported from the Drop Zone (DZ) that all were well.

Neither Lang nor anyone else in the Intelligence Section (OPS-20) knew anything of this until his Vietnamese counterpart at STD (a lieutenant colonel) called to ask for information about the team. A request for information from the OPS-30 people met with evasion, and an attempt to hide behind a wall of security. Lang called the 90th SOS in Okinawa for the DZ coordinates.

The map showed that the DZ was in a big field within view of a major highway bridge, and that there was a large Cambodian village about three kilometers away. The files showed that this village was under the control of an NVA force that occupied most of the buildings as well as a camp in the woods between the town and the DZ.

Lang went to the commander of STDAT-158 to tell him that his operations section had killed eight of his counterpart's men through sheer incompetence. The colonel summoned the deputy operations chief, a major, and asked why he had not included the intelligence section in the planning process. It became evident that like many line officers, he held MI people in low esteem and had thought it unnecessary to talk to them. "After all," he said, "I can pick DZs as well as anyone else and this way, *the whole thing was more secure.*"

The colonel asked Lang to speak.

He said that highway bridges on major paved roads *always* have a guard, and that this guard had undoubtedly reported the presence of the STD team to the enemy garrison in the nearby town. "Next time," he said to the infantryman, "let's just shoot them ourselves in the marshaling area, and save the NVA the trouble..."

The man did not seem moved by this.

"God damn it!" Lang snarled at him. "Do you think that men who will jump out of an airplane in the dark over Cambodia grow on trees?"

"That's enough," the colonel said. "That's enough." He then ordered the operations officer to never, ever do anything without the help of the intelligence section.

Intercepts the next day revealed that the NVA had run the STD team down within 24 hours, killed two in the process, captured the rest and then shot them.

The operations chief of STD came to see Lang a few days later. This Vietnamese lieutenant colonel was in his late forties. He was an old French colonial soldier. He had served with the *Deuxieme Bataillon Parachutist Vietnamien*. He had one eye and one leg and walked stiffly on his prosthesis. He had jumped into the encirclement at Dien Bien Phu and had gone into the bag at the surrender. He asked to be told of his eight men.

Lang told him that he should talk to the operations people.

The old "para" said that he had, and to the colonel commanding, but that they would not tell him. "I think that you did not know of this," he said. "I know that you will tell me. You are one of us, one of the old kind…"

Lang could see his uncle John in this battered and mutilated man. John had told him much the same thing several years before. Lang knew that he should not allow this foreign officer to see divisions among the Americans, that he should not take their side in this matter or anything else.

"They are dead, every one; all dead," he said. He wanted to say that the Vietnamese should not trust STDAT-158's judgment ever again, but he did not.

The Vietnamese paratroop officer thanked him and left.

Lang went out to dinner that night in the dining room of the Caravelle Hotel. This was located just behind the Vietnamese Parliament. Two of his counterpart Vietnamese officers from STD were invited. Lang asked the more senior of these who he preferred to work with, the French or the Americans. He knew this lieutenant colonel well. They had gone through SF training in North Carolina together. His friend said that he preferred the French. He continued that the Americans wanted too much. They wanted the Vietnamese to be Americans. In contrast, he said, the French treated the natives as children, but nevertheless, as beloved children. Lang was "processing" that when a crippled Vietnamese soldier came to the table on crutches. He wore the camouflaged battle dress of the airborne division. His parachutist's wings were prominent on his chest. He held out his hand for money. The two Vietnamese officers gestured for him to go away. Lang looked at the wall. After the day's events he was temporarily unable to deal with yet more stress. The soldier pointed to Lang's jump wings and then at his own. Lang could not look at him.

"*Vous, moi, le meme, le meme,*" the man said and then not receiving a response, he hobbled away into the street, into the night. Lang instantly understood what a terrible thing he had done. He pursued the soldier into the noise and heat of Saigon. He could not be found. He was forever ashamed of that moment.

STDAT-158 closed its doors in March 1973 when the armistice went into effect, but STD fought on without its American helpers until the end of the Vietnamese Republic in 1975. In the last months of its existence, STDAT-158 became an organization in which it was hard to get things done. Resources in men and aircraft became more and more scarce. Nevertheless, the killing and the senseless friendly deaths continued. Reconnaissance patrols continued to be launched into the border areas of the RVN by the Special Mission Force and the Vietnamese STD. Lang was decorated on one occasion for heading up an STD expedition into Cambodia which resulted in two hundred confirmed enemy killed in a base camp on which he personally placed effective air strikes from nearby. It was a long walk in the woods, in a forest filled with orchids, ferns and deep shadow. He felt relaxed, and happy in the certitude that, unlike the NVA who were mostly "city boys," he was a creature of the wild himself, and content with God's creation. His personal "body count" on the NVA continued to go up and up. STD had him awarded the Cross of Gallantry with Palm for his leadership in the Cambodia fight. The one-legged old Vietnamese colonel had recommended him for it.

Among the projects still run by STDAT-158 in the last six months of its existence was something called "Earth Angel." This was a unit of North Vietnamese Army prisoners of war who had voluntarily decided to join the American side of the war. They were paid a lot of money, were promised re-settlement in the United States and were remarkably loyal in their change of identity. They lived in a camp thirty miles outside Saigon. There they ran their daily lives as though they were still in the North Vietnamese Army. They wore NVA uniform. They ate standard NVA rations and followed the daily routine of that army. There were several genuine NVA officers among them. The most senior of these was a colonel of infantry. He ran "a tight ship." Lang spent a lot of time talking to him so as to better understand the enemy army. After a while the colonel started giving Lang career counseling.

The Earth Angels typically operated in North Vietnam and occasionally in southern Laos. They worked in small groups on really difficult missions to acquire information from the North Vietnamese that only they could obtain. US intelligence units went to a lot of trouble to obtain new NVA ID cards, ration cards, etc. This documentation changed from time to time, and it would not do to have an Earth Angel present an outdated document in a "papers" check when they were in North Vietnam.

Lang first assumed that these men were still held as prisoners by United States Special Forces, but, in fact, they all owned and kept new cars at their camp and would occasionally drive into Saigon for dinner, for female company or whatever. When they did this, one or more of the American SOG people would accompany them to keep track of what they were doing. Lang had dinner with them in fancy restaurants several times a month.

These were not "Kit Carson Scouts." That was a very different program. It placed enlisted NVA prisoners in American combat units as reinforcements. They too were volunteers and quite loyal to their new comrades.

Lang's skill as an espionage case officer led to his direct involvement from time to time in recruiting Earth Angels. From time to time he was informed of particular prisoners of war being held in the National Interrogation Center. High value PWs were held there, sometimes for months, while questioned by all the US intelligence services in Vietnam. This facility was about twenty miles outside the city.

In one instance, Lang drove there with an American sergeant who spoke Vietnamese. They sat with an enemy lieutenant for most of one day smoking French cigarettes and drinking tea. The room had whitewashed walls and smelled slightly of urine as did the whole compound. The lieutenant had served a previous tour of duty in South Vietnam. He and Lang discovered that they had actually fought each other in 1969. Lang explained what they wanted the man to do and what his rewards would be for faithful service. This Vietnamese was an Olympic Games-level rifle marksman. He had been sent home and then on to Europe to compete. After the Olympics were ended, he was sent back to the South as an infantry officer replacement. He was assigned as a company commander in the 325th Division. This would have been somewhat equivalent to assignment to the 82nd Airborne Division in the US Army. He had been captured at Hue in a night-time trench raid by South Vietnamese Marines. Concussion grenades knocked him out, and the marines carried him off as a prize. As Lang watched the man and chatted with him in French, he saw that the lieutenant no longer believed in the communist and nationalist causes. He saw that like so many other old combat men, he no longer believed in any cause. It had ceased to matter to him whether the North won, or the South won. It just did not matter. He would fight on because that was his nature and all there was in his experience, but that was all…. There was nothing else left in him.

"What did they do to you?" Lang asked.

The NVA soldier lit another *Gitane*. "Oh, they pissed away my company stupidly," he said. "Then they arrested my second in command." He laughed. "He was the political officer. They arrested him as a defeatist. Then your Vietnamese friends arrived, and I am here."

The sun was beginning to set. Lang and the sergeant gathered up their belongings.

"Tell me again what you want me to do," the lieutenant said. "I can go live in America when this is over?"

"Yes, if you live long enough."

The lieutenant nodded. "All right, let's go. I don't like the food here."

Lang summoned an MP and signed for the prisoner. They had brought clothing for him. He was still in enemy uniform. Outside, they unchained their jeep from a post.

The NVA soldier looked at the village nearby. "Show me where this is on the map. Ahh... Let's get out of here before it is night." He sat in the front seat. Lang sat behind him. The new "friend" asked for a weapon and was given an M-16. He looked at it. "I had one of these once," he said. They drove back to Saigon and went out to dinner. The next day the lieutenant met his new boss, Lang's career counselor.

The American presence in Saigon had the smell of death about it. Members of the staff began to do things from boredom that were likely to get them killed. In one illustrative case, Lang and a group of friends flew to the beach at Vung Tau (Cap St. Jacques) for the day. There was an "in county" R&R Center there that was scheduled to close in a month, and they wanted to take advantage of the place before it disappeared. After a day of spear fishing and lobster grilling, the American advisor to the Earth Angels spoke up to say that his "boys" were going to make a practice parachute jump that night at "Bear Cat," near their home base. This was northeast of Saigon. Lang asked if he could "strap-hang" on the jump. He had not jumped for a month. The advisor, a black captain of infantry, said, "I thought you'd never ask." He wanted company out in the woods that night. The advisor and Lang flew back to Saigon to get their gear for the night drop and then met at the project compound at Tan Son Nhut Air Base.

In the marshaling area, Lang looked at what he had volunteered for. There were about thirty Vietnamese. These were all members of the Earth Angel project. The jump was to be from an old Vietnamese Air Force C-47. That was OK. The Gooney Bird was always the best jump from a paratrooper's point of view, and the VNAF pilots had more than their share of "guts." They could be trusted not to shy away from ground fire. They would "bore in" and put you where you were supposed to land.

There were three Americans; Lang, the captain of infantry (not an SF man), and an SF master sergeant named Gomez. Lang and the sergeant decided that Gomez would "jumpmaster" their three-man "stick" and that the Vietnamese could handle themselves as a separate "stick" on a second pass across the DZ. The captain did not like that, but he had a total of about ten jumps to his credit. Lang had around one hundred and fifty, and Gomez something over eight hundred (he had lost count). Lang told the captain that he should feel free to jump with his Vietnamese if he chose to do so. He did not so choose.

It was an interesting flight out to the Drop Zone in the gathering red-gold twilight. Lang sat across from the open door and watched the sunlight reflected on the sides of the cumulus clouds. He was wearing a CAR-15 automatic carbine in a canvas case, a 9 mm pistol, a machete and various other bits of junk. Near Bear Cat, Gomez stood the two American officers up, hooked them up and knelt in the door to watch for the DZ safety party's bonfire on the DZ. When he saw it, he waved Lang into the door. Standing in the doorway of the small aircraft, his head was outside the fuselage. The wind was warm and pleasant and smelled of the jungle eight or nine hundred feet below. It was quite dark. As he stood there, waiting for the tap on the rump that would tell him to jump, he saw green and then yellow tracer bullets pass by the wing, fired by hostiles on the ground. Gomez grabbed him and pulled him back into the plane.

"We'll go 'round again," Gomez said after consulting with the pilot. The C-47 made a circuit and approached the DZ again, this time from a different direction. From his position in the door, the ground appeared to be very close, closer than he had ever seen it from the door of an airplane. More tracers zipped by. He saw the DZ safety party's fire under the wing.

Gomez slapped him on the butt, and he jumped. He jumped out and up, aiming to jump past the end of the wing. That was impossible of course, but the effort ensured that he would go far enough from the door that he would not strike the fuselage of the airplane. The "prop blast" seized him and turned his rigid, bent over body so that his boots pointed to the rear. He watched the tail go over his head and knew he was clear of the plane. He felt the static line drag the bag with his canopy in it off the tray on his back. He felt the pop-pop-pop of ties breaking as the canopy came out of the bag and the risers were pulled to their full length. He turned his head to watch the opening. This was a habit in old jumpers. If there was a malfunction in opening, the visual warning would provide an extra instant in which to act. He saw the white tape loop at the top of the canopy. It connected the "bridle loop" of the canopy to the end of the static line. As long as that tape held, he was connected to the airplane. It snapped with a distinct "crack!" The canopy filled from the skirt upward, billowing into the familiar mushroom shape. His speed slowed immediately.

He swung back toward the direction of flight of the C-47, then back the other way. There were bullets in the air around him. He could see the green fire in their tails; hear the buzz of their flight. The ground looked too close. He looked at the horizon to keep from tensing up on impact. He oscillated one more time, and his boots hit the ground. He was a well-trained and experienced parachutist. The unexpectedly quick landing in the dark was not a serious matter. His body took over when his boots touched earth, and he performed the rolling "parachute landing fall" that took all the energy out of the bone crushing deceleration. He lay in waist high grass. He heard the "thud" of his two friends' descent nearby. He got out of his harness and chambered a round in his carbine. The tracer bullets were now coming across the DZ about waist high. The C-47 could be seen and heard turning in a circle for another pass across the DZ. Sergeant Gomez crawled into the flattened "deer's nest" that Lang's thrashing around had made in the grass. They waited for the captain.

The airplane made its next run. It seemed impossibly low. The mass of Viet paratroopers poured out. The night sky was full of the brave little fellows. They were pursued in their descent by the green "hornets." Lang thought he saw a number of bullets hit the airplane itself. Soon there were thirty men in a circle on the ground, weapons pointing out. They searched for the captain, crawling about in the tall grass while the bullets zipped by. He was not to be found. After a while, the NVA began to "search" the DZ with mortar fire. It was time to go.

The paras crawled off the DZ into the trees and made a perimeter. The mortar fire eventually stopped, and the enemy could be heard out on the DZ, moving around. Lang decided not to open fire on them if his little "command" was not found. It was impossible to know how many there might be.

The next morning the NVA had departed, and the captain was located. He had broken a hip in the landing. Ineptitude and terror were the causes. Unlike Lang, he had watched the ground come up to meet him. He tensed for the landing. His leg went rigid and the femur of his right leg was driven into his pelvis. He had hidden under a log that had one end up on the stump. He heard people around him all night but could not decide who they were. Our Vietnamese smelled just like the enemy. They all reeked of *Nuoc Mam*. He was right to keep quiet. The NVA would have shot him at once if they had found him. They had no use for wounded prisoners.

That was the end of the war for the captain. A helicopter recovered him from the DZ, and he went home within a few days. He was a good example of someone who was dressed as a soldier but did not have the character for the role. He lacked the *vocation.* A friend who read an account of this minor night action asked Lang why he risked his life in this completely unnecessary night jump. The explanation was simple. An officer who sends men into battle without sharing the risk soon begins to resemble the politicians that all real soldiers despise.

Lang went home for two weeks leave in early December. His wife was living in New England with her mother. There were no more troop airlift flights. He bought a heavily discounted Pan Am ticket for the trip. In Honolulu, an Army lieutenant's wife joined the flight with a year old baby she was taking home to her parents. They had never seen the child. Lang was in uniform, and she assumed that he could be relied on to help her with the baby. She was correct in that judgment.

The level of hostility toward the armed forces reached by that time by a lot of Americans was impressive in its vehemence and pervasiveness. Lang was repeatedly insulted in public during this "vacation." He wanted to be with Marguerite, but when the two weeks had passed, he wanted to go back to the war. He arrived in Saigon in time for the final act of America's war in South East Asia.

A few days before Christmas, the ongoing peace talks in Paris between the North Vietnamese and Americans broke down in what seemed hopeless deadlock. Someone in Washington decided that the North Vietnamese should be pressed hard to return to "the table." Operation Linebacker II, a renewed massive air bombardment of North Vietnam, was the product of that belief. Results were mixed in the giant air operation against the North. The US Strategic Air Command was not accustomed to the experience of massive anti-air missile defenses employed against their heavy bomber force. The initial result was a great deal of ordnance delivered to targets in North Vietnam. At the same time, the number of B-52s shot down was also impressive.

Lang was asked to go to US 7th Air Force headquarters at the airport for the purpose of informing the commanding general, and he alone, of what had been done with all the aircraft operating in his Area of Responsibility.

Sitting in an anteroom with one of his assistants, Lang could hear the general screaming and yelling on the telephone. When it was his turn, he entered and standing in front of the man's desk said, "I have come to tell what we did."

The air force commander rose to his feet and shaking his fist shouted, "What *you've* done! You little intel puke! You haven't done a damned thing but sit here on your ass while my people are being shot out of the sky. OK. Tell me what *you've done?*"

So, Lang told him.

Halfway through the recital the general sat down and covered his eyes with his hands. "I had no idea, no idea. You have told me. Good day."

In the midst of all this, the bubble of Lang's confidence in the integrity of his "unit home" burst.

When SOG had officially closed down, the functions of its native personnel security section had been absorbed by an office which came under the unit's adjutant. The people in this office were Vietnamese, and the people they administered were indigenous troops, mechanics, guards, etc. US military people were managed by their respective service personnel offices around Saigon.

The head of this native personnel office was a young civilian Vietnamese man in his thirties. Working for him were eight or ten clerks, mostly women. One day, he came to see Lang with a stack of personnel jackets under his arm. These were records that he had inherited from the previous security office. He had received a mass of records from the larger SOG organization and had finally gotten around to looking at these. He gave them to Lang without a word. There were ten records. All were active STDAT-158 employees. On top of the papers in each folder was the record of a counterintelligence polygraph of the person whose file it was. In each case, the polygraph indicated deception on the subject of the involvement of this person with enemy Intelligence. These polygraph examinations had all been conducted in the context of the "security review" the previous year. There were supply clerks, bartenders in billets and the like. A number of the people involved were extremely attractive young women. The level of deception indicated by these examination results pointed to active involvement.

Lang asked if any of these people had been moved from one job to another in the last year. The answer was no. There had been no adverse action taken on any of these unresolved examinations. Several of the people involved had been given pay increases and bonuses on the occasion of SOG's closure. One of these files belonged to "Mr. Ben," the Vietnamese driver of the STDAT-158 commander.

Lang went to the colonel in command. He was also a relative newcomer and had arrived about the same time as Lang. The man was dumbstruck. He asked what Lang intended to do.

"Reopen these investigations," was the answer. The colonel accepted this. He did not have much choice in the matter, since Lang would have gone to the Inspector General at MACV Headquarters if there had been any other response.

Army MI still had a counterintelligence polygraph facility in Saigon. This was the same office that had conducted the earlier examinations. A couple of the warrant officer polygraphists who had participated in the examinations were still on hand. They remembered them well because the evidence had been clear that these "subjects" were *enemy agents.* They had turned the exams over to SOG and had no idea what happened after that. They were astonished that nothing had happened. They readily agreed to reexamine these subjects.

The first was "Mr. Ben," the colonel's driver. Lang told him that STDAT-158 would close soon and that the colonel wanted to get him a job with the Defense Attaché's office after the US withdrawal was complete. He told "Mr. Ben" that for this to happen a polygraph examination would be necessary. "Mr. Ben" did not seem very concerned with that. Lang had been sure that would be the case. After all, "Mr. Ben" had "beaten" the last one.

The polygraphists talked to him for three days. They asked him hundreds of questions. They began by interviewing him as to his "life story." After the first couple of hours, the head examiner came to talk to Lang in the usual little room watching the examination from behind a "one way" mirror. This warrant officer said that the "Mr. Ben" of the previous year had told an identical tale of his life from the time of his employment by SOG, but this year's "Mr. Ben" had evidently lived a completely different life before he hired on with SOG. According to his new story, he had been born in a different province, grown up in a different place, and gone to different schools. It seemed that he had been so sure that the "security review" crisis had passed that he had forgotten his previous story. Both the stories were completely false. Deception was indicated on both.

Over the course of the following days, a portrait of "Mr. Ben" emerged from the mass of subtle, indirect questions he was asked. "Mr. Ben" was an officer of the NVA. He had been infiltrated into SOG to direct the activities of the circle of agents delimited by the ten personnel jackets. He had been in place for at least four years. This corresponded nicely with the disastrous improvement in enemy ability to anticipate SOG operations.

Lang now saw him in a different light. He was not a chauffeur. He was a colleague, and a skilled, brave one at that. By the end of the third day, "Mr. Ben" was really upset, but Lang thought that Lieutenant Colonel Ben's (as he was now known to be) natural desire to believe that he had once again prevailed would make it possible to keep him calm enough to get him back to the headquarters. And, so it was. Congratulations, and thanks from the polygraphists were useful, especially since they made a point of telling the little man that there were a "few minor points," but nothing really important. "You must be nervous..." one said to him. "Don't worry. You did fine..."

He and all his *apparat* were arrested simultaneously the next morning by agents of the Vietnamese Army Security Service. What happened to them after that, Lang went out of his way not to know.

With this penetration discovered, the degree of accuracy of NVA knowledge of SOG activities could be easily explained by the success of the "ring" in infiltrating the air operations section itself. No amount of eavesdropping by "Mr. Ben," or bartenders or waitresses in the SOG rest camp could provide names, times, equipment counts, missions, exact coordinates of Landing Zones and DZs. Signal intercepts had shown that the NVA had all of these things.

Interviews with servicemen still present who had served for several years with SOG revealed that several of the beautiful women who were under arrest had possessed lovers in the operations section over the last years. It was pathetically, heartbreakingly clear that one or more Americans in the operations section had sold their comrades for sex. SOG Headquarters had been inhabited by a wide variety of US personnel. They were from all the services. There were few Special Forces officers or men in the headquarters. There were some very junior enlisted clerks in all the staff sections. There were also a number of drunken, reprobate, bitter, officers and senior sergeants. What must have happened seemed clear.

This situation must have become apparent during the "security review" of 1971. One could only surmise that a conspiracy to cover it up until SOG "stood down" emerged among the senior officers who were not eager to reveal that this disgrace had endured during their tenure. The survival of the polygraph records may have been an accident, or more likely, it was a mute protest by someone of conscience.

An agreement was finally reached in Paris, and the wretched war began to come to an end. A prisoner of war exchange began. There were no SOG prisoners returned by the North Vietnamese. They had killed any they took. SOG had not expected any returned prisoners. The situation had been clear from intercepts. It was a kind of compliment bestowed by the enemy. It was the measure of their fear.

As a by-product of the armistice, a four-power military commission was formed to supervise the truce. Polish, Hungarian Canadian and Indonesian officers were soon seen around Saigon. These people were also to be seen at Tan Son Nhut trying to "buy out" the USAF Base Exchange before it closed. A US helicopter company was kept in country to transport the observers. It was a remarkable experience for American pilots to fly to VC and NVA base areas.

Lang spent several evenings drinking and playing cards in the officers' club with the four power types as well as the enemy soldiers. He could not resist the opportunity to find out what they were really like. He found that they were just like his Earth Angel friends. The only difference was that these had never run out of faith.

"J'ai manqué ma chance..."
Eric von Stroheim in the role of the Rittmeister
In the film, "Grand Illusion."

The armistice immediately raised the question of what to do with the five hundred odd SMF and Earth Angel troops still under command of STDAT-158. It was obvious that they would never be accepted by either Vietnamese side.

It was decided that the "Earth Angels" would be evacuated to the States as soon as possible. Most of them settled in Hawaii or California, and a number of them opened Vietnamese restaurants.

Lang argued that the Montagnard troops in SMF should be evacuated to somewhere like the Palau archipelago where they could make a new life for themselves. This was not done. In an action reminiscent of the U.S.

Army's betrayal of its Apache Scouts after the Geronimo War, the Army just walked away from these people, abandoning its own to the enemy. These were American auxiliary native troops, not members of the South Vietnamese armed forces. They had fought like the lions they were, and this was "the thanks of a grateful nation."

To prolong the agony, SOG issued them all the weapons, ammunition and gold they could transport, and turned them loose in the Central Highlands just before the cease fire went into effect. All those not already in the Pleiku area were assembled there and then trucked to an assembly area well outside town. The trucks shuttled back and forth all day, bringing them and theirs into a defensive perimeter astride the road. At the end the native "officers" shook hands with the American officers. Among them was the Montagnard "captain" with the crippled hand.

Then, they all went into the forest. There were several hundred women and children with them. They fought the triumphant NVA for several years. They were last heard by NSA on the radio in 1977, begging for help, begging for a re-supply drop, somewhere north of Kontum. Mark Twain said that history does not repeat itself, but it does rhyme. The French had released their native GCMA troops in the same way in 1954. They, too, were last heard of on the radio begging for help.

In a splendid anticlimax, Lang spent four days destroying everything in SOG headquarters and then left. He closed the headquarters personally. He had a space reserved on the last transport out before the cease-fire. A Vietnamese soldier drove him to Tan Son Nhut. They parked in front of the operations building. Lang picked up his bag and handed the man the keys.

He had orders to the next class at the staff college. Beyond that he was scheduled to attend the language school for Arabic. The week before he left Saigon, he learned that he had been chosen for civilian graduate school.

He would be with Marguerite for years.

In any event, he now fully understood that his place was "beside the city of the Trojans." There would be no return.

CHAPTER TWENTY-TWO

Home at Last

On his last trip home from Vietnam in 1973, Lang flew to San Francisco *en route* to Boston where his wife waited. The flight arrived in California just after nightfall. He soon learned that there was a late night "red eye" flight that would arrive in Boston early in the morning. After waiting in line for an hour, he was told by the airline that there was no available seat on the aircraft. This was bad news. That was a hard time for soldiers in America. Many civilians had decided that they hated the war in South East Asia. In this they had been strongly influenced by an effective propaganda campaign driven by pro-Viet Cong forces in the American political left.

Lang believed that there were empty seats on the plane, but they were not available for him. He was in khaki and unmistakably a soldier. While sitting in the terminal and thinking through this state of affairs, he watched with amusement as travelers walked in careful circles around the place where he had "parked" himself. Women avoided his eyes. Men whispered about him at a safe distance.

A flight attendant he had met on the plane saw him as she walked to the front doors. Lang always sought the company of women. The life he led was so devoid of the gentleness of women that he hungered for their presence, and always talked to them when he could. This pretty woman came to sit with him. After hearing of his dilemma, she asked him to go with her to the station manager's office. There, she introduced him to the man on duty as "Major Lang, a nice person." She kissed him on the cheek before leaving.

"How long have you been a major?" the airline person asked, "And how old are you?"

He had to think for a moment, "Thirty-two."

"And how long have you been at that rank?"

"Three, no four years now, why?'

"I was drafted in the fifties. You were a major at twenty-eight…"

"There's been a war lately. You have heard of it I am sure. If the thing had continued, I probably would have been promoted to lieutenant colonel in a year or so."

Lang did not understand the man's curiosity, but because of the evident general attitude, it made him uneasy.

"Would you have preferred for the war to continue? I mean so that you could be promoted again so soon."

"You think I am crazy?" He rose to leave the office. "Why the hell would I want that?"

The airline manager visibly relaxed. After a moment he spoke. "I lost a cousin in this stupid war, but you are not responsible. I am going to put you in first class on the upper deck of this 747. Welcome home."

The seats were wide and comfortable. The food was good, and the woman who served him a late dinner smiled at him. After double bourbon on the rocks he slept deeply, the sleep of those who have long had the need to sleep lightly.

Someone shook him awake. A middle-aged woman was standing next to his seat. She said something about "disgrace, drunken bums, drug-soaked reprobates." She then demanded to know what he was going to do about "it."

Loud talk and wild laughter filled the compartment. He looked at his watch. It was four thirty in the morning. There was a bar in first class. One of the woman staff was making drinks there and talking to three enlisted soldiers seated around the bar. They were very drunk and very noisy.

Lang walked forward to join them. He sat among them.

They fell silent at the sight of the gold oak leaf on his collar.

"Having a good time, boys?" he enquired.

There was a three-stripe sergeant with a half dozen medal ribbons. He wore the right shoulder patch of the 1st Cavalry Division. Among his medals was the Purple Heart.

"Oh yesh, shir," this one said.

Both they and Lang knew that he could ask the pilot to radio ahead so that the military police would be waiting.

"Are they bothering you?" he asked the "bartender."

"No, not at all, not at all, they are just celebrating; you know. That it's over…"

Lang nodded.

A woman passenger spoke up to ask that they not talk anymore about the fighting.

"You hear that, gents? You are frightening these people. Understand? They are easily frightened."

The three heads bobbed up and down.

"You had better start sobering up. There will be MPs in the airport."

He went back to his seat.

The woman who had awakened him asked if that was all he was going to do.

"Yes, as long as they are not abusive, that is all I will do. I understand where they are coming from. I have just come from there as well. If you want to try to discipline them, there they are…"

At the airport in Boston he walked them through the terminal and out to the cab rank where he watched them leave for places unknown.

Marguerite was waiting for him in Boston at a hotel. His homecoming was as wonderful as he had dared to hope. His wife had been living with her widowed mother in Maine.

He had been selected to attend the Armed Forces Staff College in Norfolk, Virginia. The course would not start for several months. He spent his days while waiting on temporary duty with the ROTC detachment at a state university and then they moved to Tidewater, Virginia. The course was not difficult, and they had an idyllic six months while he absorbed the technique of planning multi-service expeditionary operations. There were a number of foreign officers in his course. He found that his abilities in the art of cultivating such people persisted.

From Norfolk they went to Monterey, California, where he and Marguerite studied the Arabic language together for a year at the Defense Department's language school. They were gifted linguists and did well. Lang had been told that he would attend graduate school in Beirut, Lebanon after language school, but during the language school course, civil war began in that country and the possibility disappeared. His assignment manager in Washington suggested several universities in the United States as possibilities. Lang decided to apply to the University of Utah in Salt Lake City. There was an excellent graduate program in Middle East studies, a large library, and the move from Monterey would be fairly painless.

Life among the "saints," was an interesting experience; the instruction at the university was good, and time passed quickly. In the course of that year, he was promoted to major in the Regular Army. His previous appointment had been temporary, and the new status meant that he would certainly be able to serve for twenty years and thus qualify for retirement. This was a great relief. The post-Vietnam decade was a time of reductions in force that eliminated many thousands of officers from the army. Lang's selection for promotion in the Regular Army meant this would not be his fate.

While he was at Utah, he had the idea of writing to Sir John Glubb, the legendary creator and commander of the Arab Legion of Jordan. His experience of serving with Montagnard soldiers and agents inspired him to do this. A few hours of research in Marriott Library led him to believe that

Glubb lived near Tunbridge Wells in Kent and on that basis, Lang wrote him a long letter filled with youthful belief in the rightness of his methods in recruiting, training and leading native troops. After sending the letter, he and Marguerite left town for a visit to relatives in Texas. When they returned, a letter from Glubb waited in their mailbox. Sir John had written to tell him that the methods that Lang had adopted in dealing with native soldiers were the same that had been used in creating Jordan's army. This letter marked the beginning of a long and satisfying correspondence that culminated in a visit to the grand old man in England.

CHAPTER TWENTY-THREE

West Point

Towards the end of the graduate school assignment he began to negotiate with Washington for a "follow on" job. He had been in school for two-and-a-half years, and at that point in his career, he needed a "real" job that would produce a "real" effectiveness report; something that would sustain his attractiveness to selection boards for competitive advancement.

To that end, he asked for a field job in the Middle East. His preferred assignment was to be assistant army attaché at the embassy in Beirut, Lebanon. One beautiful morning in Salt Lake, the phone rang fatefully. It was a man from the officer management apparatus in Washington. He announced that any possibility that Lang might go to the Middle East for a "validating" real world job was "out the window." Visions of career decline raced through Lang's brain. When he enquired as to why that might be, the answer was "USMA wants you."

Lang replied that he did not know what city or country in the Middle East "Usma" might be.

There was a slight pause and then the officer at the other end of the circuit said slowly "The United States Military Academy at West Point, New York." He was a graduate and sensitive about it.

Pat Lang laughed aloud. "What do they want me for?" he asked. "Do they need someone to run the janitorial force?" There were no USMA graduates in his family, and he had never harbored a desire to associate with the place as an officer, believing, that he would always be treated as a second-class citizen there.

"They have been required by the Secretary of Defense to begin teaching the Arabic language, and after an intensive search throughout the army, the academy says it wants you."

"My God," Lang replied. "Do you have any idea what you are asking of me?"

"You stand high in your year group's order of merit, and you have a perfect score in Arabic as tested at the language school. In any event, I don't need to know. You need to know."

"I don't want the job. I want to go to the field. I belong in the field. I didn't join the army to be a schoolteacher…" Lang was seated in the kitchen of the nice, modern apartment that he and Marguerite had found high up in the foothills of the Wasatch Range. The kitchen window looked down on Salt Lake City and the university.

Marguerite stood by the sink watching him.

He put the phone on "conference call" so that she could listen.

"Perhaps I should make myself clearer," the voice replied. "Major General Aaron, the head of Army Intelligence has released you for this assignment and no other."

"I don't know him, and he does not know me. Why would he do that?"

"Colonel Renfroe, the head of the foreign language department was his Spanish instructor, and Renfroe has asked Aaron for you."

"Ah! Was he your Spanish teacher as well?"

"No. Colonel Renfroe was my German professor."

Marguerite nodded.

"I accept."

"Good. You sit there by the phone, and Colonel Renfroe will call you."

After he hung up, Lang told Marguerite that he was sorry but that it did not appear that he had any real choice in the matter.

She said she understood.

He waited for two hours.

When the telephone rang, he heard for the first time the man who would be his boss for the next three years. Walter Renfroe was then the oldest, most senior colonel in the US Army. As a full professor at USMA, he had the privilege of staying on active duty far longer than other colonels. He was from Georgia and had been at West Point since his graduation in the 30s with the exception of a three-year absence on war service. He was a well-known translator of German and Spanish literature. He had been forced to begin teaching Arabic in his department, forced by a Texas oil man who was then Deputy Secretary of Defense. His reluctance was evident in his voice.

"You have a good record," Renfroe began, "an excellent record... You speak French and Spanish?"

"I do."

"Good, if there are no cadets who wish to study Arabic, then you can teach one of those, and I will not lose a teaching position in the department..."

This implication of doubt offended Lang. "Sir, I do not seek this assignment."

"You don't?" He sounded surprised at the thought.

"No sir, the idea had not previously occurred to me."

"But, we, I, need you. I went to Washington and went through all the records. You are the one..."

The desperation in the man's voice touched something deep and foolish in Lang. "Very, well, colonel, I will accept the job."

"I must be able to tell the Dean of the Academic Board that you are an enthusiastic volunteer."

Lang almost told him what he could do with the job, but Marguerite was frowning at him across the table. "Very well," he said. "There is nothing I want more than to teach in your department."

"Good. Good, you will receive a letter and orders. Good day," and with that the conversation ended, and they were committed to "Hudson High" for three years.

The amount of work to be done at West Point in setting up and teaching a language unknown to the place proved to be staggering in the wealth of detail and multitude of tasks involved. There was the usual bother of moving household goods across the country along with professional books, mother-in-law, dog and two cars. As a senior major by date of rank, Lang should have had his pick of a number of "sets" of quarters on the West Point reservation that were truly one of a kind. Several looked directly down on the Hudson from airy verandas. Unfortunately, the officer in the Foreign Language Department who was assigned to act as his "sponsor" and helper chose to opt for a house for the Langs that he personally would have liked. This was a two-story brick row house with a grammar school located behind along with a playground. "But I thought you would like this," the man said with a snide look on his face.

Textbooks had to be selected; lesson plans were written and reviewed by the department bureaucracy. This was comic because no one in the department knew a word of Arabic, and they could not read the writing system.

Because he was the administrative head of a sub-department of the language group, Lang was required to attend a multitude of classes that had nothing to do with teaching. Equal opportunity, drug counseling, traffic control on post; these were all among the useless necessities that soaked up time in his day.

In the midst of this frenetic activity, the academy found itself trapped in a major public scandal involving cadets cheating in their academic work. A professor of Electrical Engineering had, in the previous semester, given a whole class of cadets a take home test. The course was core curriculum. Many of the cadets had no talent for Electrical Engineering. They were required to "certify" to the separate nature of their unassisted work on this test. This was a matter of honor, and hundreds of them failed in their honor. Cheating and "cooperation' were widespread. This became known shortly after Lang's arrival. Cadets were then tried by cadet honor courts, and many were found guilty. Counsel for the convicted appealed for commissioned officer review boards. This was their right because USMA cadets are members of the US military and not simply students with a scholarship. To his surprise and dismay, Lang found himself appointed to one of the officer review boards. The case was heard, and Lang voted for dismissal from the academy as the penalty for dishonor. Several more cases were heard, and Lang voted for dismissal in each case.

The Commandant of Cadets, a brigadier general who was the actual commander of the cadet brigade, asked to speak to Lang. Colonel Renfroe accompanied him to this interview. The general explained that the academy was under pressure from Congress to graduate as many cadets as reasonably possible for budgetary reasons, etc. Lang said that he understood, but that in the system he came from, there was no possible penalty for an honor violation conviction other than dismissal, and that he could not do otherwise. After he left the room, he heard Renfroe exclaim, "We have come to a sad state when VMI must remind us of what honor is…" Lang was removed from the board the next day. He later learned that all VMI graduates had been removed from these boards after his "chat" with the commandant. There were about twenty in the staff and faculty. Whether Renfroe was still pleased with his recruitment of Major Lang never became apparent.

The next hurdle on the path leading to the beginning of classes in Arabic was recruitment of cadets from the entering class. One of the few curriculum choices available to West Point cadets at that time was a choice of foreign language to be studied. The academy taught; Russian, Chinese, German, French, Italian, Spanish and Portuguese. Arabic would be an eighth language. The entering class numbered fourteen hundred. A representative of each language group staff was given the chance to "pitch" his language in an enormous lecture hall. Lang was an expert speaker. He believed in his ability to sway young minds. At a departmental meeting, he learned that the virtually unlimited army money possessed by the academy would provide any kind of custom-made briefing aids that he wanted. Lang asked where he could procure such assistance and was told by the department executive officer that in the basement of one of the many academy buildings was a facility that employed a group of commercial artists for the purpose of making such things. He walked a few blocks to visit these people and found them hungry for an interesting task and willing to do as much of this as he wanted. This service would cost him and his department nothing, nothing at all.

He possessed a large personal library of materials concerning the Middle East and Central Asia. This included many of the beautifully illustrated books in the "Osprey" military series. He returned to the training support department and, with the help of the artists, designed a series of canvas paintings to be mounted on wooden stretchers as though for hanging in a gallery. They were ten feet by six feet in size and would be displayed on stage on large easels made by the training department. The subjects included: the history of the Arab Revolt against the Ottomans in World War One, the Arab Legion of Jordan and the great Muslim conquests of the Seventh Century AD. There were also "boards" that depicted Arab philosophers, scientists of the Middle Ages, writers and political leaders.

The West Point class of 1980 sat in massed ranks and listened quietly to the appeals of all eight foreign language instruction groups. They were still cowed by the massively alien experience of the military academy with its many demands on young people generally accustomed to indulgent treatment at home. As a group, the 1400 members of the class smelled bad. From the stage, Lang breathed the collective miasma with which they filled the room. Old dried sweat, fear, the gas generated by constipation and food different from anything mom ever cooked; they stank.

When this ordeal ended, he moved to a small room deep in the lecture hall. Each foreign language group had a room in which to receive cadets interested in studying whatever they might teach. When the class was dismissed, a sound could be heard that resembled an approaching railroad train. Colonel Renfroe had come to the Arabic reception room. It was clear that the colonel believed Lang would be lonely in his wait for cadets who were interested. This concern disappeared as plebes flooded in the door. Soon the two officers were backed into a corner by dozens of cadets who wanted to volunteer. Renfroe looked puzzled and uncertain of his own attitude toward this unexpected reaction. 250 cadets wanted to take Arabic.

The administration of the language department insisted that Lang could teach no more than three sections of cadets. Each section could have 15 students. This was quite reasonable considering the planning and administrative workload that was created in a very bureaucratic environment. The question of student selection from among the many volunteers was critical. To solve this problem, Lang visited the admissions office and obtained the verbal SAT scores of all the volunteers. A lot of them were very high.

He arranged the top hundred in descending order of promise and began interviewing. A few people with high scores were not accepted into his class because of what could only be called bad attitude. Surliness, conceited speech and behavior caused him to reject these. After having commanded troops for years, he could spot a bad actor after a few minutes' conversation. There were not many such "candidates" and in the main, the top hundred possibilities easily supplied the students needed.

Unexpectedly, Lang received a summons to the USMA library. The Librarian of the USMA book collection was a full colonel with the status of a permanent professor. This officer offered coffee and said apologetically that he had not been notified of the decision to start teaching Arabic early enough for him to have included a budget item for books and periodicals in his financial plan for the coming school year.

Professor Lang silently contemplated a necessity that had not occurred to him.

The Librarian appeared worried by the lack of response and seemed to take it as quiet reproach. He looked uncomfortable. "Well," he said, "I do have $75,000 dollars in my contingency fund that I could put into this. Would that be enough to get started? I plan to ask for half a million for next year to build a Middle East collection. Do you have a list of things you would like me to buy this year and next?"

Pat Lang had no idea how library collections were funded and built and did not realize until much later that such riches were uncommon. In 1976 money, $500,000 was a large sum. Fortunately, he had been amassing a bibliography on Middle Eastern subjects since his return from Vietnam and had several shoeboxes full of 3x5 cards. With abandon, he started giving the library lists of standard works like the "Index Islamicus" and the "Encyclopedia of Islam," and they bought them all. There was nothing like the internet in those long-ago times, and a good library was an absolute necessity for substantial learning.

One day, when he was fully occupied with preparatory work, a group arrived from B'nai Brith in New York City to inquire why he was going to teach Arabic to future US Army officers. He asked if they had permission to talk to him. They did not. He called the Foreign Language Department. They sent the department executive officer to take them away, but before he arrived, Lang informed them that if they had complaints to make they should bring them to Colonel Renfroe, the department head. He told them that the department taught Russian and Chinese and asked if they objected to that? They said nothing. They were escorted out of the building.

The first year's course went smoothly. In the middle of that year, Lang was made faculty coordinator for an inter-departmental program in Middle East studies. In addition to this, he held the academic ranks of "the Assistant Professor of the Arabic Language," and "Head of the Arabic Language Section."

In the second year of Arabic instruction, it was discovered that yet another large group of new cadets wanted to study the language. The academy searched the personnel assets of the US Army and could not identify another officer who could both teach the language and who the school wanted to have. There was a requirement that staff and faculty have high standing in their army promotion year group. They wanted this so that the faculty would serve as officer role models for the cadets. Such an officer could not be found. A search was then made for a civilian instructor. No one satisfactory was found. In desperation the Foreign Language Department asked Lang's opinion. He told them that his "roommate," Marguerite Lessard Lang had a master's degree in Arab literature and Middle East Studies. A confounded silence ensued for a few days, and then Marguerite was appointed a civilian professor of foreign languages. At the same time, an experienced foreign language professor officer was placed in language school to take up the expected third year demand.

In this second year, Lang was elected to the faculty senate. Each department had two elected members in this advisory body. Once installed, Lang discerned that the superintendent, LTG Andrew Goodpaster, was less than eager to have the advice of the group. Goodpaster had willingly given up a star and the rank of full general to return to active duty as superintendent. He had his own agenda with regard to West Point's ailments as an institution. The Electrical Engineering cheating fiasco had badly damaged West Point's reputation, and Goodpaster was determined to repair that damage without interference.

In the same year, Lang was declared to be the best classroom teacher in the USMA faculty. This happened again the following year.

In his third year at the academy, Lang looked forward to a return to what he thought of as the "real army." That third summer he took a group of cadets to Jordan to give them field exposure to an Arab Army. The trip was a grand success.

Classes reached higher and higher levels of linguistic accomplishment.

Pat Lang was promoted to lieutenant colonel.

The Commandant of Cadets asked in September for a briefing about the cadet training trip. This brigadier general listened to the briefing and then looked at the papers before him. "MI espionage officer, Special Forces, Arab World foreign area specialist, mustache; we have to make sure we don't get any more like you here…"

"Why is that, general," Lang asked.

"They will all want to be like you. We can't have that!"

"You prefer to have more of these strange women officers that have now been assigned here to keep the girls company?"

"Yes, good day, colonel."

To his surprise an offer of permanent assignment to the academy faculty was made to him by his department head. It was understood in the conversation that Marguerite's status as a civilian professor would be made permanent, and that both of them would be sent to Ph.D programs at Columbia or some other suitable university. Her interests were involved, so he asked her opinion. She was adamantly opposed to a further stay at West Point. She detested the place. She felt that West Point failed the interests of the cadets as future officers. She believed this to be true because the academy did not challenge the cadets in anything but rote recitation and problem solving. Lang informed the administration of his negative decision and contacted the Department of the Army in Washington to ask for an onward assignment when his three years had ended.

He received a call asking him to call on the Dean of the Academic Board where behind closed doors a firm proffer of permanent employment was made. This was quite irregular since such appointments were to be made in a competitive process.

He declined.

He understood that at West Point he would always be "Christmas Help." His life as a professor at USMA had been filled with reminders of his outsider status. One of the most memorable of such experiences had been a phone call from the "on-post" representative of the West Point class of 1962. This man told him that it was now "apparent" that it was only an accident of history that Lang had not been one of "them," and that "they" wished to rectify that distortion of history by making him an honorary member of the Class of 1962. It was further explained that because he had no ranking in the class, he would be ranked at the bottom for game tickets, seating at events, etc. He refused membership to the amazement of the class representative.

The Department of the Army suggested an assignment to the Republic of Yemen as Defense and Army Attaché in the US Embassy in Sanaa. He understood that this meant that he was still thought of as an "odd ball," but that was acceptable to him and Marguerite. They decided to live in Yemen for couple of years.

Orders arrived at West Point and they were soon gone.

CHAPTER TWENTY-FOUR

Yemen

Lang was Defense and Army Attaché (DATT/ARMA) in the Yemen Arab Republic for two years. The embassy was small and lodged in a multi-story mud and palm log building in the middle of Sanaa. The ambassador lived there, surrounded by beautiful gardens and many servants. The Langs established themselves in a rambling white masonry house about a mile from the embassy. It was surrounded by a ten-foot wall topped with broken glass. Water was provided by trucks that filled and refilled tanks on the roof. In time, Marguerite's garden rivalled that of the embassy. There was a guard, an aged Yemeni tribal, who although in his eighties had a large and ever-growing family. His name was Ahmad. He had every Saturday off and spent it at home somewhere making more babies. He and one of his wives produced a new one during the Langs' time in Sanaa. When asked by Lang how he managed that he replied, "Clean living, fasting in Ramadan and effort every Saturday." Ahmad was very solicitous of the memsahib's welfare and guarded the place like a lion during Lang's frequent absences in the field. Ahmad lived in a little whitewashed building by the front gate.

The office consisted of Lang, his US Army sergeant and a driver who was an employee of the embassy, but in reality, was a major in the Yemeni National Police. His assignment was surveillance of the American military attaché. His name was Abdullah al-Shami. He was a substantial person whose help was always generously given when it was requested and sometimes when it was not. He knew that Lang's work required him to "poke around" the country in places that were frequently unsafe because of banditry or some other sort of local warfare. When Lang needed to go somewhere that was probably insecure, he formed the habit of asking Abdullah's opinion. If the answer was positive, they went there together. If the answer was not, he went alone when Abdullah was away. Abdullah spoke reasonably good English having been a driver for several British officers at Aden when the United Kingdom possessed South Yemen, but Lang asked him when they first met to speak nothing but Arabic to him and he always did. From time to time, he gave Lang a verbal report as to what sort of grade his Arabic deserved. Abdullah was a wonderful companion on field trips across the mountain and desert country. On some occasions, parties of tribesmen halted their Land Cruiser truck or Peugeot 504 on country roads to demand tribute or the vehicle. Lang and Abdullah were armed with sub-machine guns in the car and Browning 9 mm automatic pistols in hidden holsters. These were formidable, but Abdullah never waved a firearm at the "bandits." He always walked back to the car's trunk and picked up two axe handles. With those in their hands they would approach the offending group. Abdullah then greeted them in a friendly way, but if the tribesmen were aggressive, he would open his jacket to show his pistol and declare, "Oh sons of donkeys, do you want to see blood?"

The tribesmen were always taken aback and inevitably settled for canned groceries brought as trade goods. On one occasion, Lang fired a magazine from an old M-3 "grease gun" machine gun into a riverbank when it was clear that there would be no violence. He had bought the weapon at a local arms bazaar. The strike of the .45 ACP bullets astounded the audience, and on an impulse Lang handed the gun to the leader as a gift. The stocky little man in native dress embraced him. As they drove off Abdullah laughed in delight. In the mirror the chieftain could be seen standing by the track holding the weapon above his head. For the rest of his time in Yemen, Lang and Abdullah knew they were safe in that little valley. On longer journeys to the south, they often "staged" through there and slept in the village after dining on a sheep or goat they had brought to these people as a token of friendship. Their safety was ensured by the tribal Arab's duty to offer hospitality and protection to friends.

Abdullah's "cover" as a driver wore thin at times. On the road, policemen sometimes saluted him and addressed him as "major." When that happened, Lang would pretend to be looking out the window at the barren countryside. Abdullah lived in a small building in the back yard of the Lang's large house and he, too, went home on the weekends.

Pat Lang was not the cookie pushing type of attaché. He was not someone who particularly liked cocktail parties although he attended many.

Yemen at that time was a lot like Arizona in the 1880s, a country inhabited by savage, heavily armed tribesmen and run by politician soldiers much like the Mexican military "brass" in the film, "The Wild Bunch."

The USSR had a 500-man military mission in North Yemen and another of similar size in communist South Yemen. This military mission was commanded by a Tank Corps major general who liked Americans. He had been a 17-year-old lieutenant in 1945 and had been among the Soviet armored men who had met the US Army at Torgau on the Elbe in Germany. He had never gotten over the experience, and when he discovered that Lang was friendly, a useful relationship developed that drove the State Department people in the embassy to lecture Lang to the effect that he should keep his distance so that the Yemenis would not think he found the Soviets acceptable company. He told them that he was there to collect information and the

Soviets had the information he needed. Others at the embassy laughed at Lang's answer and said that he was quite right.

The Communist Chinese also had a very big embassy in Sanaa. It was heavily manned with Middle East trained "spooks" who spoke beautiful Arabic. The Red Chinese also had 2,000 construction workers in North Yemen employed in continuing road projects all over the country that had been begun earlier by the US.

There were tribal wars of varying size all over the country. Some were against other tribes. Some were against the government, and some others were in combination with the government against yet other tribes. The variety was endless.

To make the "stew" even richer, there was a coalition of leftist political groups called the National Democratic Front (NDF) waging a major war against the North Yemen government. This "front" brought together: Communists, Baathists, Socialists, and just plain dissident folks who had a variety of motives. As an example, North Yemeni forces killed several NDF guerrillas who were found to be second generation Americans from Michigan. One of them had a copy of a pamphlet by Tom Paine in a pocket along with his US passport when he died. The year was 1978. The USSR supported both sides in this war between north and south largely because Ali Abdullah Salih, the Yemeni president, displayed great skill in playing the Soviets, the US and the UK off against each other to make sure that happened.

Salih, the British MI-6 station commander and Lang often went hunting together. The British fellow introduced Pat to Salih. The president often laughed aloud with the Western spies and rejoiced at the ease with which their countries were duped. He said he placed the Britisher and Lang in a different category as "people as devious as he and unlikely to be believed if they 'ratted' on him."

The United States had a six-man military mission in North Yemen and a USAF team busy teaching the Yemen Air Force to fly F-5 fighters that the Saudis had bought for them. Assisting the TAFT was a worthless group of Saudi Air Force pilots whose specialty seemed to be crashing aircraft, and a Taiwanese Air Force group seconded to the Saudi Air force to maintain the F-5s.

The US military training groups were confined by directive to execution of training tasks. Lang was not. Jobs always seemed to grow and change to match what he could and wanted to do. Lang was an experienced case officer, and that experience often opened doors for effective intelligence work.

At a steak and shrimp grill party one night, the Soviet general asked if he would like to accompany a counter-guerrilla operation conducted by 8th Yemeni Commando Brigade. He said he reckoned Lang was better at this than his own men. They had been assigned from the 106th Soviet Airborne Division, and he was sure Lang knew more Arabic than they. The general had a KGB minder with him that night, and the man's wife held her sides laughing while the spook husband choked on his steak. The general laughed as well and said to ignore him.

Lang asked DIA and was given permission. This trip to the field was often repeated and developed over time into a relationship with the Soviet commando advisers in which "Westerners" supposedly banded together against the wily NDF. After a while, Lang wore Yemeni uniform in the field as did the Soviets. The Soviet advisers with this outfit were almost all non-Russians. They were Azeris, Armenians, Georgians, Chechens, etc. Their home division's permanent station was in the Trans-Caucasus Military District. Lang could talk to the Yemenis on these expeditions, and the Soviets could not. The commando brigade made use of the American-built F-5s as well as various Soviet-provided jets for close air support on the laurel covered mountainsides in the southeast. They also had armed MI-8 helicopters in support of operations. The Yemeni pilots were dangerous to their own soldiers as well as to the targets, and it was soon agreed that Lang would vector the air support onto the targets supposedly because he had much experience in this. The 8th Commando Brigade killed many NDF fighters and lost a good many men as well. Yemenis are real fighters no matter what side they are on.

Lang's US general officer boss came to visit. Ironically, The Red Chinese ambassador told the man that Pat Lang was a hero of the struggle against Soviet hegemonic ambitions and those of the running dog friends of the Soviets as well. Pat supposed he did not know how much Lang had managed to embed himself in the Soviet advisory effort.

The Langs were sorry to leave Yemen. It had been a grand game.

CHAPTER TWENTY-FIVE

The Kingdom

A year later, Lieutenant Colonel Lang was offered the post of Defense and Army Attaché at the US embassy in Jeddah, Saudi Arabia. This was a splendid opportunity. The attaché post in that country was one of largest in the world and well placed in the most important country in the Middle East region. There were five attaché officers at the post. Two were Army, two were Air Force, and one Navy. There was an administrative warrant officer, three military clerks and three civilian secretaries. It was an important position, meant to be filled by a full colonel. Lang was still a lieutenant colonel.

It was easy to calculate that he would be considered for promotion by a competitive service- wide promotion board while on station in Saudi Arabia. If he failed to be selected for promotion, his days in the army would end. The rule for service life was "up or out." He visited the army's officer personnel center in Virginia for a discussion with the head of the colonels' assignment office. He explained to the colonel in charge that although he wanted the job, he did not want it if it was possible or probable that he would be "passed over" for promotion while on post. The man looked up from the record and said, "I don't know why you have not been promoted early. Take the job."

The Langs arrived in Jeddah a few months later. At the army's convenience, he was "frocked" as a full colonel. That meant that he was ordered to wear a colonel's insignia and call himself "colonel," but, this was, in reality, a disguise intended to make him function better in a community of principal military attachés who were all colonels or higher in grade. In a few months' time his name appeared on the army's promotion list, and after that it was just a matter of waiting until his "sequence number" on this list came up and he was promoted.

Duty in the Jeddah embassy of the United States was less enjoyable than their experience in Yemen had been. The embassy was huge. There were hundreds of Americans and local employees. The physical facility occupied a Saudi "block" as big as a Manhattan mid-town block. There was a US Army commissary store on the facility. This was a small supermarket that carried anything you could buy in the United States. There was a nine-hole golf course. There was a big swimming pool. There was a snack bar. Nevertheless, outside the walls there was Saudi society, repressive, small minded and determined to become something that looked somewhat like San Diego, California, but not in truth anything like that.

The work in this big mission was not easy. The local CIA chief was a man named Alan Michaels who claimed to have learned life from Vince Lombardi, the hyper-aggressive football coach. Michaels first attempted to intimidate

Lang into accepting de facto subordination through simple minded brutish behavior and when that failed, he lapsed into a sullen silence in which he took every opportunity to denigrate and undermine the DAO's position. On several occasions, Michaels sought to negotiate with him over functions of the attaché office. Michaels was a childish, type-A bully who in later years was convicted of "withholding information" from the FBI in the Iran-Contra affair and sentenced to a year of probation. President George W. Bush pardoned him. After all, Michaels knew where at least some of the bodies were buried.

The US military had a long history of advice and assistance to Saudi Arabia. This had begun during the presidency of Franklin Roosevelt, a distant relative of the Lang clan. At the time of Lang's assignment as Defense Attaché in Jeddah, there were several different US military missions in Saudi Arabia.

The largest of these was the United States Military Training Mission. This group had several hundred people working in different locations around the country, but its headquarters was in Riyadh, the capital. The commander of this mission at that time was a USAF major general named Neal Jenkins. A former CO of the air force demonstration flying team, "The Thunderbirds," Jenkins was a very basic fighter pilot with no grasp of the realities of life in Saudi Arabia or the complexities of Middle Eastern politics. He believed that Lang, as an independent reporter to Washington, was a threat. He was correct. Jenkins' training mission had effectively become the "servants" of the Saudi Ministry of Defense and Aviation. Many in the mission hoped for post-retirement employment by one of the many US defense contractors servicing the Saudi armed forces. A reputation as someone who criticized those armed forces would prevent that. Jenkins, himself, was simply unable to understand a situation in which he could command a Saudi-funded US military activity and yet owe the Saudis no allegiance whatever. As a result, he sought to block the acquisition by the Defense Attaché Office of any information that might make the Saudis, or him, look bad. On one occasion he challenged Lang directly by asking him how many stars his boss had. When told that the Director of the Defense Intelligence Agency was a lieutenant general (three stars), he looked crestfallen.

Lang and Jenkins had "history" before the Langs arrival in Jeddah. In the course of the Yemen experience, Pat had grown close to his French, Saudi and British colleagues. The insurgent war in the southeast of North Yemen was of great concern to the Saudi government. The notion that left wing guerrillas led by outright communists might defeat the Salih regime and arrive on Saudi Arabia's southern border was understandably worrying. The Saudi Ministry of Defense called for a US/Saudi meeting in Riyadh. Lang learned of this from the Saudi attaché in Sanaa but thought little of the matter until the US attaché office in Jeddah sent their twin engine airplane to bring him to the meeting. The night before this "pow-wow," there was a pre-meeting meeting at MG Jenkins' house in his unit's residential compound. After dinner, Jenkins tried to brainstorm the coming proceedings. Lang said little until Jenkins off-handedly asked him how long he would speak.

The Saudis had told Jenkins that they wanted Lieutenant Colonel Lang to brief.

"How long would you want me to speak, general?" was the reply. Lang was an accomplished briefer and public orator. He could make the presentation be whatever length Jenkins required.

This answer enraged the air force general. His face grew red, and he stammered until they all left.

The next day, when the Americans arrived at the Saudi conference room they found that Saudi MG Mardini, the head of their overseas military assistance program, was presiding. Lang moved to the US side of the table intending to sit as far away from Jenkins as possible.

General Mardini said, "No, no, come sit with us. We invited you."

Lang took the indicated seat next to the Saudi military attaché from Sanaa. The man reached over and held Pat's hand. This was a normal gesture of friendship in Arabia, but the Jenkins' side of the table squirmed and frowned.

When the usual meaningless talk of eternal amity ended, Mardini stated that *al-muqaddam* Lang would give the Saudi intelligence brief to begin the meeting.

Someone explained that the Arabic word meant lieutenant colonel. Jenkins face grew red again. Mardini watched him as a snake watches a bird.

"Why?" Jenkins rasped at last.

Mardini smiled. He was clearly enjoying this spectacle. "Our attaché in Sanaa, *al-muqqadam* al-Obeid is not an intelligence man. He is a… political liaison to the tribes south of Sanaa. He learns much of what he knows of the combat situation from his brother antar. Actually, Lieutenant Colonel al-Obeid suggested that *antar* brief here for us."

"Antar?" Jenkins asked

Lang pointed to his own chest. "Me," he said. That's what they call me."

"Why?"

"I don't know, sir. I did not pick the name. It is the name of one of their warrior poets."

Jenkins nodded.

Mardini, indicated with a languid hand motion that he might begin.

Lang spent 30 minutes at the map board, briefing the Yemen insurgency in Arabic. When he finished the Saudi officers asked a few questions.

Mardini said, *"Mumtaz."* "That means excellent," he told Jenkins. "I detect a slight Palestinian accent," he remarked to Lang.

"Yes, general, *qudsi.* This is from my first teacher."

"Jerusalem," Mardini told Jenkins. "Now do it in English if you please *antar...*"

At the break, several of Jenkins' officers followed their boss into the hallway to congratulate Lang.

"I did not think you could be as good at this as people said. You are a professional," Jenkins said and walked away.

The Arabs could be heard laughing in the conference room. They were pleased to see Jenkins eat dirt. It was obvious that they detested him.

The pattern was set. When Lang returned from the United States as the attaché in Saudi Arabia, he knew that Jenkins already hated him.

Lang tried to explain the Saudi mentality to Jenkins. He worked at it for a year in which they shared the same country. At the end of his time in Saudi Arabia, Jenkins told Lang that he should have listened to the advice given. In his last visit to the embassy, Jenkins said to Lang that he had had a hard time believing that when Saudi colleagues told him something they did not really expect that he would think them committed. The realization that this was true had been a great blow to him.

There were two other US military entities in Saudi Arabia at that time.

One was the US Army Corps of Engineers Middle East District. This office was busy supervising construction of a great many Saudi government infrastructure project all over the kingdom. Many of these were military; air and naval bases, large ground forces cantonments and the like, but many were essential to the emerging Saudi civil economy. The railroad system in the Eastern Province and a network of multi-lane roads that tied the country together, water sources for the kind of encyclopedic information that and sewage systems were among the larger efforts.

The other major US military entity in the country was the Saudi Arabia National Guard (SANG) project office. The function of this group was to oversee the work of an American company that was training two five-thousand man SANG light armored brigades equipped with wheeled armored vehicles. The SANG had a large full-time force outside these two brigades as well as a reserve force that functioned as a population control mechanism out in the deep desert. All these people were Bedouin tribesmen selected from the tribes thought most loyal to the government. Lang had always like tribesmen, so he began to elicit invitations to observe the SANG in training. Thus, it came to be that one frosty night he found himself standing around a fire in the *rub al-khali* (Empty Quarter) with ten SANG soldiers. The desert is mighty cold at night. He listened to the voices. After some time spent in "sorting through" the accents and vocabulary, he spoke up to tell a lieutenant across the fire that he was not a Saudi and to ask what he was.

"What do you think I am, colonel," the officer asked in English.

"I think you are an East Bank Jordanian, probably from the Amman area."

The SANG soldiers listened in puzzlement, so Lang repeated it in Arabic. They all started to laugh.

"Yes, I am from Jordanian Special Forces. I am seconded here to teach…"

"Got your coin?" Lang asked.

The lieutenant produced his "challenge coin."

"Do the Americans know you are Jordanian?"

"No sir, they never asked."

"Good, I won't tell them."

"*Ashkurak, sidi.* Thank you, sir. You must be *Antar.* Your friends speak of you at home."

Antar's relationship with the SANG and its men came to be valued by its American advisers as a bridge to a world of understanding that they could not make themselves. Even those American advisers who were Arab World specialists in the US Army had never achieved the empathy needed. Trips to the field with SANG troops were a welcome respite from embassy life and the eternal struggle with Jenkins.

The SANG project office was well run but still had "environmental problems." Lang's most excruciating experience with the SANG project occurred when a new American brigadier general was appointed to run the program. All the previous US managers that he knew of had been rather laidback cavalry types who were capable of seeing the ironic humor inevitable in their situation as "handmaiden" to a lot of desert *banditti* capable of stealing the coins off a dead man's eyes. They just grinned and ignored the graft, laziness and nepotism embedded in the system of the Saudi National Guard.

The new man was something different. He was a tough, wiry, little Italian fellow from New Jersey who had served all his army time in the artillery. He had come up from the ranks through grit, hard work and self-denial. He said he liked Lang because the attaché owed him nothing, did not care about his opinion, had no reason to flatter him, and did not do so.

One day when Lang was in Riyadh, this general asked him into his office. He was in fatigue pants and a t-shirt. His dog tags clinked on a chain around his neck. "Lang," he said, "I have discovered that one of our British electronics suppliers is overcharging the SANG for spare parts by about 1000%. I am going to tell my Saudi royal boss about this. What do you say?"

"Don't do it."

"Why?"

"Because you will probably be reporting this to the man who benefits the most from it..."

"That can't be true. They all say they want the best for their country."

"They say a lot of things, general, a lot of things."

The general reported the graft, and the Saudis asked for him to be removed from the country a week later. Their justification was that the artilleryman was cruel to his own people because some had complained of the severity of his economies. These had been intended to benefit the Saudi government's budget. This excuse was a Saudi joke and an example of their cruel humor and arrogance.

Before the artilleryman left, he asked Lang what he had done wrong. There could be no answer. Lang drove him and his wife to the airport when they left.

Among the projects conducted by the attaché office during Lang's tenure were internal war games that had scenarios depicting both Yemeni and Iraqi invasions of Saudi Arabia. These war games demonstrated conclusively the utter vulnerability of Saudi Arabia to invasion from the northeast through Kuwait and into the Eastern Province of The Kingdom. The estimated time that it would take the Iraqi Army to overrun the Gulf Coast to include the Ghawar oil and gas fields was two weeks. Six mobile divisions was the force estimated to be required. This game result, when later confirmed by DIA studies in Washington, proved to be eerily predictive of the possibilities.

Through diligent studies of available data, the Attaché Office was able to discover there were facilities in Saudi Arabia that the Saudi government did not want the United States to visit. Among them was the Intermediate Range Ballistic Missile (IRBM) site deep in the Empty Quarter desert. The Saudis had bought these missiles from China with Pakistani assistance in the belief that the nuclear warheads that normally accompanied them would be provided. China refused to provide these, but the missiles were still out in the desert, well dug into an elaborate launch and maintenance site.

Lang's service as attaché in Saudi Arabia required innovation and resourcefulness, and for this he was decorated. While he was in Saudi Arabia, he was chosen to be promoted to full colonel and to attend a senior service college in residence. He decided to attend the Army War College at Carlisle, Pennsylvania. The courses offered at all the senior service colleges were roughly the same, and he and Marguerite had lived apart from the Army for too long.

A pleasant year passed at Carlisle. His classmates were nearly all people who had passed their service lives in assignments to troop units or to the Army General Staff in the Pentagon. Their knowledge of a greater world of geopolitics and indeed of higher command in war was limited. Lang's wider experience and self-education in higher level operations served him well at Carlisle. He soon became a leader in his class and was asked by them to chair the effort to find a suitable gift to the War College from the class. He overcame the desire of some to commission a limited-edition print that could be marketed publicly and another group that wanted to build something like a pavilion at a sports field. In the end, the class presented the school with one of the lobby windows in Bliss Hall. This was the First World War Memorial window. It was not universally appreciated. A British Army officer in the class protested that the uniforms and weapons in the window were incorrect. It was explained to him that the US Army did not wear British uniforms, nor did it carry British weapons in World War I. He looked puzzled. Lang was never sure if the man had been pulling everyone's leg or not.

Around Christmas, the Department of the Army personnel branch called to inform Lang that he had been chosen for brigade command by the national selection board. There were a few days of joy until the same people called to say that he was such a valuable asset that he could not be "wasted" on command and that he would be made an "alternate" on the list. He told the caller that such a decision would be a virtual "kiss of death" for his chance of becoming a brigadier general, and that he would retire from the army as soon as he could if this arbitrary change took place. It was clear that the underlying cause for this change was the simple fact that Lang was not a "member" of the clique of officers who had acquired sponsorship within the army intelligence establishment. In the years before the Goldwater-Nichols Law made a focus on inter-service joint assignments mandatory for high rank, such assignments were a hindrance to advancement.

CHAPTER TWENTY-SIX

DIO for the Middle East and South Asia

The next week, the Director of the Defense Intelligence Agency (DIA), Lieutenant General Jim Williams called to ask if Lang would take the position of Defense Intelligence Officer for the Middle East and South Asia on his staff. In that position, he would be responsible for oversight of all that DIA did in that part of the world. This was a position that Lang had always wanted and faced with the thinly disguised hostility of the Army intelligence community, he accepted the job.

This position gave him centrality in many events in "his" region that occurred during his eight-year tenure. US retaliatory raids in Libya were at the top of the list as well as many overseas conferences in which he was Chief of Delegation.

Once in the job he discovered that he was, among many other things, the "anointed" leader of the US Defense Department liaison relationship with a section of the Israeli General Staff. The best parts of the job of liaison chief with Israel were the many trips made to the Holy Land to support the relationship. These could always be used as excuses for trips all over the region.

After he had been in the job two years, the Army decided that it wanted to take him out of the position so that he could be Defense and Army Attaché in Syria. He had performed this same duty in Yemen and Saudi Arabia and had no particular desire to do it again. In the year following his assignment in DIA, the US Army central command selection board once again chose him for brigade command, and the military personnel center once again stated that they would not allow him to command because of his "great value" in staff work.

In response, he informed the army that he would retire as soon as he had enough time in grade to hold his rank after retirement. There followed a process in which officers up to the rank of full general counseled him of his duty to remain on active duty as a colonel so long as the law would allow. His reply was to ask them if they would have done this in time of peace. Silence was the usual response.

When informed of Lang's decision to leave as soon as possible to find civilian work, Lieutenant General Perroots, the DIA director of that time asked if he would stay on as a civilian member of the Senior Executive Service. He accepted the offer.

There were many tasks to be accomplished in this position, but analysis of Iraq and its war with Iran was always the most important. Within a month or so of his assumption of the duties of DIO/ME-SA in 1985, Iraq began to intrude on a daily basis into his working life. He had never been to that country. This was a "fluke," a chance lacuna in a career filled with Arab countries and people. He was in Yemen when the war between the Iranians and Iraqis began and had watched Sana' air base fill with re-deployed Iraqi aircraft of all kinds that sought refuge from Iranian bombing. There were, among them, airplane types of Soviet manufacture that he had never seen anywhere but in a manual.

The Iran-Iraq War was so important that Lang felt he should devote a lot of effort to understanding the protracted struggle. In the course of review of the analytic work of DIA with regard to the war, he soon realized that the work that had been done at DIA was inadequate. The analytic staff tended in their writing to denigrate the fighting ability of both sides, but to be especially harsh toward the Iraqis. To correct his own ignorance, Lang studied all that he could find on the antecedents of the war, the condition of the pre-war forces, and the conduct of operations up until that time. To his surprise, the picture that emerged was different from that widely accepted in Washington. In the received wisdom of the day, the Iranian armed forces had gone into the war with Iraq in a terribly weakened state, having been repeatedly purged by the band of fanatics who held control of the Iranian state in the name of Islam, and the Iraqi military had begun the war as the instrument of a secular nationalist Arab state held in the thrall of a dictator as fearsome as any seen in the twentieth century. This was Saddam Hussein. This army had also been purged repeatedly in search of a force innocent of threat to the dictator.

The war had begun in a treacherous surprise attack by the Iraqis across the border in the southern region of Khuzistan. This region contained the bulk of the oil reserves of Iran, was largely inhabited by Arabs and was nicely flat. The objectives were the cities of Ahvaz and Khorramshar. Ahvaz was the capital of the province of Khuzistan and Khorramshar was the main port. In the first weeks and months, the campaign went well for the Iraqi Army. One force drove for Ahvaz across a series of terrain obstacles, such as rivers and the like, while another crossed into Khuzistan and encircled Khorramshar. The Iranian Army proved to be as weak an opponent as the Iraqis seemed to have expected. The *Mullahs* who ran Iran despised the "westernized" military and had done great violence to its integrity. They now paid the predictable price for this as Iranian troops fell back in disorder before the Iraqi advance.

The Iraqis, on the other hand seemed to have been able to maneuver mechanized forces at the brigade level, as well as to sustain them in the field in extended operations. They had division- and corps- sized formations, but the true level of what they had done seemed to be at brigade level, with higher echelons serving administrative and decorative functions. This was an unexpected conclusion, since the intelligence community was full of people who talked incessantly of Iraqi incapacity. The Iraqi encirclement of Khorramshar had sealed off the city and had developed into something that might be thought of as "Stalingrad With Palm Trees." The positional battle fought there was a terrible thing. The *Mullahs* found it convenient to commit to the battle a number of military units that they disliked and distrusted, among them the former Iranian Imperial Marine Corps' two infantry brigades, about ten thousand men. These were largely officered by alumni of VMI, the Citadel and the British Royal Naval College. In the course of months of fighting house to house in Khorramshahr, these units were destroyed and with them their officers.

"At the going down of the sun, we will remember them...."

In the end, the Iraqis took the town.

The advance on Ahvaz met a different fate. After crossing much of the Khuzistan desert, the corps-sized Iraqi force had halted one river short of the city. It halted on the near bank with the buildings of the objective city in plain sight across the brown water. There they sat for some two months, while the Iranians re-organized themselves. This was generally derided in analytic and journalistic circles as evidence of Iraqi ineptitude.

Lang was willing to accept that view until he noticed that the Iraqis had repeatedly sent heavily armed combat patrols across the river at night. These penetrated much of the city and brought back prisoners who said that the city was vulnerable to a serious attack. Some of the patrols crossed up stream and reconnoitered routes for an encirclement of the city. Nothing happened. The Iraqis sat before Ahvaz until enough time had passed for the Iranians to prepare a counter-offensive that drove them back nearly to the frontier.

The question that absorbed Lang in this study was simple. Why had the Iraqis not taken Ahvaz and driven on toward the Zagros Mountains where they presumably would have sought to consolidate a defensive line in the passes? The conduct of the operation up to the point at which it reached the river had been reasonably competent. The patrolling activity had been what was needed in preparation for a renewal of the advance. Why had it not happened? Iraqi communications security was always very tight and normally provided nothing useful, but after a long search, Lang found an intercepted Iranian message which reported the interrogation of a captured Iraqi major.

This man said to his captors that the corps had reached a phase line at the river where it had halted in obedience to its orders from higher headquarters. There, it had prepared to attack the city in accordance with the next phase of the existing campaign plan. The order to execute the next phase of the plan had never come from Baghdad. The major, who was a general staff trained officer, said there was a rumor that Saddam himself had prevented the needed advance. This made sense to Lang. The dictator, a civilian in a field-marshal's uniform, had lost his nerve, and unable to cope mentally with the vastness of space and resources available to the Iranians, had told the corps to stop as he told the Iraqi Army to stop many years later after the conquest of Kuwait.

If this was so, then there was no reason to accept the idea that the amateurishness of the Iraqi officer corps had been responsible for failure of the initial effort. It had been Saddam's failure just as the idiocy of the dictator Hitler had prevented the Wehrmacht from capturing Moscow forty years before. This put a new light on things, and Lang began to force DIA into a serious consideration of the Iraqi military as a developing fighting force. There was a lot of resistance to this from analysts and "managers" who feared to disagree with their civilian colleagues in the intelligence community more than they feared to be wrong in their judgments.

With the Iraqis halted before Ahvaz, the Iranians used the time given to them to create new armed forces. They consolidated the former units of the Imperial Iranian Army into new units that reflected the needs of the new regime in terms of leadership, personnel loyalty and ideology. Nevertheless, these units retained their identity and, to some extent, their "personality." As a result, it was always possible for Americans who had been advisers to these units to recognize their style of operations and to predict with some accuracy what they might do in a given situation.

These troops fought quite well once they recovered from the initial shock of the Iraqi attack and the *Mullahs'* decision to leave the soldiers "in peace" to wage their death struggle with the Iraqis. In particular, the artillery and engineers of the Iranian Army were noteworthy. These troops had officers who had been thoroughly trained at the U.S. Army artillery and engineer schools at Forts Sill and Belvoir and were superb. In later years, in conversations with Iraqi general officers, Lang was repeatedly told that these two arms were the best thing the Iranians had, and that the Iraqis wished they had benefited from similar American training.

They had not because military relations between Iraq and the United States had ended with the 1967 War in which the US had backed Israel.

These relations had never resumed. What had particularly impressed the Iraqis was the professional ease with which Iranian artillery moved by battery from one pre-surveyed position to another, firing accurately and swiftly in a tempo of operations that the Iraqis could never match with artillery trained in the Soviet method of massed, static artillery, positioned wheel to wheel in hundred gun formations and firing according to set programs. The Iranian engineers were similarly gifted. Their skill at building and maintaining the infrastructure and fortifications needed in this war was striking. The "line" armored and infantry units of the Iranian Army also fought well, but not as well as the artillery and engineers.

The Iraqis said without equivocation that the Iranian Army was the most dangerous force they faced on the battlefield. This is in direct denial of the nonsense widely written and believed that the Muslim enthusiasts thrown up by the revolution were the major element of Iranian combat power.

These enthusiasts inhabited the Revolutionary Guards Corps. This movement had emerged in the course of the revolution against the Shah as armed radicals and students who provided the muscle for the *Mullahs*. Many of them were disciples of the "Islamic" Marxist philosopher Ali Shariati. During and after the crisis which destroyed the Imperial government, the Revolutionary Guards "fought" in the streets, flogged whores, shot homosexuals, drug dealers and capitalist "profiteers" and generally made themselves useful in the same way that the SA "Brown Shirts" had been useful to Hitler before he became *Kanzler* of Germany.

After the revolution's success, the *Mullahs* suspected that the army might be the locus of counter-revolutionary plotting and successfully sought to make part of the Revolutionary Guard into a semi-militarized force to balance the power of the professional military and protect the new regime. When the war began, the rapid initial advance of the Iraqi forces and the rout of the regular army made many in the regime think that their days were numbered. As a result, they made a decision to commit to battle the "units" of the lightly armed Revolutionary Guards. The first engagements of these men against the Iraqis resulted in very heavy losses and complete failure to do anything except die well. This they were good at, attacking in massed formations with minimal support. The Iraqi decision to halt at Ahvaz gave the Iranians enough time to re-think their policy regarding the Revolutionary Guards. It was decided as a result that Revolutionary Guards "brigades" and "divisions" would be provided combat support by army armor, artillery, engineer and other troops. It was also decided that the revolution could not afford to lose so many of its most ardent and fully institutionalized defenders. In the future, Revolutionary Guards units would have a cadre of "professional" guardsmen to command and lead, but short-term volunteers given minimal training by the Guards and led by them would provide the mass of sacrificial riflemen. These were the famous "Baseej" who typically signed up for a month, two months, six months, one operation, etc. Those who survived their experience went home to school, office, farm or wherever. This method took advantage of both the large Iranian superiority in numbers and the revolutionary Islamic fervor that held the country in its grip at that time.

After the regular army's counter-offensive largely restored the frontier, it was found to be desirable by the *Mullahs* to foster a great proliferation of such Revolutionary Guards units. As the front stabilized along the Shatt al-Arab river line and in a long snaky trace up to Kurdistan in the north, they came to occupy parts of the line, usually in the quieter sectors. Trench warfare set in along the lines of WWI, and the Revolutionary Guards were good enough to act as a tripwire against offensive action until reserves could arrive to retrieve the situation. This was their major role.

The Iran Estimates (NIE) of 1985

Just after Lang arrived at DIA and was in the process of taking over as DIO from Colonel Alfred Prados, his predecessor, an ominous thing happened on the national intelligence scene. In that era, the American government made most of its foreign policy decisions on the supposed basis of "objective" assessments made by the intelligence community sitting as a "committee of the whole." In this procedure, a "National Intelligence Estimate" (NIE) would be requested of the community by competent authority. Typically, this was the staff of the "National Security Council" (NSC). This request would go to the National Intelligence Council (NIC), a body of sages entitled the "National Intelligence Officers" (NIOs). These wise persons existed to supervise the writing of NIEs. They usually were CIA personnel, protective of their agency's interest and attuned to the opinions of policymakers across Washington. In other words, they knew "which side of their bread was buttered." The usual procedure was for an NIO to appoint a "drafter" for an NIE. This analyst would produce a paper, the text of which was then "negotiated" among the senior representatives of the other intelligence agencies to produce a final version that would be voted upon by the heads of CIA, DIA, State Department

Intelligence, etc., at a meeting of the "National Foreign Intelligence Board" (NFIB), their corporate body. In fact, CIA tended to dominate the process through the simple mechanism of staffing the NIC with their own people who usually appointed CIA analysts to "draft" the text. Nevertheless, the process of negotiation over the text was often a lively "scrimmage" with both State INR and DIA forcing major revisions of the papers before they went to the NFIB for approval.

In the summer of 1985, Lang was told that the then NIO for the Middle East, Graham Fuller, had brought into being a new NIE on Iran. This had not yet been voted on by the heads of agencies and therefore was not yet official U.S. government reality. Lang asked to see the text. On review, it seemed perhaps the worst, most disaster laden piece of work that he ever saw in the government. The burden of this paper was that the Iranian revolution was not really Islamic at all, but rather was a revolution of one economic class against another, dressed up as Islamic by cynical revolutionaries in order to persuade the ignorant masses to participate.

In other words, the *Mullahs* were not really *Mullahs*, they just looked like *Mullahs* and actually had a different agenda which was a lot like the classical Marxist agenda. The paper further concluded that these pseudo-*mullahs* were under threat from true Islamic fanatics within Iran and the deteriorating economy as well as a war of catastrophic dimensions. The paper claimed that if life were not made easier for the *Mullahs,* then they would turn to the Soviet Union for assistance since they were the next best thing to communists anyway.

Much later, Lang learned that Fuller's need to produce such a paper derived from the Israeli influence exerted at the White House in favor of their Iranian friends. Lang demanded a revision of the text, knowing that to portray the *Mullahs* in this way was a farce and a cynical manipulation of the heads of the intelligence agencies by subordinates who knew better. The paper claimed that there were "moderates" among the *Mullahs* with whom the United States could "work." It was obvious to anyone who understood Islam that this was nonsense. His protests were to no avail. DIA contained a separate directorate for estimates, and the Army major who had the action for the paper in this directorate wanted nothing more than to be loved at CIA. The major's managerial superiors chose to back him to demonstrate to Lang that they, personally, were significant and Lang's predecessor, (still in charge) would not intervene. As a result, the estimate became the official truth of the U.S. government, and the basis for the infamous and foolish cooperation of the United States with the Iranian regime in what came to be known as the "Iran-Contra Affair."

Three months later, Fuller had left, and Lang persuaded the new NIO for the Middle East to write a new estimate. This new document repudiated the old one, and Lang succeeded in stuffing it down the throat of the directorate of estimates at DIA, but it was too late. Oliver North's ill-fated mission to the Iranians had begun. Israel's role in the tortured web of relations that surrounded the United States and Iraq in the 1980s yet awaits exposition.

The Arab Gulf States and Iraq

In the middle period of the war, (1983-1986) the Iranians conducted a major offensive about every six months in attempts to break through the Iraqi defenses, overthrow the Iraqi government and capture the oil fields on the south side of the Gulf. An old "saw" holds that "whatever does not kill you, makes you stronger." This rather accurately describes what occurred in the Iraqi Army. The persistent attacks of the Iranians were heavy and dangerous but not skillful enough to "finish off" the Iraqis. Even the surprise offensive that seized the Fao peninsula south of the Shatt al-Arab was not enough of a blow to kill Saddam's regime. The attacks grew and grew in size and intensity until it was a matter of multi-corps actions on either side with armored formations of two or three divisions being employed by the Iraqis and sustained in combat by them for lengthy periods of time. It was evident from the operations themselves that the Iranians were more or less "frozen" in their development in the model of Regular Army/Revolutionary Guards and Baseej volunteers. These "formations" were largely prevented by the fears and jealousies of the revolutionary Islamic regime from further professional development.

The Arab states of the Gulf were certain that the Iranian intention was conquest of the southern shore of the Gulf, and for this reason they openly backed Iraq against the Iranians. Iraqi funds for continuation and prosecution of the war came from two sources. First, there were the proceeds of their own sales of petroleum shipped mainly from the ports of the Gulf. Second were the grants and loans provided by the Arabian states of the Peninsula. These countries provided large sums of money in the hope that with these funds they were buying protection from the Shia fanatics who would, if they could, surely abolish the princely and monarchical rule typical of the Gulf. This money was spent for equipment procurement, but in nearly equal amounts went into the Iraqi research and development programs for conventional weapons, guided missiles, space technology and "special weapons." Under this rubric could be found biological, chemical and nuclear weapons. Whether or not the minor states of the Gulf knew their funds were used for this purpose is debatable, but the Saudis certainly knew, and that from an early date in the war.

Lang discovered this from a study he caused to be made of the funding of the Iraqi war machine. It showed, with crystal clarity, that the appropriate Iraqi agency maintained a large *apparat* in Europe to handle the funding and procurement actions. This *apparat* had two sets of bank accounts in Switzerland and other places. "Normal" procurement moneys went into one set and "special weapons" moneys went into the other set. Only the Saudis and Iraqis deposited money in the "special weapons" accounts, and the Saudis made these deposits *directly*. In light of later Saudi "horror" at Iraqi weapons programs, one can only marvel at the depth of their duplicity. This was rivaled by the Saudi attempt in 1986 to convince the American government that Chinese intermediate range ballistic missiles (IRBM) being brought into Saudi Arabia through Red Sea ports were intended for the Iraqis.

Senior officials of the Reagan administration were quite willing to believe this until a revealing telephone conversation between Prince Sultan bin Abd al-Aziz, the Defense Minister of Saudi Arabia and his son, Prince Bandar bin Sultan, the Saudi ambassador to Washington was intercepted. In this filial chat, the two men discussed the negotiations that had led to the purchase of these missiles from the Chinese and the Saudi *force de frappe* that would be built around them. The deal included the nuclear warheads without which the missiles made no sense in terms of their range, lack of accuracy and expense. In this deal, the warheads were to be held in storage in China until needed for war. With these missiles, Saudi Arabia imagined it would become a major "player" in world affairs. In the intercept, the two Saudis laughed at the gullibility of the Americans in accepting their explanation of the affair. With that intercept, Prince Bandar bin Sultan's influence in Washington effectively died.

As was reflected in this Saudi government conversation, the Arab states of the Gulf were solidly behind Iraq financially and politically. This was so not because they liked Iraq. Far from it, they detested the Baathist, modernist regime and society in that country and recognized in Iraq a powerful threat to the quaint, but absolute, natures of their own governments. Put simply, the ordinary people in the Gulf might see that they did not necessarily have to live with the rule of dissipated and profligate princelings. Therefore, they "held their noses" and backed Iraq from the beginning of the war in the hope that through the valor and endurance of the Iraqi soldier, the Iranian wolf would be kept from their golden doors.

Re-flagging Kuwait's Tankers

The Iranians saw Kuwait as the nearest and therefore most vulnerable of the coalition of states supporting Iraq. They also seemed to have judged that the well-known collective fecklessness of the Kuwaitis would make them easy to intimidate. Throughout the earlier years of the war, an effective air campaign had been carried out by both sides against each other's shipping, but this had been confined to Iraqi and Iranian bottoms as well as neutral ships in direct trade with the two belligerents. In 1986, the Iranians adopted a new tactic. They announced that since Kuwait was "in league" with Iraq, Kuwaiti tankers would from then on be fair game for Iranian surface and air attacks. Kuwait begged Washington for protection from the Iranians, making it clear that if help were not provided, then Kuwait would have no choice but to accommodate Iran.

The usual frantic meetings of the "interagency" ensued with much hand wringing. The difficulty was that the politicians were afraid to help Kuwait if this would be perceived as being "merely" to rescue an Arabian state. The fear was that the American public would not accept the risk of war for a lot of "rag heads." At one of these meetings, after tiring of the babble, Lang suggested that the threat be portrayed as that of Soviet intervention in the Gulf if we did not act. It seemed an elementary idea, and one that he would have been ashamed to put forward if he had been at the top of his form. The meeting solemnly considered this "judgment" and adjourned. This stupidity became the basis of the American policy of "re-flagging" the ships of Kuwait under the U.S. flag.

At that moment in the process of the dissolution of the Soviet Union and American triumph, there was no more chance of the Gulf Arabs accepting Soviet "protection" than of a cow jumping over the moon. Nevertheless, the American people were earnestly told that action was critical to prevent the entry of the Russian bear into the Gulf. To his regret and shame, Lang had no choice but to participate in this farce. In the course of the "re-flagging," the Kuwaiti ships began to wear the colors of the United States, and the expectation in Washington was that this would suffice to overawe the Iranians and prevent further attacks on these vessels.

At the urging of the Chairman of the Joint Chiefs of Staff, Admiral William Crowe, the J-2 portion of DIA took the position that the mere presence of the US flag on Kuwaiti tankers would deter Iran from attacks on these vessels. This position was published to Washington decision- makers without seeking Lang's agreement. This was a clear violation of established procedure within DIA since nothing was allowed to be published without the concerned DIO's agreement. In this case, Lang did not agree since he thought the Iranian Islamic zealots would not be deterred at all. Unfortunately for Admiral Crowe's view, not everyone saw it his way. The National Intelligence Council, (NIC) in reaction wrote a National Estimate in which the elders of the intelligence community specifically rejected the J-2's opinion.

Rep. Les Aspin was then chairman of the House Armed Forces Committee, and a bright staffer on his team challenged the difference between the two opinions. As a result, the Director of DIA, Lt. Gen. Leonard Perroots, USAF, was called before the House Armed Services committee to explain the reason for the difference in opinion since DIA was supposedly the originator of the J-2 position and had participated in the making of the National Estimate. Lang was asked by Perroots to accompany him to the hearing. A Vice Admiral who then served as the Special Assistant to Admiral Crowe went with them to ensure that they would not embarrass Crowe by abandoning his egregious opinion. In the course of the hearing, Perroots was asked by Rep. Aspin to explain the difference. Perroots replied that Colonel Lang would answer.

Up until that moment, Lang had not had any idea how this trap created by egotism and weakness could be evaded. The Vice Admiral glowered, and Aspin waited for his answer. From whence Lang could never say, the "route" to safety came to mind. He told Aspin that the National Estimate was a description of an unopposed threat, a threat in which the defensive measures of the United States were not considered to derive a "net" threat and that the J-2 threat was a net threat based on the belief that US countermeasures would virtually neutralize Iranian capabilities. Aspin looked doubtful. He asked the two "flag" officers if this was their position as well. They enthusiastically agreed, and Aspin shook his head over the sophistry of the response but let the officers go, "unscourged." Perroots was pathetically grateful in his appreciation of the manner of his escape from humiliation. Lang was chagrined and ashamed, knowing he had saved his boss with a cheap trick. Shortly thereafter the Iranians began to attack the re-flagged tankers with floating mines.

Prince Bandar and King Hussein

Throughout 1985 and 1986, Lang spent a good deal of time with Prince Bandar Bin Sultan, the Saudi ambassador to Washington. This started because Richard Armitage who was Assistant Secretary of Defense for International Security Affairs (ISA) thought that he had a good grasp of events on the Iraqi battlefront and a request from Bandar for someone to brief him had resulted in a trip to the ambassador's Chain Bridge Road mansion in Arlington, Virginia with maps. Lang and Bandar spread the maps all over the ambassador's floor, and a three-hour discussion took place about what the Iraqis were doing wrong. This visit led to many similar sessions either at the embassy across the street from the Watergate Hotel in Washington or at the ambassador's residence.

In the course of one of these meetings after a long talk about the inappropriateness of Iraqi actions, the ambassador remarked that it was too bad that Lang could not be sent to advise the Iraqis. At the time, he paid little attention to this, dismissing it as yet another of the inconsequential and nonsensical things said on such occasions. This was a mistake that became apparent when he was unexpectedly sent to Amman, Jordan to brief King Hussein on the war. The mission was mandated by Richard Armitage who told Lang that the king wanted to be brought up to date on combat developments along the whole frontline between Iran and Iraq. This was a big job, requiring a week or so of preparation. Lang arrived in Amman with a "minder" from Armitage's office and a mass of briefing materials, marked maps, satellite photographs, etc., and after a day or so of the usual "fooling around" with the embassy staff, went to see the king at the Basman Palace. The briefing was done in a reception room on the ground room of the palace. Present were Ambassador Roscoe Suddarth representing the United States, HRH Field Marshal Zaid bin Shakir then Chief of the Royal Diwan (household), Major General Abd al-Hafith al-Marei, who was Chief of Jordanian Military Intelligence and an old friend. Also present were Major Richard Francona, Lang's assistant, and a "minder" from Armitage's office.

King Hussein arrived after a few minutes. He had been riding and was dressed in Western gear; cowboy boots (snake), jeans; a red checked woolen shirt and a huge silver rodeo belt buckle in the shape of the map of Texas. He smelled of horse. He shook hands all around and seemed embarrassed by his informal dress. The rest of the group was in suits. To make a place to put down the maps and photos, a low marble coffee table was cleared of little silver dishes of nuts, framed pictures, etc. Lang started the briefing in the

North, in Kurdistan, and worked his way south to the Shatt al-Arab and the Fao peninsula, then in Iranian hands. It was a thorough job. There were lots of satellite pictures and the dispositions of both sides were clearly marked on a large map spread before the king.

King Hussein kept looking at Lang sideways during his "pitch" and seemed to have something he wanted to ask. At the end he asked what the Iraqis were doing wrong. That surprised Lang. Intelligence men were not usually asked operational questions like that. He looked at the king for a moment. Hussein turned to MG Marei and asked in Arabic, "Is this not the man the Saudis mentioned?" *Ah!* Lang thought, *Prince Bandar has been busy. That's why I am here.*

He then said to the king that there was one specific thing that was very wrong with the dispositions of the Iraqi Army. An expectant hush followed, and Lang pointed to the fact that the boundary between two Iraqi Army Corps fronting on the Shatt al-Arab River did not connect. The king asked to be shown. He put his finger on the spot. One corps had its front line on the riverbank and the other corps had placed itself kilometer back from the river. The gap beckoned to any adversary who perceived it. The right and left boundaries did not meet. How could they have made such a mistake, the king asked. Lang responded that he had no idea, but that it should be corrected as soon as possible. King Hussein asked MG Marei in Arabic if he could fly to Baghdad and brief "the brothers" about this problem. Marei smiled a little. The king looked puzzled. His cousin, bin Shakir said that it might be a good idea to include me in the conversation since I spoke Arabic. Hussein looked at me and asked, "Sah?" (Correct?) Lang said, "yes." "May I have our brother Abd al-Hafith take this map to Baghdad?" the king asked. The ambassador took a breath and looked at the ceiling. "Your Majesty," Lang replied. "Our map is your map."

The map went to Baghdad that day, and by the time Lang got back to Washington, the inter-corps boundary was firmly connected on the riverbank. The DIA staff told Lang that the troops had started to move the day following the briefing in Amman. After the business of the meeting was ended, King Hussein stood at one end of the coffee table for a moment and then said, "Does anyone remember where these things were?" He was referring to the bric a brac. His children and wife could be heard upstairs. It was a homely and endearing moment. To Lang's astonishment, the king walked him out to the car and opened the door. It was a small thing, but, although Lang was republican to the core, he would ever after feel himself to be Hussein's man. Several such trips followed in the course of which it became more and more apparent that Lang was advising the Iraqi high command "by remote control." and that the Saudis through their ambassador in Washington were responsible. This was clearly the intention of the Reagan Administration.

A couple of things should be mentioned to place the rest of this account in perspective.

The first has to do with the legality of the actions that Lang's assistants and he undertook in Iraq. Working near the end of a long career in government and its intelligence function, Lang was not a trusting soul. In his experience, superiors could be expected to "sacrifice" subordinates in any situation that threatened to damage their own careers or worse yet lead to criminal prosecution. With that belief firmly in mind, he insisted that any action taken to benefit Iraq in its war with Iran be specifically authorized by a special letter directive of the Secretary of Defense and that the actions to be carried out be briefed to the intelligence oversight committees of the House of Representatives and the U.S. Senate.

As pressure built for what amounted to a covert intervention on Iraq's side, a number of people tried to push him into acting without this protection. He refused and advised the Director of DIA to do likewise. The two refusals in the end produced a letter signed by Frank Carlucci authorizing the mission on behalf of the National Security Council. The letter was not as strong as Lang would have liked it, but it would do. The initial version of the letter stated that the assistance provided should not materially affect the outcome of the war. This was an attempt by opponents of aid to Iraq to block the program. Lang responded in writing that it would be impossible to carry out the stated objectives of the project with this restriction. As a result, the previous restriction was lifted by Carlucci, and DIA was told to make sure that what they did insured that Iraq not be defeated by Iran.

The second thing to be mentioned is that the "accepted wisdom" (still held at the time of this writing) that the U.S. supplied Iraq with military materiel with which to fight the war against Iran is simply not true. In fact, the Iraqi military was amply supplied by the Warsaw Pact countries, China and France throughout the war, and Iraq had little need of military materiel from the United States. Lang was a member of the Defense Department committee that would have approved materiel transfers to Iraq. There were no such transfers approved in that channel except for less than ten light Hughes helicopters and less than fifty heavy tank transporter trucks (HETs) made by the Oshkosh Company.

The only way that this committee could have been bypassed in transferring equipment to Iraq would have been throughout the enactment of a presidential "finding" initiating a covert action project. Lang spent so much time in Iraq throughout the latter period of the war and visited and observed so many Iraqi military units that it was clear to him that virtually no military equipment from the U.S. was in use.

A further charge levied against the U.S. in regard to provision of materiel to Iraq is that we provided the Iraqis with microbe cultures with which they developed biological weapons. As with the conventional armaments' canard, no denial will convince those who wish to believe this, but Lang served at the time on the inter-departmental board that maintained export controls over a variety of dangerous materials. The issue of export of strains of dangerous microbes was closely examined a number of times, and it was found that anthrax and several other kinds of microbes had been exported to a number of countries including Iraq for medical research in the period before the US government imposed export controls over these materials. There was no indication that there had been any American government purpose or action involved in this.

USS Stark and the Exocets

In May 1987, the US frigate Stark was struck by an Iraqi fighter in the central Persian Gulf. The ship's company fought fires aboard and performed prodigies of damage control to keep her afloat until the vessel reached Bahrain. A Joint Chiefs of Staff (JCS) investigating board was hastily convoked and sent first to Bahrain and then to Iraq to investigate the attack. Lang was still on active duty as a colonel and was selected to be the deputy head of the board under a splendid naval officer, Rear Admiral David Rogers, USN. There were five or six officers on the team, all from the Joint Staff except for Lang. The group flew first to Bahrain where they went aboard USS Stark. She was tied up alongside a float offshore three miles from the harbor of Bahrain. On the other side of the float, the flagship of Middle East Force, (MEF) the small American naval task force in the Gulf was in position. The flagship was not a combatant, but rather a transport converted to serve as a specialized vessel for headquarters purposes. The team went aboard Stark to survey the damage for themselves. It was terrible. Two Exocet guided missiles had struck the ship within a few seconds of each other. They went through the thin skin of the frigate and detonated in the crew berthing spaces. Thirty-seven men were killed and many more wounded. The interior of the ship was a burned-out reeking cavern filled with charred reminders of dead men's lives.

On board Mid East Force's flagship, the JCS panel met with the ship's officers and the captain. It was evident from the beginning of his testimony that the captain knew that the Navy would never forgive him for the damage to the ship. He was simply resigned to his fate and said that the fact that he was in his cabin sitting on the toilet when the ship went to "battle stations" would "finish him off." He was correct. The unfavorable things from the Navy's point of view were his location as well as the fact that his ship treated the approaching Iraqi fighter as "friendly." All the ship's officers were certain that their careers were at an end, and they were all correct.

From Bahrain the team flew to Baghdad in a USAF cargo jet. At the airport two complete Iraqi government convoys of vehicles and escorts waited. One was from the Ministry of Foreign Affairs and the other from the Ministry of Defense. They had been having a dispute over who would be in charge and had not been able to settle it. As a result, the Americans watched them argue like dogs over a bone for an hour until someone called to tell them that they would have joint custody. In Baghdad, the team met for several days with a mixed delegation from Iraq's armed forces and Foreign Ministry. It was quickly apparent that the Iraqi military members were all military intelligence people, and that these talks were being treated as a major political event and a possible "opening" to the improvement of relations with the U.S.A. The team sat in the Foreign Ministry and listened to presentations by the two sides (Americans and Iraqis) about what they each thought had happened in the attack. The Iraqi position was simple. They claimed that the ship had been in the wrong place, and that it had been inside the Iranian declared shipping exclusion zone that the Iraqis were using for a target designation system when they attacked it. The Iranians had declared this zone a year or so before and had held that any ship not in commerce with them that was in the zone would be treated as hostile. The Iraqis had accepted that as a great convenience and had divided the zone up into rectangular boxes that they assigned as "free fire" targets to their pilots going down the Gulf on strikes. They had modified a French built model of fighter to carry two Exocet missiles, and the procedure was for them to fly down the Gulf until opposite the "assigned" hunting box. They would then turn east, fly into the box and engage the first maritime target they saw on the principle that the Iranians had warned everyone else out of the area. The Iraqis maintained that Stark was in the pilot's box. They brought in an Iraqi Air Force pilot, a major, whom I have always thought was the actual pilot in the strike. They did not identify him as such. He explained the system and the weaponry and was quite apologetic as they all were. The US Navy insisted that the ship was not in the "box," but their case was much weakened by the fact that the ship had experienced a malfunction of its electronic equipment and had been on manual "dead reckoning" for navigation for twelve hours.

Saudi AWACS (radar and control aircraft) had identified the Iraqi strike to Stark as "friendly" because they thought of the Iraqis as friendly. They had done this before, a number of times, with no adverse effects. With the captain out of the CIC (combat information center), the ship watched by radar the single Iraqi fighter approach and listened to its internal radar for anomalies. The CIC crew did not realize that the fighter had fired at them until it turned sharply away after firing its second missile at them. The first "bird" struck Stark on the port bow while Stark was still going to "Action Stations." The range was about twenty kilometers. The missile went right through the thin skin of the frigate and burst inside a forward crew berthing compartment. The second missile struck the ship a few seconds later a little aft of the first, went through another crew living space, exploding on the way. The rocket motor had not used all its fuel and was still burning. It lodged in a stanchion on the starboard side and burned for a while like a blowtorch inside the ship. There were 37 sailors killed and many wounded.

The Iraqis insisted this was all a horrible mistake and after some discussion agreed to pay compensation for the ship and to the survivors and their families. A senior Iraqi diplomat and Lang sat up all one night checking the Arabic and English versions of the joint communiqué on the negotiation to make sure they were the same. His name was "Al-Qaisi." In the course of the night he told the American that "although the attack had been a tragedy, at least 'we and you are now speaking to each other again.'" The implication was clear. The attack might have been deliberate and intended to "break the log jam" in US/Iraq relations. Lang told him that if he loved his country he would never repeat that to anyone. He looked surprised but said that he understood the point and would be silent about this.

At a couple points in the negotiations Lang overheard (in Arabic) Iraqi officers of the General Staff ask one another if he were the officer that the Jordanians and Saudis spoke of.

As a result of these negotiations, the US and Iraq established a procedure for "de-conflicting" their operations in order to prevent another "Stark Incident." The cooperation did not go beyond making sure the two forces would not shoot each other up again. The Joint Chiefs of Staff (JCS) and US Central Command conducted this ongoing relationship, and Lang had nothing further to do with it.

"Elephant Grass"

At some point in the middle of the long Iran-Iraq War (probably in 1986), the Director of DIA (LT General Leonard Perroots USAF) approached Lang to discuss his concerns in regard to the possible outcomes of that war. They all seemed bad to him if present trends continued. It appeared to Lang that he had come to his conclusions independent of anyone else. He was afraid that the Islamic Republic of Iran might utterly defeat Iraq, conquer that country, and then move on to dominate Kuwait, Saudi Arabia and the minor states of the Gulf. The implications of such a situation seemed very bad to him. He asked if Lang thought the Iraqis were making good use of their available air power in fighting Iran.

The Iraqis then possessed a large air force equipped in the main with aircraft bought on credit from the USSR. They also had three squadrons of French-built Mirage fighters. The Soviet equipment was poorly employed. The tactical staff work and targeting needed to make it an effective military instrument was lacking, and as a result, the great bulk of the Iraqi air force was not of much use to them. In contrast, the three "French" squadrons (around sixty aircraft) were advised on maintenance and operations by Frenchmen assigned to the job by the French government and were very effective. (The Mirage that struck USS Stark was from this force.) As a result of Soviet ineffectiveness in supporting the Iraqi Air Force (IAF), eighty-five per cent of the IAF was of limited value in fighting the Iranians. These programs were kept apart by agreement of the governments involved.

Lang told Perroots that if DIA took charge of the process of selecting targets for the Soviet-provided bulk of the IAF, it would greatly benefit their war effort. This would mean looking at all available information on potential targets important to the Iranian military campaign, selecting those of critical value, and preparing "target packages" to be used by attacking fighter bomber units in planning and conducting the missions needed to destroy these targets. He told Lang to draw up a plan to do this. This was given the quaint code name "Elephant Grass" by the "wag" in charge of naming.

Perroots and Lang took this plan and proposal to the White House where Lang presented it in the Situation Room to a very senior group. They were intrigued, but non-committal. The inter-agency group thanked them. The DIA group went back to the Pentagon, filed the plan, and did not expect to hear of it again. Time passed.

The war went on with ever increasing ferocity and a growing scale of the combat. The size and scope of the fighting began to resemble both World Wars in that both positional and mobile warfare reached levels of troop and armor commitments not seen since 1945. At the same time, trench warfare became well established with the Iraqis holding their "economy of force" sectors with infantry dug in as deeply as had been seen in France in World War I. Infantry division linear defenses were normally backed up with mobile forces in reserve with the armored and motorized divisions of the Republican Guard as a national maneuver reserve.

In the winter of 1987, a great anxiety came over official Washington. The belief spread that Iraq was likely to collapse with consequent "loss" of Western influence in the Gulf. Lang thought this fear was unjustified, and that Iranian military power had passed its peak while the Iraqis were increasing in strength and capability. As is usually the case, the "policy makers" were uninterested in intelligence opinions and formed their views in a sort of mutual intellectual masturbation conducted in conference rooms and at dinner parties throughout the city. In this case, their panic seems to have been triggered by a series of articles written from Basra by Patrick Tyler of the Washington Post. The Iraqis were being attacked heavily around Basra, and Tyler wrote convincingly of the difficulty of their situation. Tyler did not exaggerate, but the danger of collapse was not as great as he thought. The mandarins' concern about the collapse of Iraq would have been justified a year earlier (the time of "Elephant Grass planning) but was excessive by the spring of 1988. Further complicating the outlook were the after-effects of the *"Iran-Contra Affair."*

The *"Iran-Contra Affair"* involved shenanigans by CIA and the NSC to obtain money from Iran for spare parts needed in the war for equipment of American manufacture. The NSC wanted to get their hands on money from a source other than Congress in order to finance their anti-Sandinista crusade in Nicaragua. Congress had passed a law forbidding the use of appropriated fund money for this and so, Oliver North, Alan Fiers and Elliot Abrams set out to illegally raise their own money. They were later convicted in federal court on this charge.

In this scheme, the NSC allowed itself to be manipulated by the Israelis into making a secret offer to Iran to help them against Iraq in the war. In that period the Israelis always acted to advance the interests of Iran against the Arab States. This Israeli inspired folly had been encouraged by the "thinking" brought on by Graham Fuller's infamous 1985 NIE on Iran (mentioned earlier). There is some question as to whether Fuller was himself swayed in creation of this estimate by Israeli influence in the White House. To "sweeten" the offer, the NSC people obtained specific military intelligence from DIA and CIA and gave it to the Iranians in meetings in Europe. This, evidently, was intended to establish their "bona fides" with the Iranians. They then invited the Iranians to "try it out" in combat. As a result, an Iranian attack was made against a divisional Iraqi sector described in the information given. In the course of this attack. the Iraqi lines were driven back a mile. The Iraqis suffered over a thousand casualties in restoring the situation and recapturing the lost ground. The NSC crew, more or less headed by Oliver North, also gave the Iranians the Iraqi estimate of Iranian intentions for the next six months of the war. This was of immense value to the Iranians and cost the Iraqis many losses and difficulties. This was also a betrayal of a trust on a scale Lang had not seen before. CIA had no knowledge that the NSC would make such use of the documents at the time they had given them to the NSC.

The *"Iran-Contra Affair"* was investigated by a special group known as the "Tower Commission." This three-member group was headed by Senator John Tower of Texas and included Senator Edmund Muskie of Maine and Lt. General Brent Scowcroft USAF (Ret.), a former National Security Adviser.

Lang was given the task of testifying as chief witness on behalf of DoD before this group as to whether or not the information and equipment provided to the Iranians by North and his henchmen had materially affected the conduct of the war and the parties to it. To that end, the CIA's Inspector General was ordered to provide him with the fruits of his investigation of the matter. This was about two linear feet of documents delivered to the DIO's Pentagon office. The Tower group wanted a military look at this because they did not trust the civilians to understand the military implications of what had happened. Lang spent three hours on the stand and told them that the effect on the Iraqis had not been fatal but had been costly. They thanked him. Lt. General Scowcroft was particularly pleasant about the result and spoke to Perroots about it at some length.

The findings of the Commission were published in an unclassified (book) form. Lang argued strenuously with the staff of the Tower Commission that the tale of treachery by the North/NSC Group should not be included. He reasoned that it would be very bad for US interests in the Middle East if this became generally known. They accepted that and did not include some of the worst things. Nevertheless, the Iraqis "pieced together" what they could learn from other sources in the media, compared this to the bad things that had happened to them and decided that the CIA had betrayed them.

This was unjust, as life often is, since it was the NSC who had betrayed them. Because of this false conclusion on the part of the Iraqi government, they refused from that time on to have anything further to do with the CIA, either in Washington or Baghdad. When this came together in early 1988 with the growing anxiety of the US government over the misperception of coming Iraqi collapse, the stage was set for "Druid Leader."

CHAPTER TWENTY-SEVEN

Druid Leader

In the early spring of 1988, Lang was informed by Perroots that the NSC wanted to take another look at "Elephant Grass." (Unbeknownst to Lang at that time, the Jordan, Saudi Arabia, Stark and Iran-Contra aspects of this story had come together in the West Wing of the White House in the form of a request from someone that he should be sent to help the Iraqis with their air force.)

Lang expected that nothing in particular would come of another briefing, but to his surprise, he heard the principals in this meeting tell Perroots to have him go "do it." He later remembered observing to the group that this was probably not necessary. They did not seem to hear. This was typical of the reaction of high level "decision makers" to intelligence people, no matter how senior the Spooks might be.

Back at the Pentagon, Perroots said that Lang could "run it" until he "screwed up." This was typical of his rather crude way of talking. Lang told him that he would not run the program unless there was a specific letter directive from the Secretary of Defense ordering us to carry out this program. Lang also insisted that DIA would brief the program to the intelligence oversight committees of Congress and get a written acknowledgement of their knowledge. Perroots was not happy with this and asked what right Lang thought he had to make conditions. Lang explained to him that he didn't want either of them to go to jail for conducting an illegal and unauthorized covert operation, and that his position would be particularly at risk since DIA was not enabled by statute to do this kind of thing. He thought about this for a minute and agreed. He was not always so easy a man to work for.

DIA's General Counsel (GC) drafted a letter for the SecDef's signature. A period of negotiation over language ensued in which SecDef's abomination of a lawyer tried to avoid giving enough language to "cover" DIA, but Lang insisted on the minimum that DIA would accept as a legal "cover." In the end he received a letter authorizing an operation to be called "Druid Leader." The letter was not on anyone's letterhead. It contained the barely minimum necessary language, but it was enough. It had Frank Carlucci's signature on the bottom. There may be copies still extant somewhere.

The initial guidance provided on this plan by Perroots was that nothing DIA did should change the outcome of the war. Lang told him that this was nonsense, and on that basis, he could do nothing. Lang also told him that this foolishness probably reflected the influence of the still powerful pro-Iran faction in the State Department. Perroots "went back to the well" and returned with a removal of this guidance. We were free to hurt the Iranians as much as seemed appropriate.

After that, Lang went to the Congress with DIA's legislative liaison. He remembered later that the House committee (House Permanent Select Committee on Intelligence--HPSCI) was non-committal about this initiative. Lang thought that was sensible since he also believed that America no longer needed to carry out such a program. At the Senate committee (SSCI), George Tenet was chief of staff. His reaction was to the effect that he had thought that DIA was already doing that. He was not correct in that belief.

Rear Admiral Bob Schmitt USN (Deputy Director of DIA) and Lang went to CIA headquarters at Langley, Virginia to "coordinate" what DIA was going to do in Iraq with the Directorate of Operations (DO). Claire George was then director of the DO. He listened with reluctance and evident hostility to the plan and kept looking at Lang appraisingly.

Lang ascertained that "Druid Leader" would be a significant change in the policy which had been to keep the Iraqis "at arms' length." This was not a surprise for a couple of reasons. First, this is a standard attitude among espionage services around the world. Typically, espionage operators are so focused on their own task of recruiting and directing foreign agent assets that they have no patience with anything else. Second, CIA is a civilian organization and as such then lacked the assets, expertise and skills needed to advise armed forces engaged in combat. In the instances in which CIA has attempted to do that. it has always been necessary for them to hire retired military people or "borrow" active duty military.

George asked if Lang really thought he could do this and was visibly uncomfortable when told, "of course." He claimed that Lang would not be welcomed by the Iraqis. Lang told him that he would have to find out for himself and inquired what the US ambassador said. The meeting ended without George having answered the question. Lang learned later that the ambassador, an old friend, had said that he would welcome his arrival.

With these "necessaries" taken care of, Lang and his deputy, Major Rick Francona USAF, set out to change history. They decided that they would attempt to bring Iraqi air power to bear not on front line targets, nor on strategic targets deep in the interior of Iran (Tehran, Isfahan, etc.) but rather on targets which were all "counter-force" (military) and located from division headquarters back to the rear boundary of army corps level formations. These would be: division and corps level operational headquarters, logistical (supply, repair, etc.) installations, troop concentrations, boats useful for river crossings, railroad and highway bridges, etc. There would be no "counter-value" (civilian population) targets.

They knew that both Iraq and Iran possessed poison gas weapons, and that the Iraqis had used them with some effect on the battlefield as an integrated part of the "fires" portion of their operations planning. So far as they could see, the Iraqis had both artillery ammunition and aerial bombs that could be used for delivery. The agents used were blister gases like Lewisite and a couple of "classic" nerve agents like Sarin and Tabun. The Iranians had a similar program which also used blister agents but had, in addition, a capability to produce blood agents like Chlorine and Phosgene.

It should be said at this point that they had no indications that the Iraqis had begun to use chemical weapons on civilians. That happened later in the history of this war. Ever since the Iran-Iraq War, it has been argued that much of the reported use of chemical weapons on civilian groups like the Kurds has been exaggerated, first by Iranian and Israeli propagandists and later by the United States because the furor created by this made a convenient "stick" with which to beat the Iraqis. At the time of the Halabja Incident in 1988, chemical analysts in DIA argued that it appeared that both sides had been engaged in combat around the Northern Iraq town of Halabja and that it was not clear to them whose "fires" had killed so many Kurdish civilians in the town. It was quite possible, they argued, that gas clouds had drifted into the town from fighting outside the inhabited area.

Nevertheless, at the time in question, it had been assumed in military planning since the First World War that *battlefield* use of gas weapons was legitimate. The logic was that bullets and gas killed soldiers equally and that to imagine that a man killed with a rifle bullet was better off than one killed with phosgene was ridiculous. This was not really an issue in our project because we were going to be concerned solely with the targets we gave them or agreed to with them and were not going to advise the Iraqis on what ordnance (bombs) to use in attacking these targets. In any event, the International Convention Against the use of Chemical Weapons had not yet taken effect.

The DIA planners knew that it was US policy that satellite photographs could not be left in the possession of foreigners. Theoretically, it was possible to deduce the characteristics of the camera system from the photos. We could use the satellite pictures for analysis, and we could bring them with us, but we could not leave them with the Iraqis. In the end the typical "target package" for "Druid Leader" consisted of: a marked map which showed the target and surrounding anti air defenses, beautifully hand-done pencil drawings of the target, often at different stages of construction (made from satellite photographs), a tabular listing of units and anti-aircraft weapons in the area and the satellite photographs.

The DIA team worked on this for a few days and based on Lang's arbitrary decision to "do" twenty "packages," the work was done in just a few days. What they had in their hands at that point were the "bare bones" of an air interdiction campaign likely to cripple Iranian offensive capability on the southern front if it was well applied. They briefed: DIA head Perroots, OSD, JCS and the NSC. They all approved, so they messaged Colonel David Lemon, the US Defense Attaché in Baghdad, and told him we were ready and waiting for an invitation from the ambassador (David Newton) and the Iraqis.

Lemon talked to the Iraqi general staff intelligence people. They were waiting for this and immediately issued an invitation. Ambassador Newton agreed. Lemon suggested that we go in through Kuwait, mainly because he had personal business to take care of there. Lang agreed. Francona and he then flew to Kuwait where Lemon met them and their sealed "tube" of documents. They drove up to the Iraqi frontier at the crossing made famous years later as the "road of death." An Iraqi MI major was waiting with a truck full of troops as escort. Lemon was dumbstruck at the courtesy. The Iraqi major, who was from the MI regional office in Basra asked if there was anything Lang would like to see during the trip. He said he had been instructed to do anything asked. Lemon was again dumbstruck. Lang told the Iraqi that he wanted to see the Iranian lines across the Shatt al-Arab in Basra. The Major said, "Yes," and they left for Basra. They drove up from the south and into the city, making their way into many different "quarters" of the town and ending up on the riverbank near the Sheraton Hotel. Lang looked at the Iranian positions across the way and climbed up on the "berm" for a better view downstream. After a minute, the escort officer stepped up beside him to suggest that he get down before the two of them died there. He was right. The party drove away through the city going north. It was on this trip to Basra that Lemon, Francona. Lemon's Iraqi driver and Lang were shelled by the Iranian artillery in the streets of Basra. They were driving along a straightaway in the middle of town when a salvo of Iranian artillery shells landed a couple of hundred yards in front of them. It was high explosive, and the six rounds "straddled" the road. The driver stopped, his hands frozen to the wheel in fright, his whole body rigid. Thirty seconds later, another salvo, probably from the same battery landed behind them straddling the road. It was evident that this battery was "searching" the road as part of their scheduled "harassing and interdicting" (H&I) fires. It was also evident that if they were following US artillery practice (they were US trained), the next salvo would land just about where the American party were. Colonel Lemon wrestled the driver over the steering wheel and jammed his foot down on the accelerator. The car rolled out of the "beaten zone' and the next salvo landed astride the street just where they had been stopped. It was a "close" thing.

They drove north from Basra passing through the marshes in which Iraqi forces were facing east, engaged with the Iranians in the kind of positional warfare that was the norm but which was interrupted by seasonal maneuver operations in which the Iranians attempted to break through Iraqi lines. Many of these attempts were massive and very bloody. Often, they were turned back and the front line restored only after a great deal of fighting and heavy Iraqi losses. Because of the limited space available, the road north passed through the divisional rear area of all the Iraqi Army divisions "in the line" facing east against the Iranians in the marshes. The highway north was actually the Main Supply Route (MSR) for all these units. For the MSR to be parallel to the front line was unusual but apparently inevitable in this geographical situation. Along the road, artillery positions and headquarters were visible on both sides. There were also large parking lots with hundreds of civilian vehicles in rows. Each parking lot had a building at its entrance. Lang later learned that these "lots" were for the use of soldiers who left their personal cars there when not absent on the periodic leave which each received every few months. There were many "tactical" signs along the way pointing in various directions to locations of facilities and units. The Arabic writing on the signs meant nothing to any of us and was apparently written in some sort of code. It was a long ride to Baghdad passing through Amara, Kut and any number of other towns. The roads were in remarkably good shape and north of the marshes much of the route was four-lane, divided and well surfaced. We passed a number of Army convoys moving up and down the main road. Our Iraqi military intelligence or security escort followed faithfully up the road and did not interfere at all except to take the lead in finding the way through large towns. The military vehicles along the way were representative of just about all the Iraqi Army vehicles seen on numerous trips into the country. They were nearly all the products of factories in Eastern Europe or China. There were a great many East German trucks, and there were "hordes" of Heavy Equipment Transporters (HET). All the HETs seen in Iraq were made in East Germany. The equipment looked well maintained and was freshly painted. The vehicles were not dirty, and it was a rare thing to pass a broken down military vehicle by the roadside. This was very different from the scene in Syria where many Syrian Army vehicles always seemed to have been abandoned on the road. Units on the road looked good with proper intervals, troops uniformly dressed, sitting in trucks with helmets on and behaving in an orderly way. Lang remembered one particular artillery battalion. It was in "march order," loaded on HETs and heavy trucks. It was a striking sight. The three batteries of Soviet built 130mm Gun-Howitzers were not being towed. They were mounted on the HETs and chained down. Additional space on the HETs was occupied by trailers, wall lockers, unit office furniture, crated equipment, etc. The troops rode in open trucks following each HET. They waved as the Americans passed. They were interested in the embassy license plates which identified the country represented in Iraq. One soldier stood up, waved and yelled, "My cousin – Floorida!" A sergeant told him to sit down.

Several times during the trip, the little convoy was passed by taxi cabs moving at high speeds. Each had on the roof a casket covered in a cloth "sleeve" printed as a large Iraqi national flag. The cabs hooted wildly on their horns and cars pulled off the road to let them past. Lemon explained that because of Muslim custom of burying the dead before sundown on the day of death, the Iraqi Army's procedure was to commandeer taxicabs at the front, pay the driver to deliver the body to "next of kin," load a coffin on the roof and give the driver the name and address of the person to whom the body was to be delivered. One can only imagine the scene at a house as the honking horn grew closer.

They rolled into Baghdad, went to register at the al-Rashid Hotel (then the best in town) and went down to the bar for a drink. The next morning Lang went to the "Diplomatic Hard Currency Store" to buy some clothes. Violating his long-standing practice, he had allowed bellmen from the hotel in Kuwait to load his personal bag in the truck while he waited in the lobby. Predictably, they had forgotten his bag somewhere. Lang had the tube with their materials tucked under his arm at the time. So, he went to the store and bought a suit. (His clothes showed up a day later by air.) At the embassy, he and Francona talked to David Newton, the ambassador. He blessed the effort and said he hoped that the project would improve the poisonous relations between the embassy and the Iraqi Ministry of Defense that had prevailed since disclosure of US plotting with Iran in the Iran-Contra Affair.

One embassy officer present at the meeting with the Ambassador was unhappy and openly showed it. He told Lang that "the Iraqis" did not want to see him and did not want to be asked about it.

Lang laughed at him, which surprised him. "Do you want to come with me," he was asked? He sputtered and said that the DIA group could not go without his permission. He was told that they were leaving for the Ministry of Defense in ten minutes. He was ready by then. At the Iraqi headquarters, the team were greeted as long-lost brothers, or as, "the cavalry" arrived to save the fort. The main conference room was adorned with flowers, food covered the table and several generals sat smiling at us while staff officers hovered. Lang listened to the Iraqis talking among themselves. "Is he the one?" was the question. "Is he the one who the Saudi brothers speak of?" That was too much for the officer accompanying Lang, and he reminded them that Lang understood what they were saying and thereby lost the Americans the advantage.

Lang briefed the program and the target set to the Iraqi military intelligence staff. These were the officers who were running the combat intelligence support to Iraqi forces in the line of battle against Iran. At some point during the presentation a brigadier asked if Lang would like to see their "holdings" on one of the same facilities that the American "packages" covered. When assured that they would, the Iraqis produced a thick dossier filled with typed reports in Arabic on one side and low-oblique aerial photographs of the place on the other. Lang looked it over while they watched expectantly. "What else do you have on this place?" Lang asked. They replied that they had biographic files on the senior Iranian personnel in the headquarters concerned, the "order of battle" file for the Army Corps involved, and that they had the "grid square" file. Lang asked what that might be. They responded that they had a dossier file on each and every one-kilometer sized grid square in the country. These described: the terrain, any installations, and known activity that had occurred within that square. It was impressive stuff. It was the kind of intelligence staff work that would have characterized a good World War II army. Lang told them that this was good work and that what we had brought would complement their efforts and allow a precise targeting of targets involved in the Iranian war effort on the southern front, *if they wanted DIA's help.*

They did not "register" that last clause for a moment, and then they looked at each other in surprise. Their head of delegation looked suspicious as he asked what was meant. He was told that the American military was not sure that Iraq wanted its help. They laughed as that soaked in. "Of course, we want your help," their "boss" replied. "We intend to begin striking these targets tomorrow, and we will strike them again and again until you tell us they have been destroyed!"

And so, it was. Over the next few months, the squadrons of the Iraq Air Force that were not advised by France devoted themselves to destruction of the military targets which DIA provided them. The three French-equipped and advised squadrons had always done well under French tutelage, and they continued to concentrate on maritime attacks against Iran associated shipping in the Gulf. DIA commented seriatim on all strikes against our target set, and the Iraqis hit them again and again until they were profoundly disrupted. This had the effect of eliminating the Iranian "threat" to the oil supplies in the Gulf that was perceived in Washington policy circles at that time. The disruption to Iranian forces in the forward areas was so severe that Iranian armed forces from that time on lost any real chance of large-scale offensive action in the war. In the middle of the active period of the project, Lang asked to have the operation code name changed because of concern over possible "leaks" in Washington, and the name was changed to "Surf Fisher."

Was the destruction of these major targets the major "contribution" to history of the project? No. The biggest effect of the project was psychological. Before the "Druid Leader/Surf Fisher" (DL/SF) project, Iraq felt isolated in the world, dependent on essentially hostile Gulf state money for the purchase of armaments, and the object of hostile attention from the United States, a country which they both admired and feared.

After DL/SF, the Iraqis believed that they had been befriended by America. This made a difference in their self-esteem, a big difference. Within a short period, US personnel began to hear from third parties in the Third World that the Iraqis had taken heart from professional American military assistance and were seriously planning offensives to re-take territory lost to the Iranians along the front including the Fao Peninsula just north of Kuwait. The Iraqis began to plan really large operations often rehearsed "endlessly" on full scale (1:1) models out in the desert.

At the same time US/Iraqi military to military cooperation increased dramatically outside the scope of DL/SF. A variety of agreements were reached between the US Department of Defense and the Iraqis for participation in conferences, sponsored training in non-lethal fields, and for a variety of technical support arrangements, none of which involved delivery of weaponry or ammunition.

As the project progressed, the level of trust on both sides seemed to rise. At one point, the Deputy Assistant Secretary of Defense for Middle East Policy came to Lang's office to say that the Iraqis had captured an Iranian artillery piece manufactured by North Korea and that the US wanted the weapon handed over. This was the "Koksan" self-propelled gun. It had been developed from the German 88mm multi-purpose gun of WWII and was mounted on a T-54 tank chassis. It had a range of 60 km. The Iranians had been shelling northern Kuwait with these weapons from the Fao peninsula southeast of Basra. It was of special interest to the United States because it had been designed for just one purpose, and that was to shell Seoul from across the DMZ in Korea. The Iraqis had captured the piece in a raid across the lines.

Lang asked the Iraqi military attaché in Washington for the gun on behalf of the US Government. He passed the request on to Baghdad and the answer was that although they would not give the US the gun, they would allow a US team to study it *in situ*. Rick Francona took a team of three or four engineers from the Army Foreign Science and Technology Center (AFSTC) at Charlottesville, Virginia to Iraq where they were given access to the gun at an artillery "barracks" just to the southeast of Baghdad. The team crawled all over the gun, measuring it in various ways and driving it around the compound for a few hours. While doing that, they noticed that a number of new types of Soviet artillery equipment were parked under open sheds along the sides of the compound. Francona asked if the American team could inspect these as well. The Iraqi Brigadier in command said that it would be disloyal to a friendly country for the Iraqi Army to allow the US access to this equipment, but that he and his men would be going to lunch shortly and would not return for two hours. The Iraqis left, all of them, and the American team inspected several new types of Soviet equipment never before seen except in Moscow parades.

As time passed, the fruits of the US/Iraqi intelligence cooperation became evident. The Iraqis launched larger and larger offensive operations against Iran. They re-captured the Fao Peninsula in a corps-sized operation which used a combination of conventional and chemical fires in the artillery and air preparation of the battlefield. The US had no part in that, but we became aware that they had used chemical fires against Iranian troops in this battle when an American military intelligence officer on the scene in Baghdad representing Lang was invited to visit the battlefield just after the completion of the capture of the front line there. He was transported to the area by Iraqi Air Force MI-8 helicopter and walked around with them in the defenses vacated by the Iranians. The broken bunkers and trenches were littered with the usual trash a military force in the field leaves behind it. The American officer found many expended atropine auto-injectors. Atropine is a drug specifically used to counteract the effects of nerve agents. Soldiers are taught to inject themselves through their clothing with these spring-loaded devices if they think they have been exposed to nerve gas of some kind. Our conclusion after examining several of the European manufactured injectors was that they had been in the hands of Iraqi troops who had injected themselves from fear of the lingering effects of their own gas fires delivered on the Iranians. This is unfortunate since atropine has a very bad effect if administered to someone not in need of it.

The major operation that re-captured the Fao Peninsula marked a true "turning-point" for the Iraqis. After that, they launched operations of ever greater scope and operational sophistication. On Lang's visits to Baghdad, he was often briefed on what they were doing and was generally treated as a colleague and friend. He particularly remembered an Iraqi MI brigadier coming red-eyed into a meeting one morning after they had been fighting to capture a mountain in Kurdistan along the Iranian border. There had been combat coverage of the assault on the peak on television the night before. It had been impressive. He shook my hand with a big smile, embraced me and said "We should have been there. It was an excellent battle!" (ma'raka mumtaza in Arabic).

On several of those trips, Francona and Lang were taken to night clubs. The Iraqis liked to "party" and drink. On every single occasion, an Iranian SCUD ballistic missile struck nearby. In every case the Iraqis sat quiet for a minute and then the music and dancing began again. We came out of the "Khan Marjan" (a medieval caravan sarai) club one night to see that a two-story building across the street had disappeared in the huge noise that we had heard earlier.

The exchange of ballistic missile fires between Iraq and Iran was called the "War of the Cities." (harb al-mudun in Arabic). This was a complicating factor in what DIA was doing because the missiles had a large "Circular Error Probable" (CEP). The people and facilities that DIA was dealing with could easily "disappear" in a roar and shower of dust at any time. Ballistic missiles have no warning sound as they are arriving. The explosion of their arrival is all that one hears. This is un-nerving at first. The first time Lang experienced one of these missiles he was asleep in the Rashid Hotel when something woke him in the middle of the night. He was wondering what it had been when the phone rang. It was Francona who asked, "What was that?" Just then there was a tremendous noise outside, and Lang went to the window to look down across the garden of the hotel, and across the four-lane street to a smoking hole where a solid masonry house had been and now was gone. It was two in the morning and the traffic sat in the street for a minute (presumably while occupants counted their parts to see if they still had them). Then they drove away. When Lang and Francona went out to run the next morning, a wooden fence had been erected around the missile strike site and the sound of machinery could be heard within. When they returned from meetings that afternoon, the fence was gone, and the lot was as smooth and debris-free as a billiard table. The Iraqis were remarkably insouciant about the prospect of sudden disintegration from above.

On one occasion, Lang was having dinner with the ambassador at his residence when a sudden "ka-whoomp!" shook the building. The ambassador, his wife and their guests abandoned dessert to walk down the street to a big hole still smoking steadily. Iraqi civilians were standing around the crater chatting and smoking cigarettes. The police arrived, and after a while one asked who the foreigners were. When told that the distinguished looking man was the US Ambassador, he became concerned and asked the ambassador to go home in case there was another 'hit" in the same area. This sometimes happened. There was nothing hostile at all about the policeman's attitude or that of anyone in the crowd. There was, as there was so often, talk about cousins in America. There was a lot of curiosity about America, a country that was clearly admired as the epitome of modernity. It must be remembered that the DIA people were associating with the "modernist" faction in Iraq, but, nevertheless, the friendly interest was remarkable. One evening, Lang's Military Intelligence (Istikhbarat 'Askariyah in Arabic) hosts sent him and a US Army Lt. Col. accompanying Lang to a "Club Mediterranee" style vacation village on Lake Habbaniyah west of Baghdad. They had a "minder" with them from Iraqi civilian intelligence and security (mukhabarat in Arabic). As is the case in every country in the world, the Iraqi military and civilian intelligence services viewed each other as the ultimate rival and often as enemies.

The odd little group walked along the lakeside boardwalk in a pretty little "town" made up of cottages and villas. There were many young couples walking hand in hand along the lake edge. My US colleague had served in Saudi Arabia and expressed astonishment at this behavior since it would have been unthinkable in that country. The Iraqis asked what the matter with him was. Lang explained, and they laughed, saying that what these Iraqi people did was their own business. It was a moment of revelation, speaking powerfully of the differences between Iraq at that time and many other Muslim countries, and especially the Mullah driven Iranian theocracy that they were fighting.

The Mukhabarat "minder" left after dinner, and the group drove back to Baghdad with their Istikhbarat escort. Baghdad was under a military curfew, and they were a little late, and the escort officer decided to take a "short cut." In the gathering dusk, they drove through a military unit deployed in a circular position on both sides of the road. It was a SCUD missile battery. This "visit" was not supposed to happen, and the captain escort suddenly looked worried. Lang looked out the window with growing interest. There were several SCUDs on mobile transporter-erectors. There were meteorology vans, radar and communications vans. There was a Soviet built mess truck. There was a group of officers sitting around a table covered in white linen and china tableware. There were soldiers lounging around on the low hills that surrounded the site.

The important thing was that this was a real artillery unit equipped with SCUD missiles, not a factory manned experimental operation. After they cleared the area, the escort officer asked what Lang thought that had been. The American told him that it had looked like some sort of training. The captain never looked back but said, "thank you." He was a nice fellow, a graduate in English Literature from Baghdad University. He had two children, a pretty wife, and very friendly and well-educated parents. Lang certainly did not want to cause him a problem.

The Iraqis continued to progress in the scale of their operations. This progression culminated in "Operation 'In God We Trust.'" (Tawakalna 'ala Allah in Arabic) This operation launched four armored and/or mechanized divisions in a corps-sized raid which swept through the Iranian lines, then swung around through their front line divisions in a half-circle and emerged within Iraqi lines twenty miles east of the initial penetration having destroyed the best part of the Iranian Army in the process. The Iranians accepted the UN proposed cease fire shortly thereafter. Iraq had "arrived" as a regional military power. The Iraqis told Lang that the operation had been named in honor of our military cooperation. There is a great irony in that. After the war the Iraqis created a new division in the Republican Guard. It was a mechanized division and it was named "Tawakalna 'ala Allah." We destroyed it utterly in the First Gulf War.

Lang was in Baghdad the day that the Iranians accepted the cease fire. He and Francona watched helicopters take anti-aircraft guns down off the roofs of tall buildings and deposit them in parking lots across the city. People wept, got drunk and hugged each other. It looked like the pictures of Times Square on VE Day.

Iranian political warfare and that of their Israeli "ally" has sought to portray the outcome of the Iran-Iraq War as a "draw." Nothing could be farther from the truth. In the last battles and campaigns, Iraq wrecked the armed forces of Iran. That is why the Iranians accepted the cease-fire. After the war, the Iraqis laid on an exhibition of equipment captured in the final battles. It was at a cantonment just south of Baghdad. The US had overhead photography of the event, but DIA people also walked around through the exhibition with all the other foreign visitors. There were hundreds of tanks, over a thousand pieces of heavy artillery, armored personnel carriers in the thousands, anti-aircraft guns and trucks as far as the eye could see. Lang later briefed this show to President Mubarak of Egypt. He asked what he was looking at in the pictures. Lang told him that it was the skeleton of a dead army.

US/Iraqi military cooperation ended the day that Iran accepted the cease-fire. On that day there were fourteen ongoing programs of military to military cooperation. They all ended the next day without announcement of the change to the Iraqis. There had always been a lot of opposition within the US Government to the concept of this cooperation. The neocon fanatics were active even then and they argued that Iraq was an obstacle to their dream of "democratization" in the Middle East. They also claimed to believe that Iraq was a client state of the USSR even though most of them knew that the only place allowed to a communist in Iraq was prison. The Iranian "lobby" at State had always opposed any such cooperation and the Zionist lobby, AIPAC, had vehemently opposed any help for an emerging Arab power.

It took the Iraqis six months or so to accept the idea that their brief "honeymoon" with the Americans was over. When they did, Saddam began to rage against the Israelis again and to threaten the Kuwaitis and Saudis. It had been understood during the war that the moneys paid by the Gulf Arabs to Iraq for war expenses would never be re-paid. The Gulf Arabs were protected from the Iranians, and the Iraqis felt that they had pre-paid the debt in blood. Therefore, when the Kuwaitis in particular began to demand repayment, the Iraqis were enraged. From that much mischief flowed. The political situation between Iraq and its neighbors ran downhill rapidly over a year or so and war almost inevitably came to the Gulf again, this time with the US and the Iraqis as enemies.

The part Pat Lang played in that war was described well by Bob Woodward in "The Commanders" and it is not necessary to dwell on it again.

There were a few footnotes to all these events involving the two wars:

Lang was awarded the "Presidential Rank of Distinguished Executive." This is the US equivalent of a knighthood in the British Civil service.

Major Francona served as general Shwartzkopf's interpreter in Saudi Arabia during the Gulf War. At the armistice ceremony at Safwan in southern Iraq, Francona met the Iraqi generals' party at the dismount point only to find that the officer who had so often been my escort was there to interpret for the Iraqis. Francona and he were touched by seeing each other again. Francona said he was happy to see that the other man had survived. Francona said he hoped that the family had not been injured and was glad to know that they had not been hurt. The senior Iraqi general interrupted to ask in astonishment if they really knew each other. When told that they did, he just shook his head and walked up the hill to sign his country's surrender.

A few months later, Lang was in Jordan for meetings and he took the occasion to ask MG Abd–al-Hafiz al-Marei to tell the Iraqis that he had nothing to do with the bombing of the headquarters where he had worked with them against Iran. The Jordanians brought back word that the Iraqis had known that must be true.

CHAPTER TWENTY-EIGHT

Defense HUMINT

(The Owl, Symbol of Defense HUMINT)

Pat Lang's eight-year tenure as the Defense Intelligence Officer for the Middle East and South Asia came to an end in 1992. It had been an eventful "ride," filled with hectic activity and accomplishments, but that came to an end with the appointment of a new director for the Defense Intelligence Agency. This man arrived with a belief that Lang was "too big for his britches," had too high a profile and should be "cut down to size." He began to restrict Lang's activities and indeed began to perform many of the overseas and high-level domestic briefings and liaison that had long been in Lang's "portfolio." This was followed by a decision to "rotate" executives throughout the upper echelons of the agency.

After some fumbling around, Lang was sent to be the head of attaché affairs at embassies around the world.

The people who sent him to this job did not seem to wish him well and seemed to expect that he would fail at this job. They had never seen him work in any capacity other than as head of analysis in the DIO job. Those who had knowledge of it seemed to have missed the import of the Iraq project with regard to his abilities. They did not seem to know that he had been an infantryman, Special Forces soldier, covert action operative and clandestine case officer.

When he arrived in the new job, he found a staff resigned to a perpetual second-class status in the US Intelligence Community. Lang, however, had extensive inter-agency experience in the Intelligence Community and knew how to overcome problems presented by other agency hegemony. He recognized that this second-class status stemmed from a broad-based failure to appreciate the unique role that DIA could provide in gaining the trust of foreign military men.

Once placed in the Defense HUMINT headquarters, he and a group of colleagues resolved to rectify these situations. This was not good news for the service intelligence chiefs (all generals and admirals) who liked the "theater" of having "spies" subordinated to them. It did not seem to matter to them that they did not have enough resources or enough unity to do anything useful with their "spooks." That did not matter at all.

Unfortunately for them, DIA as a sub-set of the General Intelligence Program owned and controlled all the HUMINT resources being misused by the service intelligence chiefs for this purpose. Lang and "associates" succeeded in building and reorganizing DIA's HUMINT, but the unexpected positive results were not without personal consequences.

These outcomes doomed Lang's prospects for more government service. The generals and admirals would not accept the loss of their "toys."

At the same time, the neocon element always present in the government, including the Department of Defense, continued to press for Lang's removal as a possible enemy of Israel and a lover of things Arab. This was amusing as Lang had never particularly liked the Arabs, their culture or language.

In My End Is My Beginning

A pretext was found, some nonsense about Lang being feared by his staff. Anything would have sufficed. The director of the day had in mind for himself a final promotion to full general, and the collective pressure of the various people Lang had annoyed or threatened by exposing their ineptitude was just too much for him. He removed Lang from the job of HUMINT chief and shortly thereafter, Pat Lang resigned from DIA and went forth into what for him was the meaningless, pointless existence called civilian life. Yet another career followed in international business and media consulting, but in truth the only life that mattered to him ended the day he left government.

It did not matter. He had kept faith with the China sailor who had trained him for his life of duty. Perhaps they might meet again on the Far Shore.

An End

Taps

https://www.youtube.com/watch?v=Bfe4TxvUOiw&t=77s

PHOTO CREDITS FOR TATOO

Title Page
1. Courtesy of Shutterstock. 2. Tattoo: Courtesy of the Office of Chief of US Army Bands.

Chapter One—The Far Shore
1. Courtesy of Aulia Teguh Pratama at unsplash.com
2. and 3. W. Patrick Lang personal photo collection.

Chapter Two—The Dancing Carabao
1. Courtesy of the Army Historian at US Army History Museum, Ft Belvoir, VA.

Chapter Three-Chrysanthemum
1. Chrysanthemum Japanese Imperial seal, Courtesy of Creative Commons Licensing. 2. Courtesy of the Department of the US Navy. 3. Courtesy of the Army Historian at the US Army History Museum, Ft. Belvoir, VA. 4. Order of the Chrysanthemum, courtesy of Creative Commons licensing.

Chapter Four—A Boot Full of Blood
1. John H Lang from the W. Patrick Lang personal photo collection. 2. USS Panay, courtesy of the www.archives.gov/historical -docs). 3. John H. Lang, courtesy of www.history.navy.mil/our-collections. 4. Courtesy of Shutterstock.

Chapter Five—Casablanca
1. USS Massachusetts, courtesy of www.history.navy.mil/content/ history. 2. The Guns of the USS Massachusetts, courtesy of US Naval Historical Center.

Chapter Six—Zebulon Pike
1. Courtesy of www.usmm.org/libertyships.html. 2. Courtesy of the collection of the United Kingdom Imperial War Museums. 3. Courtesy of Michael Dziedzic at unsplash.com. 4. Father John McDonnell, October 15, 1940, courtesy of the Lowell Sun, Lowell, Massachusetts. 5. Courtesy of the US. Army through Creative Commons licensing.

Chapter Seven—Gunning
1. Courtesy of Laura College at unsplash.com. 2. Courtesy of HMaag through Creative Commons Licensing

Chapter Eight—The Inferno
1. Courtesy of Matt Howard at unsplash.com 2. W. Patrick Lang personal photo collection. 3. Courtesy of Creative Commons licensing.

Chapter Nine-To the Last Man

1. Courtesy of the Army Historian at US Army History Museum, Ft Belvoir, VA 2. Courtesy of the Army Heritage Museum Collection. American Heritage Museum. 3. Courtesy of War in the Pacific, ibiblio. org. 4. Courtesy of curiosandrelics through Creative Commons Licensing.

Chapter Ten—Idle Hour

1. Courtesy of Adrian Diaz-Sieckel at unsplash.com. 2. Courtesy of Shutterstock.

Chapter Eleven—The Old Corps

1. Charge of the New Market Cadets by Benjamin West Clinedinst, oil on canvas, 1914, Virginia Military Institute. Courtesy of permission granted by Keith E. Gibson, Colonel, Director, VMI Museum System, Virginia Military Institute.

Chapter Twelve—Hiawatha

1. Longfellow's Hiawatha carrying Minnehaha at Minnehaha Park in Minneapolis, Minnesota through Creative Commons Licensing. 2. W. Patrick Lang personal photo collection. 3. W. Patrick Lang personal photo collection. 4. Courtesy of the Army Historian at US Army History Museum, Ft Belvoir, VA. 5. Courtesy of US Army at www. Usarc. army.mil. 6. Courtesy of US Army at army.mil. 7. Courtesy of licensing through Creative Commons. 8. Courtesy of the Army Historian at US Army History Museum, Ft Belvoir, VA. 9. Courtesy of US Army at arcent.army.mil/history. 10. Courtesy of US Army at www. Usarc.army. mil. 11. Courtesy of US Army at history.army.mil.

Chapter Thirteen—Touch Me Not

1. Courtesy of the Army Historian at US Army History Museum, Ft Belvoir, VA. 2. Courtesy of BasilioC through Creative Commons licensing. 3. Courtesy of curiosandrelics through Creative Commons licensing. 4. W. Patrick Lang personal photo collection. 5. Courtesy of the Army Historian at Army History Museum, Ft. Belvoir, VA. 6. Courtesy of the Army Historian at Army History Museum, Ft. Belvoir, VA. 7. Courtesy of commons.wikimedia.org. 8. Courtesy of https://pubs.er.usgs. gov/publication/sim3233 with permission of D. Noserale, Northeast Region Public Affairs Officer, USGS. 9. W. Patrick Lang personal photo collection. 10. Courtesy of US Army. 11. Courtesy of York Museums Trust through Creative Commons licensing.

Chapter Fourteen—Red Diamond

    1.   Courtesy of the Army Historian at US Army History Museum, Ft Belvoir, VA.

Chapter Fifteen—Lieutenant of the Infantry

    1.   Courtesy of the Army Historian at US Army History Museum, Ft Belvoir, VA. 2. Courtesy of commons.wikimedia.org. 3. Courtesy of US Air Force at the USAF Museum at Wright-Patterson AB in Dayton, Ohio. 4. Lang Wedding Photo. Courtesy of Bachrach Photography, Boston, MA.

Chapter Sixteen—Aaron Bank's Children

    2.   Courtesy of US Army Special Forces History at https://arsof-history. org/. 2. Courtesy of US Air Force. 3. National Numismatic Collection, National Museum of American History. 4. Bobby C. Hawkins through Creative Commons Licensing. 5. Courtesy of US Air Force. National Archives and Records Administration. 6. Uwharrie National Forest (N.C.), United States Forest Service, Southern Region, Library of Congress Map Division. 7. Courtesy of the Army Historian at US Army History Museum, Ft Belvoir, VA. 8. Courtesy of ARSOF History.org. U.S. Army Special Operations Command. 9. US Government. Courtesy of US Air Force. 10. Courtesy of US Army through Creative Commons licensing. 11. W. Patrick Lang personal photo collection. 12. W. Patrick Lang personal photo collection. 13. W. Patrick Lang personal photo collection. 14. W. Patrick Lang personal photo collection.

Chapter Seventeen—Ahoy the Tegrone

    1.   Courtesy of US Navy. http://www.public.navy.mil/subfor/ underseawarfaremagazine/Issues/Archives/issue_14/coldwar.html. 2. Courtesy of the Army Historian at US Army History Museum, Ft Belvoir, VA. 3. Courtesy of Maryland State Police. 4. Courtesy of the John Vachon Library of Congress Collection, Washington, DC. 5. W. Patrick Lang personal photo collection. 6. Courtesy of Hossam M. Omar at www.unsplash.com.

Chapter Eighteen—Worthy of Our Steel

    1.   Courtesy of the Army Historian at US Army History Museum, Ft Belvoir, VA. 2. Courtesy of Gerardo Guitierrez at www.unsplash.com. 3. W. Patrick Lang personal photo. 4. Courtesy of commons.wikimedia.org. 5. W. Patrick Lang personal photo collection. 6. Courtesy of the Army Historian at US Army History Museum, Ft Belvoir, VA. 7. Courtesy of Warner Pathé Archive through commons.wikimedia.org. 8. Nativity

From the 1910 short film, Nativite' by Louis Feuillade; image posted on https://centuryfilmproject.org/about/copyright/ Copyright license under Public Domain for material over 100 years old. 9. Courtesy of Shutterstock.

Chapter Nineteen-Doc Lap! Doc Lap!

1. Courtesy of the Army Historian at US Army History Museum, Ft Belvoir, VA. 2. Courtesy of the US Army from the official U.S. Department of the Army publication. 3. Courtesy of US War Department Special Series 1943. 4. Courtesy of US Air Force at commons.wikimedia.org. 5. Courtesy of US Department of Defense at commons.wikimedia.org. 5. W. Patrick Lang personal photo collection. 6. Courtesy of Shutterstock. 7. Courtesy of cia.gov. 8. Courtesy of US Navy under Creative Commons licensing. 9. W. Patrick Lang personal photo collection. 10. Courtesy of commons.wikimedia.org. 11. Courtesy of US Air Force, Creative Commons licensing. 12. Courtesy of Department of Defense.

Chapter Twenty—Murder Is Murder

1. Courtesy of the Army Historian at US Army History Museum, Ft Belvoir, VA. 2. Courtesy of John Oxley Library, State Library of Queensland, Australia at commons.wikimedia.org. 3. W. Patrick Lang personal photo collection. 4. Courtesy of David Clode at www.unsplash. com 5. Official Photo US Army 6. Courtesy of the US Army. 6. W. Patrick Lang personal photo collection.

Chapter Twenty-One—The City of the Trojans

1. Courtesy of the Army Historian at US Army History Museum, Ft Belvoir, VA. 2. W. Patrick Lang personal photo collection. 3. Courtesy of Claire Ward at www.unsplash.com (vase). 4. W. Patrick Lang personal photo collection. 5. W. Patrick Lang personal photo collection. 6. W. Patrick Lang personal photo collection. 7. W. Patrick Lang personal photo collection. 8. Courtesy of World Pictures.

Chapter Twenty-Two—Home at Last

1. Courtesy of Sarah Brown, www.unsplash.com,

Chapter Twenty-Three—West Point

1. Courtesy of Department of Defense.

Chapter Twenty-Four—Yemen

1. W. Patrick Lang personal photo collection.

Chapter Twenty-Five—The Kingdom

1. Courtesy of Daryl Figueroa at www.unsplash.com.

Chapter Twenty-Six—DIO for the Middle East
1. Courtesy of the Department of Defense.
Chapter Twenty-Seven—Druid Leader
1. Courtesy of Anonymous at Gutenberg.org through commons. wikimedia.org.
Chapter Twenty-Eight—Defense HUMINT
1. Courtesy of Luis Argaiz at Unsplash.com. 2. Courtesy of the Office of Chief of US Army Bands.

Made in the USA
Las Vegas, NV
14 May 2021

23066752R00236